FTCE PreK/PRIMARY PK-3 (053)

FLORIDA TEACHER CERTIFICATION EXAMINATIONS

Katrina Willard Hall, Ph.D.
University of North Florida
Jacksonville, Florida

Kim A. Cheek, Ph.D.
University of North Florida
Jacksonville, Florida

Research & Education Association
www.rea.com

Research & Education Association
1325 Franklin Ave., Suite 250
Garden City, NY 11530
Email: info@rea.com

**Florida FTCE Prekindergarten/Primary PK–3 (053)
with Online Practice Tests**

Published 2023

Printed in the United States of America

Library of Congress Control Number 2019930136

ISBN-13: 978-0-7386-1241-6
ISBN-10: 0-7386-1241-3

The competencies presented in this book were created and implemented by the Florida
Department of Education. For further information visit *www.fl.nesinc.com*.

Cover image: © iStockphoto.com/Wavebreakmedia

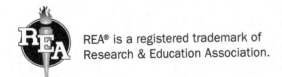

Contents

About Our Authors.. vi
About REA... vi

Chapter 1: Getting Started 1
    How to Use This Book + Online Prep..1
    An Overview of the Test 2
    PK–3 Study Schedule 6

Chapter 2: Strategies for Success 9

Diagnostic Test.. *available online at www.rea.com/studycenter*

Chapter 3: Developmental Knowledge Subtest 1 (531).......................................13
    Competency 1: Knowledge of Child Growth, Child Development, and
        Relationship with Families and the Community..13
    Competency 2: Knowledge of the Profession and Foundations of Early
        Childhood (PreK–3) Education...20
    Competency 3: Knowledge of Developmentally Appropriate Practices.....................38
    Competency 4: Knowledge of Developmentally Appropriate Curricula.....................48
    Competency 5: Knowledge of Developmentally Appropriate Intervention
        Strategies and Resources Available to Meet the Needs of All Students.................51
    Competency 6: Knowledge of Diagnosis, Assessment, and Evaluation.....................53
    Competency 7: Knowledge of Child Guidance and Classroom Behavioral
        Management...57

Chapter 4: Language Arts and Reading Subtest 2 (532).....................................63
    Competency 1: Knowledge of Literacy and Literacy Instruction..............................63
    Competency 2: Knowledge of Fiction and Nonfiction Genres Including Reading
        Informational Texts 78
    Competency 3: Knowledge of Reading Foundational Skills 83
    Competency 4: Knowledge of Language Elements Used for Effective Oral
        and Written Communication...88
    Competency 5: Knowledge of Assessments to Inform Literacy Instruction 95

CONTENTS

Chapter 5: Mathematics Subtest 3 (533) 101
   Competency 1: Knowledge of Effective Mathematics Instruction..........................101
   Competency 2: Knowledge of Algebraic Thinking..........................110
   Competency 3: Knowledge of Number Concepts and Operations in Base Ten........113
   Competency 4: Knowledge of Measurement and Data Collection and Analysis 126
   Competency 5: Knowledge of Geometric and Spatial Concepts.............................132

Chapter 6: Science Subtest 4 (534)...139
   Competency 1: Knowledge of Effective Science Instruction...............................139
   Competency 2: Knowledge of the Nature of Science 148
   Competency 3: Knowledge of Earth and Space Sciences...........................156
   Competency 4: Knowledge of the Physical Sciences 167
   Competency 5: Knowledge of the Life Sciences 172

Practice Test 1 *(also available at www.rea.com/studycenter)* 185
   Subtest 1: Developmental Knowledge (531) 185
      Answer Sheet 186
      Answer Key.............................196
      Detailed Answers 197
   Subtest 2: Language Arts and Reading (532) 203
      Answer Sheet 204
      Answer Key.............................212
      Detailed Answers 213
   Subtest 3: Mathematics (533) 219
      Mathematics Reference Sheet.............................220
      Answer Sheet 222
      Answer Key.............................231
      Detailed Answers 232
   Subtest 4: Science (534).............................239
      Answer Sheet 240
      Answer Key.............................249
      Detailed Answers 250
   Practice Test 1: Correlation with FTCE Competencies 255

CONTENTS

Practice Test 2 *(also available at www.rea.com/studycenter)* 257

    Subtest 1: Developmental Knowledge (531) 257

        Answer Sheet 258

        Answer Key 267

        Detailed Answers 268

    Subtest 2: Language Arts and Reading (532) 277

        Answer Sheet 278

        Answer Key 287

        Detailed Answers 288

    Subtest 3: Mathematics (533) 295

        Mathematics Reference Sheet..296

        Answer Sheet 298

        Answer Key 307

        Detailed Answers 308

    Subtest 4: Science (534)...313

        Answer Sheet 314

        Answer Key 322

        Detailed Answers 323

    Practice Test 2: Correlation with FTCE Competencies 327

About Our Authors

Katrina Willard Hall, Ph.D., is an Associate Professor in the Department of Teaching, Learning, and Curriculum in the College of Education and Human Services at the University of North Florida. Dr. Hall has done extensive work in PreK–3 curriculum development, especially in the reading area, focused on providing high-quality, diverse literature for the early childhood grades. Her latest project explores the ingredients for a healthy school—including the use of outdoor classrooms—designed to place children's well-being at the forefront. Dr. Hall is a recipient of the University of North Florida's Outstanding Undergraduate and Graduate Teaching Awards. She earned her Ph.D. in Curriculum and Instruction, with an emphasis on literacy, from the University of Florida. She also holds an Ed.S. in Curriculum and Instruction: Literacy and an M.Ed. in Elementary Education from the University of Florida, and a B.A. in Communications from the University of North Florida.

Kim A. Cheek, Ph.D., is an Associate Professor in the Department of Teaching, Learning, and Curriculum in the College of Education and Human Services at the University of North Florida, where she is also the Director of the Doctorate of Education Program in Curriculum and Instruction. Dr. Cheek was honored with UNF's 2020 Outstanding Faculty Service Award. She has taught math, science, and social studies in early childhood settings. Her research interests include how spatial, temporal, and numeric thinking impact science learning, teaching for conceptual understanding in science, model-based reasoning, and differentiated instruction as a means to further participation of underrepresented populations in STEM. Dr. Cheek received her doctorate in science education from Durham University in the UK. She also holds an M.S. in Geosciences from Mississippi State University, an M.Ed. in Elementary Education from Towson University, and a B.A. in Elementary and Special Education from Goucher University.

About REA

Founded in 1959, Research & Education Association (REA) is dedicated to publishing the finest and most effective educational materials—including study guides and test preps—for students of all ages.

Today, REA's wide-ranging catalog is a leading resource for students, teachers, and other professionals. Visit *www.rea.com* to see a complete listing of all our titles.

Acknowledgments

We would like to thank Larry Kling, Editorial Director, for supervising development; Pam Weston, Publisher, for setting the quality standards for production integrity and managing the publication to completion; John Cording, Technology Director, for coordinating the design and development of the REA Study Center; and Alice Leonard, Senior Editor, for project management.

We also gratefully acknowledge Diane Goldschmidt for editorial review; Dr. Norman Rose for his technical expertise; Ellen Gong for proofreading; Kathy Caratozzolo of Caragraphics for typesetting; and Jennifer Calhoun for file prep.

Getting Started

Congratulations! By taking the FTCE Prekindergarten/Primary PK–3 (053) exam, you're on your way to a rewarding career as a teacher of young students in Florida. Our book, and the online tools that come with it, give you everything you need to succeed on this important exam, bringing you one step closer to being certified to teach in Florida.

Our *FTCE Prekindergarten/Primary PK–3 (053)* Book + Online Prep package includes:

- A complete overview of the PK–3 test

- A comprehensive review for all four subject tests in the PK–3 test battery

- An online diagnostic test to pinpoint your strengths and weaknesses and focus your study

- Two full-length practice test batteries placed here in the book and also online with powerful diagnostic tools to help personalize your prep.

HOW TO USE THIS BOOK + ONLINE PREP

About Our Review

The review chapters in this book are designed to help you sharpen your command of all the skills you'll need to pass the Prekindergarten/Primary PK–3 test. Each of the skills required for all four subtests is discussed at length to optimize your understanding of what the test covers. Keep in mind that your schooling has taught you most of what you need to know to answer the questions on the test. Our content review is designed to reinforce what you have learned and show you how to relate the information you have acquired to the specific competencies on the test. Studying your class notes and textbooks together with our review will give you an excellent foundation for passing the test.

About the REA Study Center

We know your time is valuable and you want an efficient study experience. At the REA Study Center (*www.rea.com/studycenter*), you will get feedback right from the start on what you know and what you don't to help make the most of your study time. Here is what you will find at the REA Study Center:

- **Diagnostic Test**—Before you review with the book, take our online diagnostic test. Your score report will pinpoint topics for which you need the most review, to help focus your study.

- **2 Full-Length Practice Test Batteries**—Our practice tests give you the most complete picture of your strengths and weaknesses. After you've studied with the book, test what you've learned by taking the first of two practice exams (online or in the book) for each of the four subjects. Review your score reports, then go back and study any topics you missed. Take the second practice test online to ensure you've mastered the material.

Our online exams simulate the computer-based format of the actual FTCE test and come with these features:

- **Automatic Scoring**—find out how you did on the test, instantly.

- **Diagnostic Score Reports**—get a specific score tied to each competency, so you can focus on the areas that challenge you the most.

- **Detailed Answer Explanations**—see why the correct answer is right, and learn why the other answer choices are incorrect.

- **Timed Testing**—learn to manage your time as you practice, so you'll feel confident on test day.

AN OVERVIEW OF THE TEST

What is assessed on the test?

The FTCE PK–3 test is a subject area examination constructed to measure the knowledge and skills that an entry-level educator in Florida public schools must have. The test is a requirement for candidates seeking a Florida Pre-K/Primary Education certificate. Because it's a computer-administered test, the exam is available throughout the year at numerous locations across the state and at select locations nationally. To find the test center near you, visit *www.fl.nesinc.com*.

The PK–3 exam is actually a battery of four subtests, with four unique test codes:

- Subtest 1: Developmental Knowledge (531)

- Subtest 2: Language Arts and Reading (532)

- Subtest 3: Mathematics (533)

- Subtest 4: Science (534)

Below is an outline of the PK–3 exam's four subtests. The first table shows the number of questions and time allocated for each subtest.

A Snapshot of the FTCE PK–3 Test

Subtest	Competencies	Number of Items*	Time Allotted
Developmental Knowledge (531)	7	55	1 hour and 10 minutes
Language Arts and Reading (532)	5	55	1 hour and 10 minutes
Mathematics (533)	5	45	1 hour and 10 minutes
Science (534)	5	50	60 minutes
Total	22	205	4 hours and 30 minutes

The following chart shows what's covered on each subtest.

Subtest	Percentage of Subtest
DEVELOPMENTAL KNOWLEDGE: Approx. 55 questions	
Child growth, development, and relationships with family and community	14%
Profession and foundations of early childhood (PreK–3) education	12%
Developmentally appropriate practices	20%
Developmentally appropriate curricula	12%
Developmentally appropriate intervention strategies and resources available to meet the needs of all students	15%
Diagnosis, assessment, and evaluation	14%
Child guidance and classroom behavioral management	13%
LANGUAGE ARTS AND READING: Approx. 55 questions	
Literacy and literacy instruction	24%

---

* Number of test items is approximate. You will be told the exact number of questions on test day.

Subtest	Percentage of Subtest
Fiction and nonfiction genres including reading informational texts (e.g., literary nonfiction, historical, scientific, and technical texts)	20%
Reading foundational skills	24%
Language elements used for effective oral and written communication	22%
Assessments to inform literary instruction	10%
MATHEMATICS: Approx. 45 questions	
Effective mathematical instruction	23%
Algebraic thinking	16%
Number concepts and operations in base 10	30%
Measurement and data collection and analysis	15%
Geometric and spatial concepts	16%
SCIENCE: Approx. 50 questions	
Effective science instruction	19%
The nature of science	19%
Earth and space sciences	20%
The physical sciences	17%
The life sciences	25%

When should the test be taken?

Traditionally, teacher preparation programs determine when their candidates take the required tests for teacher certification. These programs will also clear you to take the examinations and make final recommendations for certification to the Florida Bureau of Educator Certification. A candidate seeking Elementary Education certification may take the appropriate test at such time as his or her Educator Preparation Program (EPP) determines the candidate's readiness to take the test, or upon successful completion of the EPP, whichever comes first. The EPP will determine readiness through benchmarks and structured assessments of the candidates' progress throughout the preparation program. Taking the appropriate FTCE examinations is a requirement to teach in Florida, so if you are planning on being a Sunshine State educator, you must take and pass these tests.

How do I register for the test?

To register for the test, you must create an account in the Pearson online registration system. Registration will then be available to you online, 24/7, during the regular, late, and emergency registration periods. Visit Pearson's FTCE website at *www.fl.nesinc.com* and follow the instructions.

What is the format of the test?

The test is organized into four subject tests and includes a total of just over 200 multiple-choice items. You may encounter non-scorable questions but you won't know which is which, so they surely aren't worth worrying about. Your final scaled score will be based only on the scorable items.

What is the passing score?

The FTCE PK–3 test is a pass/fail test. Immediately after testing, you will receive an unofficial pass/non-pass status. Official score reports are released within 4 weeks of testing.

On your official score report you will see "Pass" or "Not Pass." Your raw score and percentage of correct answers on the test are converted to what is called a scale score. The minimum passing scale score for each subtest on the FTCE PK–3 test is 200. The following table shows the approximate percentage of questions you need to get correct in order to pass:

Subtest	Approx. Percent of Correct Answers Needed to Pass
Developmental Knowledge (531)	67%
Language Arts and Reading (532)	71%
Mathematics (533)	68%
Science (534)	64%

What if I don't pass each subject area subtest?

You must pass all parts of the FTCE PK–3 test in order to meet the examination requirement for FTCE PK–3 certification. If you don't do well on every part of the test, don't panic. You can retake individual subtests after a 31-day waiting period after the first and subsequent attempts.

If you do not pass one of the FTCE PK–3 subtests, your score report will include a numeric score as well as a detailed performance analysis report that indicates the number and percentage of multiple-choice questions you answered correctly by applicable competency. Use this information to determine the sections of the test in which your performance is weakest, and then plan to do some additional studying in those areas.

How should I prepare for the test?

It is never too early to start studying for the PK–3 test. The earlier you begin, the more time you will have to sharpen your skills. Do not procrastinate. Cramming is not an effective way to study, since it does not allow you the time needed that works best for you. Be consistent and use your time wisely. Work out a schedule and stick to it.

When you take our diagnostic and practice tests, simulate the conditions of the test as closely as possible. Go to a quiet place free from distraction. Read each question carefully, consider all answer choices, and pace yourself.

As you complete each test, review your score reports, study the diagnostic feedback, and thoroughly review the explanations to the questions you answered incorrectly. But don't overdo it. Take one problem area at a time; review it until you are confident that you have mastered the material. Give extra attention to the areas giving you the most difficulty, as this will help build your score.

PK–3 STUDY SCHEDULE

Week	Activity
1	Take the online Diagnostic Test Battery at the REA Study Center. Your detailed score report will identify the topics where you need the most review.
2–3	Study the review chapters, using your Diagnostic Test score report to focus your study. Useful study techniques include highlighting key terms and information and taking notes as you read the review. Learn all the competencies by making flashcards and targeting questions you missed on the diagnostic test.
4	Take Practice Test Battery 1 either in the book or online at the REA Study Center. Review your score report and identify topics where you need more review.
5	Reread all your notes, refresh your understanding of the test's competencies and skills, review your college textbooks, and read class notes you've taken. This is also the time to consider any other supplementary materials that your advisor suggests.
6	Take Practice Test Battery 2 either in the book or online at the REA Study Center. Review your score report and restudy the appropriate review section(s) until you are confident you understand the material.

Are there any breaks during the test?

If you take at least three of the FTCE PK–3 subtests, you will receive a 15-minute break, which is built into the test. Instructions will appear on the computer screen at the appropriate time. During a scheduled break you are permitted to access personal items and you may leave the test center. You will need to show identification when leaving or re-entering the testing room. After finishing your break, the test administrator will check your ID and escort you back to your seat so you can resume your test.

If you need to take an unscheduled break during the test, the exam clock will not stop. The test administrator will set your workstation to "break" mode before you leave the room. During an unscheduled break, you are not permitted to access personal items (other than food, drink, or medications) and you are not allowed to leave the test center. After your break, the test administrator will check your ID and escort you back to your seat so you can continue your test.

What else do I need to know about test day?

The day before your test, check for any updates in your Pearson testing account. This is where you'll learn of any changes to your reporting schedule or if there is a change in the test site.

On the day of the test, you should wake up early after a good night's rest. Have a good breakfast and dress in layers that can be removed or added as the conditions in the test center require.

Arrive at the test center early. This will allow you to relax and collect your thoughts before the test, and will also spare you the anguish that comes with being late. As an added incentive to make sure you arrive early, keep in mind that no one will be admitted into the test center after the test has begun.

Before you leave for the testing site, carefully review your registration materials. Make sure you bring your admission ticket and two unexpired forms of identification. Primary forms of ID include:

- Passport

- Government-issued driver's license

- State or Province ID card

- National ID card

- Military ID card

You may need to produce a supplemental ID document if any questions arise with your primary ID or if your primary ID is otherwise valid but lacks your full name, photo, and signature. Without proper identification, you will not be admitted to the test center.

You may not bring watches of any kind, smartphones, or any other electronic communication devices, or weapons of any kind. Scrap paper, written notes, books, and any printed material are also prohibited.

No smoking, eating, or drinking is allowed in the testing room. Consider bringing a small snack and a bottle of water to partake of beforehand to keep you sharp during the test.

CHAPTER 2

Strategies for Success

1. Guess Away

One of the most frequently asked questions about the PK–3 test is: Can I guess? Absolutely! There is no penalty for guessing on the test. That means that if you guess incorrectly, you will not lose any points, but if you guess correctly, you will gain points. Thus, while it's fine to guess, it's important to guess strategically, or as the strategy is called: use process of elimination (see strategy No. 2). Your score is based strictly on the number of correct answers. So answer all questions and take your best guess when you don't know the answer.

2. Process of Elimination

Process of elimination is one of the most important test-taking strategies at your disposal. Process of elimination means looking at the choices and eliminating the ones you know are wrong, including answers that are only partially wrong. Your odds of getting the right answer increase from the moment you are able to get rid of a choice.

3. All in

Review all the response options. Just because you believe you've found the correct answer; don't neglect to look at each choice so you don't mistakenly jump to any conclusions. You are asked to choose the *best* answer; so be sure your answer is the best one.

4. Letter Choice of the Day

What if you are truly stumped and can't use the process of elimination? It's time to pick a fallback answer. On the day of the test, pick a letter choice (A, B, C, or D) that you will use for any question you can't strategically guess. According to the laws of probability, you have a higher chance of getting an answer right if you stick to one chosen position.

5. Use Choices to Confirm Your Answer

The great thing about multiple-choice questions is that the answer has to be staring back at you. Have an answer in mind and use the choices to *confirm* it. For the math subtest, you can work out the problem and find the match among the choices, or you might want to try the opposite—*backsolving*—that is, working *backwards* from the choices given.

6. Watch the Clock

Among the most vital point-saving skills is active time management. The breakdown and time limits of each section are provided as you begin each test. Keep an eye on the timer on your computer screen. Make sure you stay on top of how much time you have left for each section and never spend too much time on any one question. If you spend too much time on one question, this will limit your ability as a test-taker to successfully answer each question within the given subtest. Remember, each multiple-choice question is worth one raw point. The last thing you want on test day is to lose easy points because you ran out of time and focused too much on difficult questions.

7. Read, Read, Read

It's important to read through all the multiple-choice options. Even if you believe answer choice A is correct, you can misread a question or response option if you are rushing to get through the test. While it is important not to linger on a question, it is also crucial to avoid giving a question short shrift. Slow down, calm down, and read all of the choices. Verify that your choice is the best one, and click on it.

8. Take Notes

Use the erasable notepad and pen provided to you to make notes to work toward the answer(s).

9. Isolate Limiters

Pay attention to any limiters in a multiple-choice question stem. These are words such as *initial*, *best*, *most* (as in *most appropriate* or *most likely*), *not*, *least*, *required*, or *necessary*. Also, watch out for negative words, such as "Choose the answer that is *not* true." When you select your answer, double-check yourself by asking how the response fits the limitations established by the stem. Think of the stem as a puzzle piece that perfectly fits only the response option(s) that contain the correct answer. Let it guide you.

10. It's Not a Race

Ignore other test-takers. Don't compare yourself to anyone else in the room. Focus on the items in front of you and the time you have left. If someone finishes the test 30 minutes early, it does not necessarily mean that person answered more questions correctly than you did. Stay calm and focus on *your* test. It's the only one that matters.

11. Confirm Your Click

In the digital age, many of us are used to rapid clicking, be it in the course of emailing or gaming. Look at the screen to be sure to see that your mouse-click is acknowledged. If your answer doesn't register, you won't get credit. However, if you want to mark it for review so you can return to it later, you can do so—but only within a subtest. Before you click "Submit," use the test's review screen to see whether you inadvertently skipped any questions.

12. Creature of Habit? No Worries

We are all creatures of habit. It's therefore best to follow a familiar pattern of study. Do what is comfortable for you. Set a time and place each day to study for this test. Whether it is 30 minutes at the library or an hour in a secluded corner of your local coffee shop, commit yourself as best you can to this schedule every day. Find quiet places where it is less crowded, as constant noise can distract you and will not accurately simulate testing conditions. Don't study one subject for too long, either. Take an occasional breather and treat yourself to a healthy snack or some quick exercise. After your short break—5 or 10 minutes can do the trick—return to what you were studying or start a new section.

13. Knowledge Is Power

Purchasing this book gives you an edge on passing the PK–3 test. Make the most of this edge. Review the sections on how the test is structured, what the directions look like, what types of questions will be asked, and so on. Take our practice tests to familiarize yourself with what the test looks and feels like. Most text anxiety occurs because people feel unprepared when they are taking the test, and they psych themselves out. You can whittle away at anxiety by learning the format of the test and by knowing what to expect. Fully simulating the test even once will boost your chances of getting the score you need. As an added benefit, previewing the test will free up your brain's resources so you can focus on racking up as many points as you can.

14. B-r-e-a-t-h-e

Anxiety is neither unusual nor necessarily unwelcome on a test. Just don't let it stifle you. Take a moment to breathe. This won't merely make you feel good. The brain uses roughly three times as much oxygen as muscles in the body do: Give it what it needs. Now consider this: What's the worst that can happen when you take a test? You may have an off day, and despite your best efforts, you may not pass. Well, the good news is that this test can be retaken. Fortunately, the FTCE PK–3 test is something you can study and prepare for, and in some ways to a greater extent than other tests you've taken throughout your academic career. In fact, study after study has validated the value of test preparation. Yes, there will be questions you won't know, but neither your teacher education program nor state licensing board (which sets its own cut scores) expects you to know everything. When unfamiliar vocabulary appears or difficult math problems loom, don't despair: Use context clues, process of elimination, or your response option of the day (i.e., choose either A, B, C, or D routinely when you need to resort to a guess) to make your choice, and then press ahead. If you have time left, you can always come back to the question later. If not, relax. It is only one question on a test filled with many. Take a deep breath and then exhale. You know this information. Now you're going to show it.

Developmental Knowledge Subtest 1 (531)

This chapter focuses on the knowledge and skills needed to understand the complexity of early childhood growth and development, while recognizing the impact of a variety of factors, including nutrition, environment, temperament, diversity, and socioeconomic status. At the end of this chapter, you will find a list of resources that support each FTCE competency and set of skills. These resources come in varied forms from websites to journals, and are collected at the end of the chapter so that you may stay focused on the material at hand as you review.

Competency 1: Knowledge of Child Growth, Child Development, and Relationship with Families and the Community

Skill 1.1: Identify the major effects of genetics, health, nutrition, public policy, environment, and economics on child development.

Children's well-being and development is influenced by a variety of factors that can be difficult to isolate. The factors can be divided broadly into biological, environmental, and behavioral and all can contribute to a child's health, which includes their physical, dental, auditory, visual and nutritional development and well-being. Biological factors, sometimes called "nature," include heredity, genetics, and prenatal issues, as well as influences that occur during infancy and beyond which impact a child's overall health and temperament. Nutrition can also impact a child's development and includes not only food or nutrients, but also how the child processes those nutrients to be healthy, grow, and develop properly. Public policy decisions at several levels (e.g., federal, state, and local) can impact a child's health directly or indirectly. A child's environment, sometimes called "nurture," can vary greatly and includes the circumstances, objects, people, conditions, and the places within that environment, such as the home, the neighborhood, and the classroom. Economic factors, such as food insecurity and poverty, can also impact child development.

Skill 1.2: Identify the developmental stages (e.g., social-emotional, cognitive, language, physical) and the milestones for the typically developing child.

Developmental stages are broadly categorized as physical, social-emotional, and cognitive, which includes language, literacy, thinking, and creativity. Developmental milestones typically occur in a predictable trajectory or continuum, although the pace can vary with each person. Children develop rapidly during the first five years. Typically, developing children are somewhere in the middle of the continuum. The milestones are evaluated in increments: 0–3 months, 3–6 months, 6–12 months, 12–18 months, 18–24 months, 2–3 years, 3–4 years, 4–6 years, 6–9 years, 9–11 years, 11–15 years, and 15–21 years. The Florida Department of Children and Families (2020) provides a matrix for assessing milestones, shown on the following pages.

Table 1

3–4 Years				
Physical	**Social & Emotional**	**Cognitive**	**Indicators of Developmental Concern**	**Positive Parenting Characteristics**
• Continues to run, jump, throw, and catch with better coordination • Walks up and down stairs, one foot on each step • Rides tricycle • Uses scissors • Can button and lace • Eats and dresses by self with supervision • Uses toilet or potty-chair; bladder and bowel control are usually established	• Emotional self-regulation improves • Understands taking turns and sharing • Self-conscious emotions become more common • Forms first friendships • Shows concerns for a crying friend • May get upset with major changes in routine	• Asks "why" questions – believes there is a reason for everything and he or she wants to know it • Engages actively in symbolic play – has strong fantasy life, loves to imitate and role-play • Speech can be understood by others • Should be able to say about 500 to 900 words • Understands some number concepts • Converses and reasons • Is interested in letters • Scribbles in a more controlled way – is able to draw circles, recognizable objects	• Falls down a lot or has trouble with stairs • Drools or has very unclear speech • Doesn't use sentences of more than three words • Can't work simple toys (such as peg boards, simple puzzles, turning handle) • Doesn't make eye contact • Doesn't play pretend or make-believe • Doesn't want to play with other children or with toys • Lashes out without any self-control when angry or upset	• Provides a sense of security by maintaining household routines and schedules • Supports child's need for gradual transitioning. Example: Provides warning of changes so child has time to shift gears: "We're leaving in 10 minutes" • Points out colors and numbers in the course of everyday conversation • Encourages independent activity to build self-reliance • Provides lots of sensory experiences for learning and developing coordination— sand, mud, finger-paints, puzzles • Reads, sings, and talks to build vocabulary

4–6 Years				
Physical	**Social & Emotional**	**Cognitive**	**Indicators of Developmental Concern**	**Positive Parenting Characteristics**
• Has refined muscle development and is better coordinated, so that he or she can learn new skills • Has improved finger dexterity—ties shoes; draws more complex picture; writes name • Climbs, hops, skips, and likes to do stunts. Gross motor skills increase in speed and endurance	• Plays cooperatively with peers • Enhanced capacity to share and take turns • Recognizes ethnic and sexual identification • Displays independence • Protects self and stands up for rights • Identifies with parents and likes to imitate them • Often has "best friends" • Likes to show adults what he or she can do • Continually forming new images of self based on how others view him or her	• Is developing longer attention span • Understands cause-and-effect relationships • Engages in more dramatic play and is closer to reality, pays attention to details • Is developing increasingly more complex and versatile language skills • Expresses ideas, asks questions, engages in discussions • Speaks clearly • Is able to draw representative pictures • Knows and can name members of family and friends • Increased understanding of time	• Poor muscle tone, motor coordination • Poor pronunciation, incomplete sentences • Cognitive delays; inability to concentrate • Cannot play cooperatively; lack curiosity, absent imaginative and fantasy play • Social immaturity: unable to share or negotiate with peers; overly bossy, aggressive, competitive • Attachment problems: overly clingy, superficial attachments, shows little distress or overreacts when separated from caregiver • Excessively fearful, anxious, night terrors • Lacks impulse control, little ability to delay gratification • Exaggerated response (tantrums, aggression) to even mild stressors • Enuresis, encopresis, self-stimulating behavior—rocking, head-banging	• Encourages exploration • Applauds child's efforts • Interprets new/unfamiliar situations • Reinforces good behavior and achievements • Encourages child to express feelings and emotions • Encourages physical activity with supervision • Gives child chances to make choices • Uses time-out for behavior that is not acceptable

(continued)

6–9 Years				
Physical	**Social & Emotional**	**Cognitive**	**Indicators of Developmental Concern**	**Positive Parenting Characteristics**
• Gradual replacement of primary teeth by permanent teeth throughout middle childhood • Fine motor skills: writing becomes smaller and more legible; drawings become more organized and detailed and start to include some depth • Gross motor skills: can dress and undress alone; organized games with rough-and-tumble play become more common	• May have a special friend • Likes action on television • Enjoys books and stories • May argue with other children but shows cooperation in play with a particular friend • Self-concept includes identifying own personality traits and comparing self with others • Becomes more responsible and independent • Still obeys adults to avoid trouble • Can adapt ideas about fairness to fit varied situations	• Thought becomes more logical, helping the child categorize objects and ideas • Can focus on more than one characteristic of concrete objects • Attention becomes more selective and adaptable • Can use rehearsal and organization as memory strategies • Emotional intelligence is developing: self-awareness and understanding of own feelings; empathy for the feelings of others; regulation of emotion; delaying gratification • Vocabulary increases rapidly • Makes the transition from "learning to read" to "reading to learn" • Carries on long conversation	These indicators may be present in any child between 6–11 years: • Low self-esteem • Acts sad and/or nervous much of the time • Aggressive much of the time (hits, fights, curses, breaks or throws objects) • Exhibits poor impulse control • Has difficulty concentrating or sitting still • Scapegoated/ ignored by other children • Poor grades • Doesn't respond to positive attention/ praise • Seeks adult approval/ attention excessively • Suspicious/ mistrustful of adults; doesn't turn to adults for help/comfort • Little frustration tolerance; difficult to engage and keep interested in goal-directed activity • Cannot adapt behavior to different social settings • Doesn't understand a person's identity remains the same regardless of outward changes (e.g., costume) • Can't understand concepts of space, time, and dimension • Can't differentiate real from pretend • Can't understand the difference between behavior and intent (breaking a lamp is equally bad regardless of whether on purpose or an accident)	• Shows affection for child; recognizes accomplishments • Helps child develop a sense of responsibility—asks child to help with household tasks such as setting the table • Talks with child about school, friends, and things to look forward to in the future • Encourages child to think about consequences before acting • Makes clear rules and sticks to them • Engages in fun activities together • Praises child for good behavior • Supports child in taking on new challenges • Gets involved in child's school

Skill 1.3: Identify atypical development (e.g., social-emotional, cognitive, language, physical).

Atypical development includes those children who reach developmental milestones earlier or later than most children their age. During the first three years of development, a child's brain connections increase in complexity and external influences can have long-term effects on development. Childcare providers and teachers should pay close attention to those children who are developing slightly atypically, as those children often fall into an area where they struggle at school, but do not qualify to receive services. It is also important for providers and teachers to pay attention to those children who have moderate to severe delays, to best support the child and his/her family. The Florida Department of Children and Families also provides a list of indicators of developmental concern in their 2019 child development matrix.

Skill 1.4: Identify and distinguish the influences of substance abuse, physical abuse, and emotional distress on child development.

The CDC (U.S. Centers for Disease Control) reports that one in four children experience some trauma that may include some sort of maltreatment (physical, sexual, or emotional abuse). Parental substance abuse can have a negative impact on a child's development at each stage and is often associated with maltreatment of children. Substance abuse during pregnancy can result in impaired brain development, congenital malformations, premature delivery, low birth weight, and withdrawal symptoms after birth. In later stages, parental substance abuse can impact or impair a child's physical, social-emotional, cognitive, and language development in a variety of ways. Further, parental substance abuse can result in physical and emotional abuse or neglect of the child through exposure to toxic or negative physical, social, and emotional environments and relationships that may impact a child's future substance use (Landers, Howsare, & Burne, 2013). Physical abuse may also impact a child's development physically, socially, emotionally, and cognitively. Emotional distress may result from several factors and can also have a negative impact on a child's development. Trauma-informed care includes teachers and caregivers being sensitive to children's past traumas, their coping mechanisms, and their current issues while taking into account the whole child (physical, social-emotional, and cognitive domains).

Facts about Child Abuse and Neglect from Child Protective Services

Here's key information on child abuse and neglect from the 28th edition of the Child Maltreatment Report, January 28, 2019:

- In 2017, the latest year from which information is available, an estimated 1,720 children died from abuse and neglect.

- About 674,000 children were identified as victims of child abuse or neglect by child protective service agencies in 2017.

- In 2017, there were 4.1 million reports of child maltreatment in the United States involving more than 7.5 million children. Of these, 74.9 percent suffered neglect.

- Neglect is the most common form of maltreatment.

- Neglect is a pattern of failing to provide for a child's basic needs. It is abuse through omission—of not doing something—resulting in significant harm or risk of significant harm. There are four types of neglect: physical neglect, medical neglect, educational neglect, and emotional neglect.

- More children have died from neglect than from any other form of maltreatment in recent years. In each of these recent years, at least 1,500 children died from maltreatment.

- Of the children who experienced maltreatment or abuse, three-quarters suffered neglect; 17.2% suffered physical abuse; and 8.4% suffered sexual abuse.

Overall U.S. Child Abuse Statistics:

- 61,000 reports to Child Protective Services per week = 6 per minute.

- Of 1.5 million runaways, 85% are fleeing some form of abuse.

- Only 10% of these children do not know their abuser well.

- Abuse victims = 48% male, 52% female.

- Estimated referral to CPS for investigated response or alternative response increased by 15% from fiscal year 2013 (3,598,000) to fiscal year 2017 (4,135,000).

Skill 1.5: Identify diverse family systems and recognize their influences on children's early experiences which contribute to individual differences and development and learning.

Family and community systems can vary greatly regarding race, ethnicity, culture, economics, language, and social context, all of which may tremendously influence a child's development, temperament, and learning. Productive and nurturing relationships with family and other individuals support a child's cognitive and language skills. Children are constantly learning at home, in early childhood settings, and in their neighborhoods and communities. Daily routines, activities, and opportunities to play, explore, and imitate are all part of a child's learning. Adults can foster and enhance a child's learning and development by ensuring that basic health and safety needs are met, by engaging in conversations with them often, and by providing intentional and appropriate experiences that allow children to explore and to develop needed skills and problem-solving abilities.

Skill 1.6: Identify the influence of scientific research on theories of cognitive and social development, the principles of how children learn, and the development and implementation of instructional strategies.

A great deal of cross-disciplinary research has been done on how individuals learn and develop. Much of the work done with early childhood learning and development has been situated in psychology or clinical settings and later applied to education, teaching, and learning. It is important to acknowledge that the theories and principles that describe and explain how children grow, learn, and develop are situated in the context of the theorist's time, circumstance, culture, and values, and sometimes may not hold up over time. The term "evidence-based" practice can help alert educators to practices that have likely been shown to be sound and reliable, but it is also important to pay attention to where and when the information is published. For example, the theory of learning styles, or the idea that people learn best either auditorily, kinesthetically, or visually, has been challenged by researchers who found that individuals may have preferences, but oftentimes the way individuals learn material may be a habit or externally controlled (Willingham, Hughes, & Dobby, 2015). Several early childhood professional groups as well as state and national agencies and policy groups can be good resources.

Skill 1.7: Identify and apply strategies to involve families in their child's development and learning in all phases of school programs.

Family engagement is defined as program practices that welcome families' active participation in school and include families in all aspects of their child's learning. Research reveals that when families are involved in their children's programs, children tend to have more school-readiness skills and long-term academic success. Programs that promote family engagement typically have the following indicators:

1. Families are encouraged to offer ideas and suggestions, no matter their background, skill set, or past experiences.

2. Families have clear lines of communication and are able to collaborate and share ideas.

3. All families are invited to be part of program decisions and are invited to help with policy-making.

4. The enrollment process is simple and accessible, so that all families, including those who do not speak English as their first language or those who are homeless and do not have easy access to technology, are able to enroll with ease.

5. Staff and families are involved in creating family engagement goals.

6. Programs ensure that children have learning opportunities at home and at school that are consistent with the families' beliefs and values.

Skill 1.8: Identify and apply strategies to facilitate family and community partnerships.

According to the National Center on Safe and Supportive Learning Environments, these partnerships are a shared responsibility and a reciprocal process that should include all stakeholders. When done in culturally appropriate and relevant ways, these partnerships can positively impact children's academic, social, emotional, and physical outcomes. For example, children who feel supported by their parents are less likely to suffer from eating disorders. Further, adults who are included in meaningful partnerships with their child's teacher and school believe in and empower their children more as the children move through their lives and academic careers. Early childhood teachers and caregivers can implement strategies such as providing documents in the home language of the family, planning opportunities for parents to meet during evenings or weekends, or conduct home visits, with guidance from their administrator. They can take care to avoid academic jargon and acronyms that may be confusing. They can hold parent nights where the children can share what they are learning in a supportive atmosphere. Many schools offer a parent resource library, access to computers and the internet, or classroom take-home activity kits that allow the parents to understand what their child is learning and to help them learn. While there are many strategies that can facilitate partnerships, teachers must be careful to ensure that they keep their administrator informed that they are following laws and guidelines regarding privacy and safety.

Competency 2: Knowledge of the Profession and Foundations of Early Childhood (PreK–3) Education

Skill 2.1: Identify theorists, theories, and developmental domains (e.g., physical, cognitive, social-emotional) in the fields of early childhood education and their implications for the classroom teacher of young children.

A number of theorists, philosophers, and researchers have impacted the field of early childhood education, and as a group, have contributed to the idea that there are specific domains, or areas of human development, that broadly include development in the physical, emotional, social, and cognitive areas. Within these domains, there are broad developmental norms, or the typical characteristics of development at a given age. While there are a lot of outside influences on individual development, teachers and other professionals in early childhood can use these norms as a guide to determine the child's progress in each area. Additionally, there are developmental milestones, or sets of skills and tasks that most children can do at a certain age. These milestones can be used to develop assessments or for observations. They can influence decisions regarding teaching, learning, and support.

While not an exhaustive list, the following researchers and theorists have had a significant impact on the field of early childhood education and the more recent move toward **Whole Child Education.** Whole Child Education includes infancy through adolescence and means that the early childhood teacher or professional considers the developmental stages of the child rather than focusing simply on the cognitive domain or academic learning and achievement.

Arnold Gesell (1896–1961) developed the concept of "readiness" as he and his colleagues studied children and identified developmental norms or patterns. Gesell advanced the **Maturationist theory**, which suggests that genetic differences determine the rate at which children develop and proceed through stages. Many screening instruments and developmental charts are influenced by Gesell's work and provide guidance for caregivers and teachers as they plan, develop, implement, and assess learning and development activities and opportunities. Critics of this theory assert that the studies were too small and not diverse enough to be used in broad settings. Others have noted that environmental factors are still essential for children to develop and progress. So, while norms can be guides, caregivers and teachers must consider a child's circumstances and individual development and temperament.

Jean Piaget (1896–1980) is one of the best known cognitive theorists and developed the theory of **Constructivism**. He studied how children think, both in the laboratory and with his own children. He found that children think very differently from adults, constructing their understanding through interactions with individuals and objects or things in their environment. As they grow and develop, children revise and expand these understandings through active involvement and interaction. Piaget posited that play was the most effective way for children to learn. Through his research, Piaget identified three types of knowledge: physical, social, and logico-mathematical. Children learn physical knowledge by actively interacting with the external world. For example, a child might learn about an apple by looking at it, holding and squeezing it, and tasting it, learning much more than if he or she had just been shown a picture of an apple. Social knowledge includes language, stories, symbols, rules, and values and beliefs and is learned by observation, being told about it, and reading. For example, a child might see his parent use a hammer and learn that there are different types of hammers (e.g., claw, sledge, ball peen) that are used for different purposes. Another example is that a child might be told that in certain situations, when eating, he or she should not put elbows on the table or that the napkin should be placed across the lap. Logico-mathematical knowledge is developed as children construct their understanding of relationships through observation, comparison, and reasoning. While this knowledge requires direct experience, it is based on the internal processing of what's experienced. For example, a child playing with wooden blocks may observe that some blocks roll, some do not, and some stack better than others. He or she may develop the idea of a block as one category of toy that can have several characteristics. Piaget coined the term "schemata" to describe children's organized ways of making sense of their experiences. These schemas begin as behavioral and move to physical and mental constructs, which allow for representational thought and problem-solving ability. Piaget found that children organized their experiences through assimilation, or included the information into the existing schemata, and accommodated, or adjusted or created a new mental structure or schema.

Piaget's Stages of Cognitive Development:

1. **Sensorimotor Stage** (birth to age 2)—is reached when children begin to understand that objects exist even when they are not visible.

2. **Preoperational Stage** (ages 2–7)—Children have reached this stage when they exhibit an increased understanding of the world from the sensorimotor stage. However, their preoperational thinking still exhibits serious shortcomings. The preoperational stage is divided into two sub-stages:

   • **Preconceptual Phase** (ages 2–4)—Children have entered this sub-stage when they can identify images mentally and can identify them as belonging to the same class. But they don't always get it right. Think of a young child seeing his first cat, but calling it a dog because of the basic characteristics that can make the two types of animals appear to be the same. He doesn't understand all the properties of classes.

   • **Intuitive Phase** (ages 4–7)—At this substage, children have formed a more complete understanding of concepts. Their thinking has become more logical, although it is structured more about perception than logic.

3. **Concrete Operational Stage** (ages 7–11)—Children enter this stage when they understand the concept of transitive inference, or the ability to mentally arrange objects in a series.

4. **Formal Operational Stage** (ages 11–15)—Children have moved into this stage when they develop hypothetico-deductive reasoning, or the ability to systematically analyze and deduce outcomes based on a general theory.

Piaget noted that the stages of cognitive development and previous social experiences can affect children's moral development, noting that children move from believing that rules are fixed and from a higher authority to understanding that some rules are made by people and can be changed.

The instructional impact of Piaget's work was to help refine the concept of readiness and support the use of materials for sensory play and exploration, open-ended learning materials, a daily schedule with ample time for play, opportunities to question, problem-solve, and explore the real world. Later research has revealed that Piaget's stages may occur earlier than he had determined and may be less discrete and more gradual.

Lawrence Kohlberg (1927–1987) extended Piaget's theory of moral development, focusing on moral decisions that individuals make during their lives. He posited that there were **three stages of moral development** that were sequential and dependent on the previous stage and were based upon the individual's ongoing experiences and developing reasoning. He assumed that children moved from making decisions based on external consequences, to choosing behavior based on internal standards and principles. Level One is *preconventional morality* (ages 2–7) and presumes that children make decisions based on self-interest and emotion. By age 4, children begin to understand the concept of reciprocity, or the idea that doing something good for someone might result in a positive return. Level Two, the *conventional morality stage* (ages 7–12), assumes that people choose to conform to and follow rules because they are concerned with group approval and consensus. There is a desire to maintain the social order for the general good. Level Three is *post-conventional morality* (adolescents and older, though some do not reach this stage), and is the highest level. Kohlberg described this level as when people accept rules and laws, but may make decisions based on conscience or belief in a universal morality. Critics have noted that Kohlberg's research was done primarily with male subjects, hypothetical scenarios, and focused on Western values of individual rights. Follow-up research has suggested that males and females may make moral decisions based on caring and justice, and males may lean more toward justice and fairness than females do. Kohlberg's ideas have influenced some social-emotional curricula and have contributed to the idea that education should focus on the child as a whole individual.

Maria Montessori (1870–1952) was an Italian physician and educator who posited that children develop in six-year increments. Similar to Piaget, Montessori observed that children learned best when they moved from active, hands-on activities to more abstract ideas. In the first six years, children need opportunities to explore and play. In the second phase (ages 6–12), children develop rational thinking, problem-solving abilities, and an interest in the world around them. In the third stage, Montessori asserted that children develop a sense of social justice and begin to work to solve real-world problems. She believed that children have the desire to participate in the adult world and learn best when activities move from concrete to more abstract in reality-based, organized, aesthetically pleasing settings. Typical Montessori early childhood classrooms have kitchen areas, but the focus is on imitating real-world activities rather than imaginary, fantasy play. Teachers in Montessori schools act as directors and help support children's self-guided learning. Critics have asserted that the **Montessori Whole Child model** is less suited to a team-oriented, collaborative approach to learning and that the less structured routine can be difficult to manage well. Montessori schools have also been criticized for their lack of imaginary play; however, advocates for the model have noted that Montessori had posited that young children had an innate need to distinguish reality from fantasy and preferred real-world play opportunities (Kirkham & Kidd, 2015).

Rudolf Steiner (1861–1925) was an Austrian-born philosopher and social reformer who created a school for children of workers in the Waldorf Astoria cigarette factory in war-torn 1919 Stuttgart, Germany. Steiner studied Goethe extensively and developed the idea that individuals progress through developmental stages at seven-year intervals. In the *first stage (birth to age 7),* children develop physically and move into interacting with others socially. Like Piaget and Montessori, he posited that children needed opportunities to interact with and act on the environment. In the *second stage (ages 7–14)*, he describes children as artists, who construct their own view of the world. He describes this as when the child develops his or her "will" or persistence, curiosity, and fine and gross motor skills. At around 9 years of age, he noted that children begin to ask questions and notice the world around them more; at around 12 years of age, they become more interested in the world around them. It is during this stage that the child's development is most focused on "heart" issues, such as empathy and compassion. The *third stage (ages 14–21)* begins at the onset of adolescence and puberty and is marked by the child's ability to think abstractly and begin judging and thinking critically. It is at this stage that the child's developmental focus is on the "head" or cognitive and abstract thinking stage. The *last stage (ages 21–28)* is when the individual ideally develops completely and can integrate the previous stages seamlessly. Steiner asserted that individuals repeated these stages at seven-year intervals as they grew older. While critics have focused on Steiner's ideas of anthroposophy, or that connections to the spiritual world are possible through deep mental work, much of his practical applications have been supported by less controversial theories of children's development in the physical, social-emotional, and cognitive domains. Steiner's education philosophy was that children should move from exploration and creative play through a rich, multisensory approach that culminates in the development of ethics, social responsibility, and a mastery of rigorous subject matter. Teachers take on the role of performer, artist, and leader of the curriculum experiences. Waldorf schools and public schools inspired by his principles have become part of the Whole Child educational models. They are characterized by the use of natural materials, a focus on aesthetics and artistry, imaginary play, and curricular guidelines developed to match the emotional and cognitive development of the child (Edwards, 2002).

Lev Vygotsky (1896–1934) was a Russian psychologist whose sociocultural theory dealt with how children develop thought and language through social and cognitive interaction. Like Piaget, Montessori, and Steiner, Vygotsky believed that children should be active participants in their learning as they construct their understandings. Like Steiner, he felt that imaginative, fantasy play was a part of a child's learning. His ideas differ somewhat from Piaget's and Montessori's and align with Steiner in that he believed that children's learning was shaped by their social experiences with their peers, older children, and adults and that language was the means for creating understanding. He posited that children's social context influenced both what the children thought about, how they thought, and how they understood concepts. For example, a child who plays outside a lot may think of time as morning moving into afternoon into evening and night. A child who watches a lot of television indoors may think of time in the construct of television episodes. Vygotsky believed that children who were raised in settings where talk was the primary way to communicate would understand and organize experiences and information differently from a child raised in a home where sign language and nonverbal communication was primary. Vygotsky asserted that language development fostered the ability to organize and integrate experiences and develop conceptual understanding, and as such was essential for thinking. He suggested that adults talk to themselves internally, but in children, private speech is audible and gives them a tool for regulating their behavior. As children grow older, they move from audible to internal speech. Vygotsky coined the term *Zone of Proximal Development* to describe the behaviors that children can do independently and with help from another, more competent individual. He found that adults could support children by helping or scaffolding in the space that exists between what a child can do on his or her own and what he or she cannot yet do without assistance, similarly to how Montessori teachers support a child's learning. Vygotsky's ideas have highlighted the importance of social context for learning and the importance of family in a child's learning and has played out in the classroom through collaborative learning and fantasy and pretend play. His Zone of Proximal Development has formed the framework for teacher interaction with children and is part of the process of guided reading at the instructional level. His assertion that evaluating and assessing children should be both qualitative and quantitative has supported the use of anecdotal notes and performance-based assessments.

Erik Erikson (1902–1994) developed a psychosocial theory of development that describes eight stages of social and emotional development in the first eight years of life. He believed that each stage fostered basic attitudes and that difficulty in any stage could negatively impact the individual's mastery of the next stage. He created a continuum for each stage that ranged from unhealthy to healthy development. The first stage, *Trust vs. Mistrust* (infant), describes the period when infants learn or fail to learn that people are reliable, nurturing, and responsive or that they need to depend on themselves for nurturing. Infants learn that the world is a good and safe place if they have nurturing, responsive relationships. If they do not experience this type of care, they may not develop the ability to trust others or themselves. *Autonomy vs. Shame and Doubt* (toddler) is the second stage and is the time when toddlers aged 12 to 15 months develop a sense of autonomy, self-governance, and an ability to act on something independently. During this time, conflict regarding toilet training and self-help skills is common. If the child's behaviors and actions are received in a positive way, the child will move successfully through this stage. If the adult is harsh or punitive, or if the child is disciplined harshly for asserting his or her independence, then the child may experience more shame and doubt as he or she develops. The third stage, *Initiative vs. Guilt*, begins in the preschool years when a child typically is curious, ready to learn, and wants to actively explore and create. If the child's curiosity is perceived as negative, or the parent is overly concerned with the child being hurt or damaging things, the child may either not develop initiative or be overly worried and have feelings of guilt. The next stage, *Industry vs. Inferiority*, occurs in the school-age years and deals with a child's readiness to learn new ideas and construct things. During this stage, a child needs opportunities to interact with various materials and the chance to be successful socially, intellectually, and physically. Experiencing success can lead to a sense of accomplishment and competence. If a child repeatedly fails, he or she may develop a sense of inferiority. Because these stages occur during childhood, positive relationships with significant adults are essential and an understanding of these stages is important for early childhood educators. One caveat is that in some cultures, families may value group membership more than individualism. Therefore, teachers should be careful to select practices that honor the family's culture or values.

Abraham Maslow's (1908–1970) **Self-Actualization Theory** is based on the idea that there is a hierarchy of basic needs that impact motivation and potential. If the needs are not met or only partially met, individuals may not survive, may focus too much energy on meeting the needs, or may not thrive. The needs move from basic to growth in a pyramid shape (see the next page). The basic needs that form the base of the pyramid are called physiological and include the need for air, food, water, and shelter. The next step in the pyramid covers safety needs and includes physical and emotional security. The third step is love, which includes feeling a sense of belonging with loved ones that may include family or friends. The fourth step is esteem, which includes self-esteem and a belief that one is respected by others. The final step, which leads to self-actualization, includes the ability to understand one's self, to maintain positive relationships, to focus on giving and receiving love, and to see the world clearly and to be open to new experiences and learning. Critics have argued that Maslow's theory is founded on a Western philosophy of individualism and may not be applicable to all cultures. However, many of the ideas are applicable to education, including providing an optimal environment for learning that includes children feeling safe, not being hungry or thirsty, and believing that they are accepted and cared for.

Maslow's Hierarchy of Needs

Self-actualization

Esteem

Love

Safety

Physiological

B.F. Skinner (1904–1980) and his **Behaviorism Learning** theory has greatly influenced beliefs about how people learn. In contrast to developmental theories, behaviorism principles apply to all learners regardless of age and are founded on the belief that behavior is changed because of consequences experienced immediately following a behavior. Working with rats, Skinner developed the concept of *operant conditioning*, which is the idea that positive consequences, or rewards, will result in repeat behavior, and negative consequences, or punishment, will decrease the behavior. Behaviorism deals with isolated, observable behaviors, and while some aspects are useful in an educational setting, such as praising a child's effort, human behavior is complex, and the desired behaviors may not occur. Because behaviorism focuses on rewards, children may be motivated extrinsically, rather than intrinsically. This may result in a child not developing internal behavior control and self-motivation. Some children with challenging behaviors or learning needs may benefit from behavioral learning techniques and appropriate consequences and acknowledgment. However, more complex behaviors are usually taught more effectively using principles from developmental theories such as **Constructivism**.

Urie Bronfenbrenner (1917–2005) was one of the founders of the *Head Start* program. His *Ecological Systems Theory* suggested that children's development could be understood through the contexts of the social, political, legal, and economic systems in which a child was situated. Each of the five systems influences each other, as well as the child. According to Bronfenbrenner, the *microsystem* of family, school, and peers is where a child has the most interactions. The *mesosystem* is the next layer, and includes the family's relationship to the school or to children's peers. If a family has positive relationships with the school, then they are more likely to encourage academic success for their child. The *exosystem* layer contains the social settings that can affect the child while not actually involving him or her. These include things like a parent's job. If a parent experiences a pay cut or is required to work more hours, the parent-child relationship may be affected. The *macrosystem* is the next layer out, and includes the child's cultural setting, encompassing the behavior patterns, beliefs, values, traditions, and customs that are transmitted from one generation to another. The final *chronosystem* is the timing of events and how they impact a child's development. For instance, if a child experiences the death of a parent at a young age, his or her experience will be different from that of a child who experiences the death of a parent as the child enters adolescence. Ecological systems theory influences educational practices by basing the curriculum on aspects that are significant to a child, such as family, community, and culture.

Howard Gardner's (1943–) research in neuroscience and cognitive development has resulted in the learning theory of *multiple intelligences*. Gardner suggests that an individual's intellectual capacity is formed by several faculties that can work separately or together. While he originally identified seven intelligences, Gardner has recently posited that there are nine, and perhaps more. He defines *intelligence* as what is needed and valued within a society.

1. **Musical intelligence** is the ability to produce and respond to music and is seen in children who are sensitive to sound and who have the aptitude to play an instrument.

2. **Bodily-kinesthetic intelligence** describes children who have good coordination, are physically active, and who have a hard time sitting still; they are often good at sports or activities like dancing.

3. **Logical-mathematical intelligence** is the ability to understand cause and effect and number properties. This is typically expressed in an interest in numbers and proficiency with puzzles.

4. **Linguistic intelligence** is the ability to learn languages easily or the ability to learn new words and use language to communicate. This may be exhibited in children who love to tell stories or love reading and writing.

5. **Spatial intelligence** is the ability to form mental images and do activities such as reading maps or building structures with blocks.

6. **Interpersonal intelligence** is the ability to work with others and be empathetic. Leaders and socially outgoing children often have this ability.

7. **Intrapersonal intelligence** indicators include a child's confidence, ability to set and achieve goals, and ability to focus.

8. **Naturalist intelligence** is displayed when a child easily recognizes plants and animals and discriminates between different plants, animals, and other categories. These children often want to be outdoors and may have a desire for pets, animals or plants.

9. **Existential intelligence** is the capacity to think deeply about human existence and our purpose. Gardner found that this intelligence is not connected to a particular region of the brain, so he identified it as a half-intelligence. Teachers may incorporate aspects of this learning theory when providing opportunities for children to be successful in artistic endeavors, physical activities, and time outdoors.

Skill 2.2: Identify models of early childhood curriculum (e.g., Montessori, Creative Curriculum)

Infant Schools, established in England by Robert Owen, were originally for children ages 3 to 10 years of age; today the term describes schools for children between 4 and 7 years of age. The *kindergarten* model was developed in Germany by Friedrich Froebel for children 4 to 6 years old and was based on the idea that children love learning and need time to play. In many countries, it is used to describe all programs for young children, while in the United States, it typically describes the formal schooling for 5-year-olds. Froebel created materials such as blocks, geometric shapes, yarn balls, and furniture made of natural materials for use in his kindergartens. He called these materials "gifts."

Developmental and Child-Centered Curricula are derived from theorists including Froebel, Montessori, Steiner, Piaget, and Vygotsky. In the *child-centered* humanistic approach, the developmental stages, needs, and interests of young children are the focus of the learning. Related to this is the *Whole-Child Approach*, in which children's social, emotional, physical, and cognitive development are all considered essential.

The **Developmental-Interaction Approach**, sometimes called Bank Street because it was developed at Bank Street College in New York, is a progressive framework based on children venturing into the world and having direct experiences. Many of them are derived ideas from Piaget and Vygotsky that posit that children need opportunities to act on and with objects in their environment. Piaget observed that children learn best when they begin with concrete or real objects, which has led to many mathematical materials, called manipulatives, to be included in typical mathematical curricula for young children. Vygotsky's ideas of social learning have resulted in instructional strategies and curriculum models framed with the idea of collaboration, teamwork, and social interaction. Skinner's behaviorism theory has formed the foundation for many token economies used in behavior and classroom management plans.

The **Montessori Method** includes instructional materials that are didactic in nature, with specific rules for use. These developmental materials were designed to help children hone their senses and learn big ideas at the conceptual level and were carefully designed and sequenced. Through her observations, Montessori noted that children preferred to imitate the real world during their play; therefore many of her materials, such as child-sized sinks and dishes, were connected to daily life.

Many of Steiner's **Waldorf** materials for young children were also natural and developmental in nature, built around the idea that children needed to transition from a home-like environment into environments that focused on the aesthetic. For example, very young children have open-ended play opportunities that allow them to make choices and express creativity. His curriculum includes fine and applied arts, and the classroom teacher is expected to be a role model focused on each child's potential. His idea of teachers staying with their classes can be seen in the idea of *looping*, in which a teacher stays with the same class of students for multiple years.

High/Scope, an education approach developed in the 1960s as a model for ameliorating poverty, is based on Piaget's developmental tasks. The Reggio Emilia Approach, which was developed in Italy from the work of Loris Malaguzzi, includes a focus on family involvement and emphasizes creativity and a strengths-based approach.

These curriculum approaches to early childhood education formed the foundation for *Developmentally Appropriate Practice*, or a research-based framework of principles for practice couched in the child's social and cultural context, and which includes the child's development, strengths, interests, and needs. Diane Trister Dodge created *The Creative Curriculum* in 1978 based on developmentally appropriate practices. Today, many of her checklists and guidelines, updated regularly, are used in preschools.

Skill 2.3: Identify and analyze the impact of federal and state laws on education in the classroom (e.g., English for Speakers of Other Languages, Individuals with Disabilities Education Act).

A number of federal, state, and local laws and rules impact early and primary education. The Florida Department of Education maintains a webpage that allows educators to keep up to date with rules and regulations.

For those working with children who are not of school age, the Florida Early Learning Department maintains a webpage (*www.floridaearlylearning.com*).

For those working with children in the Voluntary Preschool Program, there is also a link on the Florida Department of Education website (*www.floridaearlylearning.com/vpk/floridas-vpk-program*).

The Florida Department of Children and Families also has a website with information for educators and families (*www.myflfamilies.com*).

Early childhood caregivers and educators may be impacted by legislation on an annual basis in a variety of ways. For example, the 2019 *Rilya Wilson Act* requires that in certain situations, teachers promptly report the absences of children enrolled in the program but who are under protective care. Named in memory of a child whose disappearance and later death led to a number of reforms, the law provides priority for childcare services for specified children who are at risk of abuse, neglect, or abandonment. Please see the list at the end of this chapter for websites with further information.

Students with Disabilities

In Florida, special education is called Exceptional Student Education, or ESE.

The *Individuals with Disabilities Education Act* (IDEA) is a federal special education law. IDEA guides how states, school districts, and public agencies provide early intervention, special education, and related services to more than 6.5 million eligible infants, toddlers, children, and youth with disabilities. IDEA was first enacted by Congress in 1975 to ensure that children with disabilities receive a free appropriate public education (FAPE). IDEA has been revised several times over the years. The most recent revisions were enacted in December 2004, with final regulations published in August 2006.

Section 504 of the Rehabilitation Act of 1973

Section 504 of the Rehabilitation Act prohibits discrimination based on a disability in programs or activities receiving federal financial assistance including public preschool, elementary, secondary, and postsecondary schools. Under Section 504, students with disabilities have rights to reasonable accommodations. These accommodations should be outlined by the school in a 504 Plan. A student with a disability is defined as a student who has a physical or mental impairment that substantially limits one or more major life activities, has a record of such impairment, or is regarded as having such impairment. Caring for one's self, walking, seeing, hearing, speaking, breathing, learning, working, and performing manual tasks are all considered major life activities.

All school districts in the state of Florida are required to identify a Section 504 Coordinator and establish policies and procedures including a complaint resolution system.

Details can be found in the Code of Federal Regulations at 34 C.F.R. 104.33

Every child with a disability who is eligible under IDEA and ESE has an Individual Education Plan (IEP). The IEP is an individualized written plan that supports the need for specialized supports and services. Parents and teachers consider the IEP to be their child's educational road map.

English Language Learners (ELLs)

Florida's *Consent Decree* addresses the civil rights of ELL students. Foremost among those is their right to equal access to all education programs. In addressing these rights, the Consent Decree provides a structure that ensures the delivery of comprehensible instruction to which ELL students are entitled.

The Consent Decree outlines the framework for compliance with the following federal and state laws and jurisprudence regarding the education of ELL students:

- Title VI and VII of the Civil Rights Act of 1964

- Office of Civil Rights Memorandum (Standards for Title VI Compliance) of May 25, 1970

- Requirements based on the Supreme Court decision in *Lau v. Nichols,* 1974

- Equal Education Opportunities Act of 1974

- Requirements of the Vocational Education Guidelines, 1979

- Requirements based on the Fifth Circuit Court decision in *Castañeda v. Pickard,* 1981

- Requirements based on the Supreme Court decision in *Plyler v. Doe,* 1982

- Americans with Disabilities Act (PL 94–142), 1990

- Florida Education Equity Act, 1984

- Section 504 of the Rehabilitation Act of 1973

Florida's authority for the implementation of the Consent Decree is found in Section 1003.56, F.S.

Additional Resources:

English Language Instruction for Limited English Proficient Students, and Rules 6A-6.0900 to 6A-6.0909, F.A.C., Programs for Limited English Proficient Students.

The League of United Latin American Citizens (LULAC) et al. v. State Board of Education Consent Decree, United States District Court for the Southern District of Florida, August 14, 1990.

Skill 2.4: Identify professional organizations, websites, and scholarly journals in the field of early childhood education.

There are a number of professional organizations, websites, and scholarly journals available, and early childhood education teachers and caregivers should make it a practice to review these regularly. Additionally, many of these organizations have annual conferences, which can positively impact an educator's instructional practice and knowledge base. Educators may join or participate in the organization in many ways. Each organization requires an annual membership fee, and while some publications are free, each has at least one journal that requires an annual subscription.

The *National Association for Education of Young Children* (NAEYC) is a major professional organization for those who work with children from birth through grade three. Their vision is that "All young children thrive and learn in a society dedicated to ensuring they reach their full potential." Their mission is "to promote high-quality early learning for all children, birth through age 8, by connecting practice, policy, and research. We advance a diverse, dynamic early childhood profession and support all who care for, educate, and work on behalf of young children." The NAEYC has an annual conference, as well as publications including the journal *Young Children*, that provide both research and opportunities for educators to contribute to the field.

The *Florida Association for the Education of Young Children* (FAEYC) is the state-level affiliate of NAEYC and the membership fee is less than NAEYC, and includes discounted access to an annual state conference. Their mission is to benefit children and families by providing leadership, advocacy, and professional development for early childhood professionals. The vision of the FAEYC is for every child and family to have access to quality services. In addition, it advocates for all early childhood professionals to be highly respected, skilled, fully supported, and equitably compensated for the valuable role they play in the lives of children and families.

The *Southern Early Childhood Association* (SECA) is a regional (Florida is one of the member states) organization focused on advocacy and policy for young children. Their membership is typically lower in cost than national or international organizations and in addition to an annual conference; they offer briefs and the *Dimensions of Early Childhood* journal.

The *Association for Childhood Education International* (ACEI) is an international organization focused on children from birth through adolescence. Their mission "is to promote innovative solutions to education challenges and inspire action that creates positive, sustainable futures for children and youth worldwide." ACEI's journals include, *Childhood Education: Innovations*, the *Journal of Research in Childhood Education*, and *Childhood Explorer*.

Skill 2.5: Interpret professional standards set by early childhood and elementary educational organizations (e.g., National Association for the Education of Young Children, National Association for Childhood Education International, National Council of Teachers of Mathematics, and Southern Early Childhood Association).

Professional early childhood and educational organizations develop standards that include a focus on all areas of children's learning, and well-being, as well as expectations for educators, staff, curriculum, family and community relationships, leadership and management. These standards can provide guidelines for centers, schools, and individuals in the profession.

National Association for the Education of Young Children

The governing board of the NAEYC is currently revising their 2009 Professional Standards and Competencies for Early Childhood Education. There are currently ten standards that are under review and relate to all areas of early childhood:

- Standard 1: Relationships
- Standard 2: Curriculum
- Standard 3: Teaching
- Standard 4: Assessment of Child Progress

- Standard 5: Health

- Standard 6: Staff Competencies, Preparation, and Support

- Standard 7: Families

- Standard 8: Community Relationships

- Standard 9: Physical Environment

- Standard 10: Leadership and Management

The 2018 draft has three levels of understanding for Introductory: Birth through age 8, Essential for birth through age 5, and Essential for birth through age 8.

The *Association for Childhood Education International* has ten universal beliefs that inform their code of ethics:

1. Education is a human right.

2. Education and development of a child is a continuum of experiences from birth onward.

3. All children can learn; therefore, inclusion of all children and consideration of their unique needs are essential in all learning environments.

4. The foundations of early learning create the foundations for lifelong learning.

5. Education, when appropriately designed and delivered, is transformational and can create better lives for learners, their families, their communities, and ultimately nations.

6. Education has a direct and lasting impact upon workforce opportunities and civic participation and engagement.

7. The process of learning is enlightening and empowering.

8. Appropriately designed education settings are inspirational places of learning that promote hope and promise for the future.

9. Innovation in education advances new approaches to teaching and learning, which prepares children for the world of tomorrow.

10. The education profession shares a global responsibility to the advancement of humankind and should, therefore, embrace interconnectedness and relationship building between schools, within communities, and across nations.

Skill 2.6: Analyze the relationships among current educational issues, trends, and legislation and their impact on the field of early childhood education.

Early childhood educators need to keep up with current issues, trends, and legislation as they can impact their profession and field. Current educational issues include the recognition that an over-emphasis on the cognitive domain can be detrimental to children's development, especially in other domains. This has led to a shift toward child-centered or whole-child models such as Montessori, Waldorf, and Reggio Emilia. Other trends in the early education field include a focus on trauma-informed care, which acknowledges that young children's learning and well-being may suffer when they are subjected to stresses and issues such as food insecurity, abuse, neglect, and physical or mental health issues. Along with this, research on the importance of outdoor activities and contact with nature has impacted learning environments and materials, with a shift toward natural light, time outdoors, and furniture and toys made from natural materials. Another trend is the integrating of STEM (Science, Technology, Engineering, Mathematics) with play as a way of deep learning for young children. Some U.S. companies now have divisions focused on helping educators with inquiry and project-based activities for young children.

The Florida Department of Education is tasked with implementing legislation and developing rules and guidelines for education. For example, recent legislation at the state level has included a requirement for physical education and daily recess in primary and elementary grades.

Skill 2.7: Analyze and apply ethical behavior and professional responsibilities as they relate to young children, families, colleagues, and the community (e.g., Florida Educator Accomplished Practices, Florida Department of Education Code of Ethics, and National Association for the Education of Young Children Code of Ethics).

The *Florida Educator Accomplished Practices* (FEAPs) are Florida's core standards for effective educators and provide valuable guidance to Florida's public-school educators and educator preparation programs on what educators are expected to know and be able to do. Established in 1998 through State Board of Education Rule 6A-5.065, F.A.C., they were updated in December 2010. The Educator Accomplished Practices serve as the state's standards for effective instructional practice and form the foundation for the state's teacher preparation programs, educator certification requirements, and school district instructional personnel appraisal systems. The Educator Accomplished Practices are based upon three foundational principles. Those principles focus on high expectations, knowledge of subject matter, and the standards of the profession. Each effective educator applies the foundational principles through six Educator Accomplished Practices. In this way, Florida educators have a common understanding of the expectations for instructional and professional responsibility.

Principles of Professional Conduct for the Education Profession in Florida

Established through Rule 6A-10.081, Florida Administrative Code, Principles of Professional Conduct for the Education Profession in Florida states that:

1. Florida educators shall be guided by the following ethical principles:

   - The educator values the worth and dignity of every person, the pursuit of truth, devotion to excellence, acquisition of knowledge, and the nurture of democratic citizenship.

Essential to the achievement of these standards is the freedom to learn and to teach and the guarantee of equal opportunity for all.

- The educator's primary professional concern will always be for the student and for the development of the student's potential. The educator will therefore strive for professional growth and will seek to exercise the best professional judgment and integrity.

- Aware of the importance of maintaining the respect and confidence of one's colleagues, of students, of parents, and of other members of the community, the educator strives to achieve and sustain the highest degree of ethical conduct.

2. Florida educators shall comply with the following disciplinary principles. Violation of any of these principles shall subject the individual to revocation or suspension of the individual educator's certificate, or the other penalties as provided by law.

- Obligation to the student requires that the individual:

  ▶ Shall make reasonable effort to protect the student from conditions harmful to learning and/or to the student's mental and/or physical health and/or safety.

  ▶ Shall not unreasonably restrain a student from independent action in pursuit of learning.

  ▶ Shall not unreasonably deny a student access to diverse points of view.

  ▶ Shall not intentionally suppress or distort subject matter relevant to a student's academic program.

  ▶ Shall not intentionally expose a student to unnecessary embarrassment or disparagement.

  ▶ Shall not intentionally violate or deny a student's legal rights.

  ▶ Shall not harass or discriminate against any student on the basis of race, color, religion, sex, age, national or ethnic origin, political beliefs, marital status, handicapping condition, sexual orientation, or social and family background and shall make reasonable effort to ensure that each student is protected from harassment or discrimination.

  ▶ Shall not exploit a relationship with a student for personal gain or advantage.

  ▶ Shall keep in confidence personally identifiable information obtained in the course of professional service, unless disclosure serves professional purposes or is required by law.

- Obligation to the public requires that the individual:

  ▶ Shall take reasonable precautions to distinguish between personal views and those of any educational institution or organization with which the individual is affiliated.

  ▶ Shall not intentionally distort or misrepresent facts concerning an educational matter in direct or indirect public expression.

  ▶ Shall not use institutional privileges for personal gain or advantage.

  ▶ Shall accept no gratuity, gift, or favor that might influence professional judgment.

  ▶ Shall offer no gratuity, gift, or favor to obtain special advantages.

- Obligation to the profession of education requires that the individual:

  ▶ Shall maintain honesty in all professional dealings.

  ▶ Shall not on the basis of race, color, religion, sex, age, national or ethnic origin, political beliefs, marital status, handicapping condition if otherwise qualified, or social and family background deny to a colleague professional benefits or advantages or participation in any professional organization.

  ▶ Shall not interfere with a colleague's exercise of political or civil rights and responsibilities.

  ▶ Shall not engage in harassment or discriminatory conduct which unreasonably interferes with an individual's performance of professional or work responsibilities or with the orderly processes of education or which creates a hostile, intimidating, abusive, offensive, or oppressive environment; and, further, shall make reasonable effort to ensure that each individual is protected from such harassment or discrimination.

  ▶ Shall not make malicious or intentionally false statements about a colleague.

  ▶ Shall not use coercive means or promise special treatment to influence professional judgments of colleagues.

  ▶ Shall not misrepresent one's own professional qualifications.

  ▶ Shall not submit fraudulent information on any document in connection with professional activities.

  ▶ Shall not make any fraudulent statement or fail to disclose a material fact in one's own or another's application for a professional position.

  ▶ Shall not withhold information regarding a position from an applicant or misrepresent an assignment or conditions of employment.

▶ Shall provide upon the request of the certificated individual a written statement of specific reasons for recommendations that led to the denial of increments, significant changes in employment, or termination of employment.

▶ Shall not assist entry into or continuance in the profession of any person known to be unqualified in accordance with these Principles of Professional Conduct for the Education Profession in Florida and other applicable Florida Statutes and State Board of Education Rules.

▶ Shall self-report within forty-eight hours to appropriate authorities (as determined by district) any arrests/charges involving the abuse of a child or the sale and/or possession of a controlled substance. Such notice shall not be considered an admission of guilt nor shall such notice be admissible for any purpose in any proceeding, civil or criminal, administrative or judicial, investigatory or adjudicatory. In addition, shall self-report any conviction, finding of guilt, withholding of adjudication, commitment to a pretrial diversion program, or entering of a plea of guilty or Nolo Contendere for any criminal offense other than a minor traffic violation within forty-eight hours after the final judgment. When handling sealed and expunged records disclosed under this rule, school districts shall comply with the confidentiality provisions of Sections 943.0585(4)(c) and 943.059(4)(c), F.S.

▶ Shall report to appropriate authorities any known allegation of a violation of the Florida School Code or State Board of Education Rules as defined in Section 1012.795(1), F.S.

▶ Shall seek no reprisal against any individual who has reported any allegation of a violation of the Florida School Code or State Board of Education Rules as defined in Section 1012.795(1), F.S.

▶ Shall comply with the conditions of an order of the Education Practices Commission imposing probation, imposing a fine, or restricting the authorized scope of practice.

▶ Shall, as the supervising administrator, cooperate with the Education Practices Commission in monitoring the probation of a subordinate.

(Rulemaking Authority 1001.02, 1012.795(1)(j) F.S. Law Implemented 1012.795 FS. History– New 7–6-82, Amended 12–20–83, Formerly 6B-1.06, Amended 8–10–92, 12–29–98, Formerly 6B-1.006, Amended 3–23–16.)

Competency 3: Knowledge of Developmentally Appropriate Practices

The National Association for Education of Young Children (NAEYC) has a position statement on developmentally appropriate practices teachers are tasked with:

- Creating a caring community of learners

- Teaching to enhance development and learning

- Planning curriculum to achieve important goals

- Assessing children's development and learning

- Establishing reciprocal relationships with families

Skill 3.1: Identify and apply developmentally appropriate practices that guide effective instruction.

Effective instruction includes the teacher's role and attitudes. NAEYC has a list of 10 effective DAP strategies that teachers can work to include in their daily interactions with children.

- Acknowledge what children do or say, but avoid giving directions or talking too much. Give positive attention, sometimes through comments, sometimes through just sitting nearby and observing.

- Encourage persistence and effort rather than just praising and evaluating what the child has done. "I love your hard work! Are you going to add more parts to your Lego structure?"

- Give specific feedback rather than general comments. "You put most of the silks in the basket. Can you go back and fix it, so that no silks are hanging over?"

- Model attitudes, ways of approaching problems, and behavior toward others, showing children rather than just telling them. Acknowledge if you make an error and correct it—such as if you have misspelled a word on a chart or paper.

- Demonstrate the correct way to do something. This usually involves a procedure that needs to be done in a certain way, such as forming a letter.

- Create or add challenge so that a task goes a bit beyond what the children can already do. This is called scaffolding and relates to Vygotsky's Zone of Proximal Development.

- Ask questions that provoke children's thinking. "If you wanted to explain to others how to copy your block house, how could you draw it?"

- Give assistance to help children work on the edge of their current competence. "I see you are writing your name. Remember that your first name has a capital letter!"

- Provide information and foster vocabulary or background meaning whenever possible. "You have stacked your block parallel to the other blocks."

- Give specific directions for children's action or behavior and avoid multi-step directions.

(Source: https://www.naeyc.org/resources/topics/dap/10-effective-dap-teaching-strategies)

Skill 3.2: Identify the components of effective organization and management, such as classroom rituals, routines, and schedules.

The term *temporal environment* refers to the timing, sequence, and length of routines and activities that take place throughout the school day. It includes the schedule of activities such as arrival, play time, meal time, rest time, both small- and large-group activities, and the many transitions that hold them all together. Predictable schedules and routines create a sense of security, help young children to learn about their world, help them to adjust to new situations, and prevent challenging behaviors. Daily routines also help young children to say good-bye to parents and to feel safe and secure within a nurturing network of caregivers. For example, establishing the routine of reading a book together every day in the same cozy corner of the room can help a child to prepare for the difficult separation from her parent.

When developing classroom routines, schedules, and rituals, it is important for teachers to recognize children's social, emotional, and physical levels and not assume that children know and can implement expectations. Many teachers call the routines "rhythms" to indicate a more relaxed schedule. Some general guidelines include:

- Give notice before the change, so that children have time to finish or stop what they are doing. This will avoid a lot of frustration. Depending on what you are doing, notice of the change could be given five minutes in advance for a large activity or 60 seconds for a simple math page. "You have five minutes before clean-up. Think about a good stopping place." This way they won't be in the middle of something when you ask them to transition.

- Develop relationships with children who are hard to transition, so that you can work on nonverbal cues or other strategies. You know who doesn't understand or like transitions. Take a moment to stop by his desk to guide him to get ready to make the change. "I want you to stop after this math problem." Or, "Don't start gluing today. You can put the things you cut out in this envelope." This helps the child cope and avoid panic. In fact, hard-to-transition kids frequently are the children who want or need extra attention anyway, so you are able to give them that attention in a positive way.

- Teach them to freeze, or at least, stop talking, through practice and variety. Hand signals, clapping patterns, call and response, spelling the word "quiet," or a sound such as clapping or ringing a chime. Call and response is when you announce a word in your teacher voice and the class responds. For example, you call "Macaroni and…" The class will reply with "Cheese!" Once you have the students quiet, wait for several seconds before you talk. You want to develop the habit of the children being quiet before you start speaking.

- Different activities take different amounts of time to clean up. Plan for that time and give children a chance to practice.

- Avoid too much empty transition time. Let everyone know what to do or where to go next. If they are done quickly, consider letting them stay put and talk quietly until you are ready to give instructions.

- Don't have the entire class move at the same time—break it into smaller groups. Use different ways of moving them, for example, by row, by those wearing blue, etc. Wait until a group is nearly to their next location before moving another group.

- Notice without naming. This trick usually works like a charm every single time. Say in your teacher voice, "I notice three children have their book open to page 3 and are ready to go. Now I see four children." Be positive and be careful not to give attention to the children who are not following rules.

- Make transitions "game-like"—such as having the students make bubbles with their mouth so they will remember not to talk in the hall or having them walk in slow motion to where they are going. Let them try to whistle as they wait. Have a quiet contest. Keep it light and they will look forward to the transitions rather than losing control.

- Don't allow children to whine or complain in a way that slows the transition. You are the boss of your classroom. A simple, "I know no one wants to stop right now, but we have more things to accomplish today," goes a long way. Practice waiting and being quiet, but don't get in the habit of arguing or going into long discussions.

- Practice, practice, practice. It takes about three weeks when school starts to get children into a rhythm. More practice will be needed at several points in the school year, so the teacher should avoid being frustrated or saying demeaning things, such as, "You know how to walk in line. You are not babies anymore." Stay consistent. While practice will still be needed, it will be less than what was needed at the beginning of the year.

Skill 3.3: Identify ways to organize furniture, equipment, materials, and other resources in an indoor or outdoor environment in order to support early childhood development and curricula.

According to the Peabody Iris Center, research reveals that safe, responsive, and nurturing environments are an important part of supporting the learning and development of infants, toddlers, and preschoolers. Such environments also help to prevent challenging behaviors and serve as a core component of interventions for infants and young children with identified disabilities. According to the Division for Early Childhood Recommended Practices (DEC-RP): "Environmental practices refer to aspects of the space, materials, equipment, routines, and activities that practitioners and families can intentionally alter to support each child's learning across developmental domains."

When organizing the physical environment, teachers need to take into account their students' needs (which may vary from year to year), safety, the curriculum, and the resources and materials available. Indoor and outdoor environments may vary from year to year and sometimes during the year, so teachers need to review frequently to best support children's development, well-being, and learning. The Florida Department of Education's Department of Early Learning has a webpage where up-to-date checklists can be accessed and can be used as a resource.

The term *physical environment* refers to the overall design and layout of a given classroom and its learning centers. Teachers should design the environment by organizing its spaces, furnishings, and materials to maximize the learning opportunities and the engagement of every child. To effectively do so, teachers can apply a concept known as Universal Design for Learning (UDL), which stresses that the environment, and the materials in it, should be accessible to everyone. Creating this accessibility might involve providing books at different reading levels, placing materials within easy reach on a shelf, or creating ample space so that a child who uses a wheelchair can maneuver around the classroom. A well-designed physical environment has different activity areas with clear physical and visual boundaries, defined by the furnishings and floor coverings. These furnishings and floor coverings should create spaces that are comfortable and that lend themselves to their intended purpose. For example, a block area might have bookshelves to set it off as a block center, and carpeting or foam flooring to muffle the sound when blocks fall on the floor. Also, the library area should have a soft, comfortable floor covering for young children and adults to sit on while they look at the books. When they arrange furnishings, teachers should:

- make sure that all children are visible to adults and that adults are visible to children, to ensure proper supervision.

- design areas with spaces for children to work and play independently or in small groups, and to gather as a community.

- establish clear boundaries to indicate where the center space begins and ends.

- consider the location of centers. Centers with high activity levels (e.g., block centers, dramatic play areas, music centers) should not be located close to centers with quieter activities (e.g., listening centers, computer areas).

- consider the number and size of centers. Make sure there is enough room for the children to be engaged in the activity without being crowded.

- create cozy, private spaces. Create safe spaces where children can retreat to rest, observe, and recharge emotionally throughout the day.

Another aspect of the physical environment includes the selection and placement of materials. The selection of materials includes choosing toys and other physical objects that are age and developmentally appropriate, as well as linguistically and culturally relevant, for the children in the classroom. For example, the block area should include a variety of blocks to allow children with varying motor skills to manipulate them, and these materials should be placed so that they are easily accessed. Teachers should also take care when it comes to:

- organizing materials and keeping them in appropriate places (e.g., art materials in art center, sensory table near sink), taking into consideration the children's development of independence skills.

- providing enough materials within the centers so that children can be engaged and not arguing over limited resources.

- having centers organized and ready to go when children arrive.

- making sure the materials represent the diversity and the ability levels of the children.

- placing heavier items on lower shelves so that children do not get hurt when they take them.

- providing safe play items that offer developmentally appropriate challenges to promote the growth of problem-solving skills.

- encouraging children to make decisions about materials.

- rotating materials both to promote children's interest and to keep the materials novel.

Light and Sound—When planning the physical environment, teachers should also consider its lighting and sound. Teachers can use lighting and sound to create a comfortable environment that is conducive to the different activities that occur throughout the day. For example, so that children can engage in both quiet and more active play activities during center time, the block area can be carpeted to reduce noise.

- Research reveals that natural lighting and windows are best for children's and teachers' well-being. Lamps can be used rather than fluorescent lights. In early learning class-rooms, including Voluntary Preschool, teachers should be sure they are following safety guidelines outlined by the Department of Children and Families. For example, using light bulbs that don't get hot and are not in a place where they can be knocked to the ground are things to keep in mind.

- Carpets and rugs can add warmth to the room. While some educational carpets may have alphabet letters, numbers, or maps, teachers may opt to go with plain rugs and make "moveable" letters or seating spaces with fabric squares or circles. Chairs with rubber leg bottoms or chairs with tennis balls over metal bottoms can also help to reduce sound, as can wall hangings, drapes, and soft furnishings. Teachers should ensure that they are following safety guidelines and fire codes with regard to fabric and hangings.

- Because some children are sensitive to loud sounds and bright lights, teachers might need to find ways to minimize noise and to create a dimly lit space for them. Accommodations might include providing headphones for children who don't like loud noises or who may get overwhelmed during center time.

Visual Material—Posters for displaying classroom rules, daily schedules, and steps to complete a routine help young children to know what to do and to better understand their environments. For example, in the block area, the teacher can label the center and use photos or pictures of the different blocks to indicate where they belong on the shelves. This will help during clean-up time. Some tips include:

- Label centers and frequently used materials in languages that represent the home languages of the children in the classroom. Because research shows that a less cluttered environment is more attractive, the teacher should use the labels sparingly and include them as part of a literacy lesson.

- Hang signs or visuals at children's eye level. If a teacher has to post visuals higher—such as putting an alphabet line around the top of the whiteboard or chalkboard, it can be useful to have a flashlight, so that children can shine a light on the letter when working with the alphabet line, or have long pointers available. It is important to go over the rules and practice using the tools safely.

- Research shows that contact with nature can positively impact children's well-being. Teachers might consider creating a seasonal nature table for children to visit. Collections from outdoor walks can be displayed and used for learning activities, including sorting, classifying, and art.

- Hang children's work to decorate the room and encourage children to express themselves individually and creatively. Provide opportunities for children to talk and comment in positive ways that extends their verbal skills and fosters language development.

- Use a visual cue for schedules and to indicate when a center is closed (e.g., visual prompts such as sheets or blankets, circles with a slash through them). Practice with the children so that they know how to recognize that the center is closed and what to do next.

- Display materials that are representative of the environment's diversity (e.g., culture, disability, language, family structures) so that children see themselves in the environment. This is also important to consider when choosing books and literacy materials.

- Have children bring in pictures of their families to display. This fosters a sense of community.

The *social environment* refers to the way a classroom environment influences or supports the interactions that occur among young children, teachers, and family. Teachers need to be careful to be culturally sensitive and consider many factors when designing the social environment.

Primary classrooms can be quite similar to preschool and kindergarten environments, but there can be some differences. For example, classroom materials may be more complex—such as having Legos in addition to wooden blocks, or puzzles with more pieces. In outdoor spaces, older children may not need gates and may be located farther from the classroom or bathrooms. Age-appropriate equipment may vary with regard to balls, tricycles vs. bicycles, the addition of scooters, etc.

Skill 3.4: Identify and analyze strategies for short- and long-term planning to set instructional goals in alignment with standards for developing teacher objectives.

When engaging in instructional planning, teachers need to both consider the long-range plans, which are the year-long objectives, and the short-term, or day-to-day objectives for each class. Both are essential to having a well-planned curriculum for the year.

Goals are broad, realistic, achievable learning outcomes that children are expected to attain at the end of specific times. Teachers can use the state and early learning standards to guide their development of the long-range goals. Sometimes called "years at a glance," these goals help with the pacing of instructional objectives. The Florida Early Learning Standards include all domains, including cognitive, and span from birth to five, birth to eight, and VPK (Voluntary Pre-Kindergarten) to eight.

The Florida Department of Education has a website (CPALMS) for academic standards for PK through grade 12.

Skill 3.5: Identify strategies for designing appropriate objectives and developing, implementing, and assessing lesson plans.

Using the long-term goals or "years at a glance," the teacher can develop short-term goals and work backward to design weekly and daily lesson plans. These short-term goals include instructional objectives, which are specific and measurable and connect back to the long-term goals. Instructional activities are organized around three major components: curriculum, instruction, and assessment. These three components impact what teachers do in the classroom. Instruction represents the methods teachers use to present the content to students. States and districts identify effective instructional practices and the types of instructional materials that can be used. In early childhood, teachers should be careful to include opportunities for play and active learning, which impacts the materials used. Assessment measures how well students learn the curriculum and reflects the effectiveness of instruction. At the classroom level, teachers can use a variety of informal assessment techniques to determine student learning, develop ongoing progress monitoring plans, and determine if all children's needs are being met.

The state also requires assessments in early learning and in the primary grades and teachers need to take these parameters into account when developing, implementing, and assessing their lesson plans. Importantly, private and public VPK, providers must also administer a number of assessments, which need to be considered in long-range planning.

Skill 3.6: Identify and select developmentally and/or age-appropriate instructional materials that enrich and extend active learning.

In recent years, many early childhood programs have moved more toward a formal, academic focus and away from a holistic model that includes a focus on all domains of learning. Because a child's cognitive, physical, social, and emotional development changes quickly in their early years, materials should encourage play, exploration, and active learning through a multisensory focus that supports artistic and musical development, social skills, and fine and gross motor skills. The term "readiness" has translated into a deficit perspective that suggests that children are "behind" and need to be ready for formal school. However, there are no critical periods in early childhood during which a child must have exposure to formal reading and math, or technology.

Developmentally appropriate materials can be divided up into categories that are aligned with cognitive learning, physical, sensory, and social-emotional development. Many of these materials can be incorporated into learning centers and dramatic play spaces.

Cognitive Learning

Literacy: High quality, diverse children's books that include images that allow children to see themselves and their culture in positive ways are essential. Magnetic letters that can be used to explore and build words also encourages fine motor control. Research on writing utensils is inconclusive, so teachers should provide a variety of types of pencils and pencil grips as well as types of paper and cardboard from which children can choose. Chalk, paint, and play-dough are also excellent for fostering literacy. Dramatic play centers can be set up with materials that foster literacy, vocabulary, speaking, and listening such as phones, menus, keyboards, order pads, etc. In the block or building center, maps, graph paper, books with construction terms, pencils and markers can encourage children to label and write about their constructions. Cooking and baking activities can build students' vocabulary and informational literacy.

Mathematics: Useful materials include objects and things to count and work with such as buttons, rocks, nuts and bolts, beads, and small animals. Teachers need to be careful that materials meet safety guidelines, which can vary by children's age. Other materials include blocks, puzzles, pattern blocks, measuring cups, clocks, and calendars. In dramatic play centers, calculators, phones, calendars and keyboards are useful. Cooking and baking activities can build students' mathematical understanding through measuring, counting, cutting, sorting, and estimating.

Science: Useful materials include water and sand tables, artistic activities that include water-color, building with clay or beeswax, microscopes, digital cameras, geometric shapes, easels, plants, gardening materials, percussion instruments, autoharp, materials to build things (cardboard tubes, boxes, etc.). Cooking and baking activities can build students' understanding of changes, properties of heat, and a variety of scientific concepts.

Social Studies: Books, artifacts and realia from other cultures, photos and pictures, maps, and other materials can support social studies learning. Social studies competencies can be infused in a variety of settings.

Physical Development: Fine motor skills can be developed through activities such as working with clay or beeswax, using tweezers or tongs to pick up objects, etc. Finger knitting with yarn is another way to foster fine motor skills as well as mathematical learning. Teachers in early learning settings should take care to review safety guidelines with yarn and activities like sewing cards. Painting with brushes and working with other tools, building materials, puzzles and other manipulatives, all foster fine motor skills. Gross motor skills can be supported with child-sized dustpans, brooms, bean bags, tricycles, balance beams, ropes, ladders, balls, and other materials for active movement.

Sensory Development: This can be fostered through baking and cooking, outdoor activities, scavenger hunts, opportunities to handle a variety of textures and materials such as sandpaper letters, water and sand tables, beads, tree blocks and cotton balls treated with smells such as lavender (taking care to be sure children have no allergies). Children with sensory issues may benefit from being able to access headphones or quiet spaces when necessary.

Social-Emotional Development: This can be encouraged through dramatic play centers, dolls and materials for creating various play settings (this could tie into themes such as farms, doctor offices, or supermarkets), vehicles, mirrors, pretend animals, pets if allowed, etc.

Skill 3.7: Apply a variety of methods of flexibly grouping children for the purposes of instruction.

Effective teachers use a variety of grouping strategies with children—whole, small, or individual—depending on the instructional goals and children's differentiation needs. Children may be grouped flexibly, based on learning goals. For example, teachers typically tell stories, read aloud, do interactive writing, calendar activities, or introduce concepts in a whole-group setting. In grades K–3, this may be called Tier 1 or whole-group instruction. Activities such as a writing workshop may be a whole group, with the teacher pulling small groups or conferencing with individuals based on their needs. Small groups, or Tier 2, are used for focused teaching at the children's instructional or learning level. Teachers can incorporate Vygotsky's principles of scaffolding and teaching at the Zone of Proximal Development, or in that space between what a child can do on her own and what she cannot do. Guided reading is typically done in small groups. Teachers may use a homogenous group or heterogeneous group, depending on the activity, concept, or learning objective. Small groups and heterogeneous grouping is often used for centers and work stations. Tier 3 or one-on-one instruction or assessment may be used for informal assessments and intensive instruction on concepts or skills.

Skill 3.8: Identify and apply characteristics of an integrated curriculum.

An integrated curriculum is one that allows children to pursue learning in a holistic way, without the restrictions often imposed by subject boundaries. In early childhood programs, it focuses upon the inter-relatedness of all curricular areas. In grades K–3, an integrated curriculum connects different subject areas. This allows teachers to focus on relevance and making learning meaningful for their students.

Skill 3.9: Identify characteristics of play as related to children's social, emotional, and cognitive development.

According to the American Academy of Pediatrics, play is essential to development because it develops the cognitive, physical, social, and emotional well-being of children and youth. Play is so important to optimal child development that it has been recognized by the United Nations High Commission for Human Rights as **a right of every child**.

Play allows children to use their creativity while developing their imagination, dexterity, and physical, cognitive, and emotional strength. Play is important to healthy brain development. It is through play that children at a very early age engage and interact with the world around them.

Social emotional development is fostered when play allows children to create and explore a world they can master and practice adult roles, developing their competency, confidence, and resilience. Undirected play allows children to learn how to work in groups, to share, to negotiate, to resolve conflicts, and to learn self-advocacy skills. Children can practice decision-making skills, move at their own pace, discover their own areas of interest, and ultimately engage fully in the passions they wish to pursue. When child-driven, children can practice leadership and group skills. Social emotional learning is best integrated with academic learning, so that children can learn kindness, empathy, teamwork, and other skills.

Cognitive development is fostered through the physical activity that allows for optimal physical development as well as the opportunity for children to act on their environment. When concepts are presented in a playful manner, children can explore and test ideas out in a non-threatening environment.

Skill 3.10: Identify strategies for building and nurturing trusting relationships with students.

Research confirms Maslow's theory and reveals that children learn best when they trust their teachers and feel safe and respected. Some strategies include:

- providing a safe structure, rhythm, and consistency; being well-prepared for each day's activities and lessons

- having an equitable management and discipline plan that is focused on strengths and social emotional development, such as Becky Bailey's Conscious Discipline model

- taking time to know each child and his or her family, respecting culture and diversity, and being interested in each child

- seeing each child through a strengths-based lens, while understanding that each child learns differently and that children's needs should be met

- incorporating storytelling and opportunities for play-based learning throughout the day

- providing opportunities for children and families to participate in school activities after school

Skill 3.11: Analyze and evaluate the use of evidence-based practices to improve student achievement.

Teachers need to keep abreast of current research and policy in order to understand evidence-based practices. The best way to analyze and evaluate these practices is to rely on professional organizations such as the National Association for Childhood Education International, as well as organizations associated with specific content areas. The Alliance for Childhood is a great resource for play. For literacy, the *International Literacy Association* is a reliable source. For mathematics, the National Council of Teachers of Mathematics is a reliable source. The National Science Teaching Association is the premier professional organization for practices around teaching science and improving achievement. For social studies, the National Council for the Social Sciences is an excellent resource.

To analyze and evaluate broad instructional practices, well-known researchers such as Robert Marzano study and publish a list of practices that have been shown to positively impact student achievement. (See references at the end of this chapter.)

Competency 4: Knowledge of Developmentally Appropriate Curricula

Skill 4.1: Analyze and select developmentally appropriate curricula that provide for all areas of child development (i.e., physical, emotional, social, linguistic, aesthetic, cognitive).

The NAEYC published a position statement on "Developmentally Appropriate Practice for Children, birth through age 8" that is currently in its 3rd edition. This is a great resource for teachers who are analyzing and selecting developmentally appropriate curricula. Additionally, national, regional, and local early childhood organizations are involved in determining the types of curricula that are most developmentally appropriate. Teachers should use the resources of their

Early Learning Coalition, the Florida Department of Education, and their district in considering which curricula to use.

Skill 4.2: Identify strategies for facilitating the development of literal, interpretative, and critical listening and thinking skills.

Teachers can foster children's development of literal, interpretive, and critical listening and thinking skills by providing their students with intentional and well-planned opportunities to play, explore, and act on their environment. Storytelling has also been shown to foster children's listening, thinking, and comprehension skills. Reading high-quality books, modeling, and scaffolding children's questions will also foster children's learning.

Skill 4.3: Determine activities that support the development of fine and gross motor skills.

Teachers can support the development of fine and gross motor skills by providing ample opportunities for active learning, limiting worksheets, and passive activities, such as computer programs and work on tablets. Children need to experience a variety of textures to fully develop their brain and the slick surface of tablets or phones may hinder that development. Further, little research has been done on the impact of children's visual and eye development when screen time replaces hands-on activities.

Skill 4.4: Select and apply strategies, including the use of technology, for presenting instruction and concepts related to health, safety, and nutrition.

The Florida Department of Education and the Florida Office of Early Learning have an approval process for curriculum that includes strategies that are evidence-based. For example, teachers can use strategies that include creating partnerships with the community to present instruction related to health, safety, and nutrition. These strategies should include time for physical activity every day and encourage children to drink enough water to be hydrated. Class gardens and field trips can provide opportunities to teach about health and nutrition. Many teachers are including instruction in mindfulness to help children learn to self-regulate their emotions. Role-playing responding to situations can be a good strategy to discuss safety and well-being. In Florida, there have been recent changes in how schools implement safety and security procedures and some districts are providing videos or other media to help present concepts related to safety. The Office of Safe Schools serves as a central repository for best practices, training standards, and compliance oversight in all matters regarding school safety and security. Their mission is to support districts in providing a safe learning environment for students and educators.

Skill 4.5: Select and apply strategies, including the use of technology, for presenting instruction and concepts related to visual arts, music, drama, and dance.

The Florida Department of Education and the Florida Office of Early Learning develop guidelines for curriculum that include effective instructional strategies for introducing these concepts. Position statements on developmentally appropriate practice can also influence decisions on how to teach these concepts to children. Keeping in mind that active learning opportunities are best for children, teachers need to also consider the needs of students who have exceptional needs. This includes those who have learning disabilities, physical disabilities, are from other cultures, or whose home language is not English.

Skill 4.6: Select and apply strategies, including the use of technology, in developmentally appropriate ways to teach reading, mathematics, science, and social studies.

For young children, integrating math, literacy, and science concepts in everyday activities enhances cognitive, social, emotional, and physical development, and thus their overall growth. Skills and concepts that children learn while they are young will expand as they gain experience and knowledge over time. In the early years, the kinds of technology used should focus on using tools, such as microscopes, that can foster later academic learning. For example, when using an apple peeler, children are learning spherical geometry at the conceptual level. When using blocks, children are learning spatial concepts that will be evidenced in the intermediate grades. Something as simple as using a watering can or hose to water plants integrates science and math concepts. When teachers intentionally include content-specific vocabulary in the activities or use recipes for cooking the apples, they are integrating reading and literacy activities. Audiobooks can also be a way to use technology effectively. Children who have exceptional learning needs or physical needs should have technology adaptations that allow for optimal learning. As children develop, technology can be used for inquiry projects and problem solving. Learning to use cameras, coding with games such as *Minecraft*, and using computers to create graphs or models, research or writing can eventually become a strong and useful life skill.

Skill 4.7: Select and apply strategies, including the use of technology, in developmentally appropriate ways to increase receptive and expressive vocabulary.

For typically developing children, strategies are aligned with developmentally appropriate and evidence-based practices such as opportunities for talk, for guided and free play, work centers, and other activities that encourage talk, questioning, prediction, and experimentation. For atypically developing children, a number of technology innovations and programs can foster receptive and expressive vocabulary. Children who have been identified as having autism or apraxia benefit from strategies that allow them to develop their receptive and expressive language. There are professional organizations that have collected the research on best strategies, and a variety of local and state resources.

Competency 5: Knowledge of Developmentally Appropriate Intervention Strategies and Resources Available to Meet the Needs of All Students

Skill 5.1: Select and analyze evidence-based instructional strategies to adapt curricula for children with diverse needs.

Teachers should rely on guidelines provided by professional educational organizations, the Florida Department of Education, and the Florida Early Learning Coalition to ensure they are using evidence-based strategies for their students. A lot of resources are available to ensure that teachers do not allow implicit bias or lack of knowledge to impair their effective teaching, but it is important that teachers take the time to do their research to prepare. These best practices may be categorized into four broad bands of strategies that include:

- demonstration of high expectations,

- implementation of culturally relevant instruction,

- establishment of caring relationships, and

- effective parent and community involvement.

Skill 5.2: Identify characteristics of children with diverse needs in order to support their learning.

Teachers of young children understand that their students will have diverse needs cognitively, physically, socially, culturally, and emotionally. Children with learning disabilities are a diverse, heterogeneous group exhibiting potential difficulties in many different areas. For example, one child with a learning disability may experience significant reading problems, while another may experience no reading problems whatsoever, but have significant difficulties with written expression. Some characteristics include attention disorders, reading difficulties, written language difficulties, oral language difficulties, poor motor abilities, social skills difficulties, psychological processing issues, quantitative disorders, and information processing difficulties. Children who have reading problems may appear to struggle with math or other content areas simply because they can't read. English language learners may appear to have learning disabilities because they don't understand the language. Teachers need to rely on their local, district, state, and national agencies to ensure they are best meeting the needs of all of their children.

Skill 5.3: Identify and select resources and procedures that support children with diverse needs and their families.

Diversity can be defined as the sum of the ways that people are both alike and different. The dimensions of diversity include race, ethnicity, gender, sexual orientation, language, culture, religion, mental and physical ability, class, and immigration status. There are a number of resources and procedures to support these children and their families. Teachers should access resources from district, local, and state agencies. In Florida, these resources include the Early Learning Coalition and the Florida Department of Education.

Skill 5.4: Identify characteristics of children at risk for school failure and select appropriate intervention strategies for these children.

There are a number of factors that play into determining children at risk for school failure. For teachers of young children, the typical factors relate to academic or learning difficulties, exceptional needs, socioeconomic factors, families with a pattern of substance abuse, parental lack of education, child abuse or neglect, domestic violence, high mobility, and homelessness. Strategies should be culturally sensitive and include the input of families and local resources. The Early Learning Coalition of Florida and WIDA (World-Class Instructional Design and Assessment) Consortium each provide guidance on students who are English language learners.

Skill 5.5: Identify major trends in educating children with exceptionalities and incorporate such trends in early childhood settings as appropriate.

Some major trends for children with exceptionalities include multi-tiered systems of support, in which the child's needs are met by the teacher, school personnel, families, and district or other agencies. This framework is focused on equity and access for all children, using a universal design model. Trauma-informed care is another trend, which focuses on all areas that can hinder learning and development.

Skill 5.6: Select and apply appropriate strategies for working with children who are in foster care and children who are migrant, transient, orphaned, or homeless.

A number of factors, including a lack of affordable housing, poverty, and domestic violence, are key elements for children who are homeless or transient. Children who are in foster care are also at risk of homelessness due to family conflict and family dynamics, sexual orientation, sexual activity, school problems, pregnancy, and substance abuse. Strategies include focusing on all domains that include treating children with respect and helping find resources and support systems. School counselors can also provide support. The Florida Department of Children and Families and local Early Learning Coalitions also provide guidance.

Strategies include providing consistent routines and conducting assessments so that children's academic needs are addressed and gaps are covered.

Skill 5.7: Identify ways for accessing and appropriately using health information to monitor children's medical needs (e.g., medications for allergies) and/or other health impairments.

Children's safety and well-being is of paramount concern, but teachers should not administer medication unless they have the appropriate permissions. Teachers should seek guidance from administration or local agencies to ensure that all FERPA and HIPAA requirements are followed. FERPA is the acronym for the Family Educational Rights and Privacy Act and is a federal law that protects the privacy of student education records. The law applies to all schools that receive funds under an applicable program of the U.S. Department of Education. FERPA gives parents certain rights with respect to their children's education records. These rights transfer to the student when he or she reaches the age of 18 or attends a school beyond the high school level. HIPAA is the Health Insurance Portability and Accountability Act of 1996 and may factor into how teachers access and use health information.

Skill 5.8: Identify needs for, and methods of, collaboration with other professionals in order to positively impact student learning.

There is so much information and research available that teachers need to collaborate with their colleagues, their school-level resources, and other agencies, including district professionals if they are to positively impact learning. The Florida Early Learning Coalition, the school district's website, the Florida Department of Education, and professional organizations are excellent resources.

Skill 5.9: Identify programs, curricula, and activities that address the language needs of children and their families with limited English proficiency.

The Early Learning Coalition of Florida and the WIDA (World-Class Instructional Design and Assessment) Consortium provide guidance on students who are English language learners. These are just two of the many organizations available to provide guidance on programs, curricula and activities to address the language needs of children and their families. Teachers using universal design principles can work to address the needs in a holistic manner.

Competency 6: Knowledge of Diagnosis, Assessment, and Evaluation

Skill 6.1: Select and apply developmentally appropriate, reliable, and valid formal and informal screening, progress monitoring, and diagnostic instruments and procedures that measure specific characteristics.

Best practices for the assessment of young children include carefully selected informal and formal strategies that measure specific characteristics over several designated periods of time and in many different contexts. Such assessment more accurately provides a broad picture of child growth, development, and learning from which wise decisions regarding the needs of individuals can be made. Formal assessments usually entail the use of standardized tests—tests that must be administered according to prescribed time limits, instructional and scoring procedures, and administration guidelines. Scores are usually compared to the scores of a normative (or comparison) group. Examples of formal assessments include achievement tests, readiness tests, developmental screening tests, intelligence tests, and diagnostic tests. Informal assessments rely more heavily on observational and work sampling techniques that continually focus on child performance, processes, and products over selected periods of time and in a variety of contexts. Portfolio systems for tracking various elements of assessment are typically utilized. Progress monitoring is simply the practice of checking regularly on a child's learning.

Skill 6.2: Identify procedures for accurately establishing, maintaining, and using formal and informal student records.

Records provide raw data that enable coherent, balanced, and objective decisions on issues such as promotion, student and staff discipline, and teaching and learning performances. Properly kept human resource records serve useful employment and planning related purposes. Teachers should be careful to do the following: keep good records, including anecdotal notes, plan a good system to maintain records, and collaborate with other teachers and resource staff to ensure confidentiality and best practices.

Skill 6.3: Interpret formal and informal assessment data to make instructional decisions about the educational needs of children.

Perhaps the most significant change to take place in early childhood assessment in recent years concerns the linking of assessment and instruction. Assessment is a dynamic process that relies on teachers collecting information from multiple sources over numerous time points through systematic observation, recording, and evaluating. Formal assessments are one component in acquiring information about the child. Analyzing the data can lead to intervention. Informal monitoring of child learning is needed to design programs and plan curricula. Teachers can learn to observe and document children's skills, knowledge, and accomplishments as they participate in classroom activities and routines, interact with peers, and work with educational materials. Curriculum-embedded or performance-based assessment allows children opportunities to demonstrate their knowledge or skills through active engagement in classroom activities. Anecdotal notes, checklists, portfolios, and other collections of children's work help teachers document learning and monitor instruction.

Skill 6.4: Identify procedures for appropriately using authentic assessments (e.g., portfolios, observations, journals) to plan instruction that further develops a child's level of learning and interest.

Authentic assessment allows teachers to gather information to understand each child's development. Gathering observation notes, photos, artistic creations, emergent writing, and dictations provides teachers with meaningful insight about each child and about the group as a whole. With this insight, teachers can plan activities and experiences that are responsive to children's interests and needs. Teachers can share their understanding of each child's growth with his or her family, while also gaining important insight from them in return. Teachers should take care to use value-free language and to carefully reflect on their assessments. When using a working portfolio, teachers should be careful to differentiate between work samples that show progress and showcase portfolios that highlight students' best work.

Skill 6.5: Identify procedures and legal requirements that provide for productive family conferences or home visits, regarding the assessment, education, and development of children, in accordance with due process (e.g., IEP, RTI) and confidentiality.

Protecting the privacy of students and safeguarding the confidentiality of their records is a responsibility that must be addressed by every public school. FERPA, or the Family Education Rights and Privacy Act, was enacted into federal law in 1974 and serves to help keep these records safe from public view. FERPA allows students and parents access to educational records. Educational records include files, documents, and other material maintained by the educational institution that is directly related to the student. A student's grades or written comments about that performance in class are examples of educational records that must be released to the child and that child's parents or legal guardians. Under FERPA, a teacher does not have to reveal any individual records they may keep for their use only. These records are considered personal and are not made available to the school or any other third party. Such records may be shared with a substitute teacher, if, for instance, they affect the way the substitute must deal with the student. Directory information, that includes such things as a student's name, address, email address, place of birth, class level, may be released without a student's or parent's consent. Everything else, known as non-directory information, must remain private until consent is obtained. Teachers cannot post test scores from the class on a bulletin board or ask another student to distribute graded papers to the class. Graded work cannot be stacked in a box for students to go through and take their papers. A teacher cannot post a list of class grades on the internet. While a student's work can be evaluated by the class for learning purposes, once it is graded by the teacher, it is off limits for public view. The Florida Family and School Partnership for Student Achievement Act was created to provide families with specific information regarding their child's educational progress and comprehensive information about their choices and opportunities for involvement in their child's education. In addition, this act creates a framework for building and strengthening partnerships among families, educators, other school-related personnel, and community organizations.

Skill 6.6: Identify methods of observing, facilitating, and extending children's play to practice newly acquired abilities (e.g., through problem solving, imitation, persistence, and creativity).

Teachers can act as observer of play where they observe and sometimes take notes. They may also take on the role of instructional leader, selecting games to develop children's academic and social abilities. In a role of participant, teachers can model play and invite others. When disputes occur, teachers may act as mediator, to reinforce the rules that were discussed. As participants or gentle guides, teachers can seek to enrich or expand on the present experience. For example, teachers helping children in the block center can take an opportunity to reinforce spatial vocabulary.

Skill 6.7: Identify different types of assessments (e.g., norm-referenced, criterion-referenced, diagnostic, curriculum-based) and the purposes of each.

There are three types of assessments: diagnostic, formative, and summative. A diagnostic assessment identifies students' current knowledge of a subject, their skill sets and capabilities, and clarifies misconceptions before teaching takes place. Diagnostic assessments can include pre-tests and interviews. Formative assessments provide feedback and information and measures student progress and how well the information was taught. Formative assessments can identify areas that need improvement and are typically not graded. Formative assessments include observations, reflections, questioning, conferencing, and in-class activities. Many districts in Florida use I-Ready math and reading assessments as formative assessments. Summative assessments take place after the learning and provide information to determine how well children learned the material. Summative assessments can include rubrics, exams, projects, portfolios, and tests such as the Florida Standards Assessment or FSA. The FSA is a high-stakes assessment administered in third grade. Students who do not score at a particular level may be retained.

Norm-referenced tests report whether test-takers performed better or worse than a hypothetical average student, which is determined by comparing scores against the performance results of a statistically selected group of test-takers, typically of the same age or grade level, who have already taken the exam.

A criterion-referenced test is a style of test which uses test scores to generate a statement about the behavior that can be expected of a person with that score. Most tests and quizzes that are written by school teachers can be considered criterion-referenced tests. Curriculum-Based Measurement (CBM) is a method teachers use to find out how students are progressing in basic academic areas such as math, reading, writing, and spelling. CBM can be helpful to parents because it provides current, week-by-week information on the progress their children are making.

Skill 6.8: Identify and apply appropriate processes for monitoring struggling students (e.g., RTI, tiered interventions) and planning and implementing intervention strategies.

There are a variety of processes for monitoring struggling readers. Response to Intervention (RTI) is a multi-tier approach to the early identification and support of students with learning and behavior needs. The RTI process begins with high-quality instruction and universal screening of all children in the general education classroom. Struggling learners are provided with interventions at increasing levels of intensity to accelerate their rate of learning. These services may be provided by a variety of personnel, including general education teachers, special educators, and specialists. Progress is closely monitored to assess both the learning rate and level of performance of individual students. Educational decisions about the intensity and duration of interventions are based on individual student response to instruction. RTI is designed for use when making decisions in both general education and special education, creating a well-integrated system of instruction and intervention guided by child outcome data. There are three tiers of intervention for RTI. Tier 1 is whole-group instruction. Tier 2 is small group instruction with a specific focus. Tier 3 is individual one-on-one intensive instruction and may occur in the classroom or in a pullout setting.

Competency 7: Knowledge of Child Guidance and Classroom Behavioral Management

Child guidance is defined as the clinical study and treatment of the behavioral and emotional problems of children by specialists that may include a psychiatric social worker, a physician or psychiatrist, or a clinical psychologist. Classroom behavioral management deals with all the factors that go into the work that teachers do to create a safe setting conducive to learning and well-being.

Skill 7.1: Identify and analyze developmentally appropriate components of a positive and effective classroom behavioral management system.

Positive and effective classroom behavioral management systems have proactive strategies for defining, teaching, and supporting appropriate student behaviors and a social-emotional focus to create positive school environments. Programs such as positive behavior support take a behaviorally-based systems approach to enhance the capacity of schools, families, and communities to design effective environments. These programs improve the link between research-validated practices and the environments in which teaching and learning occurs. *Conscious discipline* is a classroom management system focused on social emotional learning and a strengths-based approach.

Skill 7.2: Apply developmentally appropriate positive strategies for guiding children's behavior and responding to challenging behaviors.

Researchers have noted that it is helpful for teachers to think of unacceptable behavior as unintentional "mistaken behavior" rather than "misbehavior" that should be punished. Mistaken behavior suggests that children are learning to behave acceptably and may make mistakes. Rules include:

- Observe the child closely and think carefully about what the behavior means. There is always a reason for it.

- Emphasize that school is a safe place. Let children know that you will not allow anyone to hurt them and you will not allow them to hurt others.

- Offer two acceptable choices when you want children to change their behavior.

- Offer real choices such as giving a child two options rather than simply saying, "Do you want to put your trucks away?"

- Allow children to save face—don't embarrass them.

- Focus on solutions rather than causes and avoid rhetoric. Don't ask, "Why did you take that toy?" but rather, "What can we do since both of you want the toy?"

When conflict arises, teachers should remain calm, get down to the child's eye level and tell them what you observe. Ask questions and listen. Repeat what you heard them say. Ask for input to solve the situation. Then praise and reinforce positive behaviors while observing from a distance.

Skill 7.3: Identify opportunities for promoting children's positive self-concept and self-esteem, prosocial skills, and social-emotional development through interaction with peers and familiar adults.

Teachers and caregivers promote children's social and emotional health by treating children with warmth and respect. Teachers can intentionally teach and enhance these skills by using evidence-based strategies to teach, model, and reinforce positive behaviors.

Skill 7.4: Select developmentally appropriate problem-solving strategies for conflict resolution, self-regulatory behavior, and social interaction.

Teachers can help children develop their self-regulation through opportunities for practice and by encouraging other behaviors that can prevent mistaken behaviors. First, children need adequate rest and nutrition—hungry and tired children often lose their ability to self-regulate and resolve conflicts effectively. Children need to have opportunities to breathe air, play, and be outdoors. Simply breathing and moving can help children feel more positive and calm. Blowing bubbles is an easy way to practice deep-breathing which calms the body down. Blowing bubbles requires the child to breathe from the belly at a regular tempo. Yoga is another strategy for helping children to connect with their bodies and stay calm. Reading books about feelings and helping children talk about what they need are other ways to help children develop strategies for conflict resolution, self-regulation, and social interaction. Calm music can help children relax. Singing has also been shown to help children calm themselves and begin breathing more regularly.

Skill 7.5: Select and analyze appropriate strategies for teaching character development of young children.

Teachers can teach character development during free play, work time, and routines by using events that arise and talking through them with the children. Teachers can model character traits such as politeness and empathy and can read books that offer opportunities to discuss issues. Role play is also a good way to portray issues of character development that can be followed by solid discussion.

Skill 7.6: Identify the roles of early childhood professionals in collaboration with other professionals (e.g., social workers, school counselors, community liaisons) in helping children and their families cope with stressors.

Teachers of young children typically have some background in developmental domains, but their primary expertise is in cognitive and academic learning. Therefore, it is important that teachers rely on school counselors, social workers, and community liaisons, who are all instrumental in helping children and their families cope with stressors that may negatively impact children's development, well-being, and learning. For optimal learning to occur, teachers must ensure that children's emotional, social, physical, and cognitive developments, as well as their well-being, are all considered. School counselors are important members of children's IEP teams and instrumental in helping teachers identify children with needs that are not being met. Social workers are also tasked with fostering the well-being of children and families and may work closely with the Department of Children and Families.

REFERENCES

Copple, C., Bredekamp, S. (Eds.) (2008). *Developmentally Appropriate Practice in Early Childhood Programs Serving Children from Birth Through Age 8* (3rd edition).

Edwards, C. P. (2002). Three Approaches from Europe: Waldorf, Montessori, and Reggio.

Emilia. *Early Childhood Research and Practice, 4* (1).

Kirkham, J. A. and Kidd, E. (2017), The Effect of Steiner, Montessori, and National Curriculum Education Upon Children's Pretense and Creativity. *Journal of Creative Behavior, 51*: 20–34. doi:10.1002/jocb.83.

Lander, L., Howard, J., & Byrne, M. (2013). "The impact of substance use disorders on families and children: from theory to practice." *Social Work in Public Health, 28*(3–4), 194–205. doi:10.1080/19371918.2013.759005.

Willingham, D. T., Hughes, E. M. & Dobby, D. G (2015). The scientific status of learning styles theory. *Teaching of Psychology, 42*(3) 266–271. doi: 10.1177/0098628315589505.

Websites Referenced in this Chapter

Competency 1: Knowledge of Children, Families, and Community
Skill 1.8: Family and Community Partnerships

https://safesupportivelearning.ed.gov/training-technical-assistance

Competency 2: Profession and Foundations of PK–3 Education
Skill 2.3: Federal and State Laws on Education in the Classroom

Further information on the Rilya Wilson Act:

a) *www.elcgateway.org/providers/115-rilya-wilson-act-requirements/*

b) *www.leg.state.fl.us/statutes/index.cfm?A*

Access to Florida Family Services: *https://www.myflfamilies.com/*

Skill 2.5: 2018 Draft of the Three Levels of Understanding for the Education of Young Children

https://www.naeyc.org

Universal Beliefs about Childhood Education: *http://ceintl.wpengine.com/about-us*

Skill 2.6 Current Trends and Issues that Impact Early Childhood Education

https://www.microsoft.com/en-us/education

https://info.fldoe.org/docushare/dsweb/Get/Document-7967/dps-2017–85.pdf

http://www.leg.state.fl.us/statutes/index.cfm?App_mode

Competency 3: Developmentally Appropriate Practices

https://www.naeyc.org/sites/default/files/globally-shared

Skill 3.1 Link to the National Association for Education of Young Children (NAEYC)

https://www.naeyc.org/resources/topics/dap/10-effective-dap-teaching-strategies

Skill 3.2 Components of Effective Organization and Management

https://theeducatorsroom.com/ten-tips-smooth-transitions/

https://iris.peabody.vanderbilt.edu/module

3.3 Office of Early Learning Checklists

http://www.floridaearlylearning.com/statewide-initiatives

Creating Environments: *https://iris.peabody.vanderbilt.edu/module*

3.4 Florida's Website for academic Standards for PK through Grade 12

www.cpalms.org/Public/search/Standard

Florida Early Learning and Development Standards: *http://elcosceola.org/wp-content/uploads*

3.5 Designing Objectives, Implementation, and Assessments

http://www.cpalms.org/Public/search/Standard

Learning through Play: *https://www.unicef.org/sites/default/files/2018–12/UNICEF*

3.6 Developmentally and/or Age Appropriate Materials

Enriching Materials to Use in an Early Childhood Setting: *www.institute4learning.com*

3.11 Evidence Based Practices to Improve Student Enrichment

www.allianceforchildhood.org

www.literacyworldwide.org.

www.nctm.org

www.nsta.org

www.socialstudies.org

Marzano's List to Positively Impact Student Achievement (A Summary of Relevant Research Findings: *www.marzanoresources.com/research/database)*

Competency 4: Developmentally Appropriate Curricula
Skill 4.5 Instruction in Visual Arts, Music, Drama, and Dance

http://www.fldoe.org/core/fileparse.php/5574/urlt/Visual-and-Performing-Arts-Specifications.pdf

Skill 4.7 Strategies to Increase Receptive and Expressive Vocabulary with Students who Lie on the Autism Spectrum

http://autismteachingstrategies.com

Competency 5: Developmentally Appropriate Intervention Strategies and Resources
Skill 5.6 Children in Foster Care and Those Who Are Migrant, Transient, Orphaned or Homeless

https://www.myflfamilies.com/

Language Arts and Reading Subtest 2 (532)

Competency 1: Knowledge of Literacy and Literacy Instruction

Reading, writing, and the language arts (speaking, listening, viewing, presenting) are all under the umbrella term "literacy." As we learn more about the nature of literacy and how children learn, the definition has expanded. Researchers currently define **literacy** as "the ability to identify, understand, interpret, create, compute, and communicate using visual, audible, and digital materials across disciplines and in any context."

While the term "literacy" is used in a variety of contexts to indicate a basic knowledge (i.e., computer literacy), for this test framework, literacy includes the skills surrounding reading, viewing, hearing, developmental writing, the writing process, and listening and speaking. Teachers of young children, or those children between the ages of 3 and 10 years, are challenged to provide instruction along a developmental framework, accepting and meeting the literacy learning needs of their students while moving their learning forward along a continuum. Teaching effectively means that teachers need to possess a strong knowledge of literacy theory and research, evidenced-based practice, and the developmental stages of the children with whom they will work. At the end of this chapter, you will find a list of resources that support each competency and set of skills. These resources come in varied forms from websites to journals, and are collected at the end of the chapter so that you may stay focused on the material at hand as you review.

Skill 1.1: Identify the content of emergent literacy.

Emergent literacy includes the aspects of literacy that develop before formal academic instruction. It includes reading, writing, and speaking behaviors, interest in print and visuals, and motivation to communicate. The term characterizes aspects of literacy that begin to develop well before formal academic instruction, and later through an intentional and stimulating environment. Early childhood teachers must provide a variety of experiences that foster emergent literacy and be able to explain the rationale for their instructional decisions that provide rich literacy experiences, and may include:

1. **Concepts of print**

   This relates to children's understanding of print and reading before they actually are able to decode. Examples of this include an understanding that print and texts may contain illustrations and words that convey meaning. Conventions include that books in English typically have pages that are turned from right to left and print that goes from left to right and top to bottom. Marie Clay (1966) developed an informal assessment for observing a child's knowledge of print that included finding the title of the book, knowing where to start reading, directionality of print, and discriminating between print and illustrations, etc. When children are read to often, they typically pick up these concepts without much difficulty. Holdaway (1979) found that the practice of shared reading (an interactive reading experience that occurs when students join in or share the reading of a book or other text while guided and supported by a teacher) using big books (or enlarged print) helped children who did not experience a lot of "lap reading" understand concepts of print.

2. **Alphabetic principle**

   This is the understanding that there are systematic and predictable relationships between written letters and spoken sounds. There are 26 letters in the alphabet, but approximately 44 phonemes in the English language, so children must learn that there is not a one-to-one correspondence between letters and sounds (i.e., the digraph *sh* is a new sound). Teachers must be aware of specific needs of students who are English language learners (ELLs). For example, a teacher can use a picture of a cat for the initial sound /c/. However, the Spanish word for "cat" is "gato," which has a /g/ sound. Students whose home language is Spanish may be confused.

3. **Oral language (speaking and listening)**

   Oral language plays a large role in children's emergent literacy development (Dickinson & Tabors, 2001). Research reveals that language develops in phases. *Prebirth* includes the sensory stimuli that infants experience inside the womb. These sounds begin to stimulate neurological function. In *infancy*, cooing, babbling, and other noises are common. **Echolalia** is the term to describe sounds that imitate speech. The *holographic* stage of language development describes the phase when toddlers learn that the noises communicate meaning. During this phase, toddlers may use one word to communicate (i.e., "milk," "no"). *Helegraphic* describes the stage when toddlers and young children are learning more about the purposes and functions of language. At this stage, two-word phrases are common (i.e., "more cookies," "me go"). In the *preschool and primary* stage, children begin to speak in whole phrases, ask questions, take turns in conversation, refer to past or future events, use quantities or amounts, and begin to become fluent in communicating verbally.

   An essential element to developing oral language skills is that children need input that is responsive and related to what they are engaged in at the moment (Tamis-LeMonda, Bornstein, & Baumwell, 2001). For example, if a child is playing with blocks, an adult can interact to extend a child's language by commenting using descriptive language or asking questions that extend basic understanding. Rather than saying, "I see you are playing with blocks," an adult might say, "I see you have the dark blue blocks sorted by size from small to large," and, "I wonder how high you can stack those yellow and green cubes," to expand the child's vocabulary and conceptual understanding of color, size, and direction. Television and computer programs are not sufficient for fostering oral language, because children need personalized responses that will help them elaborate and extend their thinking and speech (McCabe, Tamis-LeMonda, Bornstein, Cates, Golinkoff, et al. 2013). This means that the adults in children's lives are key to helping children develop their emergent literacy skills by interacting verbally through conversation, which extends and expands children's language. Children need opportunities to talk and develop skills that are connected with later reading skills. Research has shown that children from families in the lower socioeconomic brackets come to school having heard few words (Hart & Risley, 1995). Therefore, it is essential that teachers provide rich experiences and opportunities for young children to talk during school.

- **Phonological awareness** is an umbrella term that includes an understanding of sounds and how they work, including the idea that spoken words make up sentences and that these sounds and words communicate a message. The ability to rhyme falls under the umbrella of phonological awareness. Subskills that fall under phonological awareness include a child's ability to distinguish spoken language from other environmental sounds. This includes identifying sounds that are similar and different, remembering sounds, ordering sounds, and understanding the meaning of sounds and words. Understanding that words can have one or more syllables also falls under this umbrella. An easy way to have children identify syllables in words is to have them place their hand on their chin as they say a word. They can count syllables by the number of times their chin drops. For example, "too" has one syllable and the chin drops once. "Caterpillar" has four syllables. Phonemic awareness is often confused with phonological awareness, but phonemic awareness deals specifically with identifying and manipulating the sounds in words.

- **Phonological skills in order from simplest to most complex (Moats & Tolman, 2009)**

  ▶ **Word awareness.** This includes the ability to orally count words in sentences and is usually evidenced around 4 or 5 years of age.

  ▶ **Responsiveness to rhyme and alliteration** includes the ability to recite learned rhyming words or alliterative phrases in books, nursery rhymes or songs, and usually occurs between the ages of 4 to 5 years. The ability to produce a rhyme typically occurs between 5 and 6 years of age.

  ▶ **Syllable awareness** includes the ability to count the syllables in a word, or to segment or blend syllables of a word. This typically occurs around 5 years of age.

  ▶ **Onset and rime manipulation.** The ability to produce a rhyming word depends on understanding that rhyming words have the same rime. Recognizing a rhyme is much easier than producing a rhyme, which usually occurs around 5 to 6 years of age.

- **Phonemic awareness** includes the understanding that the words we say are made up of sounds as well as the ability to work with those sounds verbally. This includes the ability to recognize the sounds in a word (*boy* starts with a /b/ sound), to isolate sounds in a word (the last sound in *dog* is /g/), to blend sounds in a word (/m//o//p/ = *mop*), to segment a sound into its parts (*mop* = /m/-/o/-/p/), and to substitute sounds in a word (i.e., "Take the /d/ from *dog* and add a /b/—the new word is *bog*"). Phonemic awareness is part of oral language development, but is sometimes confused with phonics. Phonics is the understanding that there is a relationship between sounds and letters and words. Using flash cards to teach the letters is a phonics activity. Phoneme awareness includes several components. Some children pick up on this naturally, but many need to be taught explicitly. The skills are typically mastered between the ages of 5 and 9.

▶ Identify and match the initial sounds in words, then the final and middle sounds (e.g., "Which picture begins with /m/?"; "Find another picture that ends in /r/").

▶ Blend sounds into words (e.g., "Listen: /s/ /e/ /t/. Say it fast.").

▶ Segment and produce the initial sound, then the final and middle sounds (e.g., "What sound does *zoo* start with?"; "Say the last sound in *milk*"; "Say the vowel sound in *rope*."). Segment the phonemes in two- or three-sound words, moving to four- and five-sound words as the student becomes proficient (e.g., "The word is *eyes*. Stretch and say the sounds: /ī/ /z/"). This skill is typically mastered between 6 and 7 years of age.

▶ Manipulate phonemes by substituting or deleting sounds (e.g., "Say *smoke* without the /m/."). The deletion of medial and final blends typically occurs last, around 9 years of age.

Components of Phonemic Awareness

Skill	Definition	Example	Mastery
Phonemic isolation	Ability to hear individual sounds	What is the last sound in *lap*?	Around 5 years of age
Phonemic categorization	Ability to identify similar and different sounds	Which word doesn't belong? *big, jump, ball*	Around 5 years of age
Phonemic identification	Ability to recognize same sounds	Which words have the same sounds at the end? *Rig, jig, jam*	Between 5 and 6 years of age
Onset and Rime blending	Ability to blend onset and rime	*b—all* is *ball*	Between 5 and 6 years of age
Phonemic addition	Ability to make new words by adding a phoneme	The word is *cat*. Add an /s/ and the new word is *cats*.	
Phonemic blending (chunking)	Ability to combine phonemes into a word and later chunking groups of letters into a word	Listen to the sounds and blend them to make the word /s/ /a/ /m/ = *sam*	Around 6 years of age

(continued)

Skill	Definition	Example	Mastery
Phonemic segmentation	Ability to break words into individual sounds or phonemes	Tell me the sounds you hear in *bug*. /b/ /u/ /g/	
Phonemic deletion	Ability to delete sounds	The word is *stack*. Take away the /t/ and what is the new word? *sack*	
Phonemic substitution	Ability to replace a phoneme in a word to make a new word	The word is *bat*. Take away the /b/ and add an /m/—what's the new word? *mat*	

- **Vocabulary** is the words needed to be able to communicate. Most vocabulary is learned indirectly and there are generally accepted to be three tiers of vocabulary. Tier 1 are the common, basic words that children typically know as they enter school. Tier 2 are content words used across the curriculum as well as process words such as *assess* or *determine*. Content words are essential for fostering later comprehension. Tier 3 are content-specific or domain-specific words (i.e., words connected with a "construction" unit such as *crane* or *scaffold*) that are needed for deeper understanding. Recent research has revealed that **academic vocabulary**, or those words needed in academic settings (i.e., *plot, summarize, glossary*) are also essential for emergent literacy. Children have a listening vocabulary, a speaking vocabulary, a reading vocabulary, and a writing vocabulary. The listening vocabulary is the words children learn and need to know when listening or hearing. The speaking vocabulary is those words a child needs to know to speak or to communicate a message. Listening and speaking vocabularies, part of oral language development, are fostered through rich, experiential learning activities, reading aloud, and opportunities to talk. Children's listening and speaking vocabularies are typically larger and more sophisticated than their reading and writing vocabulary. Children with opportunities to develop their vocabulary learn the nuances of meaning or the **semantic (meaning)** variances of words. Teachers should include instruction in **inference** and **figurative** language to positively impact students' later reading comprehension and writing skills (Goodson, Wolf, Bell, Turner, & Finney, 2010).

- **Syntax** in oral language is knowing how to make words into sentences, form more sophisticated sentences, and communicate a message effectively. Syntactic ability is linked with later reading and writing development.

- **Narrative discourse** is the ability to communicate an experience that includes past, present, and future events or a cause and effect (Justice, 2004). This type of discourse is different from a conversation because one speaker is conveying all the information. Recent research indicates that intentional instruction in narrative discourse and language fosters students' reading and writing of formal language.

4. **Emergent reading and writing behaviors**

There are four cueing systems linked with reading and writing that are developed during the emergent literacy stage: semantics, syntax, graphophonic, and pragmatic. All systems are needed to effectively comprehend and communicate. The difficulty of the text, the type of text, and the skill of the reader can impact comprehension if one system is used more than another.

- **Semantic knowledge** is the linguistic study of meaning, both literally and figuratively, in words and texts. Denotation and connotation are two concepts associated with semantics. **Denotation** is the literal and basic definition of a word, while **connotation** is the meaning of the word within context, or the meaning that is conveyed by the word. For example, the word *lion* denotes a species of animal related to the cat, usually with a muscular chest, a rounded head and ears, and a tufted tail. The connotative meaning of *lion* expands beyond the literal in that a lion is considered a symbol of strength, courage, and royalty, often associated with the phrase "king of the jungle." Children whose home language is not English, those who come from families where there is not a lot of interactive talk, or children who are hearing impaired may struggle with the figurative meanings of words. Good readers use their knowledge of illustrations, prefixes, other words in the sentence, and "clues" to make sense of the text.

- **Syntactic knowledge** deals with knowing the rules of sequencing words into sentences, sentences into longer sentences and paragraphs, and paragraphs into longer works that make sense. For example, many sentences are in a noun-verb form, i.e. "The dog ran." Children whose first language is not English may struggle with the order, so teachers need to be cognizant of their students' backgrounds.

- **Graphophonic knowledge** is the ability to sound out words. If children have the word in their speaking or listening vocabulary, they may know the meaning and be able to sound it out. If the word is not in the children's oral vocabulary, they may be able to sound it out, but not know what it means.

- **Pragmatic knowledge** deals with background knowledge and expectations. For example, a child who has heard fairy tales will have certain expectations when a story begins with "Once upon a time." Another example is if an adult says, "We are going to the grocery store to buy____" and a child knows that a grocery store is where one usually buys food.

Skill 1.2: Identify common emergent literacy difficulties and apply strategies for prevention and intervention.

1. **Rhyming**

Singing songs, reading poems aloud, chanting nursery rhymes, and clapping games are excellent authentic ways to expose students to rhyming words and patterns (Bryant, MacLean, & Bradley, 1990). Picture cards of objects that rhyme (i.e., a picture of a *cat* and a picture of a *hat*) can be used for rhyming practice; teachers can show students two pictures and have children identify if they rhyme or not (i.e., show pictures of a *dog* and *frog* (names rhyme) or *dog* and *cat* (names do not rhyme).

2. **Phonemic awareness**

Emergent readers sometimes have difficulty with phonemic awareness skills, particularly if they have not been read to often before starting school or if they potentially have a learning disability that has not been identified. The following strategies are suggested for prevention and intervention.

- **Phonemes:** Elkonin boxes are used to help students segment words into individual sounds, or phonemes and gain practice counting the sounds in words rather than the letters. To use Elkonin boxes, a student listens to a word and moves a token into a box for each sound or phoneme. An example of an Elkonin box for the word "shape" (3 sounds /sh/ /a/ /p/)

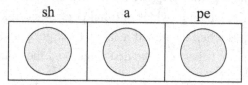

- **Onset and Rime:** An onset is the initial phonological unit of a syllable (e.g., *c* in *cat* or *sp* in *speak*). The onset is always a consonant or a cluster of consonants, so not all words or syllables have an onset (i.e., *axe* begins with a vowel and is one syllable, so there is no onset). The rime is the letters that contain the initial sound, usually a vowel, and final consonants (e.g., *at* in *cat* or *eak* in *speak*) in the word or syllable. Similar to teaching beginning readers about rhyme, teaching children about onset and rime helps them recognize common chunks within words. This can help students decode new words when reading and spell words when writing.

3. **Alphabetic knowledge**

Students who have had little exposure to print in books may come to school not realizing that words are made up of letters or groups of letters that have sounds and are spelled the same way every time. Most children come to school with knowledge of *environmental print* such as fast food signs or logos for common brands or concepts. Teachers can share photos of places that are familiar to children (i.e., a photo of a *McDonald's* or a *Walmart* sign) to help convey the idea that the name of things, places, people are spelled consistently. Another strategy is to focus on the letters in a child's name (i.e., *William* or *Shanita* are always spelled the same for that individual) or common words (i.e., *chair* is always spelled c-h-a-i-r). Teachers can also use the letters that mean the most to the children, such as the letters in their names, family or pet names, and concrete objects.

4. **Decoding strategies**

- Phonics instruction includes teaching students letters and corresponding sounds, blends (i.e., *b l* in *blue*) and rimes, also called word families or phonograms (i.e., *-ack, -og, -igh*).

- Another way to learn words is the "whole-part-whole" that includes activities such as *say, spell, cover, write, check*—which involves saying the word, spelling the word aloud while looking at the word, covering the word and writing it down, and checking the word. If the word is misspelled, the student corrects the word and repeats the process.

5. Letter formation and handwriting

- There are five components of letter writing: formation, slant, spacing, size, and alignment. Teachers need to consider how each letter is formed and break down the steps, while explaining how to form the letter. Drawing shapes such as circles, vertical, horizontal, and slanted lines can be a way to teach strokes before formal handwriting instruction. Dot-to-dot activities can help develop students' straight line skills.

- Most children begin using crayons and pencils by gripping them in their fist or five fingers to hold the pencil, often changing hands before choosing a dominant preference. Research on **pencil grip** has not shown an overall relation to writing proficiency, but a tripod grip, which provides optimal control, seems more conducive to legible writing. This grip is when the pencil rests on or slightly above the knuckle of the middle finger and the point is between the first finger and the thumb.

- Body position is important for developing legible and efficient handwriting, as is a proper chair or seat height. Typically, the paper is on a flat surface at an angle, turned away from the writing hand. If in a chair, the child should be seated comfortably with feet on the floor and the back straight. The writing surface should be at a comfortable distance away from the writer.

Skill 1.3: Apply various approaches for developing emergent and early literacy skills (e.g., oral language and listening, phonological awareness, alphabet knowledge, background knowledge, concepts of print).

Whole-to-part and part-to-whole are two approaches for developing early literacy skills. Part-to-whole involves teaching sounds, then letters, then words. Whole-to-part might involve looking at a word and breaking it into parts or sounds. For example, when trying to decode the word *caterpillar*, a teacher might draw a child's attention to words within a word (*cat, pill*) or to looking at a group of words and looking for patterns. Both approaches are necessary for teaching early skills.

Reading

1. Develop students' academic language skills, including the use of inferencing (i.e., predicting, problem-solving, brainstorming), narrative language, and vocabulary, including academic (i.e, character, plot) language. Students must be able to identify the individual phonemes that make up the words they hear in speech, name the letters of the alphabet as they appear in print, and identify each letter's corresponding sound(s) in order to decode (read words and say them aloud) and encode (convert spoken words to print).

2. Foster awareness of the segments of sound in speech and how they link to letters. Students need to be able to identify and manipulate sounds in speech in order to be able to blend and make words. The ability to isolate sounds and then link those sounds to letters will help students read about 70 percent of regular monosyllabic words (Ziegler, Stone, & Jacobs, 1997).

3. Teach students to decode words, analyze word parts, and write and recognize words.

4. Ensure that each student reads connected text every day to support reading accuracy, fluency, and comprehension.

Writing

Writing is a complex activity integrating the mental functions of the writing process, attention, memory, language, visual process, and higher-order thinking skills with the fine motor skills involved in the physical act of moving a writing tool across a surface to form letters, numerals, punctuation, and symbols. Writers visually check their output while kinesthetically monitoring the pencil grip, the position and movement of the fingers and hand, and the pace and rhythm of the process. Cognitively, the writer is pulling symbol and language knowledge from memory (Sousa, 2016).

Young children learn to encode (construct language) when they "sound out" words. Therefore, children need opportunities to write frequently for authentic reasons. Given time and opportunity, emergent writers typically move through the stages of writing with the goal of writing to communicate or for meaning.

Handwriting

Handwriting, the ability to legibly and fluently form letters, numbers, punctuation and symbols to communicate, is an essential component of early writing development (Coker & Ritchey, 2015). Research reveals that instruction in printing and cursive handwriting (not typing) involves areas of students' brains connected with reading ability, fine motor skills, attention, and academic achievement (James & Engelhardt, 2012). Letter writing and letter writing fluency is linked to word reading and spelling (Jones & Christensen, 1999). A study of preschoolers found that students who wrote words by hand were able to identify letters in words better than preschoolers who typed the words on keyboards (Longcamp, Zerbato-Poudou, & Velay, 2005). Moreover, improvements in handwriting are related to improvements in writing (Graham, Harris, & Fink, 2000).

Skill 1.4: Identify appropriate emergent and early literacy activities.

When selecting activities, teachers need to take care that they are sending the message that learning is enjoyable, while at the same time offering activities that build attention, focus, persistence, and stamina.

Learning letters and sight words can be taught through a variety of game-like activities. While a common practice, there is no scientific evidence to support the teaching of single letters in isolation or in alphabetical order. A more appropriate activity is to teach letters through the **"own name advantage"** (Schickendanz & Collins, 2013). Children pay attention to words that mean something to them, such as their name, their friends' names, names for their loved ones (i.e., "mom") and words for things they find interesting or engaging ("dinosaur"). Providing opportunities for children to write their names, such as signing in, or drawing attention to the letters in children's names through graphing or simple games such as, "If your name starts with B, please stand up." Activities such as providing cookie cutters shaped like letters of the alphabet or sandpaper letters and numbers are good ways to add tactile experience and build fine motor skills.

Dramatic play to support literacy and language development should include three components. First there are *props and objects* available that can be used to support the play. Second, the children begin to take on a *role* or *persona* associated with the scenario. For example, the children may decide to create a doctor's office where children come to get shots or medicine. This is usually familiar to most children and may involve *combining multiple roles or storylines*, which is the second component necessary for optimal literacy and language development. Third, the children create a *pretend scenario* and act out the story through talk and movement. During this phase, they may assign roles or jobs adjusting the scenario based on the ongoing verbal negotiations. Teachers can support this by providing a variety of props and dress-up materials.

Story reading and read alouds, including shared reading, are excellent ways for teachers to model fluency, teach story language, build children's background knowledge and vocabulary, and teach concepts of print. Additionally, teachers can read aloud stories and have children act them out to model story concepts such as beginning, middle, and end, plot, or character development.

Blocks, Legos, Lincoln Logs, and puzzles build literacy knowledge including sequencing, order, numbers, spatial concepts and vocabulary, as well as children's fine motor skills. When working in small groups, the activities provide opportunities for conversation and negotiation. Research suggests a link between a child's ability to build sophisticated structures and later achievement in geometry and algebraic thinking (Jirout & Newcomb, 2015).

Skill 1.5: Select specific instructional methods (e.g., whole group, small group, explicit, systematic) for developing emergent literacy.

Skill 1.5 reflects learner-based instructional approaches that focus on how the teacher can support learners in the emergent literacy stage.

Let's look at each instructional method in turn.

1. **Systematic** refers to goals-based instruction that creates a coherent literacy curriculum, reflecting solid research, theory, and practice. In other words, to guide young learners effectively, an instructor should have a confident grasp of literacy practices that can inform holistic curricular decisions as well as day-to-day class activities (Schmoker, 2019; Shanahan, 2020; Rosenshine, 1986).

   - Systematic instruction should reflect goals, objectives, and outcomes that can be implemented using a variety of learner-centered activities.

   - Instruction might integrate sequences such as a prereading and activation of prior knowledge, introduction of new vocabulary, choral repetition of new vocabulary, real-world examples of content in story books, and connections among disciplines.

- A systematic approach should integrate literacy materials that reflect learner readiness. Teachers should be aware that instructional-level materials designated for a specific grade level could trigger frustration if the learner has not reached the literacy level of the grade-designated materials.

- A systematic approach can reflect the teacher's understanding that reading is far more than simply decoding text but is instead holistic construction of meaning that pulls together experience, interest, developing linguistic proficiencies, and general comprehension.

- Systematic instruction necessarily includes authentic assessment that can be integrated into daily classroom activities with immediate formative feedback.

- Systematic instruction should integrate instruction in linguistic areas such as phonology, morphology, syntax, and semantics to support learners' growing awareness of literacy structures.

- Systematic instruction should integrate reading and writing activities in support of developing literacy.

- Systematic instruction should provide support for English Learners.

2. **Explicit** instruction can be viewed as a "showing how to" approach in which teachers guide learners to master simple through complex skills by demonstrating, observing, providing feedback, and recognizing improvement (Rosenshine, 1986). In emergent literacy settings, explicit instruction generally reflects the teacher's efforts to show learners how to apply linguistic skills, metacognitive skills, and even life experience to construct holistic meaning. Some specific types of instructional activities are recognized as good examples of explicit instruction:

- Modeling. In modeling, a teacher literally enacts/shows how something is done, ideally with explanatory commentary. In a classroom of emergent readers and writers, a teacher might stop during a read aloud to show learners how to apply phonics skills and context cues to decode a new word in an early reader science book.

- Think alouds. A think aloud is a prolific strategy for promoting learners' metacognitive skills. In think alouds, a teacher shows how to process a new text by applying skills that are already in the learners' repertoire. In a think aloud, the teacher articulates the thinking that occurs as new material is processed. For example, during a whole-group lesson to introduce a book about rivers, a teacher might comment on the expectations raised by the title of book or might comment on the illustrations on the end papers of the book. The teacher might flip to the back of the book and say, "I'm wondering if there's a list of new words that I'll need to know as I read."

- Scaffolding. Scaffolded lessons are constructed in sequenced steps of simpler to more complex learning activities. Scaffolding can be provided in many ways, including instructions, realia, pictures relevant to the content of the lesson, examples, and practice.

- Guided practice. Practice is a vital part of new learning. In guided practice, a teacher integrates time to allow learners to practice and process new skills, experiment with error, receive feedback, and try again if necessary.

- Learner involvement. Learners need to be able to *do* things to show that they are learning. For emergent readers, doing can be as simple as drawing a picture to "summarize" their takeaways from a story they just read. Even students who are still learning how to shape letters and recognize the connections between alphabetic symbols and sounds can create artifacts that show their developing literacy. For emergent readers and writers, doing can involve manipulatives, crayons, whiteboards, and a variety of other instructional supports to encourage activity.

- Direct instruction. In early literacy instruction, there must be a good bit of direct instruction where learners are explicitly taught basic concepts such as phonics skills necessary for decoding, principles such as text directionality in English texts, and the alphabetic principle. Consider, for example, the explicit instruction that must be involved in order to teach emergent readers and writers the "mysteries" of how the *ph* digraph represents the /f/ sound in English. Direct instruction is a vital component of explicit instruction although sometimes it is considered a limited approach to effective literacy instruction (Camilli & Wolfe, 2004; ILA, 2020).

Whole-group and **small-group** instructional methods allow teachers flexibility in presenting new content and providing opportunities for practice.

3. In emergent literacy classrooms, **whole-group** instruction might be used to present a focused lesson in a content area or to introduce a new skill or concept, such as distinguishing between fact and opinion or identifying key plot elements in a story. Whole group instruction, especially for young learners, should integrate opportunities for learners to practice and to seek guidance in applying new knowledge. Whole-group instruction should reflect learner readiness, the developmental level of the class, and even the configuration of the classroom. Teachers should also integrate a variety of techniques in whole-group instruction to support multiple learning styles.

4. **Small-group** instruction can be used to provide differentiated instruction in the smaller setting of randomly selected or ability-based groups. Most literacy specialists recommend against ability-based grouping as the only approach to grouping because of the stigmatizing effect it can have on learners placed in low achievement groups. However, in general, small-group instruction is recognized as a prime strategy for promoting literacy learning, especially in learners who require focused attention from the teacher including students in low SES categories, ELs, and struggling learners (Duke, 2019).

There are many recognized advantages of small-group instruction, including opportunities for young learners to develop autonomy in interacting with other learners, in selecting materials for practicing skills, and in demonstrating developing competencies. Small groups also allow learners to feel safe making errors and taking risks that are a necessary part of acquiring new knowledge.

Literacy experts recommend that a good bit of small-group instruction be worked into the blocks of instructional time devoted to literacy in a typical school day (Shanahan, 2020).

Skill 1.6: Identify the components of and techniques for creating a print-rich environment reflecting diverse cultures and the impact of such an environment on classroom instruction.

The **components of a literacy-rich environment** include print materials such as labels in different languages, alphabet charts, and reading materials that might include books, big books, magazines, catalogs, maps, and dictionaries. Tools include pencils, pens, crayons, sketch pencils, colored pencils, markers, crayons, chalk, paint brushes, paints, clipboards, dry erase boards, chalkboards, and different types of paper. Centers and work stations can include literacy components. For example, a teacher could stock the block center with books about castles, graph paper, clipboards, and pencils. Menus, calendars, and an adding machine could be added to a dramatic play housekeeping center. The listening center could include sketch books and pencils for sketching the story sequence or comparing characters. Older technology such as overhead projectors can be repurposed in the writing center with magnetic letters and dry erase markers.

Techniques for creating a print-rich environment include using word walls, anchor charts, motivational charts, artwork, photos of diverse families, songs and music from diverse cultures, and job charts that feature photos of the children matched with their names. The calendar area can be maximized for literacy instruction by including the names of the days of the week and the months of the year.

A literacy-rich environment positively impacts classroom instruction when the teacher uses the materials intentionally and thoughtfully. For example, it's important to create the word wall with the students' input. An alphabet line and number line are helpful for reinforcing children's learning. Research suggests that having the lines at students' eye level is important. When that is not possible, teachers may use pointers or flashlights to highlight the letter, sound, or numeral.

Skill 1.7: Analyze the structure (e.g., small group, whole group) and components (e.g., vocabulary, phonics) of a balanced literacy program.

1. **Structure and Format**

   - **Whole group instruction** takes place when the teacher has the students together in a whole group. For young children, it is better to have the children sitting in a manner so that the teacher can see the children's faces, in order to monitor their attention and understanding, and to help avoid distractions. Students' attention spans are generally about a minute for each year, so a 4-year-old typically has a 4- to 6-minute attention span. Teachers should plan for frequent shifts or breaks such as stopping to sing a song or stretch. Calendar time or a morning meeting are often done in a whole group and can be an effective teaching time when planned well. Mini-lessons are often done in a whole group setting. This is also called *Tier 1* instruction.

   - **Small group instruction** typically includes 3–7 students and includes differentiated instruction, guided practice, reinforcement, or review. Teachers need to be situated so that they are able to monitor the rest of the class, while teaching the small group. Flexible group membership is important, so that students are moved to another group when appropriate and determined through informal assessment. This is also called *Tier 2* instruction.

- **Individual instruction** takes place when the teacher interacts with a child individually to reinforce or to teach specific skills. This is called *Tier 3* instruction and can be done in the classroom by the teacher. Other formats include an exceptional student education (ESE) teacher "pushing" in to help while the individual is in the main class, or "pulling out"—when the student is taken to another area—so that the instruction is delivered with minimal distraction.

2. **Components**

- A **balanced literacy program** uses whole language and phonics and aims to include the strongest elements of each. Effective literacy instruction incorporates six common features, sometimes called the six Ts: time (to read and write); talk; teach; texts; tasks; and testing (Allington, 2005).

- The **components of a "balanced literacy"** approach are as follows: The read aloud, word study, guided reading, shared reading, interactive writing, shared writing, dictation, Reader's Workshop, and Writer's Workshop.

- The **read aloud** allows the teacher to model fluency, introduce students to vocabulary and content that is typically at a reading level beyond their own, and to model metacognitive thinking through thinking aloud, thus demonstrating how we monitor our comprehension and the meaning of texts.

- **Word study** is a way to teach spelling and words through a focus on patterns and rules. The instruction can take place in whole or small groups and will vary based on the needs of the students.

  ▶ Word families, rimes, and phonograms are the parts of words that typically follow the first consonant. For example, in the word *tick*, *-ick* is the rime.

  ▶ Cloze reading may be part of word study. It is a strategy in which words are removed from a text to support a student's reading comprehension. Teachers may remove words from the passage to allow students to use their analytical skills of inferring, rereading, and critical thinking—to decide what makes sense to fill in the blank.

- **Guided reading** is a small-group lesson typically about 20 minutes in length. The teacher works with students who are at about the same reading level using texts that are at their instructional level. Instructional level texts are a bit harder than texts students can read on their own, without assistance, also called their independent or recreational level. The teacher scaffolds or supports students' reading by teaching strategies or specific skills or content needed.

- **Shared reading or interactive reading** is when the teacher reads a book with student participation. This can be done in whole or small groups, and allows the teacher to model fluency and other strategies with the students' interaction.

- **Interactive writing** involves the teacher writing, modeling spelling or other concepts, and allowing students to "share the pen." For example, during Calendar Time, the student might write or copy the date on the board.

- **Shared writing** involves the teacher writing down what is said while asking questions, summarizing, and helping teach or reinforce conventions of print and spelling.

- **Dictation** is primarily when the teacher writes down exactly what a child says, in order to get the words on paper.

- **Reader's Workshop** typically spans 60 to 90 minutes and includes all of the elements mentioned above.

- **Writer's Workshop** is typically a 30- to 60-minute block of time and includes mini-lessons, time to write using the writing process (drafting, writing, revision, editing, publishing), teachers conferencing with students on skills or concepts specific to their needs, and a time for student sharing of their work. (Graves, 1994; Calkins, 1994)

Skill 1.8: Apply instructional approaches and strategies for teaching informational literacy skills (e.g., reading labels, signs, newspapers).

"Information literacy" deals with the basic communication competencies of accessing, analyzing, evaluating, and communicating information. Teaching information literacy skills includes helping students:

1. Plan research or pose a question (i.e., Why are bees important?)—This can be done as a class with the teacher modeling and directing students' comments and input.

2. Develop a way to search for the answer—Teachers can model ways to search for an answer to the questions. Students can work collaboratively in small groups, with guidance from a teacher or older students.

3. Find resources—This can be varied and may include books, internet sources, and local experts. Teachers can provide materials in the classroom or have a media specialist help students find books to answer their questions. Teachers can model how using different books on the same topic can allow the reader to gather information from a variety of sources. Using the internet provides an opportunity to discuss safety rules and how to tell the difference between a reliable source and an unreliable source.

4. Evaluating the resources and thinking critically about them—This might include looking at who wrote the book, what was the author's purpose, the publisher, and text features, etc. The teacher can model this and help students through guided practice on evaluating a resource for information. Older students can also be partnered with younger students.

5. Expressing the information learned in meaningful ways—For example, students can share their information through writing, speaking, drawing, singing, or acting. The teacher can help students create a video or record their presentations.

Skill 1.9: Identify effective methods and strategies to integrate reading, writing, speaking, listening, viewing, and presenting across the curriculum.

Project-Based Learning is a teaching method in which students gain knowledge and skills by working for an extended period of time to investigate and respond to an authentic, engaging, and complex question, problem, or challenge. The culminating project allows students to integrate reading, writing, speaking, listening, viewing, and presenting in authentic ways.

Thematic units, which are built around multiple content areas, are also good opportunities to provide assignments that allow students to integrate multiple literacy skills and demonstrate competency.

Skill 1.10: Determine effective techniques for motivating students to engage in academic and personal reading.

1. Student interest—Interest inventories are informal ways to identify student interests and preferences for types of books.

2. Opportunities to read at school—Some students do not have an opportunity or place to read outside of school. As such, teachers should provide some time for students to read during the school day. In an activity called "Sustained Silent Reading," everyone, including the adults, find a comfortable place to sit and read.

3. Self-selection and managed choice—Research shows that students prefer to select the books they are going to read and to have a choice in the books they read. In managed choice, the teacher provides a selection of books at the student's reading level, so that the student has some autonomy in choosing the books.

4. Reading goals—Can be motivational for students, who can set a goal to read a certain number of minutes, a certain number of pages, or a certain number of books.

Competency 2: Knowledge of Fiction and Nonfiction Genres Including Reading Informational Texts

Skill 2.1: Select literature (e.g., pattern books, concept books) from a variety of narrative texts that build language skills and concept development.

Teachers have a great deal of control over the books they have in their classrooms and the books they choose to read aloud and share with students (Hall, 2005). In addition to considering their students' cultural backgrounds and experiences, teachers should also provide ample access to a variety of texts on many topics, at many reading levels, and diverse genres. Pattern books and concept books are ideal for supporting early readings. Informational and narrative texts should be available as soon as students can read just a few words. Research reveals that students need lots of opportunity to read **connected text** (or text that has multiple related sentences) daily, both with and without constructive feedback, as these texts require acquisition of skills that extend beyond reading isolated words or phrases. Reading connected texts requires that readers develop the ability to read accurately, fluently, with expression, and to comprehend what they are reading. Comprehension requires readers to self-monitor their understanding, build their background knowledge, and use strategies to foster their comprehension (Foorman, et al., 2016).

Skill 2.2: Identify and distinguish the elements of various literary genres and formats of prose and poetry (e.g., multicultural literature, fables, legends, biographies, realistic fiction, fantasy).

The two primary genres of literature are **fiction** and **nonfiction** or **informational**. Under those umbrellas are a variety of genres or subgenres.

Fiction

Fiction is typically narrative writing that is imagined or made up. While it can be realistic, it is not based primarily in fact. There are a number of categories or subgenres that fall under the fiction umbrella and include:

Realistic fiction are stories that could actually happen in the real-world.

Historical fiction are stories that are set in the past and include fictional characters, settings, and events, although they could be based on real people, events, or places.

Fantasies are stories that are set in other worlds or times and often include magical or supernatural aspects.

Science fiction are stories that contain some element of science, either real or imagined, past or future and are set on Earth or elsewhere.

Poetry includes verses that have a pattern or rhythm and sometimes rhyme. Poetic elements can also be found in nursery rhymes and songs.

Folklore embraces songs, stories, myths, tall tales, and proverbs passed down through the oral tradition of storytelling. Folktales fall under this category and include stories often set in the countryside or woods. Human characters interact with animals, who are often able to talk.

Fables are stories that usually have a moral or message. They often have animals or inanimate objects as characters speaking.

Fairy tales are similar to folktales but are often set in a town or involve royalty. The stories may include fairies or other magical creatures. The characters are either good or evil and good usually prevails.

Tall tales are usually stories with humor, gross exaggerations, and larger-than-life protagonists.

Legends are stories that are said to be based on fact or history, but have fictional or magical elements mixed in.

Mythology is stories based in part on historical events that reveal human behavior and natural phenomena by its symbolism; often pertain to the actions of the gods. A body of myths can be that of a particular people or that relating to a particular person.

Drama includes literature connected with theater. This genre includes stories or scripts composed in verse or prose, usually for theatrical performance, where conflicts and emotion are expressed through dialogue and action.

Nonfiction

Narrative nonfiction is information based on fact that is presented in a format that tells a story.

Essays are short literary compositions that reflect the author's outlook or point on a particular theme or subject, usually in prose and generally analytic, speculative, or interpretative.

Biographies are written accounts of people's lives.

Autobiographies give the history of people's lives, written or told by the subject—often written in narrative form.

Skill 2.3: Analyze and compare literature with common themes written from different viewpoints and cultural perspectives.

The teacher can provide multiple versions of folk tales from diverse cultures and help students analyze the books for their central theme, lesson, or meaning. Graphic organizers can be used to compare and contrast the books.

The teacher can use literature related to a common theme as part of a larger unit of study. Graphic organizers can be used to examine different viewpoints and cultural perspectives.

Skill 2.4: Identify instructional approaches and apply strategies for developing literary analysis.

Teachers can model how to use information from the illustrations and words to analyze a text.

Teachers can create a chart comparing the points of view of characters and allow students to list ways in which the points of view are similar or different.

Teachers can provide opportunities for students to work in small groups to discuss books and analyze components of the story (i.e., character development, plot, theme).

Skill 2.5: Select appropriate techniques for encouraging students to respond to literature and informational texts in a variety of ways.

For instance:

Grade 3 focuses on use of illustrations, connections in text, and compare and contrast in informational text where the use of illustrations and the connections between the illustrations and the text are clearer and literal, making it easier for students to compare and contrast them.

Grade 3 focuses on decoding literary text and point of view in literary text.

Grade 3 focuses on text structures in informational text where text structures are more concrete.

Skill 2.6: Identify a variety of uses and purposes for multiple representations of information.

Information can be presented in multiple ways to draw attention to specific information; provide more detail; or provide a quick overview of the content of the text. Some examples include:

Tables that organize information in rows and columns and can be read more easily than narrative text.

Timelines that show the order of events in which something occurred.

Flow charts that show the hierarchy of ideas or the steps in a process.

Venn diagrams that are used to compare and contrast information.

Skill 2.7: Identify instructional methods and strategies (e.g., using graphic organizers, summarizing, oral questioning, inferring) for facilitating students' reading comprehension across the curriculum.

There are a variety of evidence-based instructional methods and strategies to support readers' comprehension. The following are a few examples:

K-W-L *(What we KNOW, what we WANT to know, what we LEARNED)* **charts** can be used with any grade level to help students' comprehension across the curriculum. The teacher begins by activating students' prior knowledge about a concept or topic. She records the information for all three columns.

A **semantic map** is a visual presentation of knowledge and experiences regarding a specific topic or concept. It is useful for activating prior knowledge, making predictions, and setting a purpose for reading, all elements needed for comprehension. The teacher begins by writing a topic or big idea on chart paper or the board and putting a circle around it. Students then verbally brainstorm related ideas or subtopics, which are recorded on the chart and connected to the main topic with lines. Then the teacher or students read the text. Under the teacher's guidance, the students revise the semantic map to reflect new knowledge or to add more subtopics. After summarizing their learning, the teacher guides the students on other ways they can use semantic maps for learning.

The **Directed Reading-Thinking Activity (DRTA)** can be used before and during reading to support students' comprehension through prediction, inference, and setting a purpose for reading. The DRTA is a discussion format that focuses on making predictions. It requires students to use their background knowledge, make connections to what they know, make predictions about the text, set their own purpose for reading, and then use the information in the text to make evaluative judgments. It can be used with nonfiction and fiction texts. First, the teacher divides the reading assignments into logical sections. Next, the teacher helps the students brainstorm what they know about the topic. The teacher then has the students preview the reading segment by looking at the illustrations, headings, figures, table of contents, and other text features. The teacher asks students to make predictions about what they will learn. These predictions can be done individually, with a partner, or as a whole group. The predictions are recorded and the students then read the selection. After reading, they discuss their predictions and whether those predictions were confirmed or not, using evidence from the text. The teacher and students repeat the process with the next reading segment that the teacher has identified. The teacher closes the lesson with a review of the text and a discussion of how to use this strategy for other assignments.

Visualization is another strategy that supports comprehension and can be used before, during, and after reading. Good readers create visual images or pictures in their minds as they are reading, which helps enhance their comprehension and memory. First, the teacher reads a short selection of a story aloud or tells the story, modeling how readers can visualize while reading or listening. The teacher then reads another short selection or tells a portion of a story, asking students to visualize as they listen. After reading, the teacher asks the students to share the images that they created in their mind and to identify the words, phrases, or ideas that triggered their image. The teacher repeats the procedure several times until the students can visualize and share their connections. The teacher then asks students to read and visualize as they are reading. Prompts can include asking about the images the students make or having them draw the image that was in their mind, along with the words or phrases that helped them make the image. The teacher then discusses how creating the images in the mind can help with remembering and comprehension.

Skill 2.8: Identify and appropriately use text structures (e.g., cause and effect, chronological order, compare and contrast) to develop student comprehension.

When students understand the format and predictable features of text, they are able to focus more on comprehension. Teachers can discuss the text structures and model the questions and signal words that help the reader determine what kind of text he is reading.

Text Structure of Nonfiction	Questions to Ask Self	Signal Words
Description	Is this describing something?	*For instance, for example*
Sequence	Is this telling me the order?	*First, second, next, before, after*
Compare and Contrast	Is this alike or different?	*Similar, both, however, also*
Problem and Solution	What's the problem and how to solve it?	*Problem, solution, issue*
Cause and Effect	Is this explaining why something happened?	*Because, as a result, therefore*

Skill 2.9: Identify informational text features and their purposes (e.g., index, glossary, heading/subheading, table of contents, bibliography, references).

Teachers can help students' comprehension by teaching the kinds of text features that are found in informational books and modeling how to use them to increase understanding.

Text Feature	Purpose
Title	Gives the reader information about the book
Cover illustration	Gives information about the contents
Table of Contents	Provides information on chapters, sections, and page numbers
Glossary	Typically found in the back of the book; gives definitions of key vocabulary words from the text
Index	Typically found in the back of the book; gives information on where to find a key word, topic, or subject
Headings and subtitles	Typically have a different font; give information about what is in that section
Sidebars	Usually on the side and set off from the main portion of the text, sidebars give additional detail on something mentioned in that section.
Photos, illustrations, and captions	Highlights important information from the text. Inset photos can also be used to show something up close or at a distance.
Diagrams	A picture of something from the text labeled to identify important elements
Figures, tables, and graphs	A way to show data related to information in the text
Maps	A way to help the reader know the location in the world related to the information in the text
Cross sections and cutaways	Allows the reader to see the inside or parts of something

Source: *http://www.readingrockets.org/article/guiding-students-through-expository-text-text-feature-walks.*

Competency 3: Knowledge of Reading Foundational Skills

Skill 3.1: Identify appropriate stages of word recognition (e.g., pre-alphabetic, partial-alphabetic, full-alphabetic) and cueing strategies (e.g., graphophonic, syntactic, semantic) that effective readers use in the decoding process.

The stages of word recognition for early readers include:

The **pseudo-reading stage** is also called pretend reading or the pre-reading stage. This describes when a child turns the pages of a book or text and tells a story, often a story previously read to the child. Children often memorize a book and pretend to read it while recalling the details from memory.

The **logographic-visual stage** is when the child uses the illustrations or letters in words to understand the text, without really knowing what the letters stand for. It is in this stage when children begin to read signs such as "Walmart" or see a big arched "M" logo and know it stands for "McDonald's" (Frith, 1985).

The **alphabetic-phonemic stage** is when the reader begins to visually represent words in a different format from other objects or symbols and the concept of letter/sound relationships develops. The child acquires an explicit knowledge of phonemes, their correspondence with letters, and how to blend sounds into words. Readers begin to develop "word attack" skills and start to decode unfamiliar words.

Children reach this stage as part of natural development, or when the act of learning to read stimulates the development of alphabetic skills. Students who have or will be identified as having learning disabilities may have difficulty transitioning from this stage and need intensive instruction.

- Students in the **partial-alphabetic substage** can recognize some letters and sounds.

- Students in the **full-alphabetic stage** recognize all letters and sounds and begin to understand patterns.

The **orthographic-morphemic stage** is when readers do not need to sound out words on a regular basis, but can recognize words automatically and understand their meaning. Repeated exposure to words enables readers to store the word in a way that they can read it automatically, and is more efficient than having a reader primarily sound the letters out to make the word. Readers who reach this stage are considered proficient readers and they only need to "sound out" unfamiliar words and learn the meaning of more words. (Hoien & Lundberg, 1988; Frith, 1985).

- Students in the **consolidated-alphabetic** or **orthographic stage** can decode unfamiliar words, sound words out, and understand patterns.

- Students in the **automatic** phase can decode easily, quickly, and fluently.

Good readers use all four cueing systems to decode and comprehend. Graphophonic, syntactic, semantic, and pragmatic systems are used in language development and are important for communication. We use all four systems simultaneously as we speak, listen, read, and write.

Skill 3.2: Identify the components of reading fluency (i.e., accuracy, automaticity, rate, prosody).

1. **Accuracy**—reading words without making mistakes is a key component of developing reading fluency.

2. **Automaticity**—when readers are able to read words or passages with speed and accuracy.

3. **Prosody**—deals with how a reader reads aloud—the musical quality that includes stress, intonation, and inflection.

4. **Rate**—the speed at which a reader reads words or passages, usually measured in words per minute.

Skill 3.3: Select instructional methods and strategies for increasing vocabulary acquisition and development (e.g., concept maps, morphemic and contextual analysis) across the curriculum.

Indirect—Most vocabulary is learned indirectly, so reading aloud books at a higher level than most of the students can read independently is one method for increasing students' vocabulary across the curriculum.

Advance—Presenting vocabulary before beginning the topic or book can help students key into the word when it appears in the text or when they hear it.

In-context—Teachers can pause when coming to an unfamiliar word or new vocabulary and quickly define for the readers without losing the pace of the reading. Modeling metacognitive strategies for monitoring comprehension when seeing unknown vocabulary, such as rereading, making a note of the word to look up later, reading ahead or reading the complete passage to see if the meaning has been embedded, followed by opportunities for guided practice can help students learn vocabulary.

Text features—Teachers can explicitly teach text features that can help children learn vocabulary, such as noting bold-faced words, the glossary, or inset frames that may provide definitions or examples.

Skill 3.4: Select effective instructional methods for teaching essential comprehension skills (e.g., main idea, supporting details, author's purpose, inference).

- As students read orally, model strategies, scaffold, and provide feedback to support accurate and efficient word identification.

- Model metacognitive thinking (thinking about one's thinking) to help students self-monitor their understanding of the text and to self-correct word-reading errors.

- Provide opportunities for oral reading practice with feedback to develop fluent and accurate reading with expression through repeated readings, timed readings, reader's theater, and other activities.

Skill 3.5: Apply instructional strategies (e.g., utilizing graphic organizers, activating background knowledge) for helping students comprehend content area texts.

1. **Activating background knowledge.** Research has shown that better comprehension occurs when students are engaged in activities that bridge their old knowledge with the new.

2. Creating **advance organizers**, graphic organizers, or semantic maps to organize information, such as using a Venn diagram to compare and contrast.

3. **Sketch to stretch** involves drawing a picture of the content of the text—creating visual images to help make links to the content.

4. **Visualization** of the content can help comprehension of the material.

5. **Summarizing** sections of text verbally and in writing helps with comprehension.

6. **Peer teaching** allows students to synthesize the information from the text to share with a peer.

Skill 3.6: Identify instructional strategies (e.g., making connections, questioning, summarizing) for developing critical-thinking skills (e.g., critiquing, analyzing, problem-solving).

1. **Model** how to develop an essential question to answer—open-ended question or one that cannot be answered with a "yes" or "no."

2. **Ask a lot of questions** or brainstorm before beginning to read or study a new topic. One strategy is to ask "Why?" five times.

3. **Model making connections** from the reading to the real world, to other texts, or to oneself, and provide opportunities for students to practice.

4. **Don't provide an immediate answer**—allow time for the student to think and problem-solve, or wonder.

5. **Provide opportunities to play and explore**, especially when introducing a new topic of study or content area.

6. **Help students learn how to make inferences** from information provided.

Skill 3.7: Select and apply instructional methods for developing reading fluency (e.g., practice with high-frequency words, timed readings, repeated readings).

1. **Repeated readings** help students develop reading fluency. Speed is not the goal. Focus on expression, intonation, inflection, and precision.

2. **Reader's theater** activities allow students an opportunity to practice their fluency and expression.

3. **Teach the vocabulary before reading.** Then model the reading of several sentences that use the vocabulary terms as a preview for the text. Have students practice reading aloud the same sentences.

4. **Have students record themselves** reading a text aloud, repeating until they are happy with their fluency.

5. **Provide opportunities to practice reading aloud,** such as with partners or younger students.

Skill 3.8: Apply effective reading strategies to comprehend complex literature and informational texts (e.g., stories, drama, poetry, biographies, technical texts).

Research shows that teachers need to explicitly teach comprehension strategies by explaining the strategy, modeling how to use the strategy, providing opportunities for guided practice, and allowing the students time to practice using the strategy until they are proficient.

1. **Monitoring comprehension** involves stopping while reading, rereading a sentence or passage that doesn't make sense, and looking up vocabulary that is unclear in the context.

2. **Metacognitive thinking** involves thinking about one's thinking and identifying areas where the comprehension issue arises, asking questions about the text, slowing down and rereading, etc.

3. **Graphic and semantic organizers** are ways to brainstorm, make predictions, and organize information that can be used to confirm or adjust understanding.

4. **Understanding the text structure**—different genres and types of texts vary in their structure and teachers can explicitly model the features and structure to show how this can help comprehension.

5. **Summarizing**—being able to summarize information is one way to determine if the reader understands the text.

6. **Answering questions** is a great way to stay focused and monitor comprehension. There are four types of questions that will help:

   • Right there—these are questions where the answer is found right in the text.

   • Think and search—these are questions that require some thinking, but the answer is in the text.

   • Author and you—these are questions that require the reader to use their prior knowledge as well as the information in the text.

   • On your own—questions that are based on the reader's experience and may not have the answer in the text, but rather be related to it in some way.

Competency 4: Knowledge of Language Elements Used for Effective Oral and Written Communication

Skill 4.1: Distinguish among the developmental stages of writing (e.g., drawing, scribbling, letter-like formations, strings of letters).

Children typically proceed through identifiable stages of writing, although they may move at different rates and sometimes may revert to a previous stage or display a combination of stages.

Pre-Literate Stage

1. **Random scribbling** describes children typically between 15 months and 2½ years of age who are exploring art materials in a playful way, making circles and random marks that don't communicate a message. The more that children scribble, the more controlled their scribbling becomes, so the development is dependent upon the opportunities a child has to work with writing utensils.

2. **Controlled scribbling** typically occurs around 2 to 3 years of age and describes the state when children are becoming more proficient at holding the pencil and are able to make repeated marks such as a grouping of horizontal lines. They may not be making letters at this point, but they may make squiggles that resemble features in letters and may look like mock letters. During this stage children may practice with both hands to determine dominance (deciding whether they are left- or right-handed) and learn to hold a pencil. The children may name their scribbles, showing that they are beginning to understand that what they are drawing has meaning.

3. The **symbolic stage** happens when children about 3 and 5 years of age begin to draw objects, animals, and people. Children move from the drawing stage where their objects "hang" in space and people look like "tadpoles" (big heads with few features or exaggerated features like big eyes, rounded bodies, sometimes sticks for legs and arms) to more sophisticated drawing.

Emergent Stage

During this stage, children between 3 and 5½ years of age, typically:

1. **Begin to write strings of random letters** that may go left to right; may begin to use letter sequences (i.e., can write their name); begin to use capital letters; and may write the same letters in many ways. They may group letters with spaces in between to resemble words.

2. **Label pictures**—matching beginning sounds with the letter to label a picture.

3. **Practice environmental print**—copy letters/words from environmental/classroom print; commonly write letters or words backwards.

Transitional Stage

As children enter this stage (from 4 to 6 years of age), they begin to do the following as their writing develops in a way that adults can begin to decipher it.

1. Use the first letter of a word to represent the whole word.

2. Move to hearing and writing the beginning and ending sounds of words, spelling phonetically, and incorporating medial vowels.

3. Begin to use some known words, may use more conventionally spelled words, attempt to put spaces between words, use capital letters for proper nouns, and start sentences.

Fluency Stage

This stage may begin around 5 or 6 years of age, but often is not fully developed until later. At this stage children begin to use:

1. Word and phrase writing. At this stage, students combine letters into words and words into sentences that convey meaning, and may be linked with their accompanying drawing.

2. Sentence writing. In this stage, students are able to construct one or more sentences using the words they know combined with their knowledge of encoding. The writing is readable and often focused; there may be punctuation and a logical structure of sequence.

3. In the last step of the fluency stage, students are able to write using appropriate conventions, voice, ideas, word choice, fluency, and organization.

Skill 4.2: Identify developmentally appropriate writing strategies for developing concepts of print and conventions, including spelling and punctuation.

Reading aloud and explicitly discussing concepts of print—Before reading a book, a teacher can talk about the cover, endpapers, spine, table of contents, dedication, or other concepts. The children may notice that the teacher is turning the pages from left to right, but the teacher can draw attention to that, while at the same time explaining how illustrations work with print.

Using big books to point out conventions of print and punctuation—The teacher can use *big books* to demonstrate conventions of print such as the use of capital letters for names or for the first word in a sentence, or calling on children to come up and identify punctuation. In *framing*, the teacher asks a child to put his hands around the word. The big books can later be put in a center, where the teacher can write sentences on sentence strips, cut them up, and let the students put the strips together to reform the sentences.

Reading the room—Teachers provide children with pointers so they can "read" charts, signs, posters, the word wall, or labels in the room. This allows them to practice reading left to right and top to bottom.

Wordless books are excellent for students to use to write.

Spelling can be taught through *rimes*, also called phonograms or word families. The **rime** is typically the part of a syllable containing the first vowel and all that follows it. Activities such as word sorts and matching games allow students an opportunity to learn spelling patterns. For example, students might sort words into those that end in *-ack* and those that end in *-og*. After sorting, the student can practice reading the words aloud (*"If I can read sack, I can read mack. If I can read mack, I can read tack."*).

Spelling can also be taught through the *Look, Say, Cover, Write, Check* strategy. The steps are to have the student write the word; look at the word noticing the letters and shape of the word, close her eyes and visualize the word; say the word as she looks at it; cover the word; write the word. Then check the word and correct it if it is incorrect. Teachers can also have students make the word with magnetic letters or letter stamps.

Magnetic letters can be used for a variety of phonics instruction, including making words, substituting, deleting, and adding letters to make new words, and for spelling. While the letter shapes are best, teachers can also use letter cards or write the letters on index cards, wooden tiles or transparent glass gems used for floral decorating, or small stones that can be purchased at home improvement stores.

Skill 4.3: Determine the stages of the writing process (e.g., prewriting, editing, publishing).

There are four generally accepted stages of the writing process. While we have begun moving toward keyboarding and writing using a computer, teachers of young children still guide their students through the stages manually, so that the children have a basic understanding of the writing process. Even though there are four stages, it is important to understand that writing is **recursive** in nature, meaning that at any point, the writer may move back and forth between stages.

1. **Prewriting and brainstorming**—During this stage, students generate ideas and begin jotting down thoughts, facts, or information to help their writing. First drafts are started at this stage. Teachers often have students keep writers' notebooks to help keep track of their ideas and learning.

2. **Revision**—During this stage, students work on their writing and focus on making it better. Teachers may conference with students during this stage and offer suggestions; older students may pair up with peers to read and discuss the pieces.

3. **Editing**—In this stage of the writing process, students review their product and check it for organization, conventions, content, and other components. Teachers may provide checklists or rubrics to help students learn to edit their work.

4. **Publishing**—This final stage of writing involves the student creating a final product. Not every piece of writing gets to this stage. Publishing can be done in a variety of modes, but the purpose is to have it in a form to share with others.

Skill 4.4: Identify and distinguish characteristics of various modes of writing (e.g., narrative, expository, persuasive, descriptive).

1. **Narrative writing** tells a story and includes characters, a setting, and a plot, typically with a beginning, middle, and end.

2. **Expository writing** explains, describes, or informs. Expository writing is organized logically and includes a topic sentence, a thesis statement, subtopics that relate to the main topic, transitions, evidence, examples, and a conclusion that restates the topic and summarizes the thesis. The types of expository writing include cause and effect, problem and solution, how-to or process, compare and contrast, and define or explain. Letter writing and recipes are often included in this genre.

3. **Persuasive writing**, also called opinion writing, helps convince a reader that the author's view is correct. Characteristics of persuasive writing include an opening statement or paragraph that clearly states the writer's position, a body that includes at least three sources of evidence to support the argument, and a conclusion that restates the author's opinion or viewpoint.

4. **Descriptive writing** includes a focus on the five senses and allows the author to create a picture of a person, place, event, or thing in the reader's mind. Characteristics include organization, precise (rather than general) words, figurative language, and sensory details.

Skill 4.5: Select and analyze the appropriate mode of writing for a variety of occasions, purposes, and audiences, and use textual support, reader response, and research as needed.

There are four main modes of writing:

1. **Expository writing** is used to explain something. This type of writing can be used for writing directions, recipes, or lists. Report writing requires the writer to research an idea or position. Letter writing is a form that can be taught under the expository mode.

2. **Descriptive writing** is expository writing, but incorporates imagery and uses the five senses.

3. **Persuasive writing** can be used to ask or convince the reader of a position or stance. Students might write the principal to ask for different snack foods in the vending machines or might write an op-ed piece or letter to the editor of the local newspaper to support local environmental protection.

4. **Narrative writing** typically has a beginning, middle, and end. Writing memoirs or stories use this mode.

Skill 4.6: Identify developmentally appropriate strategies for enhancing writers' craft (e.g., supporting details, dialogue, and transition words).

1. High-quality children's literature or "mentor text" offers an excellent opportunity to teach children concepts of writers' craft.

2. Author and illustrator studies provide students with real-world examples and models.

3. Mini-lessons as part of a larger writers' workshop, allow teachers to target specific areas of writers' craft or draw students' attention to aspects of the craft.

4. Opportunities to write for a variety of purposes, including writers' notebook and journals for content areas, are authentic ways for students to have an opportunity to write their ideas and understandings without fear of too much focus on their spelling or grammar. Pen pals are another authentic writing opportunity.

5. Integrated units of study offer a variety of ways to focus on writers' craft for fiction and informational writing, in order to develop writer's craft. For example, students may learn to write recipes as part of a math or science lesson.

6. Center activities that include writing such as children making a map of their block or town or creating stage directions for the dramatic play are additional examples of providing developmental opportunities for children to write.

7. Teachers may adapt a model such as the **6+1 Trait Writing Model of Instruction & Assessment®** developed by Education Northwest to foster students' learning. (*https://education-northwest.org/traits*). The traits include

   - **Voice**—the tone of the piece

   - **Ideas**—main message and supporting features

   - **Conventions**—spelling, punctuation, capitalization, grammar/usage, and paragraphing

   - **Organization**—the internal structure of the piece

   - **Word Choice**—the vocabulary used to convey the meaning

   - **Presentation**—how the writing appears on the page

   - **Sentence Fluency**—the rhythm and flow of the piece

Skill 4.7: Determine effective strategies for comprehension and collaboration (e.g., following multiple-step directions, following group rules, participating in group discussions).

   Listening and speaking are intricately linked. **Active listening** requires the listener to focus and be interested in what the speaker is communicating. It involves looking at the speaker, and restating or paraphrasing through conversation or questioning in order to understand the message. **SLANT** or **Sit up, Lean forward, Ask and answer questions, Nod your head, and Track the speaker** is a simple acronym for students to quickly monitor their body position to ensure they are sitting in a way that can help maximize their listening and comprehension. Teachers can help students develop good techniques for monitoring their listening through developing speaking strategies that include

   - Questioning—how to ask good questions; be specific and clear

- Paraphrasing—how to restate an idea without repeating verbatim

- Extemporizing—how to respond to an idea by expressing one's own thoughts in a way that clearly connects with the conversation

Conversation—Teachers can help students learn how to have conversations through modeling and guided practice that includes looking at the speaker's face, responding appropriately in nonverbal and verbal ways, and opportunities for talk on various subjects and in various situations. Other strategies include games such as *Telephone, Simon Says, I Spy, Red Rover, London Bridges,* and other traditional games. Teachers may teach their students how to tell *jokes,* which are a good way to practice skills such as timing and pace.

Oral story-telling is a great way to develop students' listening skills as well as their speaking skills (such as oral expression). Teachers may start with traditional stories that have a beginning, middle, and end, a simple plot and storyline. As part of that, the teacher can foster students' development of articulation, inflection, expression, intonation and other oral expression skills, as well as looking at the audience, facial expressions, and gestures.

LAPS or **Listen, Ask, Picture, and Summarize** is one strategy that integrates listening, speaking, and writing. Students are given the topic prior to the speaker presenting and generate questions about the topic. They then listen to the speaker. As they hear the answers to their questions, they sketch their answers. Then they have time to ask the questions that they haven't heard answered. They then summarize what they heard, writing a paragraph based on their sketches and notes.

Think Pair Share is a strategy that involves students listening to the teacher read about or present a topic. The teacher then pauses and presents a question or idea. The teacher then asks the students to think about their response, then partner with another student, and share their responses with each other.

RAP or **Read, Ask, Put** is a strategy that includes students first reading a passage silently. Next, they ask themselves what the passage means. They then write the main idea and details in their own words.

Literature Circles

Literature circles are groups of individuals who meet to discuss ideas related to a common text, usually with at least several chapters. This shared reading allows students to support each other's comprehension (Daniels, 2002; Daniels & Steineke, 2004). Typically done around third grade, the teacher may opt to have students have roles or jobs in the literature circle. Typical roles include the:

Discussion Director—facilitates the discussion and ensures that each student is able to participate and that the group stays on target.

Connector—makes links from passages in the book to the students, other texts or media, content areas, or the outside world.

Literary Luminary—chooses interesting or provoking passages, lines, or words from the book to highlight or share with the group.

Vocabulary Enricher—chooses vocabulary or figurative language from the text, defines and shares with the group.

Illustrator—sketches a scene from the text to share with the group.

Summarizer or Checker—helps keep the group on task and summarizes the events of the circle.

Inquiry Circles

Inquiry circles are groups of individuals who read and discuss an informational text to enhance and extend their comprehension of the topic (Harvey & Daniels, 2009). Each group member contributes by preparing strategies ahead of time as a guide for the discussion. The teacher provides as much managed choice as possible—allowing students to choose the text and their contribution to the circle. The students support each other's critical thinking and understanding of the text through reading and writing activities (McCall, 2010).

Readers' Theater involves students reading aloud from a script but props, costumes, sets, or memorization are not involved. The strategy allows students to collaborate on a shared text and develops fluency, expression, and fosters comprehension.

Skill 4.8: Identify key elements in students' presentations of ideas (e.g., visual and digital components, organization of ideas, clarity of thought).

There are several key elements that teachers can teach explicitly, model, provide opportunities for guided practice, and opportunities for practice until mastery.

- Ability to choose specific words and word order for intended effect and meaning

- Ability to present information, findings, and supporting evidence, in a way that is clear to the reader or listener

- Ability to convey a clear, organized, and developed substantial message in a style appropriate to purpose and audience

- Ability to adapt speech to a variety of contexts and tasks, demonstrating a command of formal English when indicated or appropriate

- Ability to use digital media in effective and appropriate ways

Skill 4.9: Analyze the increasing complexity of conventions of English (e.g., common prepositions, personal and possessive pronouns, compound and complex sentences).

Teachers can help students understand the more complex conventions of English by explicitly teaching:

1. **Prepositions**—words or groups of words that relate to and usually precede a noun or pronoun and express a relation to another word or element in the clause (i.e., She went *under the bridge*.)

2. **Personal possessive pronouns**—words that refer to something owned by someone—*mine, yours, ours, hers, his.*

3. **Compound sentences**—have more than one subject or predicate. *She left early; she wanted to beat the traffic.*

4. **Complex sentences**—sentences that contain a subordinate clause. *She left early to beat the traffic.*

Skill 4.10: Compare characteristics and uses of formal and informal language (e.g., oral, written).

1. **Oral language** or speech is the system by which we express ideas, information, and feelings. Informal oral language includes conversational language such as the way children might speak with each other or family members. Formal language describes the way we might speak with a person in authority. Teachers can help students improve their oral language by allowing opportunities to talk and listen; modeling syntax and explaining figurative language; explaining how tones of voice and facial expressions can impact a verbal message's meaning; and explaining common practices and customs (i.e., using a surname such as *Mr.* or *Ms.* with a teacher). Speech is typically less formal and more temporary—related to a moment—rather than written language.

2. **Written language** is a way of communicating through visual or tactile forms and is typically more permanent than oral language. Written language often contains more sophisticated sentence structures and more formal language. Authentic writing tasks such as writing friendly letters and business letters allow students to practice informal and formal written language.

Competency 5: Knowledge of Assessments to Inform Literacy Instruction

Skill 5.1: Identify appropriate oral and written methods for assessing individual student progress in reading and writing (e.g., fluency probes, conferencing, rubrics, running records, portfolios).

1. **Conferencing** takes place between the student and the teacher and is typically done one-on-one during writers' workshop or writing time. The teacher may conference with the student at any point during the writing process. It allows the teacher to informally assess the student and provide feedback specific to the student's needs.

2. **Rubrics** are tools that define expectations for an assignment by explaining requirements and criteria for different levels of quality. Instructional rubrics can be used by the teacher to rate students, by students to rate themselves and each other. There are two general types of rubrics. The first are **holistic**, which assess the work globally with components that contribute to the whole. The second type are **analytical**, which break down the assignment into smaller components, which are assessed individually. Weighted rubrics fall under the analytical category and are used when the teacher wants to put more emphasis on a particular aspect of the assignment. With young children, holistic rubrics are typically used more often, as they have fewer parts and simple guidelines (Andrade, 2001). Fountas and Pinnell (2016) developed a rubric to measure six components of a child's oral reading fluency, including rate, phrasing, pausing, intonation, stress, integration, and overall impression.

3. **Fluency probes or checks** are brief, timed oral reading passages that measure students' fluency. They can be used to determine students' instructional reading level. The short passages can also be used for students to improve their fluency through **repeated readings**.

Oral Reading Rates for Readers without Visual Impairment

Grade	Oral Reading Rate End of Year Ranges (WPM)
1	75–116
2	90–148
3	100–166
4	120–184

4. **Running records** are a quick way to assess student reading levels. It is an individually conducted formative assessment that allows teachers to informally assess a student's reading behaviors, strategies, and word attack skills (Fountas and Pinnell, 2016).

5. **Writing portfolios** are collections of student work that show growth or progress across time. The portfolio contains pieces selected from a student's writing folder and can be a "working" portfolio focused on a particular assignment and growth across time, or a "showcase" portfolio to highlight the student's best work across genres.

Skill 5.2: Interpret and analyze data from informal and formal reading assessments using qualitative and quantitative measures (e.g., screening, progress monitoring, diagnostic) to guide differentiated instruction.

Data-driven or data-informed decision making means that teachers use all the information available as they plan instruction for their students that is targeted at the students' needs and reading and writing levels. Most teachers keep data notebooks that allow them to track individual learning and class progress. Summative assessments measure the learning at the end of the instruction or year, while formative assessments provide data to guide instructional decisions.

Formative assessments are ongoing, informal, and provide feedback to the teacher with information to guide instruction or to assess learning or progress. Most formative assessments are not graded. Informal assessments are also described as *criterion-referenced*, meaning mastery of objectives or criteria; or *performance-based/authentic*, meaning that the student can demonstrate understanding through a task or activity. Formative assessments should match standards and lesson outcomes.

Some examples of formative assessments are:

- **Informal reading inventories** are diagnostic tools administered one at a time and provides insights into readers' comprehension level, accuracy, and reading levels. The three reading levels are the frustration level (where the text is too hard for the student), the instructional level (texts that students can read with scaffolding from the teacher), and the independent level (texts that children can read on their own).

Reading Level	Characteristics and Types of Texts
Independent or Recreational	Student can read the text without assistance. The oral reading fluency is 99% or above in word accuracy. The silent reading has little finger-pointing and little to no subvocalization. Comprehension is 90% or higher.
Instructional	Student can read the text with some teacher assistance. The oral reading fluency is 85% for grades 1–2 and 95% accuracy for grades 3 and up. The comprehension is 75% or higher for oral and silent reading.
Frustration	Student cannot read without teacher assistance and the oral reading lacks fluency. Student may display nonverbal or verbal tension or frustration, or may give up. The comprehension is less than 50%.
Listening Comprehension/ Capacity	Listening comprehension is typically higher than a reader's reading comprehension. The capacity indicates the level at which a student's comprehension is 75% or higher.

- **Running records** are informal assessments to measure a student's speed and accuracy.

- **Rubrics, teacher-made tests, quizzes, exit cards, projects, and reports** are other ways of assessing learning informally.

Summative assessments are administered at the end of a unit or grade to assess whether instructional goals and learning outcomes were met. **Benchmark tests** are periodic tests which measure learning and may predict performance on end-of-year tests. Most summative assessments are **formal, standardized assessments** that measure overall achievement in a specific content area. Typically, these are commercial assessments that have been tested with controlled populations.

Tests may be norm-referenced, meaning that they were used with a variety of populations and in different geographical areas, so that the average scores represent the **norm**. The results are used to draw statistically valid conclusions about group and individual achievement and results are reported as *standard scores*, such as *percentile rankings*. For example, if a student scores at the 90 percentile, that means the student scored better than 89 percent of the population used for standardization. Ten percent of the population scored higher than the student. **Stanine scores** divide scores into nine ranges. The scores of 1–3 are below average; 4–6 are average; and 7–9 are above average. **High-stakes tests** are summative assessments whose purpose is accountability. Results from the tests are viewed at the local, state, or federal level to make decisions on whether teachers or schools are effective and if students have attained learning goals.

References

Andrade, H. G. 2001. The Effects of Instructional Rubrics on Learning to Write. Current Issues in Education, 4. Retrieved from *https://cie.asu.edu/ojs/index.php/cieatasu/article/view/1630*

Bryant, P., MacLean, M., & Bradley, L. 1990. "Rhyme, language, and children's reading." *Applied Psycholinguistics, 11,* 237–252.

Calkins, L. 1994. *The Art of Teaching Writing*. Portsmouth, NH: Heinemann.

Camilli, G., & Wolfe, P. 2004. Research on reading: A cautionary tale. *Educational Leadership, 61*(6). *http://www.ascd.org/publications/educational-leadership/mar04/vol61/num06/Research-on-Reading@-A-Cautionary-Tale.aspx.*

Clay, Marie M. 1995/2016. *Literacy Lessons Designed for Individuals* (2nd ed.). Portsmouth, NH: Heinemann.

Christakis, E. 2016. *The Importance of Being Little: What Preschoolers Really Need from Grown-ups*. New York, NY: Viking Press.

Coker, D. L., & Ritchey, K. D. 2015. *Teaching beginning readers and writers*. New York, NY: Guilford Press.

Coulmas, F. 1999. *The Blackwell Encyclopedia of Writing Systems*. Oxford, England: Blackwell Press.

Daniels, H. 2002. *Literature circles: Voice and choice in book clubs & reading groups*. Portland, ME: Stenhouse Publishers.

Daniels, H. & Steineke, N. 2004. *Mini-lessons for Literature Circles*. Portsmouth, NH: Heinemann.

Duke, N. K., with Varlas, L. 2019. Turning small reading groups into big wins. *ASCD Education Update, 61*(7). *http://www.ascd.org/publications/newsletters/education-update/jul19/vol61/num07/Turn-Small-Reading-Groups-into-Big-Wins.aspx.*

Fletcher, R. 2017. *The Writing Teacher's Companion: Embracing Choice, Voice, Purpose & Play.* Scholastic.

Foorman, B., Beyler, N., Borradaile, K., Coyne, M., Denton, C. A., Dimino, J., Furgeson, J., Hayes, L., Henke, J., Justice, L., Keating, B., Lewis, W., Sattar, S., Streke, A., Wagner, R., & Wissel, S. 2016. Foundational skills to support reading for understanding in kindergarten through 3rd grade (NCEE 2016–4008). Washington, DC: National Center for Education Evaluation and Regional Assistance (NCEE), Institute of Education Sciences, U.S. Department of Education. Retrieved from the NCEE website: *http://whatworks.ed.gov.*

Fountas, I., & Pinnell, S. 2016. *The Fountas & Pinnell Literacy Continuum, Expanded Edition: A Tool for Assessment, Planning, and Teaching, PreK–8.* Heinemann.

Frith, U. 1985 Beneath the surface of developmental dyslexia. In K. Patterson, J. Marshall, & M. Coltheart (Eds.), Surface Dyslexia, Neuropsychological and Cognitive Studies of Phonological Reading. (pp 301–330). London: Erlbaum. *https://sites.google.com/site/utafrith/publications-1/reading—spelling-and-dyslexia.*

Graves, D. 1994. *A Fresh Look at Writing.* Portsmouth, NH: Heinemann.

Goodson, B., Wolf, A., Bell, S., Turner, H., & Finney, P. B. 2010. "The effectiveness of a program to accelerate vocabulary development in kindergarten" (VOCAB) (NCEE 2010–4014). Washington, DC: National Center for Education Evaluation and Regional Assistance, Institute of Education Sciences, U.S. Department of Education. Graham, S., Bollinger,

Hall, K.W. 2008. "Reflecting on our practices: The importance of including culturally authentic literature." *Young Children, 63* (1), 80–86.

Harvey, S. & Daniels, H. 2009. *Comprehension and Collaboration.* Portsmouth, NH: Heinemann.

Hart, B. & Risley, T. R. 1995. *Meaningful Differences in the Everyday Experience of Young American Children.* Baltimore, MD: Paul H. Brookes Publishing Company.

Hoien, T. & Lundberg, I. 1988. "Stages of word recognition in early reading development." *Scandinavian Journal of Educational Research 32,* 163–182.

International Literacy Association [ILA]. 2020. Literacy glossary. *https://www.literacyworldwide.org/get-resources/literacy-glossary.*

James, K. H. & Engelhardt, L. 2012. "The effects of handwriting experience on functional brain development in pre-literate children." *Trends in Neuroscience and Education, 1* (1), 32–42.

Jirout, J. J. and Newcombe, N. S. 2015. "Building blocks for developing spatial skills: evidence from a large, representative U.S. sample." *Psychological Science, 26*(3):302–10.

Justice, L. 2004. "The connection between oral narrative and reading problems: What's the story?" *Tempo Weekly Reader.* *http://www.literacyhow.com/wp-content/uploads/2015/03/TheConnectionBetween-Oral-Narrative-and-Reading-Problems.pdf*

Longcamp, M., Zerbato-Poudou, M. T., & Velay, J. L. 2005. "The influence of writing practice on letter recognition in preschool children: A comparison between handwriting and typing." *Acta Psychologica 119* (1), 67–79.

McCabe, A., Tamis-LeMonda, C. S., Bornstein, M. H., Cates, C. B., Golinkoff, R., Hirsh-Pasek, K., et al. 2013. *"Multilingual Children: Beyond myths and towards best practices. Sharing child and youth development knowledge,"* 27(4), 3–21. Society for research in child development.

McCall, A. 2010. "Teaching powerful social studies ideas through literature circles." *Social Studies,* 101, 152–159.

Moats, L, & Tolman, C. 2009. *Language Essentials for Teachers of Reading and Spelling (LETRS): The Speech Sounds of English: Phonetics, Phonology, and Phoneme Awareness (Module 2).* Boston: Sopris West.

Rosenshine, B. V. 1986. Synthesis of research in explicit teaching. *Educational Leadership,* 60-69. *http://www.ascd.org/ASCD/pdf/journals/ed_lead/el_198604_rosenshine.pdf.*

Schickendanz, J. A., Collins, M. 2013. *So much more than the ABCs: The early phases of reading and writing.* Washington, DC. National Association for the Education of Young Children.

Schmoker, M. Focusing on the essentials. *Educational Leadership, 61*(6). *http://www.ascd.org/publications/educational-leadership/sept19/vol77/num01/Focusing-on-the-Essentials.aspx.*

Schutz, K. M., & Rainey, E. C. 2019. Making sense of modeling in elementary literacy instruction. *The Reading Teacher, 73*(4), 443-451. *https://ila.onlinelibrary.wiley.com/doi/10.1002/trtr.1863.*

Sousa, D. A. 2016. *How the Special Needs Brain Learns* (3rd ed). Thousand Oaks, CA: Corwin Press.

Tamis-LeMonda, C. S., Bornstein, M. H., & Baumwell, L. 2001. "Maternal responsiveness and children's achievement of language milestones." *Child Development, 72(3),* 748–767.

Ziegler, J. C., Stone, G. O. & Jacobs, A. M. 1997. *Behavior Research Methods, Instruments, & Computers.* 29: 600. *https://doi.org/10.3758/BF03210615*

Mathematics Subtest 3 (533)

Competency 1: Knowledge of Effective Mathematics Instruction

This chapter describes effective strategies for teaching mathematics to young children. It explains the mathematical concepts students learn from PK to third grade. At the end of this chapter, you will find a list of resources that support each competency and set of skills. These resources come in varied forms from websites to journals, and are collected at the end of the chapter so that you may stay focused on the material at hand as you review.

Skill 1.1: Identify and analyze developmentally appropriate strategies for presenting mathematical concepts progressing from concrete to semi-concrete to abstract.

Young children need many opportunities to experience mathematics in the preschool and primary years. Like other areas of the curriculum, mathematics is best taught through play. Children can solve problems using concrete physical models (manipulatives) and drawings long before they are ready to use paper and pencil. Initial experiences with all aspects of the mathematics curriculum should involve real objects that can be touched. Children can count, perform simple addition and subtraction, and group objects into sets. They can investigate the properties of shapes in the block center, for example. Drawings and pictures are semi-concrete representations of real objects. An **array** is a common drawing used in third grade to solve multiplication problems. An array is a group of objects, often circles or x's, that are arrayed in rows and columns. The rows can indicate the number of groups and the columns can show how many objects there are in each group. Commercially produced worksheets often contain pictures or drawings. Overall, it is best not to force children to move too quickly to semi-concrete representations. Instead, have physical models (manipulatives) available for children who want to use them.

This array has three rows and five columns.

Mathematical vocabulary, expressions, and symbols like "plus" and "equals" can sound foreign to young children. With preschoolers it is best to use language such as *four and five make nine* instead of *four plus five equals nine*. Teachers can begin to introduce mathematical words like "plus," "minus," and "equals" as children move through the early grades. As new concepts are introduced, children should have access to concrete representations before moving to abstract symbols.

Skill 1.2: Identify and apply related mathematical concepts, computation, problem-solving, and reasoning.

Mathematics is the science of pattern and order (Van de Walle, Karp & Bay-Williams, 2015). That means that mathematics contains many related concepts. The Standards for Mathematical Practice (SMPs) from the Florida Mathematics Standards (discussed below) underscore the importance of developing **conceptual understanding** and the relationships among mathematical ideas. Composing, or putting things together, and decomposing, or taking things apart, are two important concepts that apply throughout mathematics. Children in the primary grades begin to compose and decompose whole numbers, fractions, and geometric shapes to solve mathematics problems. They learn the various meanings of the four operations. They also use the knowledge that addition and subtraction are inverse operations, as are multiplication and division, to develop flexible problem-solving strategies. They learn to reason about numbers. For example, a second grader who can reason about the size of numbers can look at the following problems and see why the answer does not make sense.

$$\begin{array}{r} 48 \\ + 67 \\ \hline 1015 \end{array}$$ The answer could not be correct because you cannot add two two-digit numbers and get a four-digit number as your answer.

Procedural fluency means students know how to use mathematical rules and procedures to solve problems. They understand the meaning of mathematical symbols—an important goal of mathematics instruction. Children who have good procedural fluency are not limited to using standard algorithms to solve problems. Instead, they can use flexible strategies based on their understanding of mathematical concepts. It is not a choice between conceptual understanding and procedural fluency. Both are important in the PK/Primary classroom.

Skill 1.3: Identify and analyze opportunities and strategies to integrate mathematics with other subject areas.

Children's literature provides a source for realistic problem-solving activities in mathematics. A simple internet search will provide an early childhood teacher with many lists of appropriate books that span the topics taught in PK to third grade. For example, kindergarten teachers can begin a lesson on adding within 10 by reading aloud a book such as *Ten Black Dots* (Crews, 1986). Children can then use counting cubes to investigate all the ways they can make 10. *Billions of Bricks: A Counting Book About Building* (Cyrus, 2016) has catchy repetitive verse about grouping bricks by twos, fives, and tens. *Seeing Symmetry* (Leedy, 2013) shows how to create symmetrical images by flips, slides, and turns.

Mathematics problem-solving journals or notebooks are an effective way to integrate writing and mathematics. The children have notebooks in which to draw and/or write their solution strategies to mathematics problems. They justify their reasoning, which connects writing to several of the Standards for Mathematical Practice (SMPs). Composition books that have a place to both draw and write are especially good. This activity can help children develop writing skills in tandem with mathematical understanding.

Mathematics and science are natural partners. Measurement and data analysis are the two most common areas in which PK–3rd grade teachers can connect the two subjects. Children can use standard or nonstandard measurement units to measure the height of a plant they are growing for science. They can use a thermometer to measure the temperature outside the classroom, then make a class bar graph of the number of sunny, cloudy, windy, snowy, or rainy days during the month. They can ask and answer questions to compare the number of days with each type of weather.

Geometry, measurement, and data analysis are good ways to connect mathematics with social studies, too. As children are learning about communities of long ago, they can tessellate simple polygons to make paper quilt squares. They can sequence events in chronological order. Children can use play money to buy and sell goods in the dramatic play center.

There are many ways to integrate mathematics with the creative arts and movement. Children can investigate repeating patterns using musical instruments. They can use cut-out geometric shapes to make collages. Children can count how many times they can jump in a given amount of time, or measure how far they can kick a ball.

Skill 1.4: Identify mathematical concepts appropriate for the PK–3 curriculum.

In PK, children begin to recognize numerals 0–10 and learn the corresponding number words. They practice rote counting, or saying the number words in order. Children practice rational counting with small sets and develop an understanding of one-to-one correspondence and cardinality. (The last number said tells how many objects have been counted.) They begin to use ordinal numbers, i.e., first, second, third. They practice using objects to solve simple addition and subtraction problems. Children in the PK years learn to recognize simple AB patterns and extend and create those patterns themselves. They sort objects based on measurable attributes and can recognize, name, and construct common two-dimensional shapes. In the K–3rd grades, mathematics instruction builds upon what children learn in the PK years. The table below lists mathematical concepts addressed in the Mathematics Florida Standards (MAFS) for grades K–3rd.

Mathematical Concepts in K–3 in the Mathematics Florida Standards (MAFS)

Curricular Area	K–3rd Grade Competencies
Counting and Cardinality	Understand one-to-one correspondence and that the last number spoken tells how many objects are counted (cardinality); know the count sequence; count by ones and tens; count on; read and write numerals
Operations and Algebraic Thinking	Recognize patterns and nonpatterns, extend and create patterns; use manipulatives and/or numerals to solve problems, progressing from one-step to two-step problems; understand various meanings of the four operations; use properties of operations to solve problems; determine the unknown in an equation
Number and Operations in Base Ten	Compose and decompose numbers into ones, tens, and ultimately hundreds; use place value understanding to add, subtract, and multiply; skip count; read and write numerals to 1,000; use place value understanding to round numbers; fluently add and subtract within 1,000 and multiply within 100
Number and Operations—Fractions	Develop an understanding of the meaning of unit fractions; represent fractions on number lines
Measurement and Data	Compare objects with measurable attributes; use nonstandard and standard U.S. customary and metric units to measure length, volume, and mass; choose appropriate tools to measure particular objects; estimate lengths in U.S. customary and metric units; know the value of coins and paper money and add money; tell time using an analog and digital clock and solve problems involving time; calculate area and perimeter and solve problems involving measurement; construct picture graphs, bar graphs, and line plots; use graphs to compare data
Geometry	Identify and describe two-dimensional and three-dimensional shapes; compose and decompose shapes; partition circles and rectangles into halves, fourths, and thirds; identify defining and non-defining attributes of shapes and draw shapes with given attributes; recognize that some shapes are examples of other shapes, i.e., rectangles are parallelograms

Skill 1.5: Select and apply the appropriate use of available tools, including technology (e.g., interactive white boards, computers) and manipulatives in teaching mathematics.

Early childhood teachers have an array of available tools for teaching mathematics. The classroom should be full of a variety of physical models (manipulatives) students can choose from to solve problems. The table below lists some, though not all, of the manipulatives often used in PK–3rd grade mathematics classrooms.

Mathematics Topic	Possible Manipulatives
Counting and Cardinality	Buttons, beads, beans, counting bears or dinosaurs, counters, tiles, Unifix cubes, plastic or foam cubes, dot dice, number cubes
Place Value	Beans, Popsicle sticks or coffee stirrers, base-10 blocks, money, 10-frame
Four Operations	Buttons, beads, beans, counting bears or dinosaurs, counters, tiles, Unifix cubes, plastic or foam cubes, dot dice, number cubes, math balance, dominoes, 10-frame
Measurement	Play money, learning clock, capacity containers, rulers and tape measures, attribute materials, balance scale, trundle wheel, cash register, thermometer, magnetic calendar
Fractions	Fraction circles and tiles, Cuisenaire rods, geoboards, tangrams, pattern blocks
Geometry	2-D and 3-D shapes, geoboards, tangrams, building blocks, pattern blocks

Young children regularly interact with technology outside of school. Virtual manipulatives and online geometry tools can supplement children's use of physical manipulatives. Students can use laptops or iPads to interact with virtual mathematics content or the images can be displayed on an interactive whiteboard. Whiteboards can be tools to help students use oral language to express their mathematical thinking, perhaps as students are using polygons to compose new shapes. Children can show the shapes they have created on the interactive whiteboard and describe the shapes they used to compose their new shape. Calculators should not be a substitute for learning basic number facts, but they can aid students in learning and practicing those facts.

Skill 1.6: Identify the use of mathematical practices to promote critical thinking (e.g., construct viable arguments, make use of structure, express regularity in repeated reasoning).

Learning mathematics is more than simply knowing facts or being able to follow procedures. Students need to engage in the practices of mathematics. The Standards for Mathematical Practices in the Mathematics Florida Standards (MAFS) and the Common Core State Standards for Mathematics (CCSSM) contain eight standards for mathematical practice (SMPs). These standards apply to all topic areas in mathematics and are important at all grade levels. They are:

- **Make sense of problems and persevere in solving them:** Mathematics involves solving problems and discussing solution strategies. Young children learn to explain the meaning of a problem to themselves rather than depending upon the teacher to explain it to them. Concrete models (manipulatives) and drawings help children conceptualize a problem and plan how to solve it. Students can monitor their problem solving by asking themselves if their answer makes sense. If a current strategy is not working, they can try another one. They listen to the strategies of others and are willing to try new approaches to solve a mathematical problem.

- **Reason abstractly and quantitatively:** In the early childhood years, students comprehend that a number represents a definite quantity. They associate the written symbol with the quantity and can represent a problem. They use properties of operations and manipulatives to solve problems rather than simply following a memorized procedure.

- **Construct viable arguments and critique the reasoning of others:** Students in PK/Primary classrooms often construct mathematical arguments using concrete models (manipulatives), drawings, pictures, or actions. They explain their own thinking and problem-solving strategies and listen attentively to classmates' explanations. They respond to their classmates' ideas and decide if the explanations make sense.

- **Model with mathematics:** Young children learn to represent real-life problems in multiple ways [e.g., concrete models (manipulatives), drawings, words, numbers, acting it out, charts, lists, tables, or equations]. They evaluate their results and ask themselves if their answer makes sense in light of the problem's context. They then can revise their model if needed.

- **Use appropriate tools strategically:** There are many tools grades PK–3rd students use to solve problems (e.g., paper and pencil, ruler, concrete model, protractor, calculator, geometry software). Children become familiar with the tools appropriate to their grade level and make decisions about when to use each of them. They recognize the strengths and limitations of the tools they use. For example, kindergartners can use a calculator as a "two more than" machine. They enter a number between 0 and 10 into the calculator and predict what number is "two more than" the number they entered. They then press + 2 and = to check their answer. Calculators are sometimes *not* the most efficient way to solve problems, however. Children should learn flexible computational strategies that build upon their understanding of place value and properties of operations.

- **Attend to precision:** Students use clear and precise language to describe their mathematical thinking. They use age-appropriate mathematical vocabulary. When measuring, they include units.

- **Look for and make use of structure:** Let's look at that concept calling mathematics the science of patterns (Van de Walle et al., 2015). There are patterns in how we write numerals in the base-ten system. Properties of operations express patterns. Children may observe that $3 + 7$ and $7 + 3$ both equal 10. The order of the addends doesn't affect the answer (commutative property). They can use this property to make problems easier to solve. It is much easier to add on three more to seven than it is to add on seven more to three. There are patterns in both columns and rows in the 100s chart. Composing (putting together) and decomposing (taking apart) numbers can help students take advantage of our number system's structure. Learning about multiplication in third grade introduces students to new number patterns.

- **Look for an express regularity in repeated reasoning:** Proficient mathematics students notice when calculations are repeated. A kindergartner may notice that each successive number in the counting sequence is one more or $+ 1$. Older children may realize that counting by tens means repeatedly adding one more group of ten.

Skill 1.7: Select and analyze uses of a variety of assessments to plan instruction.

Teachers use **assessment data** to monitor student progress, make instructional decisions, and evaluate student achievement and program effectiveness. Teachers should assess both conceptual understanding and procedural fluency. If students understand mathematical procedures, they will be able to make decisions about which procedure is appropriate for a particular problem. Teachers can also assess facility with the eight Standards for Mathematical Practice (SMPs). These include how students see themselves as mathematical learners.

Diagnostic assessments are given prior to instruction. They are used to determine students' prior knowledge about a topic so a teacher can effectively plan instruction. **Formative assessments** are given throughout the learning process. Teachers use them to identify students' progress toward meeting learning outcomes and to identify gaps in a student's knowledge. They are used to plan and modify instruction to address gaps in students' understanding. **Summative assessments** are given after instruction is completed. They are used to measure students' mastery of learning outcomes.

Listed below are a number of ways early childhood teachers can assess their students.

- **Observations and checklists:** These are especially good for the SMPs. When making observations, it is good to have a rubric that indicates which students are meeting the target and which are not there yet. Checklists limit the amount of writing the teacher has to do while making the observations. Checklists and observation forms should include a small place for comments.

- **Mathematics journals and writing prompts:** Children need to learn to explain their solution strategies and justify their mathematical reasoning. Mathematics journals and writing prompts are ways for them to practice doing so. These also reinforce literacy skills. Mathematics journals for young children usually include pictures and invented spelling. Some early childhood teachers create a class journal to which students contribute.

- **Interviews:** A powerful way to assess children's mathematical thinking is through diagnostic interviews. They are time-consuming but provide teachers with rich data about students' mathematical thinking. When interviewing a child, bring a variety of materials: paper, pencils, crayons, and manipulatives that the child can choose. Create a scoring rubric ahead of time. Ask the student to solve a problem. As each child works, ask them to explain their thinking to you. Use probing, follow-up questions to better understand their thinking.

- **Performance tasks:** Performance tasks are ones that enable students to engage in problem-solving activities. They are contextual problems that require children to use mathematics to find a solution to a real-world problem.

- **Portfolios:** These are a collection of a student's work over time that shows progress toward meeting learning outcomes. A portfolio includes children's self-reflection of their learning.

- **Tests/quizzes:** Tests and quizzes may always be a part of educational assessment; however, these should not be the main ways young children are assessed.

Skill 1.8: Select and analyze structured experiences for small and large groups of students according to mathematical concepts.

When planning instruction in mathematics, early childhood teachers must decide how to group students for learning activities. **Flexible grouping** means that teachers vary the composition and size of the groups in which children are working based upon the task. Some tasks are best done in pairs. Sometimes trios or even groups of four are appropriate because there are enough tasks for each student to have a job to do. At times, teachers may use whole class instruction. Overall, working in small groups of various sizes fosters collaboration, an important life skill that children can begin to develop during the PK/Primary years.

- **Small-Group Instruction:** Children can solve many mathematics problems in small groups, ranging from 2 to no more than 4 children. Students can be grouped **heterogeneously**, with students of mixed ability, or **homogeneously**, with students of similar ability.

- **Whole-Class Instruction:** This is most appropriate when a teacher is modeling a mathematical procedure. Teachers need to keep in mind the attention span of young children and keep whole-class instruction brief.

- **Learning Centers:** Learning center time is a hallmark of the PK classroom. Students might work individually or in groups no larger than four to explore mathematical ideas through play. The block center is a good example. Children can investigate shapes or practice buying and selling in centers. Primary grade teachers often have center time built into their mathematics block. Many teachers differentiate centers by ability levels, but they can also be differentiated by topic. During center time, the teacher typically works with one of the groups while the others practice the concept in pairs or small groups.

- **Tiered Lessons:** In tiered lessons, all students are expected to achieve the same learning outcome, but the task is adapted to make it accessible for the range of learners in the classroom. Lessons can be tiered by the amount of assistance provided. One group might be provided with examples while another is not. Teachers can increase or decrease the open-endedness of the task. The complexity of the task can also be tiered. For example, students may be working on adding with regrouping. One group could solve the problem 7 + 9. Another could work on 23 + 48, while a third group might solve 56 + 77.

- **Jigsaw:** Children begin in one group, usually their table group. Each then becomes part of another group where they become the "expert" about some topic, perhaps a type of triangle. They return to the original group to share what they learned.

Skill 1.9: Identify and analyze attitudes and dispositions underlying mathematical thinking.

Students' dispositions for mathematical thinking relate to their attitudes about themselves as mathematical learners and the learning process. Several of the Standards for Mathematical Practice (SMPs) focus on dispositions because they impact how learners respond to challenging tasks. What are important dispositions for young mathematics learners? Students in the early grades can begin to develop the attitudes that:

- **Mathematics makes sense.** Instruction should focus on sense-making, not on following arbitrary rules. The reason many adults view mathematics as a mystery is because they were not encouraged to make sense of mathematics problems. Instead they memorized many formulas and procedures without learning why those procedures made sense. For example, when students are solving word problems, they should be encouraged to understand and make sense of the problem, **not** search for key words to decide how to solve them.

- **Mathematics is useful in the real world.** Students can solve real-world problems in PK–3rd grade classrooms. Procedural fluency is important, of course, but students should primarily engage in authentic problem solving. In fact, authentic problem solving provides students with a reason to develop procedural fluency. Mathematical sense-making helps them develop problem-solving skills.

- **They can solve mathematics problems and improve my mathematical thinking if they keep working at it.** It is important for students to see themselves as competent mathematics learners. Young children are introduced to an array of problem-solving strategies, such as drawing a picture or using a physical model. They benefit from being given the freedom to investigate which model will be the best tool to help them solve a particular problem. The mathematics classroom should be a place where failure is not only permitted, but embraced and seen as a stepping-stone to greater understanding. Young children benefit from sentence starters they can use when they get stuck on a problem and want to ask for help.

Competency 2: Knowledge of Algebraic Thinking

Skill 2.1: Identify and extend simple number and nonnumeric repeating and growing patterns using words, variables, tables, and graphs.

Algebraic thinking is an important part of everyday mathematics because it involves finding patterns and generalizing from them. Patterns in the early childhood years can involve a range of attributes including numbers, letters, shapes, colors, or even sounds.

Repeating Patterns

One way young children engage in algebraic thinking is through investigating patterns. **Repeating patterns** are ones in which a series of elements is repeated over and over again, such as circle, square, triangle, circle, square, triangle. The shortest set of elements that repeats is known as the **core**. Repeating patterns are often named using letters or variables. The pattern just described is an ABC pattern. A pattern in which two elements repeat is an AB pattern. PK students are often introduced to repeating patterns using objects like counting dinosaurs. The teacher may put out a red dinosaur, blue dinosaur, red dinosaur, blue dinosaur, red dinosaur and then ask children what comes next. This is an AB pattern. Determining what comes next is an example of **extending a pattern**. As children move through the PK–3rd grades, they can practice extending a variety of repeating patterns. Teachers need not always stop at the end of the core each time when asking students to extend the pattern. In the example above, the teacher made an AB pattern but put out ABABA. Students would extend the pattern by adding B (the blue dinosaur).

An important idea when working with repeating patterns is that two patterns made with different objects may be the same pattern. Square—circle—square—circle is an AB pattern. So is the oral pattern clap—snap—clap—snap. Children need multiple experiences with visual, auditory, and tactile patterns to be able to generalize that all are the same type of pattern.

Core

Growing Patterns

Growing patterns, which are formally known as **sequences**, are a way to introduce young children to functions. Growing patterns can be arithmetic. These patterns increase or decrease by adding or subtracting the same fixed number. Geometric patterns increase or decrease by multiplying or dividing the same fixed number. Arithmetic patterns are more common in PK–3rd grade classrooms than geometric patterns, but some third graders may be ready to work with geometric patterns.

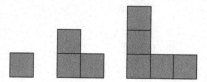

Skill 2.2: Determine and apply the concepts of equality and inequality in real-world situations (e.g., balancing and comparing quantities).

One of the most challenging concepts for children to develop is an understanding of the equal sign. It is common for children to say these equations are incorrect.

$$4 = 1 + 3 \qquad 7 + 2 = 5 + 4$$

Why are they confused? To many children, "=" means "Here comes the answer." (Carpenter, Franke & Levi, 2003.) That is because teachers often present problems exclusively as $8 - 3 = $ ____ or $6 \times 2 = $ ____ with the unknown after the equal sign. A robust understanding of the equal sign is built on an understanding of part-part-whole relationships. One way to help children understand the equal sign is to think of it as a balance. Children can use a pan balance (scale) to investigate equality. They can put different combinations of objects into each pan to make it balanced. They can also investigate inequality using the same balance by determining what to put in each side of the balance so it is not balanced. This can be done with objects like pattern blocks, counting bears, or weights for a pan balance. Teachers can purchase commercially made number balances that children can use to practice basic facts.

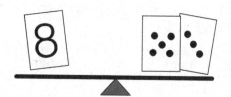

As children develop facility with determining equivalency with manipulatives, they can use paper and pencil to draw a balance, showing ways to make each side equivalent. Teachers should also introduce children to equations that are *not* always set up like the $8 - 3 = $ ___ above. Instead they should encounter problems such as:

$$\text{____} - 3 = 5 \qquad 8 - \text{___} = 5 \qquad 4 + 2 = \text{___} + 3$$

Skill 2.3: Identify and apply function rules using addition and subtraction (e.g., input-output machines, tables).

A mathematical **function** is a rule that specifies one and only one output for each input (Beckmann, 2014). Functions represent sequences. In the primary grades, functions are often introduced through the use of a function, or input-output machine. Teachers either use a real box or draw one on the interactive white board. In the first example below, students can be asked for the output if they put a 3 in the box and the machine adds 2. They can determine the outputs for different inputs using the same rule.

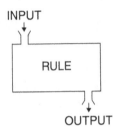

INPUT

RULE

OUTPUT

Children can also determine the rule the input-output machine is using if they know the input and the output, or they can determine the input if they know the rule and the output. In the first example below, students can see that if the input is 4, the output is 1, and if the input is 7 the output is 4. Therefore, the rule the machine is using is -3. In the second example, children can see that the rule is $+3$ and the output is 9. Therefore, the input must be 6.

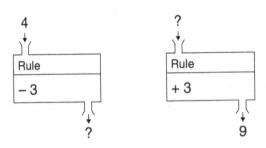

Primary grade children can also use a table to explore functions. Here is an example of a table showing a function in which the rule is -4.

Input	Output
12	8
9	5
13	?
?	2

Skill 2.4: Identify and analyze appropriate instructional strategies (e.g., draw a picture, make a table, act it out) to facilitate student understanding of problem solving.

Young children develop facility with the standards for mathematical practice (SMPs) by solving realistic mathematics problems. They can solve problems using pictures, tables, or by acting out the mathematical processes long before they can solve problems using abstract mathematical symbols. For example, children in the early primary grades can often solve the following problem using a drawing or by acting it out: *I have a large cookie that I want to share fairly with my friend. How much of the cookie do we each get?* Children will often draw a circle like the one below and then draw a line down the center to divide the cookie in half. They could also take a paper cookie or a real cookie and physically divide it in two equal pieces.

Tables are useful for solving problems, especially those related to functions. A child who wanted to determine how much flour is needed for 3 batches of cookies if each batch calls for 2 cups of flour could create a table like the one below.

Batches	Cups of Flour Needed
1	2
2	4
3	6

Competency 3: Knowledge of Number Concepts and Operations in Base Ten

Skill 3.1: Identify the cardinal number for a set, various ways to count efficiently, (e.g., counting by ones, skip counting, counting on, counting backwards, counting collections) and ordinal numbers.

The **cardinal number** for a set is the last counting number spoken when counting each object in the set. The cardinal number tells how many objects are in the set. It is common for young children to make errors when counting. They might continue counting after they have counted all the objects in a set. They might count one object twice, or they might skip an object when counting.

A child's first experience with counting is counting by ones. When counting by ones, each number said represents one more object than the previous number. This makes sense to children because each object is associated with one number word. When children skip count, they are counting by multiples of the number they start with. So when counting by twos, a child starts with 2 and then says 4, 6, 8, etc. Children in the PK–3 years practice skip counting by 2s, 5s, 10s, and eventually 100s. Skip counting lays a foundation for multiplication. Counting by 5s and 10s is especially useful for developing place value understanding. Counting by 10s helps students connect basic multiplication facts like $4 \times 3 = 12$ to the extended fact $4 \times 30 = 120$. Counting by 5s, 10s, and 25s helps children when counting coins.

Counting on is an important skill children practice in the early grades. When children count on, they start from one number and then continue counting from there, without needing to start over at one. When they count backwards, they start at a specific number and then count backwards from that number. Both are challenging, but children usually find counting backwards more difficult than counting on. Many kindergarten teachers encourage children to count on and count backwards when solving simple addition and subtraction problems.

Subitizing is the ability to recognize a common pattern or collection of objects, like dots on a die and immediately recognize the total number without needing to count each one. Subitizing helps children with counting on. Dot plates are a useful tool to help children learn to subitize. When they are constructed with two different color dots, they can also help children learn basic addition facts.

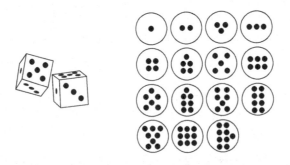

Ordinal numbers, like 1st, 2nd, 3rd, and 4th, are related to seriation. Ordering numbers in a series builds upon the ability to order objects serially based on a particular attribute (e.g., small to large or long to short). PK teachers can begin to introduce ordinal numbers when children are standing in line or when helping children sequence the temporal order of daily events—*First we have circle time. Second we have center time. Third we have snack.*

Skill 3.2: Identify pre-number concepts, 1-to-1 correspondence, conservation of numbers, constructing sets to match given criteria, and rote counting.

Pre-number concepts are important for later mathematics learning. Sorting and classifying objects by their attributes such as *big, small, short,* or *tall* lays a foundation for comparing quantities.

There are two ways to count: **rote counting** and **rational counting**. Children use rote counting when they say the number words in order but without matching the number word with the object being counted. Children can rote count to a greater number than they can rationally count. The MAFS expects kindergarteners to rote count by ones and tens to 100, but rationally count to 20. **Rational counting** is when children demonstrate both one-to-one correspondence and cardinality. When counting, one-to-one correspondence means that each object gets one count and each number word goes with one object. **Cardinality** means that the last number said when counting a set of objects tells how many are in the set.

Matching activities help children develop one-to-one correspondence. When passing out cups at snack time, each child gets one cup. Children can practice matching objects that are different from each other, such as children and cups. They can also match objects that are identical (e.g., each sock matches another sock). Young children find matching tasks easier when there are the same number of both objects, such as one cupcake for each child. They find the task more challenging when the sets are uneven (2 more cupcakes than children). The size of the sets used for matching activities should be determined by the age of the child. Longer sets are more difficult to match than shorter sets.

Skill 3.3: Use knowledge of place value to name, compare, and flexibly represent numbers in base ten (e.g., 22 = 2 tens and 2 ones, 1 ten and 12 ones, or 22 ones).

Children learn many things about place value in PK–3rd grade. There is procedural knowledge about how multi-digit numbers are written and spoken. They also learn how the number system is organized (base-ten). Children's first ideas about numbers are based on counting objects by ones. The idea of grouping numbers into tens and hundreds seems strange to many children. Being able to understand 10 as a collection of ten single objects as well as one group of 10 objects is a major achievement for children in the early grades.

Two-Digit Numbers

In English, the names for the teen numbers must be memorized. Unlike in some other languages, there is no connection between the name of the number and its value. Two-digit numbers greater than nine can be decomposed (broken apart) into tens and ones. The number 34 can be thought of as a collection of 34 countable objects. This represents counting by ones, and is a child's first understanding of numbers. Thirty-four can also be represented as three groups of ten or three tens and four ones. That is not the only way to decompose 34. It can also be thought of as one ten and 24 ones or two tens and 14 ones. Being able to decompose numbers in a variety of ways helps children understand the logic behind the standard algorithms for addition and subtraction. It also enables them to use flexible computational strategies. Three-digit numbers can be decomposed into hundreds, tens, and ones.

A variety of models can be used to help children develop place value understanding for multi-digit numbers. Ten frames are useful for introducing young children to two-digit numbers. They can use the ten frame to represent a number, such as 13, as a group of ten with 3 left over. Because the number words for the teen numbers in English do not offer clues to the values of the numbers, ten frames are a good model to make the relationship between tens and ones explicit.

There are three types of place value models: groupable proportional, pregrouped proportional, and nonproportional models. Popsicle sticks, coffee stirrers, and straws are examples of groupable proportional models. Ten individual popsicle sticks can be bundled together with a rubber band to make a group of ten. A bundle of ten can be unbundled to make ten ones. Ten bundles of ten can be grouped together to make 100. They are a proportional model because the group of ten is ten times larger than a single popsicle stick. Ten frames and base ten blocks are examples of pregrouped proportional models. Students cannot physically make groups of blocks by joining base-ten blocks together. If each unit cube is worth one, students must trade ten unit cubes for a long (worth 10), which is the same length as ten unit cubes. When they have ten longs, they must trade them for one flat, worth 100.

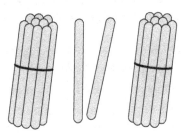 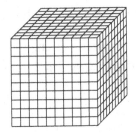

Money is an example of a nonproportional base ten model. It is nonproportional because a physical dime is not ten times larger than a penny. A physical dollar coin or a one-dollar bill is not ten times larger than a dime. Young children often believe the size of the coin indicates its value, but a dime is much smaller than a nickel! Some children do benefit from using money to model place value concepts, perhaps because of their everyday familiarity with coins.

Skill 3.4: Use place value (e.g., flexibility of numbers) and properties of operations (i.e., commutative, associative, distributive, identity) to solve problems involving addition and subtraction of multi-digit numbers and multiplication facts through 100.

Place value and computation

Knowledge of place value combined with facility with the properties of operations enables children to use flexible strategies to add, subtract, and multiply. When children are adding two whole numbers they do not have to use the traditional algorithm. There are a number of strategies they can use that both capitalize on their understanding of place value and help them improve their place value understanding. Here are several strategies for addition and subtraction. These are not the only strategies children can use, but these are common ones.

- Add tens, add ones, then add together.
  37 + 56 =
  30 + 50 = 80   Add the tens
  7 + 6 = 13   Add the ones
  80 + 13 = 93   Add them together

- Add the tens, then add the ones
  43 + 22 =
  43 + 20 = 63   Add on the tens
  63 + 2 = 65   Add on the ones

- Move some to make a ten:
  63 + 39 =
  62 + 1 + 39 = 62 + 40   Take one from the 63 and give it to the 39 to make a friendly number (a multiple of ten).

  62 + 40 = 102

- Use a friendly number (a multiple of ten) and compensate:
  63 + 39 =
  63 + 40 = 103   39 is close to 40. 40 is a friendly number that is easy to add.
  103 – 1 = 102   Now, compensate. You added one more than you were supposed to so you have to give it back.

- Subtract more tens, then give back.
  83 – 58 =
  83 – 60 = 23   58 is close to 60, and 60 is an easy number to subtract.
  23 + 2 = 25   You took away 2 more than you were supposed to, so you have to give them back.

- Solve an equivalent problem.
  42 – 38 =
  44 – 40 = 4   You can add two to each number. If you count on, you can see that the difference between 38 and 42 is the same as the difference between 40 and 44.

  42 – 38 = 4

FTCE PreK–3

Properties of Operations

Properties of operations are important. They help children flexibly perform the four basic mathematical operations (addition, subtraction, multiplication, division). All the properties can be expressed algebraically, but PK–3rd grade teachers don't share those algebraic expressions with students. It is, however, important that teachers know the names of the properties and how they work. While young children do not need to know the formal names of the properties, it *is* important that students can use the properties to flexibly solve mathematical problems.

The **commutative property** is also known as the "turnaround" property. The **commutative property of addition** says that if you add two numbers, you can change the order of the addends and the answer stays the same (e.g., $3 + 4 = 4 + 3$, $a + b = b + a$). The commutative property of addition helps students with **counting on**. If you have the problem $2 + 9$, it is much easier to turn it around to $9 + 2$. Now you can count on from 9 (10, 11). Students are more likely to make a mistake if they try to count on from 2 (3, 4, 5, 6, 7, 8, 9, 10, 11). There is also a **commutative property of multiplication**. If you multiply two numbers, you can change the order of the factors and the answer stays the same. This relates to **skip counting**. It is much easier to skip count by fives than sevens. If students forget the answer to 7×5, they can turn it around to 5×7 (e.g., $c \times d = d \times c$). Now they can count by fives to find the answer. The commutative properties of addition and multiplication are very useful for learning basic facts. Students do not need to memorize $8 + 1$ *and* $1 + 8$ as two separate basic facts. They can simply use the commutative (turnaround) property to switch the addends.

Subtraction and division are *not* commutative. $5 - 2$ is not the same as $2 - 5$. $16 \div 4$ is *not* the same as $4 \div 16$.

The **associative property of addition** states that if you add three or more numbers, it doesn't matter which two you add first. Your answer will be the same. Suppose you are adding $6 + 2 + 4$. You could first add $6 + 2$ and get 8. You could then add 4 to your answer and get 12. Instead, you could first add $6 + 4$ and get 10 (a friendly number). You can then add 2 to get 12. You may have seen this property written as $(a + b) + c = a + (b + c)$. This flexibility enables students to work with number combinations they know. There is also an **associative property of multiplication.** If you multiply three or more numbers, it doesn't matter which two factors you multiply first. Suppose you are solving the following problem:

Tyler has four boxes of granola bars. Each box contains two rows of granola bars with three bars in each row. How many granola bars does Tyler have?

One way to solve the problem is $(4 \times 2) \times 3$. Many students find it easier to first multiply $4 \times 3 = 12$ and then multiply by 2 to get 24. You may have seen the associative property of multiplication written as $(a \times b) \times c = a \times (b \times c)$. The associative property of multiplication enables children to use basic facts to learn extended facts. 3×3 and 3×30 are related to each other. The associative property is the reason why this is the case. Third graders would not be expected to write the expressions below. It is good for teachers to understand why the procedure works, however. When teaching basic and extended facts, it is important for teachers to *not* tell children that we just "add a 0 at the end." Doing so creates many problems when children are introduced to fraction and decimal multiplication in higher grades.

$$3 \times 30 = 3 \times (3 \times 10)$$
$$= (3 \times 3) \times 10$$
$$= 9 \times 10$$
$$= 90$$

Subtraction and division are *not* associative. The order of the numbers does matter.

The **distributive property of multiplication over addition**, which is usually called the distributive property, is especially useful for facilitating flexible computation strategies. The distributive property says that if you are multiplying a number (*a*) by two other numbers (*b* and *c*), you can either add the two numbers first (*b* + *c*) and then multiply by *a* or you can distribute the first number (*a*), multiply it by each addend (*b* and *c*) and then add the two products together. This is a very useful computational strategy because it enables you to split either one or both factors apart (decompose them) into two or more parts. You can then multiply each part separately and add all of them together. You may have seen the distributive property written like this: $a(b + c) = ab + ac$. Here is an example of how this property could be useful in a third grade classroom. Suppose you want to multiply 8 × 13.

$8 \times 13 = 8 \times (10 + 3)$	Break the 13 apart. (Decompose it into $10 + 3$.)
$(8 \times 10) + (8 \times 3)$	Distribute the 8 to both the 10 and the 3.
$80 + 24 = 104$	Now, add the two products together.

The **identity property of addition or subtraction** is also known as the zero property. This means that $6 + 0 = 6$ and $14 - 0 = 14$. While this may seem obvious to an adult, children need multiple problem-solving opportunities to investigate this property with sets of counters where they add and subtract 0 counters from the set. Avoid simply telling children a rule like, "If you add or subtract 0 from a number, it stays the same." Allow children to discover this rule as they solve problems in which they add or remove 0 objects from a set.

The **identity property of multiplication and division** is also known as the one property. This means that $12 \times 1 = 12$ and $36 \div 1 = 36$. Again, avoid telling children a rule. Instead, provide opportunities for children to solve equal groups problems with 1 group and *d* objects in each group, as well as *d* groups with 1 object in each group. (Use arrays—1 row of flowers with 5 flowers in the row or 5 rows of flowers with 1 flower in each row.)

The **zero property of multiplication and division** can be quite confusing for children to understand. Let's consider multiplication first. The zero property means that $9 \times 0 = 0$. We could interpret this as 9 baskets with 0 oranges in each basket. Even more challenging for children is a problem in which 0 is the first factor. Zero groups with 8 kittens in each group is an example of this type of problem. Now, let's think about division. The zero property says that $0 \div d = 0$. If you have 0 crayons that you want to divide equally into 3 boxes, each box will get 0 crayons. You can model three boxes with 0 crayons in each box. What about $d \div 0$? This problem does *not* have an answer. Again, teachers should avoid simply telling children the problem can't be solved. They will not understand why it can't. Instead pose problems like, "You have 4 cookies. You want to share them equally with 0 friends. How many cookies does each friend get?" The problem can't be solved because there are 0 friends. There is no way to model 4 cookies divided among 0 groups.

Here's another way to understand why $0 \div 5$ can be solved and $5 \div 0$ can't. Recall that multiplication and division are inverse operations.

$0 \div 5 = ?$ means the same as $5 \times ? = 0$. What number must you multiply by 5 to get 0? The answer is 0.

$5 \div 0 = ?$ means the same as $0 \times ? = 5$. What number must you multiply by 0 to get 5? There isn't a number that you can multiply by 0 to get 5 because any number multiplied by $0 = 0$. Therefore, the problem has no solution.

Skill 3.5: Differentiate between problem-solving strategies that use models, properties of operations, and the inverse relationship of operations.

Children can use many strategies to solve problems in mathematics. Ideally, we want children to be able to choose the strategy that is most appropriate for a particular problem rather than relying on a single strategy for every problem.

Using Models

Models, which include physical models (manipulatives) and drawings, can help children visualize a problem and use reasoning to solve it. A table earlier in this chapter listed common manipulatives used in PK/Primary classrooms and the mathematics topics for which they are most appropriate. Mathematics instruction in the early childhood years often begins with direct modeling to represent a problem. Children should have access to a variety of materials to use as models. They should be able to make decisions about which model is most appropriate for a particular problem and justify why that model is a good one. As a general rule, problem solving with models should precede the use of abstract mathematical symbols in the early childhood classroom.

Some early childhood teachers use a model called strip diagrams with their students. This is a strategy called Singapore Math because it is a problem solving approach used by teachers in Singapore (Beckmann, 2014). Children draw strips to represent different quantities in a problem. Here is an example.

Shante found 23 shells at the beach. Her friend, Yolanda, found 4 more than Shante. How many shells did the girls find all together?

A problem like this can be challenging because some children will simply add 23 + 4. The strip diagram helps them more clearly see how many seashells Yolanda found.

$$\boxed{} \quad 23 \qquad \text{Shante's shells}$$

$$\boxed{|\,} \quad 27\ (23 + 4) \qquad \text{Yolanda's shells}$$

$$23 + 27 = 50$$

Using Properties of Operations

Examples of how to use properties of operations to solve mathematical problems were described above. The table below lists those properties and examples of ways to use them to make problem solving easier.

Property	Explanation of Property	Example	Notes
Commutative Property of Addition (Turnaround Property)	When adding two numbers, it doesn't matter which addend comes first. The answer is the same.	2 + 9 = ? Turn around to 9 + 2 = 11	If you want to count on, it is easier to start from 9 and add 2 more than it is to start at 2 and add 9 more. Mistakes are more likely when counting on from 2 than from 9.
Associative Property of Addition	When adding three or more numbers, it doesn't matter which two addends are added first. The answer is the same.	8 + 9 + 2 = ? Rewrite as 8 + 2 + 9 = 19	Making 10 is a good strategy when adding. Instead of adding left to right, it is easier to first add 8 + 2 and then add the 9.
Identity Property of Addition and Subtraction (Zero Property)	If you add or subtract 0 from a number, it will not change the number.	11 + 0 = 11 8 − 0 = 8	Encourage children to add and subtract 0 objects from a set rather than telling them a rule to memorize.
Commutative Property of Multiplication (Turnaround Property)	If you are multiplying two numbers, it doesn't matter which factor comes first. The answer is the same.	7 × 5 = ? Turn around to 5 × 7 = 35	Because the order of the factors doesn't matter, children do not need to memorize 5 × 7 *and* 7 × 5. They can merely turn it around in their head.

(continued)

Property	Explanation of Property	Example	Notes
Associative Property of Multiplication.	If you are multiplying three or more numbers, it doesn't matter which two factors you multiply first. The answer is the same.	$4 \times 2 \times 3 = ?$ Rewrite as $4 \times 3 \times 2 =$ $12 \times 2 = 24$	Most children find multiplication facts with 2, 5, and 10 to be the easiest facts to learn. Multiplying 12×2 is often easier than multiplying 6×4.
Distributive Property of Multiplication over Addition	If you are multiplying a number by the sum of two other numbers, you get the same answer by first multiplying each addend by the initial number and then adding the products together.	$3 \times 24 = ?$ Rewrite as $(3 \times 20) + (3 \times 4) =$ $60 + 12 = 72$	It is difficult to multiply 3×24 mentally. If you break apart (decompose) 24 into $20 + 4$, it is easier to multiply each one by 3 and then add them together.
Identity Property of Multiplication and Division (One Property)	If you multiply or divide a number by one, it will not change the number.	$13 \times 1 = 13$ $7 \div 1 = 7$	Encourage children to create sets with 1 group or 1 object in each group rather than telling them a rule to memorize.
Zero Property of Multiplication and Division	If you multiply a number by 0, the answer is 0. If you divide 0 by a number the answer is 0. You cannot divide a number by 0.	$5 \times 0 = 0$ $0 \div 15 = 0$	Encourage children to create sets with 0 groups or 0 objects in each group. See explanation above for why we cannot divide a number by 0.

Inverse Relationships

Addition and subtraction are **inverse operations**. So are multiplication and division. This is especially helpful when students are acquiring basic facts. Because subtraction is the inverse of addition, any subtraction problem can be viewed as a "think addition" problem. This means that if students are trying to solve $16 - 9 = ?$, they can think of the problem as "What must I add to 9 to get 16?" For many students counting on is easier than counting backwards, making the problem easier to solve if it is viewed as "think addition." Similarly, division can be thought of as "think multiplication." If students want to solve $28 \div 4 = ?$, they can see the problem as, "What must I multiply by 4 to get 28?" In both cases, students can use addition or multiplication facts they have memorized to solve subtraction and division problems.

Skill 3.6: Use area, set, and linear fraction models (e.g., number lines) to represent fractions, including fractions greater than one.

Fractions are one of the most challenging mathematical concepts for learners and are also one of the most important. Instruction in PK–3rd grade classrooms focuses on helping children develop a conceptual understanding of the meaning of fractions rather than fraction computation. Children need many opportunities to work with a variety of fraction models. Avoid only posing problems about pies or pizzas. No matter which model students are using, it is important for teachers to emphasize the whole in each model. Avoid saying, "1 is the whole," because that is not always correct.

Area Models

Area models are ones in which the fractions represent parts of an area that can be divided into smaller pieces. Pie pieces, pattern blocks, rectangular area pieces, geoboards, grid or dot paper, and paper folding are all examples of area models for fractions. The fraction tells us what portion of the total area we have or are considering. For example, look at the rectangle below. The entire rectangle is the whole which has been divided into 4 equal parts. Three parts are shaded, which means that we have 3 out of 4 equal pieces. Therefore, the fraction of the rectangle that has been shaded is $\frac{3}{4}$.

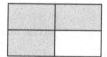

Linear Models

Teachers frequently use area models to represent fractions, but they are not the only fraction models. A second type of fraction model is called a **linear** or **length model**. These are ones in which the fractions represent length measurements. Number lines, Cuisenaire rods, rulers marked off in the U.S. customary system, and fraction strips (either commercially produced or handmade) are examples of linear models. Children compare lengths instead of areas when using these models. Linear models help students learn that a fraction is a number and *not* one number over another number. They also help students develop flexible thinking about fractions because any length can represent one whole. Linear models make it easier for children to compare and order fractions. It is common for children to say $\frac{1}{4} > \frac{1}{3}$ because $4 > 3$. Using a linear model in which children can place a $\frac{1}{4}$ strip next to a $\frac{1}{3}$ strip enables them to see that $\frac{1}{4} < \frac{1}{3}$.

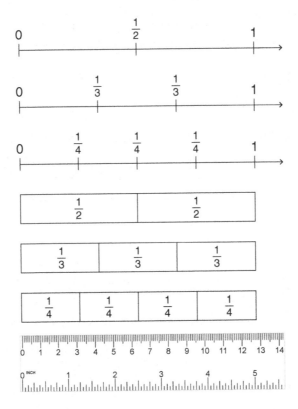

Set Models

In a **set model** for fractions, the whole is a group of objects rather than a single object. Four objects are $\frac{1}{3}$ of a set of 12 objects. The notion that a group of 12 objects could represent one whole is challenging for some learners. Two-color counters are often used as a set model. In the example just given, students could put out a set of 12 counters, 4 of which are turned to the red side and 8 of which are turned to the yellow side. The question is, "What fraction of the counters are red?" Some students will count the total red and total yellow counters and say, "$\frac{4}{8}$" or maybe "$\frac{1}{2}$." Teachers need to direct students to first determine the whole, which in this case is a set of 12 counters. Then, students can be directed to think about the number of equal sets in the whole—in this case 3. Because one of those sets is red, the fraction is $\frac{1}{3}$. In upper elementary and middle school, students will learn about fractions as ratios, but in the PK/Primary grade years, teachers should *focus solely on fractions as parts of a whole*.

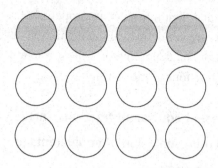

Skill 3.7: Relate the size of the fractional part to the number of equal-sized pieces in the whole.

There are several different meanings of fractions that students learn in K–12. In the early childhood years, we focus on the meaning of **fractions** as equal-size parts of a whole. All parts must be the same size, but they may not be the same shape. It is common to hear a child say, "I want the bigger half of the cookie." This child may think that anytime we divide something into two pieces, even if they are not the same size, each piece is $\frac{1}{2}$. It often helps young children if teachers ask how the shape can be divided fairly so everyone gets the same. Squares, circles, and rectangles are generally easy for children to divide into equal-size pieces. They also find it easy to partition objects in $\frac{1}{2}$'s or $\frac{1}{4}$'s. They find it far more difficult to divide shapes like triangles or to partition objects in $\frac{1}{3}$'s.

We write fractions as $\frac{a}{b}$, where a and b are integers, and $b \neq 0$. b cannot be 0 because it is not possible to divide a number by 0. The b tells us how many equal-size parts we have partitioned our whole into and is called the denominator. It is *not* correct to say the denominator tells us the size of the whole. Recall our examples above. In the rectangle, the whole is the entire rectangle, not 4. The a tells us how many parts we have and is called the numerator. In an area model, the fraction tells us what region of the model we have.

Unit Fractions

Unit fractions represent one part of the whole and are written as $\frac{1}{b}$. Just like counting whole numbers lays a foundation for adding and subtracting them, counting with fractions lays a foundation for adding and subtracting fractions which children learn in upper elementary grades. This is known as **iterating.** When we iterate, or count fractions, we take our unit fraction, say $\frac{1}{4}$, and repeat it as many times as we need to get to one whole. It takes four $\frac{1}{4}$'s to equal 1. The denominator tells us what we are counting (fourths). The numerator tells us how many fourths we have. Iterating also helps students begin to think about improper fractions and mixed numbers. Teachers do not need to start first with proper fractions and then introduce improper fractions and mixed numbers. In fact, early experiences with fractions greater than 1 can help children develop concepts about the whole and the meaning of the numerator and denominator. Linear fraction models are especially good for iterating because they connect fractions to measuring.

Skill 3.8: Use models to represent equivalent fractions, including fractions greater than one, and numerical representation of equivalents (e.g., $\frac{1}{2} = \frac{2}{4} = \frac{3}{6}$, the same amount is shaded in the whole).

Two fractions are **equivalent** if they represent the same amount or quantity. Fraction equivalence is challenging because it is the first exposure a child has to the notion that a single quantity can have multiple (infinite) names. While teachers should use all the fraction model types discussed earlier to help students learn about equivalent fractions, area models are a good place to begin. In the figure on the left, the rectangle has been divided into three equal parts. One part is shaded, so the fraction of the rectangle that is shaded is $\frac{1}{3}$. In the second rectangle each of the $\frac{1}{3}$'s has been divided in half. This means that the entire rectangle has now been divided into six equal parts. Two parts are shaded, so the fraction of the rectangle that is shaded is $\frac{2}{6}$. Notice that the same amount of the rectangle has been shaded in both figures.

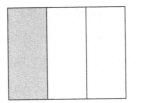 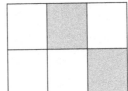

Third graders can represent equivalent fractions that are greater than one, too. Pattern blocks and Cuisenaire rods are good models to use because children can place blocks on top of or next to each other to show equivalence.

Competency 4: Knowledge of Measurement and Data Collection and Analysis

Skill 4.1: Identify the use of measurable attributes and the appropriate use of metric and customary units to measure and compare length, area, perimeter, and volume.

Objects have **measurable attributes**, such as length, width, height, volume, perimeter, or weight. Those attributes are measured using a unit that has the attribute they want to measure. For example, length can be measured with a ruler or meter stick, both of which have length. Measurement is a useful skill, but one that can be confusing. One reason is because in the U.S. students must learn two measurement systems: the U.S. customary system and the metric system.

U.S. Customary System

The U.S. Customary System is used in many facets of life in the U.S. It can be confusing for children because there is no standard way to compare measurement units for a particular attribute. The table below provides a useful reference for PK–3rd grade teachers. Young children should not be expected to memorize or use unit conversions, though. It is far better for them to develop a "feel" for measurement by linking measurement units to familiar referents (e.g., "A paper clip is about an inch long").

Attribute	Common Units	Relationships among Units
Length	Inch, foot, yard, mile	12 in. = 1 ft. 36 in. = 1 yd. 3 ft. = 1 yd. 5,280 ft. = 1 mi. 1,760 yd. = 1 mi.
Mass/Weight	Pound, ounce, ton	16 oz. = 1 lb. 2,000 lb. = 1 ton
Volume	Cup, pint, quart, gallon	2 c. = 1 pt. 2 pt. = 1 qt. 4 qt. = 1 gal.

Metric System

The **metric system** is based on tens, which makes it analogous to our base-ten number system. It is widely used across the world. Some things in the U.S. are measured in metric units, like soda. The basic unit of length in the metric system is the meter. All other units of length are based on their relationship to a *meter*. That is also true for units of mass (basic unit is the *gram*) and volume (basic unit is the *liter*). Because the metric system uses the same prefixes for units no matter the attribute, it is more straightforward than the U.S. Customary System. The table below shows common metric units.

Prefix and Its Meaning	Base Unit(s)	Relationship to Base Unit
Milli- (thousandth)	Meter (length)	1/1000 of base unit
Centi- (hundredth)	Gram (mass or weight)	1/100 of base unit
Kilo- (thousand)	Liter (volume)	1,000 times base unit

Teaching Measurement

Young children should have the opportunity to use metric measuring tools as well as U.S. Customary ones, as the metric system is essential for later instruction in science. There are several ways children measure objects to compare them. In the preschool years, children often use direct comparison. They put two objects side-by-side to determine which is longer. They pour water from one container to another to see which holds more. Children can also use **tiling** to measure. This involves using as many copies of the unit as needed to measure the object. Measurement always involves **units**. It is meaningless to say the length is 4.4 what? Unit cubes, inches? The numerical measurement only has meaning when it is associated with a unit. Measurement in the early years is often introduced using nonstandard units. Children can measure with unit cubes, paper clips, index cards, or drawings of their feet. When measuring the length of a table with index cards, a child might place index cards end-to-end and then count how many it took to measure the length. Another way to measure is to iterate units. This involves taking a unit and repeating it again and again until the object is measured. Here the child might take a single index card and keep moving it until the length of the table is measured. There are several important ideas about measuring that are not immediately obvious to children.

1. The spaces on the measuring tool are important.

2. When measuring, use units of the same size.

3. Cover or fill the space completely with no gaps or overlaps.

4. Count the units.

5. Decide what to do with any leftover parts.

Perimeter is a measure of length. It can be thought of as the distance required to "walk around" an object. Two-dimensional objects have area or the amount of space they cover up. Area uses square units, e.g., in^2, ft^2. Children at this age should not be encouraged to use a formula to find perimeter or be told area is length × width or base × height. That is because those formulas only apply to certain shapes. Children can use shapes drawn on grid paper or one-inch tiles to fill in the space on a shape. They can count the tiles used or the grids covered to determine a shape's area.

Most children are able to understand length before they can conceptualize volume. They are fooled by the shape of a container, usually asserting that a tall, thin container must hold more than a short, fat one. The water table is a great place for young children to learn about volume. Provide an assortment of containers children can use to pour water from one to the other.

Skill 4.2: Identify effective instructional activities for estimating, telling, and writing time; calculating elapsed time; and counting money.

Time is an abstract concept. It is often a difficult concept for young children to understand. Time involves duration or how long an event takes (elapsed time). It is perceived subjectively, so even adults do not always judge elapsed time accurately. Time also involves sequence or the temporal order in which events occur. Young children's concepts about time are related to repeating patterns of morning, afternoon, evening, day, and night. They can sequence familiar, daily events, *i.e., I brush my teeth after breakfast*, but often have difficulty with longer time periods. Weeks, months, and years are associated with events such as a birthday or holiday. As students move through PK–3rd grade classrooms, they learn to read and write time using analog and digital displays, estimate time, and determine elapsed time.

Telling Time with Analog and Digital Clocks

Learning to read a clock is important, but it is not fundamentally related to understanding the concept of time. On an analog clock children must differentiate between the hour and minute hands and know when to count by ones or by fives. They must deal with fractional parts that are read forwards and backwards (e.g., "quarter till," "quarter past"). Analog clocks contain two, and sometimes three hands. On a two-handed clock the longer of the two hands is the minute hand. The shorter of the two is the hour hand. When an analog clock has a third hand, it is typically a different color from the minute and hour hands. Digital clocks are easier to read but children often have difficulty understanding what they mean. For example, it is not obvious to a child that 3:59 is almost 4:00.

Many early childhood teachers introduce children to telling time using an analog clock with the minute hand removed. Children can then notice that it is "about 3 o'clock" or "a little after 7 o'clock." When the minute hand is added, the teacher can ask children to notice what happens to the minute hand as the hour hand moves. Commercially produced cardboard clocks with moveable hands allow children to make times on the clock and read times that someone else has made. They are preferable to worksheets as the ability to physically move the hands on the clock reinforces the movement of the hands as time passes. Students can also make their own clocks using paper plates, strips of cardstock for the hands, and a paper fastener.

When introducing the minute hand, it is best to begin with 5-minute intervals. This should be connected to counting by fives. Twelve children can either make a human clock or they can line up. Count by fives and ask students to notice which child would represent 25 (the fifth one).

On a digital clock, the hours and minutes are separated by a colon. Because digital clocks are more difficult to understand, early childhood teachers usually begin instruction using analog clocks. When introducing digital clocks, it is good to show children an analog clock and ask them to show what the display would look like on a digital clock. Then, they can do the reverse. Teachers can create or find commercially produced matching games that children can use to equate analog and digital displays.

Elapsed Time

Children are expected to determine **elapsed time** beginning in third grade. Calculating elapsed time is a multi-step process that requires students to account for a.m. and p.m. Sometimes they must calculate elapsed time from the start and end times. Other problems may give students the elapsed time and either the start or end time. They then calculate the unknown value. One of the most effective strategies for dealing with elapsed time is an open timeline. Imagine the following problem:

Your family is driving to Grandma's today. The trip takes 3 hours and 20 minutes. If you leave at 9:30 a.m., what time will you get there?

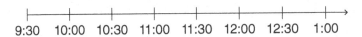

9:30	10:00	10:30	11:00	11:30	12:00	12:30	1:00

One way to solve the problem is to start at 9:30. Jump 30 minutes to 10:00. Now jump 2 hours to 12:00 noon. Jump another 30 minutes to 12:30 (½ hour + 2 hours + ½ = 3 hrs). Now, jump 20 minutes to 12:50.

Elapsed time in the early childhood curriculum is not just about calculations, though. Children should have the opportunity to estimate how long certain activities take, like cleaning up the block center.

Counting Money

Recognizing coins and their values is fundamentally not a mathematical skill. Students must be able to count on and skip count to determine the value of a collection of coins. Children sometimes believe that larger coins have more value than smaller ones, thereby reasoning that a penny is worth more than a dime. They also have difficulty understanding that 10 pennies have the same value as 1 dime or that a particular amount of money can be represented using different combinations of coins. Start by counting pennies, which reinforces counting by ones. When using more than one coin, begin by only using two different coins. Practice skip counting by 5s, 10s, and 25s to help children count money. Many teachers use calendar time as a way to reinforce counting money. On the first day of the month, they put out one penny and continue adding another penny each day. When they get to the fifth day of the month, they emphasize that the 5 pennies could be traded for one nickel. When they get to the 10th day, they note that we can either use 10 pennies, 5 pennies and 1 nickel, or 1 dime to represent 10. The dramatic play center is a good place for children to practice using play money.

Skill 4.3: Select effective methods to organize, represent, and interpret data (e.g., bar graphs, line plots).

One of the first ways children learn to organize data is through **tally charts**. Tally charts connect to skip counting by 5s. Real graphs use actual objects like M&M's, leaves, or pebbles. Picture graphs (or pictographs) use drawings to represent the objects. When using real graphs or picture graphs, it is important to place the objects inside a square or rectangle so that children can easily compare how many of each object are present. Bar graphs are more symbolic than either real or picture graphs. They use blocks or bars to represent data. Real, picture, and bar graphs are all used for discrete data. They show data in which the order of the categories doesn't matter. If we are graphing how many of each color of M&M's candies is in a bag, it doesn't matter what order we put the colors in.

A **bar graph** has a horizontal *x*-axis and a vertical *y*-axis. The categories go on the *x*-axis (e.g., M&M's colors) and the frequency or how many of each color we have goes on the *y*-axis.

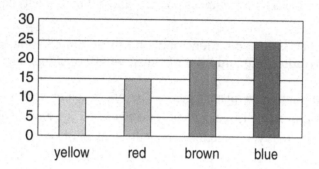

A **line plot** uses a number line to show data, such as the number of pets in each family. To make a line plot, students first draw a number line. Then each data point is indicated on the line plot by making an X above the data element. If three children have 3 pets each, 3 X's would be drawn above the 3 on the line plot. Line plots are easy to read because children can count how many X's there are above each data element.

```
                  X
                  X
                  X            X              X
   X              X            X       X      X
   X              X      X     X       X      X
  <++++++++++++++++++++++++++++++++++++++++++++++>
   0      1       2      3      4      5
```

Skill 4.4: Solve problems analyzing data sets, drawing conclusions, and making predictions.

Data analysis is an important skill. We can ask three basic types of questions about data displays. The first are questions that require children to read something directly from the display such as, *What is this graph about? How many red M&M's were in the bag?* A second type of question requires children to compare information in the graph. *How many more children want to make pudding for snack than want to make fruit cups? Which color of M&M's is the most common? How many maple and oak leaves are there all together?* The third type of question requires children to think beyond the information that is in the graph to use it to make predictions. *If we surveyed Ms. Smith's class, do you think more children would have a dog or a cat?*

Competency 5: Knowledge of Geometric and Spatial Concepts

Geometry is the area of mathematics that focuses on space, objects in space, and the relationships among them. Geometry in the early grades does not emphasize zero- and one-dimensional space. Instead, children focus on two-dimensional and three-dimensional shapes.

Skill 5.1: Identify and classify two-dimensional and three-dimensional shapes, according to defining attributes (e.g., number of sides, length of sides, measure of angles).

Two-dimensional shapes are plane figures. They have length and width but no thickness. **Three-dimensional shapes** are also known as solid figures. They have length, width, and thickness. The name of a shape tells you something about the number of sides or angles it has. *Tri-* means three, so a triangle is "three angles." *Quad-* means four and *later* means sides, so a quadrilateral is a four-sided polygon. A pentagon has five angles because *penta-* means five. The names of three-dimensional figures also tell you information about their attributes. A triangular prism is a prism that has triangles for its bases. A square pyramid has a square base.

Shapes can be described by their attributes. Some attributes like color, size, or texture are called non-defining attributes. They are not essential. Defining attributes are the "must haves" for a shape.

Triangles

Triangles are polygons (closed figures composed of line segments). They have three sides and three angles. No matter the type of triangle, if you add the measure of all three angles together you always get $180°$. Triangles can be classified by the lengths of their sides or by their angles.

Some triangles are classified by the length of their sides. An **equilateral triangle** is one in which all three sides are equal. This means that all three angles are also equal. Since the angles in any triangle add up to $180°$, this means that each angle in an equilateral triangle measures $60°$. It is important for young children to have experience with many different types of triangles in order to develop ideas about defining and non-defining attributes, not just triangles that are equilateral. An **isosceles triangle** is a triangle that has two equal sides. By this definition, an equilateral triangle is also an isosceles triangle. Because it has two equal sides, it also has two equal angles. A **scalene triangle** is a triangle with no equal sides or angles.

Type of Triangle	Defining Attributes	Example
Equilateral	3 equal sides, 3 equal angles	
Isosceles	2 equal sides, 2 equal angles	
Scalene	0 equal sides, 0 equal angles	
Right	One 90° angle	
Acute	All angles < 90°	
Obtuse	One angle > 90°	

Triangles can also be classified by their angles. A triangle with one 90° angle is known as a **right triangle**. Recall that all the angles in a triangle add up to 180°. Therefore, in a right triangle, the remaining two triangles must each be < 90° (acute). An **acute triangle** is one in which all three angles are < 90°. An **obtuse triangle** has one angle > 90°. What does this mean about the remaining two angles? They must each be < 90°.

The challenge is recognizing that shapes can have more than one name as the table below illustrates.

Type of Triangle	Must also be . . .	Might also be . . .	Will never be . . .
Equilateral	Isosceles, acute	—	Scalene, right, obtuse
Isosceles	—	Right, equilateral, acute, obtuse	Scalene
Scalene	—	Right, acute, obtuse	Equilateral, isosceles
Right	—	Isosceles, scalene	Equilateral, acute, obtuse
Acute	—	Equilateral, isosceles, scalene	Right, obtuse
Obtuse	—	Isosceles, scalene	Equilateral, right

Quadrilaterals

A **quadrilateral** is a four-sided polygon. The table below lists the defining attributes for common quadrilaterals.

Type of Quadrilateral	Defining Attributes	Example
Trapezoid	1 pair of parallel sides	
Parallelogram	2 pairs of equal and parallel sides, opposite angles are equal	
Rectangle	2 pairs of equal sides and 4 right angles	
Square	4 equal sides and 4 right angles	
Rhombus	4 equal sides and opposite angles are equal	

Some quadrilaterals are special types of other quadrilaterals. The Venn diagram below illustrates the relationships among quadrilaterals. You can see from this figure that all rectangles, squares, and rhombuses are parallelograms. Squares are examples of rectangles and rhombuses. Not all rectangles are squares, though, and not all rhombuses are squares. Students need experience with lots of different examples of each shape. Otherwise they develop the misconception that all rectangles have two long and two short sides.

Quadrilaterals

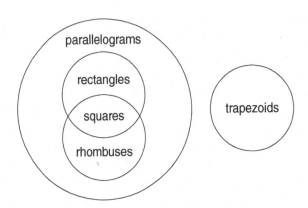

Skill 5.2: Identify the composition of a complex figure using basic two-dimensional and three-dimensional shapes (e.g., squares, circles, triangles, spheres, cones, prisms).

There are different types of three-dimensional figures. One that is composed of polygons is known as a polyhedron (plural: *polyhedra*). The polygons that make a solid figure are called its **faces.** Two faces meet at an **edge.** A corner where several faces meet is called a **vertex** (plural: vertices). A sphere is a three-dimensional object that is perfectly round like a ball. Cylinders are shapes with two bases that are closed figures. Cones have one base that is a closed figure. Spheres, cylinders, and cones are not polyhedral. That is because they are not composed of polygons.

There are several classes of three-dimensional objects that children encounter in daily life.

Type of Figure	Defining Attributes	Example
Cylinder	Has 2 parallel bases that are circles or ovals that are joined by a curved surface	
Prism	A polyhedron with two parallel bases that are joined by parallelograms. Prisms are named for the shape of their bases. A triangular prism has bases that are triangles. A rectangular prism has bases that are rectangles. A cube is a type of prism with bases that are squares. All faces of a cube are squares.	triangular prism, cube, rectangular prism
Cone	Has a single base that is either a circle or an oval that is joined to a point in space by a curved side. The point is called a vertex.	
Pyramid	Is a polyhedron with a single base that is joined by triangles to a point in space called the vertex.	

Children in the early grades need many opportunities to work with shapes to observe their properties and construct understanding of the relationships among shapes. Pierre van Hiele and Dina van Hiele from the Netherlands developed a five-level hierarchy to describe how people reason about shapes and their properties (Van de Walle et al., 2015). PK–3rd grade children will almost exclusively be at the two lowest levels (0 and 1). Children at Level 0 can begin to classify shapes that are similar. It is especially important that they see many different examples of particular shapes. For example, students should work with a variety of triangles, not just equilateral ones. The Mathematics Florida Standards expect children to be reasoning at Level 1 in third grade. Students at Level 1 can think about multiple examples of a shape, not just the one in front of them.

Skill 5.3: Analyze and distinguish examples of symmetry and non-symmetry in two dimensions.

Shapes can be moved in space. When shapes are moved in space or bisected they may have symmetry.

One type of symmetry is known as **line symmetry** or reflection symmetry. Think about the hearts children often make for Valentine's Day. Typically they fold a piece of paper in half, draw half of a heart, and cut it out. When they open the paper they have a heart that looks the same on either side of the fold. This is an example of line or reflection symmetry. An object has line symmetry if it can be folded in such a way that the two sides are mirror images of each other. Circles have line symmetry. So do equilateral and isosceles triangles. Scalene triangles do not. Rectangles and rhombuses have line symmetry. Since a square is both a rectangle and a rhombus, it has line symmetry, too. Parallelograms that are not rectangles or rhombuses do not have line symmetry. A trapezoid may have line symmetry. Note, however, that not all lines that cut a shape in half are lines of symmetry. A rectangle has a vertical and a horizontal line of symmetry. If you draw a diagonal line and fold the rectangle along the line, the two sides are not mirror images of each other. A rectangle's diagonal is not a line of symmetry.

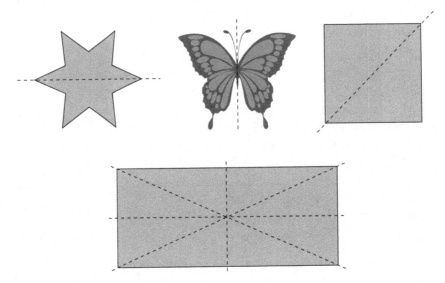

Children can work with cut out shapes that they can fold in multiple ways to determine whether or not they have line symmetry. In addition to investigating line symmetry with polygons, many early childhood teachers also use capital letters or pattern blocks. Geoboards are another great way for children to create shapes and investigate line symmetry. One rubber band should be placed vertically or horizontally on the geoboard. Then children can construct a shape on one side. They can then determine how to make the "mirror image" shape on the other side. For an extra challenge, students can also use a diagonal line of symmetry on the geoboard.

Two-dimensional shapes can have **rotation symmetry**. This means that the shape can be rotated in space any amount < 360° and the shape looks the same. Equilateral triangles and parallelograms (which include rectangles, rhombuses, and squares) have rotation symmetry. Isosceles and scalene triangles, as well as trapezoids, do not. Geoboards are good models for children to investigate rotation symmetry. Cardstock shapes that students can trace around and then rotate to investigate their "footprint" are also good.

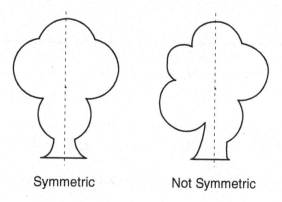

Symmetric   Not Symmetric

Skill 5.4: Identify spatial concepts (e.g., above, below, hidden view, through) and vocabulary (e.g., line, angle, ray, plane) useful for teaching geometry in real-world situations.

Spatial concepts are the notions people have about the spatial properties of objects and the relationships among objects. Children can be introduced to spatial concepts prior to entering preschool. *I Spy* is a wonderful game to help children learn spatial vocabulary like *above, below, inside, behind*, etc. As children are playing in centers, PK teachers can take advantage of the opportunity to introduce spatial vocabulary. Children's literature can be another great way to emphasize spatial vocabulary.

A **point** in geometry specifies a location. It has no length, width, or depth. To a young child, a point is a dot. Teachers should use the term *point* when referring to a location in space, but it is not necessary to introduce the idea that a point is dimensionless. A **line** has no thickness. It is straight and extends in both directions without end. A portion of a line is a **line segment**. A **ray** is a portion of a line that has one endpoint and extends forever in the other direction. An **angle** is the area that is between two rays with the same endpoint, which is called a vertex. Children typically refer to angles as points. Again, teachers can model the use of the word *angle*, but it is unwise to have PK–3rd grade children memorize a definition for angle. Children at this age can investigate angles by using two strips of card stock joined with a paper fastener. This allows them to measure angles and compare two angles without emphasizing the abstract concept of degrees.

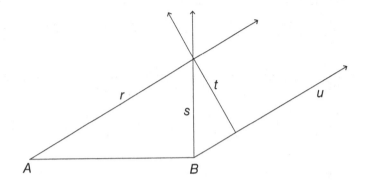

References

Beckmann, S. (2014). *Mathematics for Elementary Teachers, with Activities* (4th ed.). Boston, MA: Pearson.

Carpenter, T. P., Franke, M. L., & Levi, L. (2003). *Thinking Mathematically: Integrating Arithmetic and Algebra in Elementary School*. Portsmouth, NH: Heinemann.

Crews, D. (1986). *Ten Black Dots* (Redesigned and rev. ed.). New York: Greenwillow Books.

Van de Walle, J., Karp, K., & Bay-Williams, J. (2015). *Elementary and Middle School Mathematics: Teaching Developmentally* (9th ed.). Boston, MA: Pearson.

CHAPTER

6

Science
Subtest 4 (534)

The goal of science is to construct explanations about how the natural world works. Scientists ask questions and then investigate them, both systematically and informally. Young children are inherently curious about how the world works. Effective science instruction in the PreK/Primary classroom provides children with many opportunities to engage in authentic inquiry and construct their own developmentally appropriate explanations about scientific phenomena. At the end of this chapter, you will find a list of resources that support each competency and set of skills. These resources come in varied forms, from websites to journals, and are collected at the end of the chapter so that you may stay focused on the material at hand as you review.

Competency 1: Knowledge of Effective Science Instruction

Skill 1.1: Analyze developmentally appropriate strategies for teaching science practices (e.g., observing, questioning, designing and carrying out investigations, developing and using models, constructing and communicating explanations).

Science instruction in the early childhood years takes advantage of children's innate curiosity about the world. Young children develop proficiency with science and engineering practices by having regular opportunities to investigate the world around them. The block center, the water table, and a classroom garden are all locations in which children's curiosity can be nurtured. Productive questions (Harlen, 2001) promote children's reasoning skills and help them construct scientific explanations. They are important tools teachers use to support children in various science practices. Examples of productive questions include:

- What do you notice about. . . ?

- What makes you think that?

- Why do you think that?

PreK/Primary teachers don't always have to ask questions to foster children's reasoning. Conversational prompts such as *Tell me more about that* or *I'm curious about what you're thinking* can remove the pressure some children feel to always have the "right" answer. When teachers use conversational prompts, they demonstrate interest in children's ideas.

The questions children ask are based on their sensory experiences. During the PreK/Primary years they can begin to consider which questions can be answered by conducting a scientific investigation. With teacher support, they can collaborate with others to plan an investigation and make observations. They can record their observations in a manner commensurate with their writing skills. Through individual or class discussion they can help decide what kind of data should be collected to answer the question they are investigating.

Reasoning with models is an authentic science practice. Young children can be encouraged to describe how a specific scientific model is different from the object or process it represents. They can create their own models, which could be drawings or physical objects. Children naturally use one object to stand for another when engaged in free play, so it makes sense to allow them to do so in science. Models are a way for children to communicate their science ideas. Quality early childhood science instruction encourages children to talk about their science ideas with each other and the teacher. When teachers welcome children's ideas and engage in active listening, children feel supported.

Children's writing skills across the PreK/Primary years and within a single classroom can differ widely. Science notebooks in which children can draw, write, or even dictate their observations enables all children to communicate their science ideas. Rather than taking away from the literacy block, science instruction that focuses on constructing explanations creates an authentic context for developing young children's oral and written language skills. As they read informational texts in science they learn about text features and how to gain information from images such as graphs or diagrams.

Skill 1.2: Identify strategies and skills for facilitating children's experiences in ways that support their active inquiry, naturalistic exploration, talk and argument, and conceptual development.

An early childhood classroom that emphasizes play is one of the best ways to promote children's learning in science. Play is not frivolous. It is the way children learn about the world. Play should be a feature of primary education. Learning centers encourage children's self-directed, active inquiry. Centers can include materials (living and/or nonliving) to observe, tools for observing, and questions to guide observations. Materials within a science center can be rotated throughout the school year so children can observe many science phenomena. Walking field trips around the school grounds and to nearby locations can be ways for children to explore the world around them. Of course, when taking children outside, teachers always need to follow appropriate procedures to keep the children safe.

An **anchor chart** is a tool that the teacher and students create together during a lesson. It is then displayed prominently in the classroom so children can refer to it as needed. It "anchors" the most important content. Anchor charts in science are especially good ways to support children's science talk and scientific argumentation. An anchor chart with sentence starters can help them engage in respectful conversation with their peers. Some teachers use anchor charts to post class observations from investigations during a science unit. As children are developing and refining their conceptual understanding, they can consult the chart to remind them of evidence that supports their claims. Using pictures as well as words on this type of anchor chart makes the information accessible to children with varying literacy skills.

Skill 1.3: Identify and analyze strategies for formal and informal learning experiences to provide science curriculum that promotes children's natural curiosity about the world (e.g., active hands-on experiences, active engagement in the physical world, student interaction).

When children engage in active learning, they construct new knowledge through sensory experiences with actual objects and interacting with others to reflect on their experiences. It is more than simply hands-on experiences. Active learning requires children to think about their experiences and make meaning from them. Many active learning experiences have a problem-solving dimension to them. Suppose a child tries to put a lid on a container but finds that the lid falls into the container. The child may then search until a lid that fits the container is found. Experiences like this can help the child realize the need to consider the size of the opening of a container when choosing the right lid to fit it.

Most learning in schools is **formal learning** that is based on curriculum standards. Teachers have specific learning objectives for students and there may be little student choice in what is learned or how learning occurs. In contrast, **informal learning** is learning that is student-directed, which means that it is flexible. It focuses on what the learner wants to learn. Informal learning is sometimes known as experiential learning. It is the way humans learn on a day-to-day basis outside formal education.

Early childhood educators can do several things to encourage children's informal learning in science. One way is to provide time in the day for children to engage in unstructured self-directed learning through play. Play can help children develop social skills as they negotiate sharing materials and making decisions about how to use those materials. A second way is to encourage parents and caregivers to foster informal learning at home. Schools can provide families with lists of local resources for informal learning such as zoos, museums, etc., or lists of science informational texts they could read with their children. Schools can also share generic questions that parents/caregivers can ask children to guide their thinking while reading with them or investigating the natural world. Science take-home activity bags that contain a science informational text and a science activity for children and caregivers to complete together is a way to integrate literacy and science. Whether we are considering self-directed learning in the early childhood classroom or at home, it is important for adults to remember that learning can sometimes be messy.

Skill 1.4: Identify ways to organize and manage the early childhood classroom for safe, effective science teaching and learning (e.g., procedures, equipment, layout).

The list of safety precautions for early childhood science classrooms is based on the *National Science Teachers Association* position paper on safety in the science classroom (NSTA, 2015). Additional information that is specifically applicable to PreK/Primary classrooms has been added.

- Wear safety goggles when working with any objects that could damage or splash and irritate anyone's eyes.

- Wash hands before and after handling living things (plants or animals) or Earth materials, such as soil.

- Remind children not to eat or drink during investigations unless instructed by the teacher that it is safe to do so. Overall, it is best to not eat or drink in the same area of the classroom where science investigations are conducted.

- To the extent possible, use non-breakable measuring instruments and storage containers (beakers, etc.). If something spills or breaks have a procedure in place for reporting it to the teacher immediately.

- When outside, be prepared with emergency treatments for students who may need them (e.g., Epipen). If taking children outside visit the area first to identify hazards such as holes or broken glass so you can alert children to be careful.

- Be aware of children's allergies and take appropriate precautions.

- Place science materials at a level where children can safely reach them. The exception would be potentially hazardous materials. These should be stored safely out of the reach of children.

- Pay attention to spills, such as around the water table. Wipe them up as quickly as possible so no one slips and falls.

- Organize the classroom so children, including those with mobility issues, can move about freely.

Introducing live animals into the classroom can be an educative experience for young children. Any animals brought into the classroom should be examined by a veterinarian to be certified for their safety. This is especially important with reptiles who may carry salmonella. Because some children may be allergic to specific animals, a teacher should obtain permission from parents or guardians for their children to be around animals in the classroom. The teacher is ultimately responsible for the safety of the animal as well as the children. Teachers need a plan for care of and interaction with animals in the classroom. They need to model appropriate ways of interacting with animals and monitor children's interactions with them to keep everyone, including the animals, safe.

Skill 1.5: Identify and select developmentally appropriate formal and informal assessments to evaluate prior knowledge, to guide instruction, and to evaluate the impact of science experiences on student learning.

Early childhood teachers use assessments in science to monitor student progress, make instructional decisions, and evaluate student achievement. Teachers not only assess students' understanding of science concepts, they also assess children's ability to engage in science and engineering practices and apply concepts across science topics at age-appropriate levels. Assessments are also used to evaluate program effectiveness. In Florida, state assessments in science are given in fifth grade. Nonetheless, early childhood teachers play a key role in giving young children the foundation they need to be successful in science classrooms at higher grades.

There are many ways to characterize assessments. One way is based upon when the assignments are administered.

- **Diagnostic assessments:** given prior to instruction; used to determine students' prior knowledge about a topic for instructional planning.

- **Formative assessments:** given throughout the learning process; used to identify students' progress toward meeting learning outcomes and gaps in a student's knowledge; also used to plan and modify instruction to address learning gaps.

- **Summative assessments:** given after instruction is completed; used to measure students' mastery of lesson learning outcomes and state curriculum standards.

There are many ways early childhood teachers can assess their students in science. Using multiple types of assessments as a teacher increases the likelihood that you will be able to make instructional decisions that will more consistently and effectively help improve student learning. Here are a few:

- **Observations and checklists:** Teachers often use a rubric and clipboard when using observations as assessments. The rubric provides documentation of which students are meeting the target and which are not. Checklists are good because teachers do not need to write a lot while making observations. When designing a checklist or observation form, include a place for comments.

- **Science notebooks:** Practicing scientists use notebooks to record the questions they are investigating, make observational drawings and record written observations, make scientific claims, and write new questions they are wondering about. Young children can use science notebooks in the same way. Science notebooks reinforce emergent literacy skills. Young children's science notebooks usually include pictures and invented spelling. The primary focus should be constructing explanations and the use of science and engineering practices, rather than undue attention to neatness or coloring. Many teachers create and photocopy recording sheets that students glue into their notebooks to save precious class time. Children should be encouraged to make observational drawings in science realistic, but teachers also need to take account of children's developmental level and not expect the kind of precision that would be expected of older learners. Early childhood teachers can model how to create science observational drawings. For example, when making an observational drawing of a marigold, it is important to use realistic colors and not draw a face on the flower. Some early childhood teachers also create a class science notebook to which students regularly contribute.

- **Interviews:** Another way to assess children's conceptual understanding in science is through an interview. This can be time-consuming, but often yields rich data about a child's thinking. When conducting interviews, it is good to audiotape or videotape them (with parental permission) for later analysis. Ask open-ended questions to find out what students are thinking. Provide realia, models, and paper, pencils, and crayons that children can use to illustrate their explanations.

- **Performance tasks:** Performance tasks in science are ones that require students to use science concepts and science and engineering practices to solve a real-world problem. Project and problem-based learning tasks are examples of performance tasks. When students work in teams to design a house that can withstand hurricane-force winds, for example, they must use what they have learned about weather to design an appropriate structure.

- **Portfolios:** These are a collection of a student's work over time that shows progress toward meeting learning outcomes. A portfolio includes children's self-reflection about their learning.

- **Informal assessments:** Many teachers rely on a variety of informal assessments to track student progress. One minute papers, thumbs up-thumbs down, bell-ringers, questioning, etc., can be used to assess children's understanding at different points during a lesson.

- **Tests/quizzes:** Tests and quizzes will probably always be a part of educational assessment. They should not, however, be the main ways young children are assessed.

Skill 1.6: Select and analyze small- and large-group strategies to help students explain the concepts they are learning, provide opportunities to introduce formal science terms, and to clarify scientific concepts and misconceptions.

Science classrooms should be language-rich environments. Science conversations can be informal ones that children engage in among themselves or ones they have with the teacher while engaging in inquiry. Those conversations can also be more formal ones that occur after children have completed an investigation. Helping children develop their oral communication skills is an important goal of early childhood teachers. Learning to take turns speaking, listening to the ideas of others, appreciating alternative perspectives, and disagreeing respectfully require time and support. Children begin practicing these skills at the beginning of the school year and continue refining them throughout the year. Many teachers create an anchor chart with sentence starters and questions children can refer to as they practice how to engage in respectful science classroom conversation. Here is a sample of some possibilities:

- I agree with _____ because _____.

- I disagree with _____ because _____.

- Can you please repeat what you said?

- I have a question about _____.

- I observed that _____.

- I predict _____ because _____.

Teachers also rely on various talk strategies to give more children an opportunity to share their ideas. **Turn and talk** is a strategy in which children are encouraged to share their ideas with someone sitting next to them (their shoulder partner). In **think-pair-share**, children are told to first think of an answer to a question but not say anything just yet. They then share their thoughts with a partner. Finally, they share them with the larger group.

Science vocabulary is best introduced in the context of authentic inquiry rather than prior to an investigation. As children are sharing their observations and their thinking, the teacher introduces the science vocabulary word. The teacher can place new vocabulary words on a science **word wall.** Children can refer to the word wall as they are explaining science concepts. Pairing the word with a picture can be helpful for emergent readers and ELLs.

Young children come to school with fairly sophisticated ideas about how the world works (National Research Council, 2012) based on their prior experiences. These ideas may be well-connected or they may be incorrect. Some ideas (even incorrect ones) can be building blocks to scientific understanding. Thus, it is important for children in the PreK/Primary years to begin to develop scientific explanations which can be refined as they progress through K–12 schooling.

Students' incorrect ideas are known by several names. One is **misconceptions.** A misconception is an incorrect idea that is based on faulty reasoning. They are very common. One way teachers find out about children's misconceptions is to ask them to explain their thinking. Many of the assessment strategies listed previously in Skill 1.5 can be used to elicit student thinking. Using models to aid student reasoning is another useful strategy to help children correct their misconceptions. Instruction that causes students to confront misconceptions by placing those ideas side-by-side with accurate conceptions can help them embrace the scientifically accurate ones.

Skill 1.7: Select and apply safe and effective instructional strategies when using curricular and instructional tools and resources such as physical and conceptual models, scientific equipment, realia, and print and digital representations to support and enhance science instruction.

Reasoning with models is one of the eight science and engineering practices. Children can draw models or use physical models to construct scientific explanations. A physical model uses familiar, everyday objects to represent unfamiliar objects or events. Many models are used in early childhood science. A styrofoam ball and a flashlight can be used to model moon phases. Models can be used to construct explanations or to make predictions. All models have strengths and weaknesses. Because they are never exactly like the real thing, they do not behave exactly like the object they represent. Young children can be asked to think about the strengths and weaknesses of the models they use in science. They can also construct their own models. The important point is that a model should be used to develop scientific understanding. They are not merely arts and crafts projects. Making a paper flower is an enjoyable activity, but it is not a scientific model.

Children will usually need instruction in how to use scientific equipment like hand lenses or measuring tools. Provide measuring tools that use metric and U.S. customary units so children can develop facility with both measurement systems. Overall it is better to use plastic containers rather than glass with PreK/Primary students. Appropriate safety procedures should be followed when using scientific equipment (see Skill 1.4).

As often as possible, early childhood teachers should use realia when teaching science concepts to children. When learning about plants, children can investigate real plants. They can plant their own seeds and track the plant's growth over time. They can use a hand lens to examine the parts of the plant and compare how a specific part looks different on different plants. This is preferable to looking at a picture of a plant, having the teacher show children an artificial plant, or watching a video of a plant.

Print and digital resources are a good choice when realia is not available or when processes cannot be investigated in the classroom. Interactive digital resources enable children to see what happens when they manipulate factors in a system. For example, children can change the food supply for one organism in a food web and see how that affects all the other organisms in the web. When using online resources, it is important to observe safety precautions for visiting websites. Many schools have firewalls that do not allow children to visit inappropriate sites. Teachers should check out their school's policies before allowing children to visit new sites.

Skill 1.8: Apply scientifically and professionally responsible decision-making regarding the selection of socially and culturally sensitive science content and activities.

Students in contemporary Florida classrooms are a diverse group. They come from different racial, ethnic, cultural, language, and economic groups. They may live in rural, suburban, or urban areas. Some students attend schools that mirror the diversity found in the larger society, while others attend schools that are more homogeneous. Some learners have intellectual, physical, communicative, behavioral, or sensory exceptionalities. Early childhood classrooms should embrace the social and cultural diversity of the U.S. This is true not only for classrooms with diverse populations but should also characterize classrooms with more homogeneous populations. All students need equitable access to science curriculum and should be encouraged to believe they can become scientists when they grow up, if they so desire.

Exposing children to scientists who represent the diversity within the scientific community through informational texts, videos of scientists, or visits to the classrooms by scientists are good strategies. They are not enough, however. The term **culturally relevant pedagogy** was coined by Gloria Ladson-Billings in 1995. Culturally relevant pedagogy enables students to achieve academic success, situates learning in the context of students' culture, and empowers them to challenge the norms and values that perpetuate social inequities. Science investigations can take advantage of students' local context. Choosing examples with which children are familiar is important. PreK/Primary teachers can utilize outdoor spaces around the school or in the neighborhood to investigate living things. When choosing science informational texts for the reading center, it is good to find books that portray the diversity that exists within the scientific community.

A PreK/Primary classroom culture of inquiry through play benefits all learners. Learning centers are a great way for children to investigate and explore science phenomena and concepts. It is important for teachers to encourage all students, girls as well as boys, to play in the science center and to engage in science inquiry activities. Children in wheelchairs may need to have science materials brought to them. When taking children outside, make sure the area to which you are going is wheelchair accessible. Children with emotional and behavioral disorders will benefit from positive support to enable them to engage in active science inquiry.

Read-alouds using science informational texts are beneficial for ELLs. If possible, a parent who speaks the child's home language can translate the book. The teacher and the parent can take turns reading each page aloud. In addition to giving children vocabulary in both languages, the practice affirms the value of children's language backgrounds. Like all children, ELLs benefit from a print-rich environment. It is important to speak slowly and use visual representations and realia as much as possible. Some children may come from cultures where students are discouraged from speaking or participating in class. A supportive environment where they are encouraged, but not forced to speak, will enable them to feel more comfortable. A science word wall that displays science vocabulary along with a picture of the object or concept is good for all young children, but especially ELLs.

Competency 2: Knowledge of the Nature of Science

Skill 2.1: Identify and apply basic process skills (e.g., observing, inferring, classifying, measuring), and developmentally appropriate science practices (e.g., analyzing and interpreting data, constructing explanations, engaging in argument from evidence).

Like all disciplines, science and engineering have their own ways of approaching, investigating, and communicating results. Scientists and engineers in different fields differ from one another in terms of the questions they ask, the tools they use, the scale at which they work, the evidence they collect, how they evaluate that evidence, and how they communicate it to others both within and outside their specialized field. At the same time, there are certain practices in which scientists and engineers engage regardless of their specific field. The *Next Generation Science Standards* (NGSS, 2013) and *A Framework for K–12 Science Education: Practices, Crosscutting Concepts, and Core Ideas* (National Research Council, 2012) upon which the NGSS are based emphasize the importance of three-dimensional learning. Science instruction should not simply be about acquiring factual or even conceptual knowledge in science. It must also be about engaging in authentic practices of science and engineering. These two documents outline eight science and engineering practices (SEPs).

Science and Engineering Practice	What It Looks Like in Early Childhood Classrooms
1. Asking questions (science) and defining problems (engineering)	Children ask and recognize questions that can be investigated in science. They begin to differentiate between testable and non-testable questions. They formulate a simple problem that can be solved through designing a new or enhanced object, process, or system.
2. Developing and using models	Children create and revise their own models and can tell how a model is different from the object or process it represents. They begin to determine the strengths and weaknesses of a particular model.
3. Planning and carrying out investigations	Children collaboratively plan and conduct investigations with guidance. They use science process skills to observe, measure, predict, and infer.
4. Analyzing and interpreting data	Children record observations, claims, and evidence using pictures, data displays, and age-appropriate writing. They begin to notice patterns in data and use reasoning to analyze data to construct claims.
5. Using mathematics and computational thinking	Children determine when to use quantitative or qualitative data. They measure attributes of objects and describe patterns using numbers and counting. They create and interpret data displays.

Science and Engineering Practice	What It Looks Like in Early Childhood Classrooms
6. Constructing explanations (science) and designing solutions (engineering)	Children construct scientific explanations based on evidence they collect during investigations. They can compare multiple solutions to a problem.
7. Engaging in argument from evidence	Children construct scientific arguments that are supported by evidence. They begin to evaluate the evidence used to support a claim. Children listen to and critique their classmates' claims.
8. Obtaining, evaluating, and communicating information	Children read and comprehend developmentally appropriate science informational texts. They use text features and begin to read and interpret non-text information like diagrams and graphs. They communicate information orally and by using developmentally appropriate writing skills.

Young children use many science process skills when engaging in these eight science and engineering practices. As they plan and carry out investigations, they do the following:

- **Observe:** Children use their senses to gather information about the natural world. PreK students' observations are often qualitative. As children move through the early childhood years, they use tools like hand lenses, rulers, and measuring cups to extend their senses and make quantitative observations.

- **Infer:** Children make a claim or draw a conclusion about some aspect of the natural world based upon their observations and prior knowledge. Inferences in science are never merely guesses (wild or otherwise). Young children need support to learn to make inferences based on *evidence,* rather than simply guessing.

- **Predict:** Children predict when they use patterns in their observations to forecast what will happen next. A prediction is also not a guess; it is a reasonable inference of what might occur next based on prior evidence.

- **Classify:** When children group or sort objects based on one or more properties, they are classifying. Objects that share a specific property are placed in the same group. Young learners often begin by classifying things based on observable qualitative properties, such as color. This is a good place to begin. Children will need support to be able to classify the same objects based on a different property. Classifying objects in multiple ways based upon different properties can lead to more interesting questions to investigate.

- **Measure:** Young children use nonstandard and/or standard units to measure observable attributes of objects. When measuring with standard units in science, children should have the opportunity to use metric units as well as U.S. customary ones. (Chapter 5 in this book discusses important concepts PreK/Primary children learn about measurement.) Carefully measuring things more than once is also a good practice.

Skill 2.2: Evaluate and interpret pictorial representations, charts, tables, and graphs of authentic data from scientific investigations to make predictions, construct explanations, and support conclusions.

There are many ways for children to record and display data in early childhood classrooms. One is a **tally chart**, which is a way to record frequency data, such as how many birds came to the bird feeder outside the classroom window this morning. Graphs are a way to organize data. There are several types of graphs that are commonly used in PreK/Primary classrooms. **Real graphs** use actual objects. Suppose you take the students in your class outside to collect leaves. They can make a real class graph to show how many of each type of leaf they collected. **Picture graphs** are slightly more abstract than real graphs because they use pictures to represent objects. **Bar graphs** are more abstract than picture graphs. They use bars to represent data. Young children can use **line plots** to show data along a numeric scale, such as daily high temperatures for one week. They can use **line graphs** to record the height of a plant over a two-week period.

Data displays like pictures, charts, tables, and graphs enable children to notice patterns in data. First, they must pay attention to the title of the graph. It provides information about what data is being displayed. They also need to notice the labels on the x- and y-axes. Children can make predictions. Suppose you have the children in your class drop a tennis ball from 100 cm, 80 cm, and 60 cm above a table and measure how high it bounces. They graph this data on a bar graph. They observe that each time the ball bounces about half the height from which it was dropped. They can use this information to predict how high the ball will bounce if it is dropped from a height of 40 cm. Students can also compare the predictions they made before completing an investigation to their actual results.

Data displays help students construct explanations and support their conclusions. After placing plants in several different locations around the classroom, children can measure their height each day and construct a graph to display the data. They can construct an explanation of the types of conditions under which plants grow best. They can refer to their graph to support their conclusions. The important point is that data displays must be interpreted. We can notice that more robins than blue jays came to the bird feeder every day last week, but scientists want to know why that might be the case. Possible explanations for the discrepancy could lead to new investigations that further increase our understanding of bird behavior.

Skill 2.3: Analyze the dynamic nature of science as a way of understanding the world (e.g., tentativeness, replication, reliance on evidence).

What makes science unique from other academic disciplines? When people talk about the nature of science (NOS), they are referring to the way science generates knowledge and the values and assumptions that underlie the practices of science. Some important characteristics of science as a way of knowing are:

- Its focus on the natural world: Science produces explanations about the natural and physical world. It does not answer questions about the supernatural.

- It assumes that pattern and order exist and can be discerned: The world is understandable because there are patterns that can be observed and explained.

- It relies on evidence: Scientists base explanations on evidence. Accurate observations and precise measurements are important for generating scientific explanations. Science is not based on beliefs or opinions—although admittedly scientists have beliefs and opinions about many things, including the value of their own work and that of their colleagues. Theories and explanatory models in science, however, emerge from the results of many investigations by individuals and teams of scientists. They are scrutinized all the time by other investigators to see if they still are our best ideas about particular phenomena and are refined as new evidence is collected.

- Its durability and its tentativeness: Because scientific knowledge is based on evidence, it is durable and can be trusted at any given point in time as the best explanation for how different aspects of the world work or function. Nonetheless, science is open to the possibility that new evidence may require modifications of a scientific theory, and in rarer instances, the replacement of one scientific theory with a new one.

- The need for replicability: Scientists should be able to investigate the same question using the same methods and achieve similar results. Replicability is vitally important to science because it increases the strength of the evidence used to support a scientific explanation. Replicability also helps scientists understand the limitations of any particular set of studies by showing situations in which the scientific principle does not apply.

Skill 2.4: Identify and select appropriate tools, including digital technologies, and units of measurement for various science tasks.

Measurement is an integral part of science that enables children to apply what they learn in mathematics about measurement in authentic contexts as well as developing a "feel" for which tool (or perhaps tools) is appropriate for a given situation. It is important that they have an opportunity to use a variety of measuring tools for different tasks, not just rulers to measure length. Students must choose the correct tool for a specific attribute (e.g., volume is measured with a measuring cup, not a ruler). When measuring an attribute, they must determine which tool measures that attribute most appropriately. For example, it is more appropriate to measure the length of the playground with a trundle wheel rather than a ruler. Young children also need to learn how to properly read measuring instruments (e.g., read a measuring cup, beaker, or graduated cylinder at eye level). Nonstandard units of measurement enable children to focus on the measuring process. Children can create their own rulers, wind vanes, or anemometers. (The mathematics chapter in this book discusses other important ideas about measurement that students learn in the PreK/Primary years.)

Science Tools for PreK/Primary Classrooms

Tool	Use
Ruler, meterstick, or trundle wheel	Measures lengths and distances in metric or U.S. Customary units. Children can also use nonstandard measuring tools such as Unifix cubes or index cards to measure length.
Thermometer	Measures temperature in Celsius or Fahrenheit.
Measuring cup, spoon, graduated cylinder, or beaker	Measures capacity of a container or volume of a substance in metric or U.S. Customary units.
Hand lens or microscope	Magnifies object being observed to enable students to see greater detail.
Binoculars or telescope	Enables user to see objects that are far away; telescopes are used to see objects in space.
Balance or scale	Measures the mass of objects. It can be a pan, triple-beam, or electronic balance, but you can also use a bathroom scale for objects with large masses.
Wind vane	Measures wind direction.
Anemometer	Measures wind speed.
Digital camera	Records observations, especially when accurate drawings are difficult.
Calculator	Performs mathematical calculations, especially when calculating by hand would detract from the learning outcome.
iPad, tablet computer, or smartphone	Performs functions of digital camera and calculator. Also enables students to create data displays, share data with others, and measure elapsed time, can access online resources.
Digital probeware	Collects and records data with a high degree of precision and creates data displays.

Many young children use digital tools regularly outside of school. Calculators are useful in science when children need to perform calculations that are beyond their current level in mathematics or when doing the calculations by hand would take so long that they would detract from the lesson's science learning outcome. Children can use digital cameras to record observations of living things around the school. The images can be used as evidence for students' claims. Smartphones, iPads, or tablet computers allow students to use a single device to perform the functions of a calculator and digital camera, as well as create data displays, share data with others in the class, and measure elapsed time. They can use a stylus to draw or write on the screen, drawing attention to specific features in digital images or data displays.

Several companies produce digital probeware systems suitable for children. They are comprised of sensors to measure attributes like temperature, motion, pressure, light, etc., that connect to handheld or desktop computers so data can be collected and displayed in real time. Young children need practice using and reading measuring tools, so digital probeware should not replace tactile experiences in early childhood classrooms. Probeware can supplement those concrete learning opportunities and give young children practice with simpler versions of the types of tools used by practicing scientists and engineers.

Skill 2.5: Evaluate the relationship between claims (e.g., including predictions), evidence (i.e., scientific knowledge, observations), and explanations (i.e., linking claims to evidence, drawing conclusions).

Scientists use reasoning to construct scientific explanations based on the evidence they collect. Some PreK/Primary teachers use the Claims-Evidence-Reasoning (CER) framework to teach children about the relationships among these three constructs (Zembal-Saul, McNeill, & Hershberger, 2013). A **claim** is a statement that answers a testable question or problem. A student might predict the answer to the question. **Predictions** are based on prior knowledge and reasoning. They are *not* simply guesses. As students complete a scientific investigation, they make **observations** and collect **evidence** or scientific data. They use that data to support the claim. Very young children can link claims with evidence. By third grade they can begin to draw on scientific principles or scientific knowledge to tell how specific evidence supports a claim. This part involves scientific reasoning and the ability to draw conclusions, more sophisticated tasks than linking claims to evidence.

Skill 2.6: Identify and analyze attitudes and dispositions underlying scientific thinking (e.g., curiosity, openness to new ideas, appropriate skepticism, cooperation).

Scientific habits of mind are the dispositions or values, attitudes, and skills that foster scientific thinking skills. Scientists and children are curious about how the world works. It is important for PreK/Primary teachers to provide children with many opportunities to ask and investigate questions about the natural and physical world. Scientists are open to new ideas and are willing to modify their conceptions in the face of new evidence. Young children need to be encouraged to conduct investigations that challenge their current ideas and to view changing their ideas as a result of new evidence positively. Scientists are appropriately skeptical. They do not accept new theories simply because they are popular. Rather, they evaluate the strength of the evidence for the new theory. Emphasizing the importance of evidence can help young children begin to balance openness to new ideas with appropriate skepticism. Scientists seek opportunities to cooperate and collaborate with others. For PreK/Primary children, this means learning to listen to the ideas of others, waiting one's turn to speak, sharing materials and responsibilities, and considering a classmate's point of view. Early childhood teachers can foster a classroom climate in which children are encouraged to question the teacher's ideas in an appropriate, respectful manner and, in turn, the teacher shows openness to new ideas grounded in evidence.

Skill 2.7: Identify and analyze ways in which science is an interdisciplinary process and interconnected to STEM disciplines (i.e., science, technology, engineering, mathematics).

Science is not simply a subject students learn in school. Many jobs in the 21st century will be in the areas of science, technology, engineering, or mathematics. STEM education recognizes the interconnectedness of science, technology, engineering, and mathematics and can help prepare students for careers in those fields. Rather than teaching each subject separately, STEM education integrates them using real-world contexts. This is the approach taken by the Next Generation Science Standards (NGSS, 2013) discussed earlier. Scientists construct explanations of how the natural world operates. Engineers apply knowledge of the natural world to design and create solutions to perceived human problems. Scientists and engineers use mathematics and technology to record and analyze data. Many fields, like meteorology, employ complex computer modeling to construct explanations and make predictions. Scientists and engineers both use the tools that engineers create. In recent years, many have advocated for changing STEM to STEAM to recognize the role of the arts and design in innovation.

An integrated STEM approach in PreK/Primary classrooms focuses on inquiry and problem-based learning. Play fosters curiosity and is the primary way young children investigate the natural world. Children generate questions as they play which they can then investigate. They naturally use what they are learning to engage in engineering design, such as by modifying a ramp so a car will roll farther once it leaves the ramp.

Skill 2.8: Analyze considerations of science technology in society including cultural, ethical, economic, political, and global implications.

Humans have long been curious about the natural world. Ancient societies like the Egyptians, Chinese, and Greeks all made observations and constructed explanations about the physical world. Scientific discoveries have impacted the way we view the world around us and our quality of life. As scientific investigations became more methodical, the demand for new technologies to enhance scientific research has grown. Inventions like the compound microscope, telescope, electron microscope, and computer, to name a few, have all impacted the ability of scientists to study the natural world.

The needs of individuals or societies often drives scientific and technological research. Widespread deaths from diseases like smallpox or cholera wiped out many communities. Learning that pathogens like viruses and bacteria cause many diseases has greatly improved human life expectancy. Improved understandings about electricity have led to the development of electric lights that enable us to read at night, refrigerators to preserve our food, and air conditioners that allow us to feel comfortable in hot weather. Sometimes developments in scientific and technological fields result in new inventions that create "wants" which quickly become "needs"—like smartphones.

Thanks to the development of sophisticated manufacturing, transportation, and distribution systems, humans can purchase food and manufactured goods produced far from their homes. Moreover, they can receive those goods quickly—often only a day or two after ordering them. These systems have increased global trade and have influenced where and how goods are manufactured. Human desire for more efficient ways to communicate with others at a distance led to the development and improvement of the telegraph system, landline phones, cell phones, and ultimately smartphones.

Sometimes politics influence scientific priorities. The space race between the U.S. and the Soviet Union in the latter part of the 20th century is an example. The Soviet Union's ability to successfully launch a human into orbit and return him safely to Earth shocked the U.S. and its allies. President John F. Kennedy gave a speech in 1961 in which he set a goal of the U.S. putting a person on the Moon and safely returning the astronaut to Earth by the end of the decade. The U.S. government provided significant funding for scientists and engineers working on developing the necessary technologies to achieve that goal.

All technological advances have trade-offs. Some people argued during the height of the space race that money spent on space exploration would be better spent solving human problems such as poverty. Transportation systems enable us to transport goods rapidly across great distances but they have increased air and water pollution. Smartphones have greatly increased the capacity for communication, entertainment, and productivity. At the same time, concerns have been raised about their impact on social interactions, sleep patterns, distraction, and users' privacy.

Scientific understanding can inform policy at local, state, national, and international levels. City governments may decide to restrict water usage during droughts. State and national legislatures may pass laws restricting greenhouse gas emissions from factories. The Paris climate agreement adopted in 2015, is an international attempt to reduce greenhouse gas emissions and keep global mean temperature increases to less than 2°C above pre-industrial levels. The 2°C figure was determined based upon scientific consensus regarding the likely impact of increased global mean temperatures on climate change.

Scientists study the natural world to better understand how it works. Technological advances are often a by-product of original scientific work, but there are also examples of new technologies being created when scientific understanding of why it works the way it does still eludes us. It is also true that not all technological advances have used scientific understandings for the good of humanity. Some technologies have depleted resources, increased pollution and disrupted ecosystems, or been used to develop weapons of mass destruction. Scientists and engineers increasingly dialogue with philosophers and ethicists to better understand the ethical dimensions of their work. These discussions have led to the creation and adoption of ethical standards for research practices, communication of results to academic and general audiences, and review of research projects by people outside of the research team to ensure that the proposed activities comply with agreed-upon standards of conduct.

Competency 3: Knowledge of Earth and Space Sciences

Skill 3.1: Identify the living and nonliving composition of the Earth's surface and the properties of the nonliving materials that make up Earth's surface (e.g., soil, minerals, rocks, water).

Earth's outer layer, or crust, is composed of rock. About 70% of its surface is covered by water. Of that, about 97% is in the oceans. The remaining 3% is divided between water in lakes and streams, groundwater, glacial ice, in living things, and the atmosphere. Water is essential to life. Water is unique because it is the only substance that occurs naturally as a solid, liquid, and gas at Earth's surface. Water is the primary agent that changes Earth's features.

There are three different types of rocks found at Earth's surface. Each one is named for the way it is formed. **Igneous rocks** are formed from liquid rock or magma that cools. When magma cools slowly below Earth's surface, it produces rocks with larger, visible crystals like granite. Magma that erupts at Earth's surface either from a volcano or fractures in Earth's crust is known as lava. When lava erupts at the surface, it cools quickly so crystals are small. **Sedimentary rocks** form from sediments of other rocks of any type. As rock is weathered at Earth's surface, sediments get moved and deposited in new locations. Material near the bottom gets compacted. Over long periods of time, sedimentary rock is formed. Because sedimentary rock forms at the surface, a lot of rock outcrops are sedimentary. **Metamorphic rocks** are also formed from preexisting rocks; however, they are formed below Earth's surface as a result of heat, pressure, or the presence of chemically active fluids. When metamorphic rocks form, the texture of the minerals that make up the rocks changes, and sometimes the chemical composition of the rocks changes too.

Rocks are mixtures of **minerals.** Sometimes people think the words *mineral* and *rock* are synonyms, but that is not correct. Minerals are the ingredients for rocks in a manner that is similar to the ingredients in a tossed salad. Not all tossed salads are the same, and not all rocks are made of the same mixture of minerals. Minerals are naturally occurring, nonliving solids that have a definite crystalline structure and chemical composition. Minerals can be identified by their physical properties. The table below lists some common properties of minerals.

Mineral Property	What it Means
Streak	The color of the powder left behind when you rub a mineral on an unglazed porcelain tile.
Hardness	The measure of a mineral's resistance to being scratched.
Luster	The way a mineral reflects light; minerals that look like metals have metallic luster; nonmetallic minerals could be glassy, pearly, silky, or dull, to name a few.
Fracture or Cleavage	Some minerals break along smooth lines. They are said to have cleavage. Minerals that do not break along uneven or sometimes curved surfaces display fracture.
Color	Color is the most visible of all properties, but it is the least reliable way to identify a mineral. That's because some minerals, like quartz, come in a variety of colors.

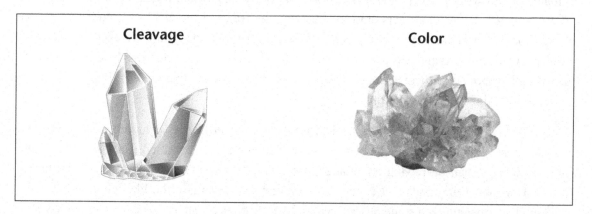

Cleavage   **Color**

The main component of **soil** is sediment, which is weathered rock and mineral fragments. Soil also contains air, water, and the decayed remains of plants and animals. Soils vary from place to place depending upon the topography of the land, drainage, the type of mineral and rock fragments, climate, the presence of plants and animals, and the length of time the soil has been forming. Because of these factors, soils are different colors. They also differ in their ability to retain water and support the growth of plants. Weathered rock and mineral sediments are classified according to their size. Some soils contain rock fragments of various sizes. The three smallest particles in soil are sand, silt, and clay. Sand is the largest of the three. Sandy soil doesn't hold water well; water drains right through it. Silt feels like flour. Its grains are smaller so it holds water better than sand. Clay is the smallest particle. Clay soils often feel sticky.

Soil forms when rocks are weathered physically and chemically. Leaves, twigs, and decomposed animals and microorganisms are examples of organic matter that is another part of soil. As animals burrow in soil they expose it to more weathering, form passages for water to move through, and introduce air into the soil. There are different layers of soil, with the top layer containing a lot of organic matter and the bottom-most layer composed of underlying bedrock from which the soil is formed.

Skill 3.2: Identify the processes that change the surface of the Earth.

Earth's surface is constantly changing as a result of constructive and destructive processes. Physical and chemical weathering are destructive processes that change Earth's materials physically or chemically. **Physical weathering**, which is also known as mechanical weathering, breaks material into smaller pieces, but the chemical composition of the material does not change. This is akin to you taking a sledge hammer and breaking a rock with it. The rock shatters into pieces but its chemical composition does not change. Physical weathering can occur in several ways. In cooler climates, liquid water seeps into cracks in rock. Water expands when it gets close to its freezing point. When the temperature gets close to freezing, the water in the cracks expands and pushes outward on the rock, breaking it into pieces. When igneous rock like granite is exposed at Earth's surface, outer layers expand and peel away in sheets. This occurs because there is less pressure on the rock from above than there is from below. *Half Dome* in Yosemite National Park in California is an example of this type of weathering.

Biologic activity can also cause physical weathering. Plant roots, including trees, grow into cracks in rock. As the plant grows, the roots exert pressure on the rock and cause it to break into smaller pieces. Small burrowing animals expose rock at the surface where it can be weathered further. Humans create roads that expose rock outcrops and increase the likelihood they will be weathered. Temperatures in some desert locations can vary as much as 30° C in a single day. The thermal expansion and cooling of rocks in an environment with large daily temperature changes can cause them to break apart, though this type of physical weathering is not as significant as scientists once thought it was.

Rocks can also undergo **chemical weathering**, which causes them to change their chemical composition. Certain minerals, like limestone, dissolve in slightly acidic rainwater. This dissolution is responsible for the sinkholes that are common in Florida. Minerals that are rich in iron or those that contain silica both react chemically with water. Although the specific reactions are different, both result in the breakdown of rock into new materials. Weathering rates and the type of weathering a rock undergoes are influenced by the characteristics of the rock and the climate.

Erosion and weathering are sometimes confused, but they are different processes. Erosion is the movement of Earth materials by water, wind, or ice. Every time a raindrop hits Earth's surface it moves tiny particles of soil. Surface runoff after a rainstorm carries sediment into streams and rivers. Some of that sediment eventually makes its way to the ocean. The size of the particles and the amount and speed of water influence rates of erosion and the type of material that will be eroded. Water is the most significant agent of erosion even in desert climates that get little rainfall each year. Wind can also erode Earth materials but it usually moves smaller particles than water and generally does not carry them as great a distance. Glacial ice erodes Earth materials as it moves. Significant portions of Long Island in New York are made up of material that was left behind when a glacier covering that area retreated northward about 20,000 years ago.

When material is transported by water, wind, or ice via erosion, it is ultimately deposited somewhere else. **Deposition** is a constructive process that produces new landforms. Deltas, like the Mississippi River delta in Louisiana, and portions of Long Island, New York, are examples of depositional landforms.

Skill 3.3: Analyze the effects of the law of gravity on objects on Earth and in space.

The law of gravity states that every object in the universe attracts every other object. The size of the force between two objects depends upon the mass of each object and how far apart they are. Gravity is a pulling force. It is what keeps us from floating off into space. All objects at or near Earth's surface are pulled toward Earth's center due to gravity. Because Earth is so massive, it exerts a greater gravitational pull on you than other objects. Even when you temporarily overcome gravity by throwing a ball up into the air, it will ultimately fall back to Earth.

The force of gravity exerted by the Sun is the force that keeps the planets and other solar system objects in their orbits. Without gravity, the planets would fly off in a straight line. The gravitational pull between the Earth and the Moon keeps the Moon in its orbit around Earth and satellites of other planets around their respective orbits.

Skill 3.4: Identify and distinguish distant objects seen in the daytime and nighttime sky (e.g., Sun, stars, planets, Moon).

The Sun, Moon, stars, and other planets are always present, but whether we can see them depends on the Earth's position in space. The Sun is the closest star to Earth and the only one in our solar system. As a result, we can typically only see the Sun during the daytime. The exception is the Moon, and occasionally Venus, Mars, and Jupiter. Within a week of the full Moon, the Moon is faintly visible. Look in the sky opposite to the Sun's location. The planets Mercury, Venus, Mars, Jupiter, and Saturn can be seen with the naked eye at night for much of the year, if you know where to look in the sky. As a general rule, planets appear in the sky as bright disks, whereas stars appear to twinkle.

Skill 3.5: Identify and analyze the causes and effects of atmospheric processes (e.g., weather, wind, water cycle).

Global weather patterns are caused by the uneven heating of Earth's surface by the Sun and the transfer of heat energy from the equator to the poles. The equator receives more heat energy from the Sun than the North and South poles do. Earth's atmosphere acts as a conveyer belt to move warm air from equatorial regions to the poles. Air in the atmosphere moves both horizontally (from the equator to the poles) and vertically. Daily and seasonal temperature, precipitation, and air pressure changes are related to this movement. Smaller-scale atmospheric circulation patterns also impact weather. Warm air rises in the atmosphere and creates an area of low atmospheric pressure. Cool air sinks in the atmosphere and creates an area of high atmospheric pressure. Low pressure is associated with precipitation and high pressure is associated with clear skies. Wind occurs when there are horizontal air pressure differences at Earth's surface. Air moves from areas of high pressure to areas of low pressure.

Water moves above, at, and below Earth's surface via the water or hydrological cycle, which plays a major role in our changing weather. There are four main parts to the water cycle.

Process	What it Means
Evaporation	Water evaporates, or becomes water vapor, when water in oceans, rivers, lakes, or soil is heated by the Sun's energy. Water vapor is a gas that rises in the atmosphere. Plants release water vapor into the atmosphere in a process called transpiration.
Condensation	When water vapor cools sufficiently, it condenses into liquid water. Clouds are formed when water vapor in the atmosphere condenses. Fog is an example of condensation that happens at the surface. When you go outside in the morning and find dew on the grass, this is another example of condensation of water vapor. In northern climates, frost occurs when water vapor goes directly from a gas to a solid (ice).
Precipitation	Precipitation occurs when ice crystals or water droplets (in warmer climates) in clouds become large and heavy enough to fall toward Earth's surface. The air temperature near the ground will determine whether the precipitation is rain, snow, sleet, or freezing rain.
Collection or Filtration	When precipitation falls to Earth, it ends up in lakes, rivers, or oceans. Some falls directly into a body of water. Some soaks into the ground and eventually makes its way to a river or ocean. Another possibility is that the precipitation doesn't soak into the ground but instead runs along the surface into a body of water. Some precipitation might not be collected. Instead, it might evaporate from the leaves of plants, for example.

The model of the water cycle below is an idealized model. There is not a single pathway that all molecules of water follow through the cycle.

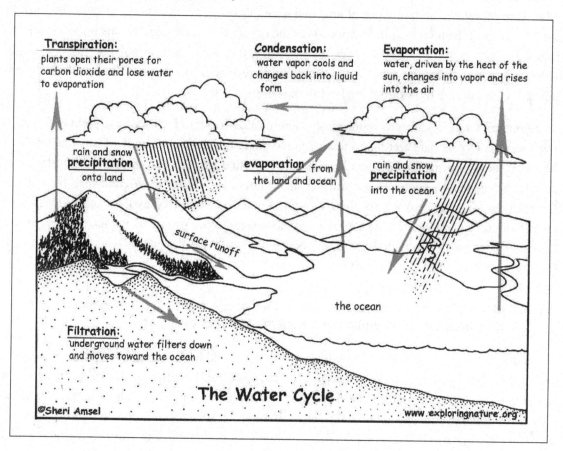

Transpiration:
plants open their pores for carbon dioxide and lose water to evaporation

Condensation:
water vapor cools and changes back into liquid form

Evaporation:
water, driven by the heat of the sun, changes into vapor and rises into the air

rain and snow **precipitation** onto land

evaporation from the land and ocean

rain and snow **precipitation** into the ocean

surface runoff

the ocean

Filtration:
underground water filters down and moves toward the ocean

The Water Cycle

©Sheri Amsel   www.exploringnature.org

Skill 3.6: Interpret and predict the direct and indirect effects of the Sun's energy on Earth, including plants, animals, water, land, and air.

The Sun's energy is the ultimate source of the heat and light living things need to survive. In fact, the cycling of energy through the living and nonliving parts of the Earth system begins with the Sun. The amount of sunlight an environment receives determines what plants and animals live there. Plants use energy from the Sun to produce their own food through photosynthesis. Not all plants require the same amount of sunlight. If a plant receives either more or less sunlight than it needs, it will not thrive. Some plants go dormant during times of the year when they receive less light and heat energy from the Sun. Warmer temperatures and more light cause them to begin growing again.

Animals depend on sunlight for their survival. Animals that eat plants or those that eat other animals that eat plants benefit indirectly from photosynthesis. Cold-blooded animals like snakes sometimes sit in the Sun during the day to raise their body temperature. Sunlight produces Vitamin D, which helps maintain strong bones. If an organism doesn't get enough sunlight, its bones may become brittle and break easily. Too much sunlight can also be a problem. Harmful UV rays can cause sunburn and skin cancer.

Sunlight warms water, land, and air. When the Sun's energy reaches Earth's atmosphere, some of it is reflected back into space and some is scattered in the atmosphere. About 30% is absorbed by either land or water. Different types of land and water absorb the Sun's energy at different rates. In turn, the air over them warms. In locations near the ocean, the air over land heats up more quickly during the day than the air over the water. Warm air over the land rises and cooler air from the ocean rushes in, creating a sea breeze. At nighttime this is reversed. The air over the land cools more quickly. A land breeze blows from the land to the ocean.

Some land surfaces absorb more solar radiation than others. That's why a parking lot feels much warmer to your bare feet than a nearby grassy area. Proximity to a body of water affects how the Sun's energy warms a place. San Francisco, California, and Wichita, Kansas, are at the same latitude. Yet generally, summers are warmer and winters are colder in Wichita than they are in San Francisco. That is because the climate of San Francisco is affected by the Pacific Ocean. The amount of sunlight an environment receives influences the types of organisms that can live there. The ocean becomes colder with depth. That's because less of the Sun's energy reaches deeper areas. Soil is cooler the deeper you dig for the same reason.

Skill 3.7: Identify the components and significance of space research and exploration (e.g., timelines, tools and equipment, benefits and cost to society).

In the 20th century scientists developed rockets that could be launched into space, initially for military use. The space race took off in earnest during the Cold War after World War II. In 1957, the Soviet Union launched *Sputnik I*, the first artificial satellite to orbit Earth. This caught Americans off guard and raised concerns that the U.S. was falling behind the Soviet Union in terms of technology. The U.S. followed by launching its first satellite in 1958. The Soviets also sent the first human into space when Yuri Gagarin orbited the Earth for 108 minutes in 1961.

U.S. Manned Space Flight

The U.S. Congress established the National Aeronautics and Space Administration (NASA) in 1958. Alan Shepard became the first American in space in 1961, and the next year John Glenn was the first American to orbit the Earth. A major goal of the U.S. Apollo program in the 1960s was to land a person on the Moon. After a series of missions in which astronauts orbited the Moon, Neil Armstrong and Edwin "Buzz" Aldrin became the first humans to step on the Moon's surface in July 1969. The final Moon landing took place in 1972.

One problem with early manned spacecraft was that they could only be used once, which was expensive. In the 1980s, the U.S. began using space shuttles, reusable vehicles that could transport humans and materials to and from space. A shuttle takes off like a rocket and then lands back on Earth like an airplane. Shuttle missions were launched from Cape Canaveral in Florida. Many have landed there, but if weather conditions were not favorable in Florida, shuttles landed in other locations such as Edwards Air Force Base in California. In all there were 135 shuttle missions, and 133 of them ended successfully. Human space travel has risks, though. In 1986, the space shuttle

Challenger was launched from Cape Canaveral. On board was Christa McAuliffe, who was to be the first teacher in space. There was tremendous excitement surrounding this shuttle mission and many classrooms across the U.S. tuned in to watch the launch. A little more than a minute after lift-off the shuttle exploded, killing everyone on board. Then in 2003, the shuttle *Columbia* broke apart on reentry into Earth's atmosphere, killing the entire crew. The space shuttle program ended in 2011.

A space station is a satellite that orbits Earth and enables scientists to research a variety of topics including how the human body responds to being in space for long periods of time. The Soviet Union launched and used the first satellites in the 1970s to the end of the century. In 1998, 15 countries, including the U.S., developed the International Space Station. Current plans call for the ISS to be operated through at least 2024.

Unmanned Space Exploration

Humans have traveled to the Moon, but space travel to other parts of the solar system is not currently possible. The trip could take years or decades, and conditions on other objects in the solar system are dangerous. Scientists have turned to unmanned space vehicles to explore those locations. Space probes are essentially robots that either fly by or land on a planet or moon. Probes take photos and send data back to Earth for scientists to analyze. The New Horizons **space probe** arrived at Pluto in 2015 and began sending data back to Earth. **Orbiters** travel to a planet and orbit around it. Like probes, orbiters take photos and send them back to Earth for analysis. Both the U.S. and the European Space Agency have sent orbiters to Mars.

Timeline of Key Events in Space Exploration

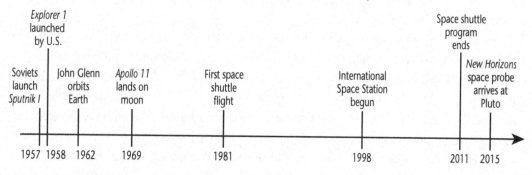

Benefits and Costs of Space Exploration

The space industry has benefited humankind in several ways. It is responsible for many technological advances. Technologies originally developed for the space program have revolutionized communication. Materials developed for spacesuits have been adapted for sports equipment and uniforms and gear for firefighters. A material originally designed for use in parachutes for spacecraft landing on other planets is now used in radial tires. Prosthetic limbs and robotic surgery both have links to the space program. The space program led to an influx of people to Florida, which attracted new businesses to the state.

Arguments about the downside of space exploration often center on the cost. Congressional funding for NASA was at its peak during the 1960s during the Apollo program. Since then funding levels have decreased. Nonetheless, NASA's current yearly budget is around $21 billion per year. Some argue that money could be better spent on addressing societal issues on Earth.

Skill 3.8: Identify and describe repeated patterns in the Sun-Earth-Moon system (e.g., the day-night cycle, phases of the Moon, seasons).

To an observer standing on Earth, it *appears* as if the Sun rises from the horizon in the east, moves across the sky, and then sets in the west each day. The real reason we experience day and night is because Earth rotates on its axis every 24 hours. As Earth rotates different locations on Earth face the Sun and experience daylight. As Earth continues to rotate, those same locations no longer face the Sun and experience night.

Earth experiences seasons due to its revolution around the Sun. In everyday speech, people often use **rotate** and **revolve** as synonyms. They are *not* synonymous when referring to Earth's movement in space. The Earth rotates when it spins on its axis. It revolves around the Sun as it travels in its orbital path. Earth is tilted on its axis approximately 23.5°. When the north pole is oriented toward the Sun, locations north of the equator experience summer. The Sun's rays strike the northern hemisphere more directly and for more hours each day (days are longer). When the north pole is oriented away from the Sun, locations north of the equator experience winter. The Sun's rays strike the northern hemisphere at a lower angle and for fewer hours each day (days are shorter). The longest day of the year in the northern hemisphere occurs around June 21 and is known as the **summer solstice**. The shortest day is around December 21 and is known as the **winter solstice**. Seasons are opposite in the northern and southern hemispheres. When it is winter in the northern hemisphere, it is summer in the southern hemisphere and vice-versa. Many people incorrectly think that seasons occur because the Earth is farther from the Sun during the winter than it is in the summer. Distance is not a factor in seasonal temperature change. In fact, when it is summer in the northern hemisphere, Earth is closer to the Sun than when locations north of the equator experience summer. Seasonal temperature differences are greater closer to the poles than closer to the equator. That is because even in winter, the Sun's rays still strike Earth's surface at fairly high angles at lower latitudes. During spring and autumn neither pole is oriented toward the Sun so neither hemisphere is receiving more direct sunlight than the other. Days and nights are about the same length. We use the word "equinox" to signify equal time periods. The **spring equinox** occurs on March 20 or 21, and the **autumnal** (or **fall**) **equinox** can occur from September 21 to 24.

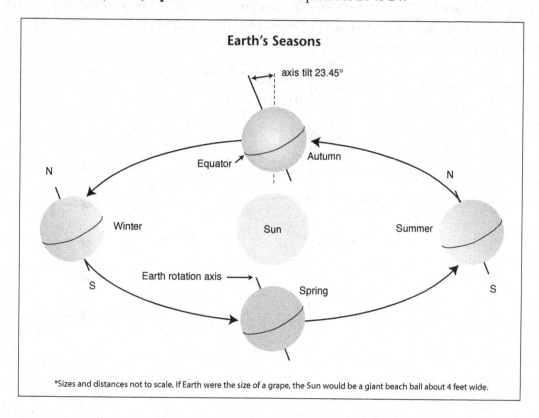

Earth's Seasons

axis tilt 23.45°

Equator
Autumn
N

N

Winter
Sun
Summer

S

Earth rotation axis →
Spring

S

*Sizes and distances not to scale. If Earth were the size of a grape, the Sun would be a giant beach ball about 4 feet wide.

If you regularly observe the Moon, you know that it does not always appear the same in the night sky. Moon phases are caused by a changing pattern in the relative positions of the Sun, Earth, and Moon as it orbits around Earth. The Moon does not produce its own light. Instead it reflects light from the Sun. One-half of the Moon is always illuminated by the Sun, but observers on Earth do not always see all of the entire lit portion. When the Moon is positioned between the Sun and Earth, the lit portion is not visible from Earth, and we have a new Moon. As the Moon continues to revolve around the Earth, we see more and more of the lit side of the Moon, which means the Moon is **waxing**. Waxing means that to an Earth observer the right side of the Moon becomes increasingly visible each night. A few days after the new Moon we can see a small sliver on the right side, which is called a waxing crescent. When the Moon is about ¼ of the way through its path around the Earth, the entire right side of the Moon is visible. This is called the first quarter. A waxing gibbous Moon is one in which more than half, but less than the entire face of the Moon, is visible. When we can see the entire face of the Moon, we have a full Moon. This occurs when the Earth is positioned between the Sun and the Moon. For the first half of its cycle, we see more and more of the Moon each night. As the Moon continues in the second half of its orbit, we see less and less of the lit portion, which means the Moon is **waning.** When we see more than half of the left side of the Moon, but less than the full Moon, we have a waning gibbous Moon. The third quarter occurs when we see the entire left side lit. This occurs about ¾ of the way through the Moon's orbit around the Earth. When we can see only a sliver on the left side, we have a waning crescent Moon.

The Moon takes approximately 27 days to orbit the Earth, but it is about 29 days from one new Moon to the next. What is the reason for the discrepancy? It is due to the fact that the Moon and Earth are both moving. This means the Moon must travel a little farther than 360⁰ so that it is between the Earth and the Sun.

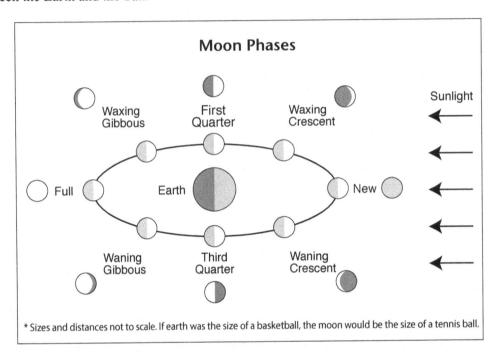

Skill 3.9: Analyze the impact of human activity on renewable and nonrenewable resources and natural events, including preparation for severe weather related events (e.g., hurricanes, tornadoes, flooding).

Humans use Earth's resources daily. **Renewable resources** are ones that are replenished over timescales of decades or less. **Nonrenewable resources** require millions of years to be replenished because the processes by which they form take a very long time. Fossil fuels, like coal, oil, and natural gas are examples of nonrenewable resources. Many aspects of modern life such as transportation and industry rely on the burning of fossil fuels. Air pollution, acid rain, and a rise in global temperatures due to CO_2 emissions are all by-products of burning fossil fuels. Hydraulic fracking—pumping high-pressure water into rocks—is increasingly being used to "squeeze" and extract natural gas and oil from rock layers. There has been an increase in earthquake activity in recent years in some areas where large-scale fracking occurs.

Human activity impacts many of Earth's processes. When natural vegetation is removed to build roads, sidewalks, and parking lots, surface runoff increases. More sediment gets washed into streams. Water that used to soak into the ground now runs into streams and rivers, increasing the volume of water in them, leading to a greater likelihood of flooding.

An overall rise in global sea temperatures is associated with an observed increase in hurricane activity. That is because hurricanes get their energy from moving across warm ocean waters. Their impact is also often felt more acutely in well-developed areas.

People can prepare for severe weather-related events. Tornadoes, floods, and hurricanes all occur in Florida. Tornadoes are associated with severe thunderstorms. Pay attention to weather reports and get weather alerts on your phone. If you are inside, go to a small interior room on the first floor. If you are outside and cannot get to shelter, lie face down on the ground. Get as far away from trees and buildings as you can. During the tornado cover your head and neck with your arms. If possible, wrap blankets around you or shield yourself with furniture. This is because even small fragments of wood or other items are moving so rapidly in the winds (100–200 mph) that they can be deadly. Keep monitoring weather reports to know when it is safe to come out.

Flooding generally occurs after significant rain or as a result of storm surge from a hurricane. If you are in an area that is under a flood warning and are told to evacuate, you should do so. Put all important documents in a waterproof container. Never drive, walk, or try to swim through flooded areas. If you are unable to evacuate, move to the highest floor of the building.

Floridians are well-acquainted with hurricanes. Hurricane season is from June 1 to November 30 (which does not mean this is the only time they happen; it is just when they generally occur). Be aware of evacuation routes and know the location of emergency shelters. When a hurricane is forecast, keep your gas tank at least half full. Every household in Florida should have a hurricane preparation kit. Include a battery-operated radio, flashlights, matches, batteries, a three-day supply of water and non-perishable food for each person in the household, medicines, important documents (including IDs) in a waterproof container, personal hygiene items, and a first-aid kit. Bring objects like trash cans, patio furniture, and bicycles inside. Board up windows. If you are in an evacuation zone, evacuate when told to do so. Return to your home only when told it is safe to do so.

Competency 4: Knowledge of the Physical Sciences

Skill 4.1: Sort matter by its observable qualitative properties (e.g., shape, color, states, texture, hardness) and quantitative properties (e.g., mass, volume, temperature, weight, density).

Matter is what makes up everything in the universe. A sample of matter can be described by its properties. Qualitative properties can be observed, but they are generally not measured numerically. A substance (type of matter) might be round, rectangular, be made of one color, more than one color, or be colorless. It could be smooth or rough, hard or soft. It might be so small that you need a magnifier to see it, or it might be larger than the Earth. On Earth, matter can be in one of three states: **solid**, **liquid**, or **gas**. A substance's properties can change, as when it changes states.

A property may be true for a specific sample of matter. For example, a sample of water can be the size of a single drop or the size of a large lake. Both are still water. Some properties hold true regardless of the size of the sample. These are known as **characteristic properties.** They can be used to identify a substance. Boiling point and freezing point are examples of characteristic properties. A mineral's hardness is another characteristic property.

Quantitative properties are ones that can be measured numerically. All matter has mass and volume. **Mass** refers to the amount of matter in an object. **Weight** refers to the force of gravity on an object. An object's mass remains the same no matter where it is in the universe, but its weight does not. The gravity on Jupiter is much greater than it is on Earth, so you would weigh more on Jupiter than you weigh on Earth. However, your mass would remain the same. You would still contain the same amount of matter. In the early childhood years, teachers do not distinguish between weight and mass. That is dealt with in upper elementary and middle school.

An object's **volume** is the amount of space it takes up. All matter—solids, liquids, and gases—have volume. Third graders learn to calculate the volume of rectangular objects in mathematics by multiplying *length × width × height*. The volume of irregular objects is generally measured by displacement. Suppose you want to find the volume of a small pebble. Place a specific volume of water in a graduated cylinder. Place a container at the mouth of the cylinder to catch overflow. Now, drop the pebble into the cylinder with water. Notice the new water level in the cylinder. Subtract the *original volume of water* from the *volume of water and the pebble*. Your answer is the volume of the pebble. Mass and volume are true for a specific sample of matter. They are not characteristic properties.

Density is the relationship between an object's mass and its volume. It is defined as the amount of mass in a given volume of a substance. Mathematically, you can calculate density by dividing the object's mass by its volume.

$$Density = Mass \div Volume$$

Children in the early childhood years do not calculate density mathematically. Instead, they compare densities qualitatively, by investigating floating and sinking. Water's density is 1.0 g/mL (1.0 g/cm³). Objects whose density is greater than 1.0 g/cm³ sink when placed in water. Those whose density is less than 1.0 g/cm³ float. It is important that early childhood teachers not say or reinforce the idea that heavy objects sink and light objects float. If that were strictly true, an ocean liner (which weighs 20,000 to 60,000 tons) could not float. Instead, density is the ratio of the amount of matter in an object (its mass) to the amount of space it takes up (its volume). Density is a characteristic property and can be used to identify a substance. In fact, density is one property scientists use to identify minerals.

Temperature is another measurable property of matter. The particles in any substance—solid, liquid, or gas—are constantly in motion. Temperature is a measure of the average energy of motion of those particles. The faster the particles move, the greater the temperature. We use a thermometer to measure temperature. A thermometer is made of a glass or plastic tube sealed at both ends, with a bulb at the bottom containing colored liquid. As the temperature around the bulb increases, the colored liquid rises in the tube.

Skill 4.2: Categorize matter as an element, compound, or mixture and compare the similarities and differences among them.

Matter is anything that has mass and takes up space. Everything in the world—living and nonliving—is made up of matter. **Elements** are substances that are made up of only one type of matter, so they have definite properties. Elements cannot be chemically broken down into other substances. Two or more elements that are chemically combined are known as a **compound**. Like elements, compounds have definite properties. The properties of a compound are very different from the elements that form it, however. Hydrogen (H) and oxygen (O) are both invisible gases. When combined, they form water (H_2O). There are a little more than 100 recognized elements, but they combine chemically to form a great variety of compounds. A compound can only be separated by chemical means.

Two or more substances that are mixed together, but not chemically combined, are known as **mixtures.** A tossed salad is an example of a mixture. So is sweet tea. Substances in a mixture retain their individual properties. The tomatoes in your salad keep the properties of a tomato. Mixtures can be separated by physical means. Some mixtures are so well mixed that people sometimes think they are a single substance. These are called **solutions.** Sweet tea is an example. Even though a solution may appear to be a single substance, each part still retains its individual properties. The sugar is still sweet. You can separate the tea and sugar by boiling the sweet tea. You will be left with just the sugar.

Skill 4.3: Identify and differentiate between physical and chemical changes in matter.

Physical changes modify the form of a substance, but do not change it into a new substance. The substance retains its properties. Physical changes include things like cutting, tearing, folding, dissolving, and changing from one state of matter to another such as melting, freezing, boiling, or condensing. **Chemical changes** result in a new substance with different properties. Burning, rusting, and digesting food are examples of chemical changes. During some chemical changes one substance is broken down into two or more substances. In other chemical changes, two or more substances combine to form a new substance or substances. In all cases, the substances produced after a chemical change have different properties from the original substances.

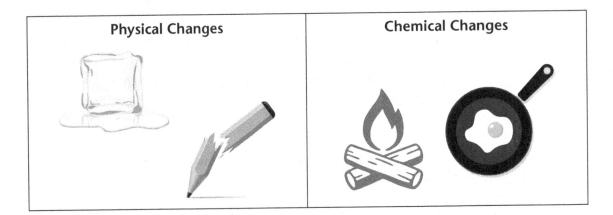

Physical Changes | Chemical Changes

Skill 4.4: Identify and compare types, characteristics, and functions of energy.

Scientists define energy as the ability to do work or cause a change in matter. There are two basic types of energy: **kinetic** and **potential.** Kinetic energy is energy of motion. A football traveling through the air has kinetic energy; so does a ball rolling down a hill. Potential energy is stored (on tap) or "possible" energy. It is the energy something has because of its position or condition. A skateboarder at the top of a ramp has potential energy.

Energy can come in many forms. **Mechanical energy** is sometimes confused with potential and kinetic energy. Mechanical energy is the sum of the energy of an object due either to its motion or its position. That means it is the sum of the object's potential and kinetic energy. **Chemical energy** is produced when bonds between atoms are broken during a chemical reaction. When you burn wood logs in a firepit, chemical energy is released and gets converted to **light** and **heat energy**. Light energy is one kind of radiant energy. The ultimate source of light energy is the Sun. Humans convert other forms of energy into light energy to enable us to see when it would otherwise be dark. **Sound energy** is caused when an object or substance vibrates. When you strike a drum with a drumstick, the head of the drum vibrates. The vibrations cause molecules in the air around the drum to vibrate. Eventually, sound waves reach your eardrum. **Heat (thermal) energy** is produced when molecules in a substance bump against each other. As thermal energy increases, the molecules move faster and the substance feels warmer. We use heat energy to cook our food and keep us warm when the weather is cool. **Electrical energy** is created by the flow of electrons. It is used to power electronic devices, machinery in factories, and many appliances. It is converted to other forms of energy to heat and light homes and businesses.

Skill 4.5: Identify and analyze ways energy is transferred between objects or the surrounding air.

Any form of energy can be converted into any other form or transferred from one place to another. According to the **law of conservation of energy**, energy is not created or destroyed. It is just transferred to a different form. Potential energy is converted to kinetic energy in several ways. When you stretch a rubber band, you give it potential energy. When you release the rubber band, it flies through the air due to its kinetic energy. A downhill skier at the top of a hill also has potential energy. When she starts down the hill, the potential energy is converted to kinetic energy.

The fact that energy can be transferred from one form to another is very important. Chemical energy contained in batteries is transferred to mechanical energy to power toys or electrical energy for a flashlight. Mechanical energy from falling water in a waterfall can be used to generate electricity and power factories. Thermal energy heats homes and enables us to cook our food. Energy transformations occur within and between organisms. Energy transfers within organisms enable cells to carry out their basic functions so the organism survives. Energy transfers between organisms occur as one organism eats another in a food chain.

Skill 4.6: Analyze and compare the relationship between forces (e.g., push or pull) and an object's change in position, direction, and/or speed.

A **force** is a push or pull on an object that occurs due to its interaction with another object. When a force acts upon an object, energy is transferred. Sometimes objects need to be touching to exert a force, such as when your foot strikes a soccer ball. This is known as a **contact force**. Sometimes objects do not need to be touching to exert a force. Place a paper clip on a table. Now, slowly move a magnet toward it. At some point the paper clip will move toward and attach to the magnet. Magnetism is an example of an **at-a-distance force**.

When a force is applied to an object, the object changes its position, direction, and/or speed. Isaac Newton developed three laws of motion that describe the relationship between forces and resulting motion. According to **Newton's First Law** (the law of inertia), objects tend to keep doing what they are doing unless acted on by an outside force. This means that objects that are stationary remain stationary and objects in motion remain in motion at the same speed and direction until a force acts on them. Suppose you have a backpack sitting on the front seat of your car. The backpack and the car are moving at the same speed down the road. An animal darts out in front of you and you hit the brakes. What happens to the backpack? It flies off the seat onto the floor. Why? When you applied the brakes to the car (a force), the car changed its motion. No force was applied to the backpack so it continued at the same speed in the same direction. The more massive an object, the harder it is to change its motion. That is why it is harder for a large truck to stop moving than it is for a small car. **Newton's Second Law** says that more massive objects require a greater force to change its motion. If you throw a baseball and a bowling ball with the same force, the effect on the baseball will be greater. Forces always come in pairs. **Newton's Third Law** states that for every force (action) there is an equal and opposite force (action). When you sit in a chair, the pull of gravity exerts a downward force on you toward the center of the Earth. At the same time, the chair exerts an upward force on you that is equal to the downward force of gravity. If that didn't occur, you would be unable to sit in the chair.

Competency 5: Knowledge of the Life Sciences

Skill 5.1: Identify how plants and animals respond to their environment.

All living things respond to their environment. Something that causes an organism to respond is known as a **stimulus.** Stimuli can either be external or internal. A living thing's ability to sense and respond to a stimulus helps it thrive. The ability of a population to adapt to changing environmental conditions over time enables the species to survive.

Plants respond to the environment when roots grow downward due to gravity or when a plant grows toward a light source. Some plants also respond to touch. The stems of various vines wrap around objects they touch. In response to cooler temperatures, some trees stop producing chlorophyll. When that occurs, the tree's leaves change color and fall off the tree. Seeds generally germinate better in warmer temperatures; however, if temperatures are too high, germination slows. Plants do not all have the same optimal temperature range for growing. That is why plants that grow well in one climate often do poorly in another with very different temperature ranges.

Animals detect changes in the environment through their senses. Some animal responses to stimuli result in changes to their physical characteristics, while others lead to changes in behavior. Some animals grow thicker fur in the winter to survive colder temperatures. In others, the color of the fur changes from brown to white to better camouflage them from predators or prey. Some species migrate to warmer climates in the winter and then return in the spring. Others eat additional food to store up fat for the winter and then hibernate. If food supplies dwindle, animals may move to a location where food is more readily available.

All animals respond to immediate changes in the environment. Some flee in the face of danger, others fight, and still others remain completely still (or engage in a combination of the three depending on further changes in the environment). They might immerse themselves in the water when hot or find shelter during a storm. Some organisms change color to protect themselves from predators or in response to heat or humidity. Animals also respond to changes in their internal environments. When thirsty, they search for water and drink. When hungry they find and consume food. When tired, they sleep. These are but a few of the many ways animals respond to changes in their environment.

Skill 5.2: Identify basic concepts of heredity (e.g., why offspring resemble their parents).

Heredity is the passing on of traits from parents to their offspring. Organisms can reproduce **asexually or sexually.** Some can reproduce in both ways. Asexual reproduction occurs when a new organism is produced from the cells of a single parent. Many plants can reproduce asexually from their stems. In sexual reproduction, two parents contribute genetic material to the offspring.

(Asexual and sexual reproduction are discussed more fully in Skill 5.9 later in this chapter.) Members of the same species vary. Often children have observable physical traits similar to their parents, but sometimes they do not. Humans do not all have the same eye color. When a person with brown eyes and a person with blue eyes have a child, each person contributes equally to the child's DNA. What is the probability that the child will have blue eyes?

Genes that encode for specific traits come in pairs, known as **alleles.** Each parent contributes one of those alleles to the offspring. Some alleles are dominant. This means that if that allele is present, the offspring will always have that trait. Other alleles are recessive. This means that the trait is masked if a dominant allele is present. The offspring will only have the recessive trait if both parents contribute a recessive allele to the organism. In humans, the allele for brown eyes is dominant and the allele for blue eyes is recessive. A Punnett square is used to show all the possible combinations of alleles and their probabilities when someone with brown eyes and someone with blue eyes have a child. In the Punnett squares below, B = brown eyes and b = blue eyes.

When one parent has both alleles for brown eyes (BB), all the offspring will have brown eyes. This is because that parent can only contribute a brown eye allele to the offspring. When one parent has a brown eye allele *and* a blue eye allele (Bb), the parent will have brown eyes because brown is dominant. They can, however, contribute either a brown eye allele *or* a blue eye allele. This means there is a 50% probability that their offspring will have blue eyes. Finally, when both parents have a brown eye and a blue eye allele, both parents will have brown eyes. There is a 25% chance that their offspring will have blue eyes.

	B	B
b	Bb	Bb
b	Bb	Bb

	B	b
b	Bb	bb
b	Bb	bb

	B	b
B	BB	bB
b	Bb	bb

Skill 5.3: Classify plants and animals into major groups according to characteristics (e.g., physical features, behaviors, development).

Classification is the process of grouping things based on their similarities. By organizing living things into groups, scientists can more easily study them. In the 1750s, Carolus Linnaeus, a Swedish physician, developed a classification system for living things based on physical features. Evolutionary theory has changed the way scientists classify living things. Scientists realize that specific organisms are similar to one another because they share a common ancestor. Today's classification system contains six kingdoms. Sorting is based upon their type of cells, the number of cells in their bodies, and whether they produce their own food.

Classification in the PreK/Primary years focuses on two of those kingdoms: plants and animals. Children learn to classify organisms within those kingdoms based on their physical characteristics and behaviors.

Plants can be classified as either **vascular**, those that use roots and stems to transport nutrients, and **nonvascular**, those that do not transport nutrients via roots and stems. Trees and flowers are examples of vascular plants. Mosses are a type of nonvascular plant. Vascular plants can be further divided into those that produce seeds to reproduce and ones, like ferns, that reproduce via spores. Seed-producing plants could be **flowering,** like a rose or peach tree, or they could be **nonflowering,** like pine, fir, and spruce trees. The diagram below shows how the plant kingdom is further classified.

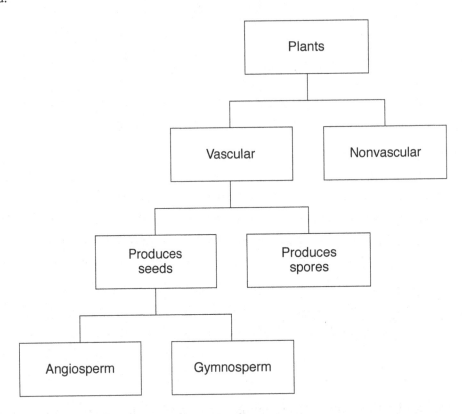

Animals are classified into two major groups, **vertebrates** and **invertebrates.** Vertebrates are animals with an internal skeleton with a backbone. Invertebrates do not have an internal skeleton with a backbone. While you are probably most familiar with vertebrate species, invertebrates make up over 90% of all animals on Earth. Worms are invertebrates. So are clams, oysters, and shrimp. **Arthropods** are another type of invertebrate. They account for an estimated 80% of all Earth's species. This group includes insects, spiders, scorpions, and centipedes. Because they have an **exoskeleton** on the outside of their body that acts like a hard shell or suit of armor, they must grow a new shell periodically and shed the old one as they grow. Arthropods all have segmented bodies.

Vertebrates have an **endoskeleton,** which is an internal one that provides support, helps the organisms move, and protects internal organs. They have muscles attached to their bones, and circulatory and nervous systems. Vertebrates can be divided into several groups as the table that follows shows.

Vertebrates

Type of Vertebrate	Characteristics
Fish	Cold-blooded which means their body temperature changes in response to temperature changes in their environment, get oxygen through gills, most have scales, fins, and lay eggs
Amphibians	Cold-blooded, most breathe with gills in water when young, go through metamorphosis, breathe through lungs as adults, and lay eggs
Reptiles	Cold-blooded, breathe through lungs, most lay eggs and have scales or plates
Birds	Warm-blooded, which means they have a fairly constant internal temperature regardless of temperature changes in their environment, breathe through lungs, have beaks, two wings, and two feet, lay eggs
Mammals	Warm-blooded, breathe through lungs, have live births, produce milk to feed babies, have fur or skin

Skill 5.4: Compare the ways living things meet their basic needs through interaction with and dependence on one another when sharing an environment (e.g., competition, predation, pollination).

Animals and plants that share an environment interact with one another to meet their basic needs. All animals, whether herbivores, omnivores, or carnivores, ultimately depend upon plants for their source of food. It may seem that it only benefits the animals, but that is not the case. When vegetation in an area is thick, the plants compete for water, nutrients, sunlight, and space. As animals eat some of the plants and thin out the vegetation, more resources are available to the remaining plants to meet their basic needs.

Animals in the wild may use plants for shelter. Humans cut down trees for shelter and fuel. They use plants for medicines and dyes, and make clothing from both plants and animals. Animals of the same species and sometimes of different species often compete with one another for food. When food supplies are depleted, some animals migrate to new locations, while others may die out. Some animals prey on others in their environment. Predator-prey relationships maintain balance in populations. If an animal's natural predators are no longer in the environment, the population of that species may increase for a time. If the population reaches the point where supplies of food, water, and space are insufficient to accommodate the increased population, organisms will die because their basic needs are not being met.

Plants depend on animals in other ways. Bees, bats, and birds all pollinate flowers, which enables plants to reproduce. The relationship between bees and flowers is an example of a mutualistic relationship. Bees benefit because they get nectar from the flowers which they use to make food. When they land on a flower, they get pollen on their bodies. When they land on the next plant, they deposit some of the pollen, thereby pollinating that flower. Seed dispersal enables seeds to germinate and survive. If a seed falls to the ground by the parent plant, it may not have sufficient resources to grow. Water and wind disperse plant seeds, but so do animals. They might carry seeds on their feet, noses, or fur. When animals eat fruit, the seeds are not digestible. They become part of animal feces.

Skill 5.5: Identify basic characteristics of living and nonliving things.

Young children in Florida are expected to be able to discriminate between living and nonliving things, a task that is more challenging than it might appear. It is important to present information about how living and nonliving things differ in developmentally appropriate ways that do not lead to misconceptions.

All living things share a common one-celled ancestor that lived about four billion years ago. You can find lists of characteristics of living things like the ones below, but not all living things possess **all** these characteristics. Living things are very diverse and may possess all or some of the following characteristics:

- **Made up of one or more cells:** They may be single-celled organisms like amoebas or composed of trillions of cells like a human. Living things have an organized structure so they are also called **organisms.** The parts of a cell have specific functions. In multicellular organisms like humans, cells are organized into tissues, organs, and body systems that work together to keep the organism alive. Young children do not learn about cells or body systems. They do learn that the parts of living things have specific jobs that keep the organism alive.

- **Need and use energy:** Living things take in materials from the environment and convert them to energy for bodily functions. Most living things, including plants, take in oxygen. When children are told all living things eat food, they often think this means that plants "eat" soil, but that is incorrect. Most plants produce their own food through a process called **photosynthesis** that requires light energy from the sun, water, and carbon dioxide. Animals get their food from plants and other animals. As living things convert food into energy, waste products are produced. This means that all living things also get rid of wastes.

- **Respond and adapt to the environment:** Living things sense changes in the environment and respond to them so they can survive. Many plants grow toward the light. Some animals change color when seasons change. You pull your hand away if you touch a hot stove.

- **Move:** Children sometimes think plants don't move, so they must not be living things. Plants do have internal movement. Materials like oxygen, nutrients, and waste products move through a plant.

- **Grow:** Living things grow and change through their life cycle. Some nonliving things like icicles "grow," but they do so by adding matter from the outside. Living things grow from the inside. Growing involves both getting larger and repairing damaged parts. If you break your arm, new bone cells are produced to repair the break.

- **Reproduce:** Living things do not exist indefinitely like some nonliving materials. They must reproduce so organisms like them continue to inhabit Earth. When living things reproduce, they pass on their traits to their offspring.

- **Control their internal environment:** All the characteristics listed above enable living things to maintain balance and control their internal environment, a process called **homeostasis.** When it is cold outside, you shiver; when you are hot, you sweat. This is how your body maintains a relatively constant internal temperature no matter what the temperature is outside.

Nonliving things are generally defined by what they don't do—reproduce, move, etc. Children develop misconceptions when we teach that nonliving things don't possess any of the characteristics of living things. Car engines convert gasoline into energy to enable the car to move. Children often view cars as more capable of movement than plants. Storm clouds grow larger as an afternoon thunderstorm nears. Nonliving things may possess some, but never all the characteristics of living things. There are two groups of nonliving things—ones that were never alive, like rocks, and ones that were alive at one time, such as coral that has been made into jewelry or paper.

Living and nonliving things share some similarities, too. Both are made of matter. They have mass and volume. Both are composed of elements on the periodic table that are found at Earth's surface.

Skill 5.6: Identify and describe the basic structures, behaviors, and functions of plants and animals that allow them to carry out their life processes (e.g., grow, reproduce, and survive).

All living things are composed of **cells**, which are the basic units of structure and function in organisms. Cells in plants and animals are organized into **tissues**, which are groups of similar cells that perform a particular function.

Plants have basic structures that enable them to carry out their life processes. Vascular plants have roots that anchor the plant in the soil and absorb water and nutrients. Stems carry water and nutrients from the roots to the leaves. They also provide support for the plant. The leaves use carbon dioxide, water, and light energy from the Sun to produce their own food in a process called photosynthesis. Many plants also have flowers. Their main function is to produce seeds so the plant can reproduce. Fruit is the fleshy material that covers and protects the seeds. Animals eat the fruit, which aids in seed dispersal. Seeds contain an embryo which can develop into a new plant if it germinates. Some nonflowering plants produce seeds while others reproduce via spores.

Seed germination begins when a seed absorbs water from the surrounding soil. The seed uses stored food to begin growing. First a root grows downward, then a stem and leaves begin to grow upward. Light, water, temperature, and the presence or absence of nutrients all determine how well a plant will grow. A change in any of those factors will either limit or enhance the plant's growth. Nonvascular plants, like mosses, do not have true leaves, stems, flowers, or roots.

flowers

leaves

roots

Like plants, animals are multicellular organisms. Their cells are organized in ways that enable them to carry out their basic life functions. Groups of similar cells are organized into tissues that together perform specific functions. Muscle tissue and connective tissue are two examples of tissues in an animal's body. **Organs** are made up of one or more types of tissue. The heart, lungs, and stomach are examples of organs. Groups of organs that work together to carry out one of the organism's life processes are called **organ systems**. The digestive system takes in and breaks down food into energy that can be used by the organism's cells. The excretory system rids the body of wastes. The reproductive system enables organisms to reproduce and pass their genes on to the next generation.

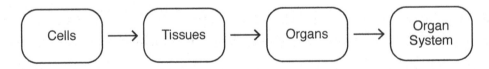

Skill 5.7: Identify and compare the structure and functions of major systems of the human body.

The human body is a complex, dynamic organism. Organs in the human body are organized into systems that perform a set of functions to keep the organism alive. Children in upper elementary grades in Florida learn about eight major systems of the human body. Children in the primary grades learn about specific organs, but it is important for their teachers to understand how those organs are part of a larger system. You will notice in the table on the next page that some organs play a role in more than one system. This illustrates how all the cells, organs, and tissues in the body work together so it can thrive.

System	Major Components	Function
Circulatory	Heart, arteries, veins, capillaries, blood	The circulatory system transports nutrients and wastes to and from the body's cells. The heart pumps blood to the lungs where CO_2 is exchanged for O_2 and then pumps the oxygenated blood to the body via arteries. Blood containing CO_2 travels back to the heart via veins. Nutrients are picked up by the blood in the small intestine and transported to cells throughout the body. Nutrients and waste products enter and leave blood through the walls of capillaries.
Respiratory	Lungs, nose, trachea, bronchi, diaphragm	Our bodies need O_2 to produce the energy necessary to keep us alive. When our diaphragm flattens, air containing O_2 gets forced into our nose or mouth, down our trachea and into the lungs where it flows into the bronchial tubes. The O_2 passes into red blood cells to be carried back to the heart and then to the rest of the body. Cells produce the waste product CO_2 which passes from red blood cells as they pass through the lungs and is then exhaled when we breathe out.
Digestive	Mouth, esophagus, stomach, small intestine, large intestine, liver, anus	Digestion is the process of breaking down the food you eat into nutrients that are used by the cells in your body to perform their basic functions. Digestion begins in the mouth as you bite and chew your food. Saliva begins breaking down starches into simple sugars. From the mouth, food travels down the esophagus to the stomach. Here food is further broken down physically and chemically. Next, food moves to the small intestine where it is further broken down. The liver produces bile, which helps break down food in the small intestine. From here nutrients are carried throughout the body by the bloodstream. Undigested parts of food move to the large intestine and are eventually eliminated through the anus.
Nervous	Brain, spinal cord, sensory organs, nerves	The brain is the control center of the body. It receives messages from your body and the wider world and then figures out how to respond to them. The brain directs voluntary functions you need to think about, like wiggling your toes and involuntary ones you don't have to think about, like your heart pumping blood. It enables you to think and have emotions. Messages travel to and from the brain via a network of billions of nerves and the spinal cord. The sensory organs (eyes, ears, nose, skin, mouth) take in information from the environment, which is carried to the brain via nerves so the brain can determine how the body should respond to the information it receives from the senses.

(continued)

System	Major Components	Function
Musculoskeletal	Muscles, bones, tendons	The musculoskeletal system provides support and enables the body to move. Bones also protect internal organs and produce blood cells. Tendons connect muscles to bones. Some muscles are voluntary, which means they are consciously controlled. Together they enable you to do things like kick a ball or tie a shoe. Smooth muscles are involuntary, which means you don't have to think about them. Involuntary muscles help control breathing, movements in the stomach, and the heartbeat.
Excretory	Kidneys, bladder, large intestine, skin	The excretory system removes wastes from the body. The kidneys filter waste products from the blood. The liquid waste, or urine, then travels to the bladder where it is stored until it is eliminated from the body. Solid wastes from undigested food are stored in the large intestine and then eliminated through the anus. Some liquid waste is removed through the skin when you sweat.
Immune	Skin, white blood cells, lymph nodes, spleen	The skin is the body's first line of defense against harmful substances. Coughing and sneezing help remove harmful pathogens from the body. White blood cells attack disease-causing pathogens and destroy them. Lymph nodes remove germs from the body. The spleen produces some white blood cells and antibodies that fight infection.
Reproductive	Male: testes, penis; Female: ovaries, uterus, fallopian tubes	Some living things reproduce asexually, which means one parent produces an offspring that is identical to itself. Humans reproduce sexually, which means two parents—a male and female—each contribute DNA to the offspring. Male testes produce male reproductive cells called sperm. Female reproductive cells, called eggs, are released by the ovaries and travel through the fallopian tubes to the uterus. When sperm are ejaculated from the male penis during intercourse, a sperm cell may fertilize the egg. If so, the fertilized egg cell implants on the wall of the uterus. Under normal circumstances, after nine months' gestation, the fetus is born. Because the infant contains DNA from both parents, it is not genetically identical to either parent.

Skill 5.8: Identify and compare the predictable ways plants and animals change as they grow, develop, and age.

All living things have a life cycle. They are born, grow, generally reproduce, and ultimately die. Some species live longer than others. A mosquito lives for about two weeks, while Koi fish can live more than 200 years. In general, larger organisms have longer life cycles. In some species like dogs, the juvenile organism's appearance is fairly similar to the adult. In frogs, a tadpole looks nothing like an adult frog. Organisms like frogs are not cared for by a parent after birth, but dogs and humans need parental care to survive. Reproduction is essential for the survival of a species. Fish may lay hundreds to thousands of eggs at a time, though many do not survive. Other species reproduce only once in their lifetime. Below are examples of plant and butterfly life cycles.

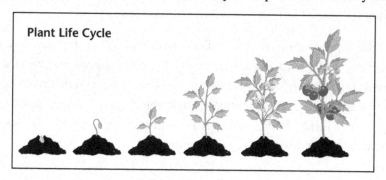

Plant Life Cycle

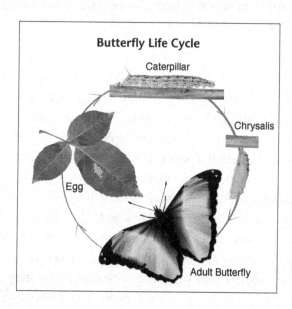

Butterfly Life Cycle

Caterpillar

Chrysalis

Egg

Adult Butterfly

Skill 5.9: Identify and compare the processes of sexual and asexual reproduction in plants, animals, and microorganisms.

Asexual reproduction occurs when one parent produces an offspring that is genetically identical to itself. One way this happens is when the cell divides into two identical cells. This is the way unicellular organisms reproduce. A second way is when an organism breaks into pieces and each piece develops into a new organism. Starfish can reproduce in this way. Asexual reproduction can occur artificially, too. Gardeners take cuttings from a plant, usually the stem, and place them in water where they grow new roots.

While plants and some animals (like starfish) can reproduce asexually, other organisms reproduce sexually. **Sexual reproduction** involves two parents. Each produces reproductive cells that contain half the number of chromosomes found in all other cells in their body. During fertilization, the two reproductive cells unite and form a new cell that contains chromosomes from both parents. The organism grows by a process of repeated cell division. In flowering plants, sexual reproduction occurs in the flower.

In animals, male reproductive cells are called sperm and female reproductive cells are called eggs. In some species, fertilization occurs externally. Sperm and eggs are released into water and a sperm cell must swim to an egg cell to fertilize it. In other species, fertilization occurs internally. The male releases sperm cells inside the female's reproductive tract, where fertilization can occur. The fertilized egg grows inside the female's uterus in most mammals until it is born. Some organisms, like birds and many reptiles, lay eggs that are hatched.

Skill 5.10: Identify the variety of habitats within ecosystems and analyze how they meet the needs of the organisms that live there.

An ecosystem includes a group of interacting living organisms and the nonliving characteristics of the area in which they live. All ecosystems share certain characteristics. Living things need energy to carry out basic life functions. They get this energy either by manufacturing their own food or by consuming other organisms in the ecosystem. There are three types of organisms within an ecosystem: **producers, consumers,** and **decomposers.** Producers make their own food, which is then converted into energy to keep the organism alive. Consumers get their energy by consuming other organisms in the ecosystem. Some (herbivores) eat only plants. Others (carnivores) only consume other animals in the ecosystem. Omnivores eat both plants and animals. Some organisms within an ecosystem feed on dead or decaying plants and animals. They are called decomposers. Earthworms, ants, beetles, and millipedes are examples of decomposers. Ecosystems contain **food chains,** which describes who eats whom. In the natural world, food chains rarely exist in isolation. Most organisms do not eat only one type of food, and typically have more than one predator who eats them. A complex web of interconnected food chains that describes all the possible feeding relationships in an ecosystem is called a **food web.**

Basic Food Chain

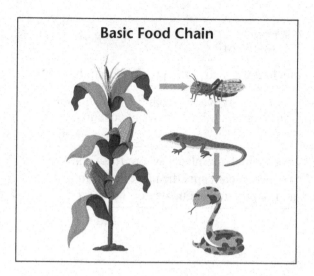

Terrestrial Food Web

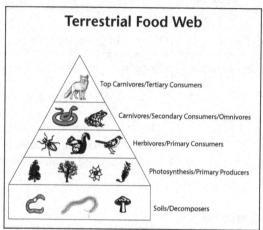

The nonliving characteristics of an environment impact the ability of organisms within the ecosystem to survive. Nonliving factors are things such as temperature or amount of precipitation, light, or oxygen. Living factors within an ecosystem also impact an organism's ability to survive. The presence or absence of predators and organisms that compete for the same food sources also influence whether organisms thrive. Different organisms survive better in different environments. When those conditions change over short or long timescales, some organisms die out, while others are better able to survive.

A **habitat** refers to the physical surroundings where a species lives. Species have their own unique habitats which contain the characteristics they need to survive. People sometimes confuse a habitat with a **biome.** A biome is a more inclusive term than habitat. It refers to a geographic area that has similar weather and vegetation. It describes the habitats of multiple organisms. Below are the major categories of biomes found on Earth.

Type of Biome	Characteristics
Rainforest	Could be tropical or temperate (e.g., northwest Washington state); receives lots of rain, lots of vegetation, great variety of species
Forest	Found in temperate or colder climates, receives moderate rainfall; may have trees that lose their leaves and/or trees with needles
Desert	Receives less than 25 cm of rain per year, occurs in cold climates, including at the poles, as well as warm ones; temperatures change significantly in a 24-hour period
Grassland	Contains deep, rich soils, generally not enough rain for trees to grow; home to large grazing animals

(continued)

Type of Biome	Characteristics
Tundra	Very cold ground that's frozen much of the year; little precipitation; thin soils
Freshwater	Includes ponds, lakes, streams, and rivers; types of vegetation and animals depend upon water temperature, amount of sunlight, flow, and chemistry of water
Marine	This largest biome includes estuaries which are places where fresh and saltwater mix, coral reefs, and the open ocean; specific plant and animal species depend upon latitude, water depth, and chemistry of the water

References

Gloria Ladson-Billings. (1995). "But that's just good teaching! The case for culturally relevant pedagogy." *Theory into Practice, 34*(3), 159–165.

Harlen, W. (2001). *Primary Science: Taking the Plunge.* Portsmouth, NH: Heinemann.

National Research Council. (2012). *A Framework for K–12 Science Education: Practices, Cross-cutting Concepts, and Core Ideas.* Washington, D.C.: The National Academies Press.

NGSS, Lead States. (2013). *Next Generation Science Standards: For States by States.* Washington, D.C.: The National Academies Press.

Zembal-Saul, C., McNeill, K. L., & Hershberger, K. (2013). *What's Your Evidence? Engaging K–5 Students in Constructing Explanations in Science.* Boston, MA: Pearson.

PRACTICE TEST 1

FTCE PreK–3 Developmental Knowledge
Subtest 1 (531)

Also available at the REA Study Center (www.rea.com/studycenter)

This practice test is also offered online at the REA Study Center. We recommend that you take the online version of the test to simulate test-day conditions and to receive these added benefits:

- **Timed testing conditions**—helps you gauge how much time you can spend on each question

- **Automatic scoring**—find out how you did on the test, instantly

- **On-screen detailed explanations of answers**—gives you the correct answer and explains why the other answer choices are wrong

- **Diagnostic score reports**—pinpoint where you're strongest and where you need to focus your study

Developmental Knowledge
Practice Test 1: Answer Sheet

1. Ⓐ Ⓑ Ⓒ Ⓓ   21. Ⓐ Ⓑ Ⓒ Ⓓ   41. Ⓐ Ⓑ Ⓒ Ⓓ

2. Ⓐ Ⓑ Ⓒ Ⓓ   22. Ⓐ Ⓑ Ⓒ Ⓓ   42. Ⓐ Ⓑ Ⓒ Ⓓ

3. Ⓐ Ⓑ Ⓒ Ⓓ   23. Ⓐ Ⓑ Ⓒ Ⓓ   43. Ⓐ Ⓑ Ⓒ Ⓓ

4. Ⓐ Ⓑ Ⓒ Ⓓ   24. Ⓐ Ⓑ Ⓒ Ⓓ   44. Ⓐ Ⓑ Ⓒ Ⓓ

5. Ⓐ Ⓑ Ⓒ Ⓓ   25. Ⓐ Ⓑ Ⓒ Ⓓ   45. Ⓐ Ⓑ Ⓒ Ⓓ

6. Ⓐ Ⓑ Ⓒ Ⓓ   26. Ⓐ Ⓑ Ⓒ Ⓓ   46. Ⓐ Ⓑ Ⓒ Ⓓ

7. Ⓐ Ⓑ Ⓒ Ⓓ   27. Ⓐ Ⓑ Ⓒ Ⓓ   47. Ⓐ Ⓑ Ⓒ Ⓓ

8. Ⓐ Ⓑ Ⓒ Ⓓ   28. Ⓐ Ⓑ Ⓒ Ⓓ   48. Ⓐ Ⓑ Ⓒ Ⓓ

9. Ⓐ Ⓑ Ⓒ Ⓓ   29. Ⓐ Ⓑ Ⓒ Ⓓ   49. Ⓐ Ⓑ Ⓒ Ⓓ

10. Ⓐ Ⓑ Ⓒ Ⓓ   30. Ⓐ Ⓑ Ⓒ Ⓓ   50. Ⓐ Ⓑ Ⓒ Ⓓ

11. Ⓐ Ⓑ Ⓒ Ⓓ   31. Ⓐ Ⓑ Ⓒ Ⓓ   51. Ⓐ Ⓑ Ⓒ Ⓓ

12. Ⓐ Ⓑ Ⓒ Ⓓ   32. Ⓐ Ⓑ Ⓒ Ⓓ   52. Ⓐ Ⓑ Ⓒ Ⓓ

13. Ⓐ Ⓑ Ⓒ Ⓓ   33. Ⓐ Ⓑ Ⓒ Ⓓ   53. Ⓐ Ⓑ Ⓒ Ⓓ

14. Ⓐ Ⓑ Ⓒ Ⓓ   34. Ⓐ Ⓑ Ⓒ Ⓓ   54. Ⓐ Ⓑ Ⓒ Ⓓ

15. Ⓐ Ⓑ Ⓒ Ⓓ   35. Ⓐ Ⓑ Ⓒ Ⓓ   55. Ⓐ Ⓑ Ⓒ Ⓓ

16. Ⓐ Ⓑ Ⓒ Ⓓ   36. Ⓐ Ⓑ Ⓒ Ⓓ   56. Ⓐ Ⓑ Ⓒ Ⓓ

17. Ⓐ Ⓑ Ⓒ Ⓓ   37. Ⓐ Ⓑ Ⓒ Ⓓ   57. Ⓐ Ⓑ Ⓒ Ⓓ

18. Ⓐ Ⓑ Ⓒ Ⓓ   38. Ⓐ Ⓑ Ⓒ Ⓓ   58. Ⓐ Ⓑ Ⓒ Ⓓ

19. Ⓐ Ⓑ Ⓒ Ⓓ   39. Ⓐ Ⓑ Ⓒ Ⓓ   59. Ⓐ Ⓑ Ⓒ Ⓓ

20. Ⓐ Ⓑ Ⓒ Ⓓ   40. Ⓐ Ⓑ Ⓒ Ⓓ   60. Ⓐ Ⓑ Ⓒ Ⓓ

Practice Test 1: Developmental Knowledge

TIME: 70 minutes
60 questions*

> **Directions:** Read each question and select the best response.

---

1. Not having proper foster care can negatively impact children's development. This statement is related to what concept?

   A. nature

   B. nurture

   C. environment

   D. heredity

2. The type of test intended to measure how well a person has learned a specific body of knowledge and skills is called a

   A. criterion-referenced test.

   B. norm-referenced test.

   C. high-stakes test.

   D. formative test.

3. The Florida statute that indicates that teachers should teach the qualities of patriotism, responsibility, citizenship, kindness, respect for authority, life, liberty, and personal property, honesty, charity, self-control, racial, ethnic, and religious tolerance, and cooperation is part of

   A. character development.

   B. civics courses.

   C. social studies.

   D. kindness curriculum.

4. HIPAA limits how teachers access and use

   A. student education records.

   B. student health information.

   C. multi-tiered systems of support.

   D. guidance records.

5. The concept of "readiness," which suggests that genetic differences determine the rate at which children develop and proceed through stages, is credited to which theorist?

   A. Piaget

   B. Vygotksy

   C. Bruner

   D. Gesell

6. A holistic approach to a child's well-being may include trauma-informed care. What is the best definition of this approach?

   A. Practices that promote a culture of safety, empowerment, and healing.

   B. Providing a nurse on staff to be sure that all children have access to medical care.

   C. Creating family nights that focus on the law and rights of children.

   D. Sending home brochures that provide numbers for local agencies who can help with need.

---

* This practice test presents slightly more items than you are likely to see on test day. The actual test contains approximately 55 questions. You will only learn exactly how many questions you will get after you take the FTCE tutorial and sign the non-disclosure agreement on test day.

7. Miss Erin notices that one of her 5-year-olds seems to have significantly poorer fine motor skills than the other children in the class. She checks the developmental indicators and confirms that she is observing atypical development. Which of the following is this a characteristic of?

   A. a possible learning disability

   B. a sign that he needs more fine motor skills practice

   C. that he has had too much screen time

   D. that he probably has better gross motor skills

8. Children who have been identified as having learning disabilities are required to have

   A. IEPs.

   B. 504 Plans.

   C. IDEA.

   D. TLAPs.

9. Planning a workshop for parents, Judy includes a slide on Piaget's preoperational stage. In this stage, children

   A. may have difficulty taking the viewpoint of others.

   B. are beginning to think logically and internally problem solve.

   C. can think about abstract concepts.

   D. know that an object can exist, even if it's hidden from view.

10. The Centers for Disease Control has determined that many children have experienced trauma that may include some sort of maltreatment. That number is

   A. one in five.

   B. one in ten.

   C. one in four.

   D. one in two.

11. The Florida Family and School Partnership for Student Achievement Act

   A. provides families with information regarding their child's educational progress and opportunities for participating in their child's education.

   B. provides families with information on how to navigate standardized tests and annual assessments.

   C. provides families with ways to become more involved in school activities that will foster their child's achievement.

   D. provides a template for family engagement agreements at the school level.

12. What agency provides guidance to address the needs of families with limited English proficiency?

   A. Early Learning Coalition

   B. National Association for the Education of Young Children

   C. International World Literacy Alliance

   D. World-Class Instructional Design and Assessment Consortium

13. Finding a peaceful solution to a problem is called

   A. negotiation.

   B. team building.

   C. conflict resolution.

   D. social emotional skill.

14. The idea that language development fostered the ability to organize and integrate experiences was developed by which theorist?

   A. Piaget

   B. Montessori

   C. Erikson

   D. Vygotsky

15. Mr. Joseph is considering putting his third graders' names and test scores on the classroom door to motivate them to study hard for the upcoming week's test. This may be a violation of which of the following?

A. HIPAA

B. FERPA

C. WIDA

D. IDEA

16. While observing a 2-year-old playing with a basket of plastic animals, Dawn hears the child pick up a dog figure and call it a "doggy." The child then picks up a plastic cow and calls it "doggy." Dawn sits down next to the child and observes for a minute or so. The child points to the two figurines and says "doggy." Dawn smiles and picks up the cow and says, "This looks like a dog, doesn't it? But it's a cow." She picks up the dog and says, "They are kind of alike. They have four legs. She puts the cow down and points to each of the cow's legs as she counts "1-2-3-4." She then goes on to describe how cows and dogs are similar and different. The 2-year-old nods her understanding and points to the cow as she says "Cow." What is the child demonstrating?

A. assimilation

B. accommodation

C. confusion

D. concrete thought

17. According to the Florida Department of Children and Families, teachers can help children who are in foster care by

A. having consistent routines.

B. inviting social workers into the classroom.

C. getting books about diversity.

D. conducting home visits.

18. Second grader Tomás is having trouble staying focused on the science activity that he is doing with his group. He keeps walking away to look out the window. His teacher writes a quick observation. What is this behavior linked to?

A. executive function

B. organizational ability

C. attention deficit disorder

D. social immaturity

19. You are a teacher in a class of two-year-olds with various learning needs. One child is visually impaired and the parent asks for advice in helping her child at home. What advice would you give her?

A. To provide opportunities for safe play, so that she can touch, smell, feel, and hear. Talk with her about her experiences. For example, add measuring cups and other utensils to her tub toys; use the correct terms for utensils; sing songs with her as she plays.

B. To get a workbook with large print and start working on identifying the letters with her. Build up to recognizing sight words correctly.

C. To work on an audible phonics program together. Learning the alphabet and sight words through music can help the information go into her long-term memory.

D. To get Braille flash cards so that she can begin learning the letters by feel.

20. Ms. Latisha is teaching a small, guided reading group of second graders. The children have their leveled texts open on the table and are beginning to whisper read. The child to her right is reading and mistakes the word "bread" for "bed." Ms. Latisha has him go back to the word and asks him to look at it again. He hesitates and she says, "Put your finger under the beginning of the word. What do you see? Yes, a 'b' and an 'r'. So it can't be just a /b/ sound. Let's say it together slowly. '/b//r/'." The child then reads the word as "bread." What concept does this scenario best illustrate?

A. internal processing

B. zone of proximal development

C. linguistic intelligence

D. emergent literacy

21. Ms. Taylor has a child with apraxia in her class who seems to have trouble listening to or understanding directions. When planning her lessons, she decides that she needs to plan for

    A. using technology to communicate.

    B. intentional opportunities to work on receptive language.

    C. using direct instruction to foster his literacy skills.

    D. intentional opportunities for mindfulness.

22. Mr. Miller notices that one of the girls in the dramatic play center has stopped to include another child in their pretend store. This is an example of what?

    A. prosocial behavior

    B. team player

    C. kindness

    D. emotional intelligence (EQ)

23. Purposeful collections of student work that exhibits the student's efforts, progress, and achievements in one or more areas is called

    A. an anthology.

    B. culminating work.

    C. a portfolio.

    D. work samples.

24. Parents can find high-quality care and early education programs through which Florida state agency?

    A. Florida's Child Care Resource and Referral Network

    B. Department of Children and Families Referral Network

    C. Early Learning Access Network of Florida

    D. Department of Health and Human Services

25. Over the course of a few days, Ms. Lopez observes a few first-grade children repeatedly fighting over toys in the dramatic play center. Which would be the most developmentally appropriate way to address the issue?

    A. Call their parents.

    B. Role play a similar situation during circle time and brainstorm problem-solving ideas.

    C. Close the center, as they are not ready for it or using it appropriately.

    D. Have the principal come into the classroom and talk with the class.

26. Ms. Jones has a kindergarten student who experienced war trauma and was recently adopted after spending time in a resettlement camp. He often becomes anxious during center time, when he has an opportunity to make decisions and interact with others. He sometimes becomes aggressive and at other times becomes withdrawn, particularly when he is expected to share with other children. Ms. Jones talks with the school counselor for suggestions on what could be done to help him become more self-reliant and confident. What would be the most appropriate treatment to explore?

    A. play therapy

    B. talk therapy

    C. medication to ease his anxiety

    D. family counseling

27. Ms. Thomas is observing her 3-year-olds playing in the transportation center. She notices that one child is sorting the vehicles by the number of wheels. The child puts a toy bicycle and motorcycle together. He then puts all the vehicles that have four wheels together. He has a toy tractor-trailer rig that he separates from the others, but is still in the group. The child is demonstrating what type of knowledge?

    A. logico-mathematical

    B. physical

    C. sorting

    D. kinesthetic

28. Which organization provides guidance on developmentally appropriate practices?

    A. Association for Childhood Education International

    B. National Association for the Education of Young Children

    C. National Science Teachers Association

    D. International Literacy Association

29. Assessment is what type of process?

    A. static

    B. dynamic

    C. objective

    D. formative

30. Which of the following might be a member of the IEP team?

    A. school counselor

    B. teacher

    C. social worker

    D. All of the above

31. Assessments that provide a quick snapshot to help identify delays or atypical development in speech, language, or fine and gross motor skills are called

    A. evaluations.

    B. screenings.

    C. diagnoses.

    D. tests.

32. Ms. Davidson's lesson plans include having her 4-year-olds practice writing letters of the alphabet on primary paper. She notices that a few children are struggling with holding the pencil and staying on task. She decides to modify the assignment. Which modification would be most developmentally appropriate?

    A. She provides the children with a larger pencil and gives more time to do the assignment.

    B. She brings out play dough and lets children choose to make dough letters instead.

    C. She turns on quiet music, so that children can relax and focus.

    D. She provides paper with more space between the lines.

33. The method of discipline focused on social-emotional learning and helping children achieve behavioral goals without token systems is called

    A. CHAMPS.

    B. conscious discipline.

    C. classroom economy.

    D. multi-tiered systems of support.

34. The number of children who fail at least one grade in school because of a disability is

    A. one in three.

    B. one in five.

    C. one in eight.

    D. one in ten.

35. An assessment that allows teachers to determine how their students are progressing in math is called a

    A. curriculum-based measurement.

    B. observational assessment.

    C. rubric.

    D. quiz.

36. Mr. Anthony is planning a parent workshop on phonological awareness and early literacy. What is likely the focus on his workshop?

    A. rhyming songs

    B. sight words

    C. alphabet games

    D. letter formation

37. When adapting curricula for children with diverse needs, teachers should consider

    A. culturally relevant instruction.

    B. effective parent/community involvement.

    C. Both (A) and (B).

    D. None of the above.

38. The pedagogy that acknowledges, responds to, and celebrates cultures and offers full, equitable access to education for students from all cultures is known as

    A. anti-bias curriculum.

    B. diverse pedagogy.

    C. culturally responsive teaching.

    D. culturally reflective teaching.

39. The idea that there are critical periods in early childhood when exposure to formal reading is necessary is inaccurate, but has been attributed to what concept?

    A. developmental domains

    B. learning sequences

    C. readiness

    D. constructivism

40. Ms. Georgia is sitting on the floor in the block center building a block fence to hold some miniature plastic animals. She is creating corrals for each type of animal. Jamir comes and sits next to her and begins building along with her. In this role, Ms. Georgia is

    A. a companion.

    B. an observer.

    C. a participant.

    D. an instructional leader.

41. Which of Erikson's eight stages is typically evidenced when a child is no longer an infant but has not learned to speak (i.e., the toddler stage)?

    A. Trust vs. Mistrust

    B. Autonomy vs. Shame and Doubt

    C. Initiative vs. Guilt

    D. Industry vs. Inferiority

42. Concise, objective narratives about a student are called

    A. anecdotal notes.

    B. observational notes.

    C. a reflective journal.

    D. developmental narratives.

43. The practice of using a variety of teaching methods to remove any barriers to learning and give all students equal opportunities to succeed is known as

    A. developmentally appropriate practice.

    B. universal design for learning.

    C. equitable learning design.

    D. responsive teaching.

44. Which professional organization has a list of "10 Effective Developmentally Appropriate Practice Strategies"?

    A. Association for Childhood Education International

    B. Early Learning Association of America

    C. National Association for Childhood Education International

    D. National Association for the Education of Young Children

45. If a teacher believes there is physical abuse of a child, she should contact the

    A. Department of Health.

    B. Department of Children and Families.

    C. Early Learning Coalition.

    D. Florida Department of Education.

46. The process of starting with the long-term goals and developing instructional objectives is called

    A. backward design.

    B. universal design.

    C. curriculum planning.

    D. thematic unit planning.

47. Mr. Courtney's director told him to begin working with 3- and 4-year-olds on forming letters. Which would be the most developmentally appropriate activity to meet his directive?

    A. providing big pencils and paper with no lines so the children can practice making the letters

    B. providing play dough and alphabet letters, along with an illustrated alphabet line, so that children can explore

    C. providing crayons and markers and primary lined paper, so that children have a choice of writing utensils

    D. providing alphabet books for the children to look through

48. Child development can be impacted by factors broadly categorized as biological, environmental, and

    A. nutritional.

    B. developmental.

    C. familial.

    D. behavioral.

49. When an adult helps the child work on a task that is just above what she can do independently, it is called

    A. scaffolding.

    B. guidance.

    C. support.

    D. tutoring.

50. The idea that children should have sand and water tables to understand scientific concepts is best associated with what theorist's work?

    A. Piaget

    B. Maslow

    C. Vygotsky

    D. Bruner

51. What is Maslow's hierarchy of basic needs called?

    A. ecological systems theory

    B. stages of development theory

    C. self-actualization theory

    D. autonomy theory

52. The World-Class Instructional Design and Assessment Consortium is a resource to help students who

    A. are English language learners.

    B. have exceptional learning needs.

    C. have been identified as gifted.

    D. have been identified as being in foster care.

53. Vygotsky's zone of proximal development is best defined as

   A. the range of abilities that a child can perform with assistance, but cannot yet perform independently.

   B. the range between the ability to think abstractly and begin judging and thinking and judging using proximity.

   C. the management style of using distance to help alert a child to an undesired behavior (also called proximity control).

   D. the range of abilities that a child can do on his own without help from another.

54. Piaget's idea of cognitive development was extended into the area of moral development by

   A. Maslow.

   B. Steiner.

   C. Kohlberg.

   D. Montessori.

55. The term "temporal environment" refers to

   A. the outdoor and nature areas where children have spaces to play.

   B. the timing and length of routines in the day.

   C. the temperature and lighting of the classroom.

   D. the mindfulness activities that foster cognitive well-being.

56. The overall design and layout of a classroom and the learning centers is called

   A. temporal environment.

   B. learning space.

   C. physical environment.

   D. teaching space.

57. Third grade teacher Mr. Sebastian wants to design his classroom so that there are no barriers to learning for anyone. Knowing that students have different needs, he decides to ask for desks that can be adjusted so students can sit or stand. He also has clipboards for students who want to work while sitting on the floor. What concepts would he pull from?

   A. principles of universal design

   B. principles of accommodation and modification

   C. principles of exceptional education

   D. developmentally appropriate practices

58. Ms. Keller is teaching her third graders the standard of "Understanding Motion and Factors that Affect Motion" and is focusing on the indicator that students will be able to "infer changes in speed or direction resulting from forces acting on an object." What lesson would be best to begin?

   A. Watch a video and create a vocabulary game that includes the terminology.

   B. Put out a marble run, matchbox cars and ramps, and balls and inclines, and let them explore before discussing the concepts and related terminology.

   C. Have children play a video game that allows them to simulate bowling, rolling objects down hills, and other motion and forces.

   D. Put the students in teams and have them look up vocabulary words that are aligned with the standards.

59. According to the American Academy of Pediatrics, which of the following is essential to children's learning and development because it develops cognitive, physical, social, and emotional well-being?

   A. play

   B. exercise

   C. tummy time

   D. being read to

60. Tommy is a first grader who needs work with blending sounds and words. What is the best way to work with him?

   A. Work with him individually using Elkonin boxes.

   B. Work with him on a computer program for phonics.

   C. Let him play with letter blocks in the learning center.

   D. Have him practice matching pictures with letters.

Developmental Knowledge
Practice Test 1: Answer Key

Test Item	Answer	Competency
1.	B	1
2.	A	6
3.	A	7
4.	B	5
5.	D	2
6.	A	1
7.	A	5
8.	A	7
9.	A	3
10.	C	1
11.	A	6
12.	D	5
13.	C	7
14.	D	2
15.	B	6
16.	B	3
17.	A	5
18.	A	7
19.	A	1
20.	B	2
21.	B	5
22.	A	7
23.	C	6
24.	A	4
25.	B	7
26.	A	5
27.	A	2
28.	B	5
29.	B	6
30.	D	7

Test Item	Answer	Competency
31.	B	6
32.	B	3
33.	B	7
34.	B	5
35.	A	6
36.	A	1
37.	C	4
38.	C	5
39.	C	3
40.	C	6
41.	B	2
42.	A	6
43.	B	4
44.	D	3
45.	B	1
46.	A	3
47.	B	4
48.	D	1
49.	A	3
50.	A	1
51.	C	2
52.	A	4
53.	A	3
54.	C	2
55.	B	3
56.	C	3
57.	A	3
58.	B	4
59.	A	3
60.	A	4

Developmental Knowledge
Practice Test 1: Detailed Answers

1. (B)

Nurture includes all environmental factors (e.g., family, nutrition, and the physical environment) that can impact children's development. Choices (A) and (D) are incorrect because they are "opposite" the correct choice. Choice (C) is incomplete. (Competency 1)

2. (A)

Criterion-referenced tests assess how well a person has learned a defined body of information, such as a particular set of math or reading skills. It is not intended to be used to compare students or to compare schools. (Competency 6)

3. (A)

All the qualities listed are part of character development. The curriculum of character development might include civics, social studies, and social-emotional skill-building. (Competency 7)

4. (B)

HIPAA (Health Insurance Portability and Accountability Act) affects the type of health information that is accessible to teachers. (Competency 5)

5. (D)

Gesell studied and defined "typical" milestones of development. (Competency 2)

6. (A)

Practices that promote a culture of safety, empowerment, and healing identify a holistic approach to a child's well-being. Choices (B), (C), and (D) might be included in trauma-informed care, but are not complete by themselves. (Competency 1)

7. (A)

It is possible that this child just needs more fine motor experiences, but it would be best to consider the possibility of a learning disability. Choices (C) and (D) are simply guesses and are not particularly useful in this situation. (Competency 5)

8. (A)

Children with identified learning disabilities must have Individual Education Plans, or IEPs, that school staff can use to give appropriate instruction and support. (Competency 7)

9. (A)

The correct response is (A). In the preoperational stage (2–7 years), children's thinking is still egocentric. Children in the sensorimotor stage (birth–2 years) understand the idea of object permanence, which is knowing that an object exists even if they can't see it. Children in the concrete operational stage (7–11 years) are able to think logically and can figure things out in their head. Children in the formal operational stage (11 years and older) are able to think about abstract concepts. (Competency 3)

10. (C)

One in four children may have experienced trauma. (Competency 1)

11. (A)

The Florida Family and School Partnership for Student Achievement Act provides families with information regarding their child's progress as well as information on educational choices and requirements for their child. (Competency 6)

12. (D)

WIDA is the organization that focuses on English language learners. (Competency 5)

13. (C)

Conflict resolution involves finding a solution to the conflict that satisfies all parties and contributes to cognitive and social development. Conflict resolution might include team-building, negotiation, and the use of social-emotional skills. (Competency 7)

14. (D)

Vygotsky asserted that a child's language development is supported by rich experience, especially when there is an older individual on hand who talks about the experience with the child. (Competency 2)

15. (B)

FERPA is the Family Educational Rights and Privacy Act which guarantees privacy for students' information and grades. Parents of minors have access to the information, and teachers have limited access. The other choices are acronyms for other policies and organizations. (Competency 6)

16. (B)

The child's behavior demonstrates accommodation. She was able to take the new information provided by the teacher and adjust her schema. When the child initially called the cow a dog, she was demonstrating assimilation—she had a concept and was overusing it. (Competency 3)

17. (A)

Consistent routines are important for children's sense of security and safety. Choices (B) and (D) are not appropriate, and choice (C) is not relevant to the issue. (Competency 5)

18. (A)

Attention is a primary executive function. A child who has trouble with attention might have attention deficit disorder, might be socially immature, or might have trouble organizing thought and action. (Competency 7)

19. (A)

Children need to have opportunities to play and experience things with all their senses. This would be particularly true for sight-impaired children. (Competency 1)

20. (B)

The zone of proximal development (ZPD) is the space between what a child can do alone and what he can do with someone with more expertise. An effective teacher would use this concept to guide a child to correct a mistake, using skills the child already has, rather than just telling the child the correct word or making the child figure out the correct word with no help. (Competency 2)

21. (B)

Students with apraxia would benefit from specific opportunities to work on receptive language (understanding what another person says). (Competency 5)

22. (A)

This is prosocial behavior, which often involves acts of kindness, generosity, and inclusion. Individuals with high emotional intelligence (EQ) often exhibit prosocial behavior. (Competency 7)

23. (C)

Portfolios are collections of work that can be reviewed to assess progress and achievement. They contain artifacts such as work samples, photos, videos, etc. (Competency 6)

24. (A)

The Florida Child Care Resource and Referral Network is a statewide service that focuses on information related to quality child care. (Competency 4)

25. (B)

Role play followed by discussion would give children an opportunity to observe, process, and problem-solve the issue. The other choices do not give children an opportunity for developing cognitive and social skills. (Competency 7)

26. (A)

The most developmentally appropriate intervention is likely play therapy. A therapist trained in play therapy can provide play materials that will allow the child to explore his feelings in a safe way through play. Talk therapy (B) is more suited for older children; medication (C) is not a first resort; and while family counseling (D) might be a great option, it would be done as a supplement. (Competency 5)

27. (A)

Piaget described the ability to sort by category as an early part of logico-mathematical thinking. Choices (B) and (D) involve motion, but not categorical thinking. Choice (C) is a behavior, not a type of thinking or knowledge. (Competency 2)

28. (B)

The National Association for the Education of Young Children (NAEYC) focuses on all aspects of early developmental learning. (Competency 5)

29. (B)

Assessment should be dynamic, ongoing, and always used to foster students' learning. Many assessments are formative in order to evaluate progress, but sometimes assessments need to be summative. Of course, they should always be objective and used without bias. (Competency 6)

30. (D)

All of the individuals listed can be members of an IEP team. (Competency 7)

31. (B)

The answer is (B), screenings. A developmental screening is typically done across a group of children and can signal when more assessment is needed. Assessments may lead to a diagnosis. The entire process is called an evaluation. (Competency 6)

32. (B)

The teacher knows that manipulating the dough will help build children's finger and wrist strength, while still accomplishing the goal of forming letters. This will likely keep children on-task. She can document the work through photos. (Competency 3)

33. (B)

Conscious discipline involves helping students build social-emotional skills rather than using rewards and punishments or tokens. It can work alongside instructional management approaches such as CHAMPS. (Competency 7)

34. (B)

One in five children fail a grade due to a disability. (Competency 5)

35. (A)

A curriculum-based measurement (CBM) is a way of assessing how well a child has learned a body of knowledge in a particular content area, such as math. It requires an assessment method that is more formal than a quiz or an observation. (Competency 6)

36. (A)

Rhyming songs are best because they develop phonological awareness, rhythm, sequence, listening skills, and receptive vocabulary, and are enjoyable. The other choices would not be appropriate for phonological training. (Competency 1)

37. (C)

Both culturally relevant instruction and effective parent/community involvement are essential to match instructions with diverse perspectives and needs. (Competency 4)

38. (C)

Culturally responsive teaching attempts to include culture fully in every aspect of learning and strives to make learning equitable to all. It should include anti-bias curriculum, teaching to diversity, and culturally reflective teaching. (Competency 5)

39. (C)

Readiness has been translated into the idea of getting children "ready" for formal schooling, although it is meant to be related to an assessment of cognitive and social skills needed for classroom life. Teachers of young children will have a range of "readiness" in their classroom and need to accommodate a diversity of social and academic abilities, including assessing for formal reading readiness. (Competency 3)

40. (C)

Since the teacher is not intentionally instructing, she is a participant in play. Because of her role in the classroom, she cannot be a companion, and in this situation, she is not an observer. (Hopefully she stops to observe the actions of all her students periodically.) (Competency 6)

41. (B)

Autonomy vs. shame and doubt is the second of Erikson's life stages. This is when toddlers develop a sense of autonomy, self-governance, and the ability to act on something independently. Toilet training is included in this stage. Choice (A) represents infancy and choices (C) and (D) represent older stages of preschool and school-age children, respectively. (Competency 2)

42. (A)

Anecdotal notes are brief notes used to document a student's learning or behavior. It uses observation, but only for a particular purpose. It can be used to find or follow a trend and for record-keeping for future conferences and diagnostics. It is not reflective, but simply descriptive. (Competency 6)

43. (B)

Universal design for learning is the concept that is inclusive. It should include or be accompanied by the other choices. (Competency 4)

44. (D)

The National Association for the Education of Young Children (NAEYC) has developed a list of appropriate strategies for teaching young students. (Competency 3)

45. (B)

Teachers have a legal responsibility to report possible abuse to authorities at the Department of Children and Families. (Competency 1)

46. (A)

Backward design means starting with the end in mind and asking, "What do the children need to know or be able to do by the end of the learning unit?" Then the teacher plans activities that will bring students to the needed level of learning. (Competency 3)

47. (B)

Materials that allow young children to build their fine motor skills are best for learning letter formation. Not all children at this age can work well with pencils or crayons. Alphabet books are helpful, but passive, and cannot provide hands-on practice. (Competency 4)

48. (D)

Behavior is the third broad factor that impacts development and learning. (Competency 1)

49. (A)

Scaffolding is the practice of guiding a child to master the "next step" in a learning sequence. It can be considered a specific type of guidance or support. Tutoring is a strategy for general support in a content area, not specific to a single task. (Competency 3)

50. (A)

Piaget advocated a hands-on, experimental learning environment so young children could discover and build on basic concepts. Maslow was concerned with children having needs met to progress toward psychological health. Vygotsky was concerned with parents and teachers helping children complete their own tasks and building language skills. Bruner was also concerned with making learning more hands-on and experiential, but his emphasis was on older children. (Competency 1)

51. (C)

Maslow proposed five levels of need that built on each other, and if successfully navigated, resulted in the individual's self-actualization or the ability to understand one's self, to maintain positive relationships, and be open to learning and new experiences. (Competency 2)

52. (A)

WIDA is an organization focused on English language learners. (Competency 4)

53. (A)

These abilities are called "proximal" because the individual is close to mastering them, but needs more guidance and practice in order to perform these actions independently. ZPD is not specifically related to cognitive tasks or behavioral issues. (Competency 3)

54. (C)

Kohlberg extended the idea of moral development through cognitive stages. His work has been criticized for not taking into account diverse backgrounds. (Competency 2)

55. (B)

"Temporal" refers to the routines and schedules that impact children's learning and well-being. (Competency 3)

56. (C)

The physical environment includes both inside and outside spaces. It does not include the timing of events (temporal). Hopefully, learning takes place throughout the environment, but that cannot be guaranteed just by the way the space is arranged. (Competency 3)

57. (A)

"Principles of universal design" refers to planning and instruction that is inclusive and attempts to meet all learning needs and preferences. (Competency 3)

58. (B)

A marble run is a way to explore all the concepts experientially rather than theoretically, passively, or virtually. (Competency 4)

59. (A)

Play is essential for developing all domains, since it involves building on and using cognitive, physical, and social skills. All the other choices might be included in various types of play. (Competency 3)

60. (A)

Using Elkonin boxes allows the teacher to monitor Tommy's understanding and spot specific problem areas. Choice (B) may or may not give the kind of practice the Elkonin boxes give, and choices (C) and (D) are for letter recognition, not phonetical issues. (Competency 4)

PRACTICE TEST 1

FTCE PreK–3 Language Arts and Reading
Subtest 2 (532)

Also available at the REA Study Center (www.rea.com/studycenter)

This practice test is also offered online at the REA Study Center. We recommend that you take the online version of the test to simulate test-day conditions and to receive these added benefits:

- **Timed testing conditions**—helps you gauge how much time you can spend on each question

- **Automatic scoring**—find out how you did on the test, instantly

- **On-screen detailed explanations of answers**—gives you the correct answer and explains why the other answer choices are wrong

- **Diagnostic score reports**—pinpoint where you're strongest and where you need to focus your study

Language Arts and Reading
Practice Test 1: Answer Sheet

1. Ⓐ Ⓑ Ⓒ Ⓓ	21. Ⓐ Ⓑ Ⓒ Ⓓ	41. Ⓐ Ⓑ Ⓒ Ⓓ
2. Ⓐ Ⓑ Ⓒ Ⓓ	22. Ⓐ Ⓑ Ⓒ Ⓓ	42. Ⓐ Ⓑ Ⓒ Ⓓ
3. Ⓐ Ⓑ Ⓒ Ⓓ	23. Ⓐ Ⓑ Ⓒ Ⓓ	43. Ⓐ Ⓑ Ⓒ Ⓓ
4. Ⓐ Ⓑ Ⓒ Ⓓ	24. Ⓐ Ⓑ Ⓒ Ⓓ	44. Ⓐ Ⓑ Ⓒ Ⓓ
5. Ⓐ Ⓑ Ⓒ Ⓓ	25. Ⓐ Ⓑ Ⓒ Ⓓ	45. Ⓐ Ⓑ Ⓒ Ⓓ
6. Ⓐ Ⓑ Ⓒ Ⓓ	26. Ⓐ Ⓑ Ⓒ Ⓓ	46. Ⓐ Ⓑ Ⓒ Ⓓ
7. Ⓐ Ⓑ Ⓒ Ⓓ	27. Ⓐ Ⓑ Ⓒ Ⓓ	47. Ⓐ Ⓑ Ⓒ Ⓓ
8. Ⓐ Ⓑ Ⓒ Ⓓ	28. Ⓐ Ⓑ Ⓒ Ⓓ	48. Ⓐ Ⓑ Ⓒ Ⓓ
9. Ⓐ Ⓑ Ⓒ Ⓓ	29. Ⓐ Ⓑ Ⓒ Ⓓ	49. Ⓐ Ⓑ Ⓒ Ⓓ
10. Ⓐ Ⓑ Ⓒ Ⓓ	30. Ⓐ Ⓑ Ⓒ Ⓓ	50. Ⓐ Ⓑ Ⓒ Ⓓ
11. Ⓐ Ⓑ Ⓒ Ⓓ	31. Ⓐ Ⓑ Ⓒ Ⓓ	51. Ⓐ Ⓑ Ⓒ Ⓓ
12. Ⓐ Ⓑ Ⓒ Ⓓ	32. Ⓐ Ⓑ Ⓒ Ⓓ	52. Ⓐ Ⓑ Ⓒ Ⓓ
13. Ⓐ Ⓑ Ⓒ Ⓓ	33. Ⓐ Ⓑ Ⓒ Ⓓ	53. Ⓐ Ⓑ Ⓒ Ⓓ
14. Ⓐ Ⓑ Ⓒ Ⓓ	34. Ⓐ Ⓑ Ⓒ Ⓓ	54. Ⓐ Ⓑ Ⓒ Ⓓ
15. Ⓐ Ⓑ Ⓒ Ⓓ	35. Ⓐ Ⓑ Ⓒ Ⓓ	55. Ⓐ Ⓑ Ⓒ Ⓓ
16. Ⓐ Ⓑ Ⓒ Ⓓ	36. Ⓐ Ⓑ Ⓒ Ⓓ	56. Ⓐ Ⓑ Ⓒ Ⓓ
17. Ⓐ Ⓑ Ⓒ Ⓓ	37. Ⓐ Ⓑ Ⓒ Ⓓ	57. Ⓐ Ⓑ Ⓒ Ⓓ
18. Ⓐ Ⓑ Ⓒ Ⓓ	38. Ⓐ Ⓑ Ⓒ Ⓓ	58. Ⓐ Ⓑ Ⓒ Ⓓ
19. Ⓐ Ⓑ Ⓒ Ⓓ	39. Ⓐ Ⓑ Ⓒ Ⓓ	59. Ⓐ Ⓑ Ⓒ Ⓓ
20. Ⓐ Ⓑ Ⓒ Ⓓ	40. Ⓐ Ⓑ Ⓒ Ⓓ	60. Ⓐ Ⓑ Ⓒ Ⓓ

Practice Test 1: Language Arts and Reading

TIME: 70 minutes
60 questions*

Directions: Read each question and select the best response.

---

1. A child who understands that when reading English, we read from left to right and top to bottom and that every book has an author and sometimes an illustrator, is demonstrating which of the following?

   A. directionality

   B. concepts of print

   C. book handling skills

   D. alphabetic principle

2. Most vocabulary is learned

   A. directly.

   B. indirectly.

   C. before school.

   D. in school.

3. Which graphic organizer would be best to activate students' prior knowledge?

   A. concept map

   B. Venn diagram

   C. story map

   D. T-chart

4. Which is NOT an effective way to foster communication and collaboration?

   A. turn-and-talk

   B. literature circles

   C. popcorn reading

   D. buddy reading

5. A visual representation of knowledge or experiences regarding a specific topic is called a

   A. KWL chart.

   B. semantic map.

   C. mind map.

   D. Venn diagram.

6. The understanding that letters and sounds have a systematic relationship is

   A. phonological awareness.

   B. phonemic awareness.

   C. alphabetic principle.

   D. concepts of print.

7. A stanine score of 3 is considered

   A. average.

   B. above average.

   C. below average.

   D. the norm.

---

* This practice test presents slightly more items than you are likely to see on test day. The actual test contains approximately 55 questions. You will only learn exactly how many questions you will get after you take the FTCE tutorial and sign the non-disclosure agreement on test day.

8. When readers read words or passages with speed and accuracy, what are they demonstrating?

    A. comprehension

    B. accuracy

    C. automaticity

    D. prosody

9. Singing and clapping songs are a good strategy for teaching which emergent literacy skill?

    A. rhythm

    B. rhyming

    C. syntax

    D. sounds

10. Teaching vocabulary to children who are English language learners is best done

    A. explicitly.

    B. indirectly.

    C. through phonics.

    D. informally.

11. The instructional activity that involves students reading aloud from a script with no props, costumes, sets, or memorization is called

    A. storytelling.

    B. literature circles.

    C. dramatic theater.

    D. reader's theater.

12. An example of a literary device is a

    A. metaphor.

    B. concept map.

    C. plot.

    D. glossary.

13. Writing multiple paragraphs with transitional phrases and temporal words typically begins to occur in which grade level?

    A. Pre–K

    B. kindergarten

    C. second grade

    D. fourth grade

14. What is an effective instructional strategy to integrate reading, writing, speaking, and listening skills?

    A. project-based learning

    B. author and illustrator studies

    C. learning journals

    D. literature circles

15. A sentence that has a subordinate clause is called a

    A. complex sentence.

    B. compound sentence.

    C. prepositional phrase.

    D. subordination.

16. A beginning third grader reading at grade level would typically be reading what types of books?

    A. concept

    B. pattern

    C. repetitive

    D. series

17. A child who recognizes the Publix supermarket chain logo is demonstrating what stage of word recognition?

    A. pseudo-reading

    B. logographic-visual

    C. pragmatic

    D. visualization

18. The alphabetical list of names and subjects typically found at the end of a book is called a

    A. glossary.

    B. index.

    C. bibliography.

    D. table of contents.

19. Conventions of print such as capitalization and punctuation are best taught through

    A. exposure to print.

    B. reading aloud.

    C. direct instruction.

    D. visualization.

20. An instructional activity that can help students segment words into sounds is

    A. word writing.

    B. an Elkonin box.

    C. reading books aloud.

    D. matching words with picture cards.

21. Stories that are based in part on historical events, contain symbolism and pertain to the action of gods are called

    A. tall tales.

    B. fables.

    C. myths.

    D. fantasies.

22. "Which" and "Who" are examples of which of the following?

    A. adjectives

    B. adverbs

    C. pronouns

    D. nouns

23. A visual representation of knowledge and experiences is called a

    A. plot line.

    B. story summary.

    C. semantic map.

    D. flow chart.

24. Figures can

    A. show data related to the text.

    B. provide information on the chapters.

    C. give information about the sections.

    D. allow the reader to see the inside or parts of something.

25. Initial reading instruction in grades K–3 should include

    A. phonemic awareness, oral language, phonics, fluency, comprehension, and vocabulary.

    B. phonological awareness, semantics, syntax, and orthographonics.

    C. phonics, phonological awareness, fluency, vocabulary, and logographic.

    D. oral language, phonics, fluency, comprehension, and phonological awareness.

26. The stages of the writing process include

    A. prewriting, revision, editing, publishing.

    B. prewriting, brainstorming, editing, revision.

    C. narrative, expository, persuasive, descriptive.

    D. opinion, expository, fiction, nonfiction.

27. Stereotypes are typically found in what genre?

    A. science fiction

    B. fairy tales

    C. fiction

    D. myths

28. Which of the following genres is typically more appropriate for kindergarten retelling?

    A. science fiction

    B. mythology

    C. folklore

    D. graphic novels

29. Stories that typically have animals as main characters and a lesson to be learned are called

    A. fables.

    B. folk tales.

    C. fairy tales.

    D. fantasy tales.

30. Periodic assessments that measure learning and may predict summative performance are

    A. standard assessments.

    B. benchmark assessments.

    C. rubrics.

    D. summative assessments.

31. The words "bright" and "bite" are an example of what?

    A. rhyme

    B. rime

    C. onset

    D. sound

32. To help students compare and contrast, a teacher might use which graphic organizer?

    A. Venn diagram

    B. K-W-L chart

    C. mind map

    D. concept map

33. Events in chronological order are often depicted in

    A. tables.

    B. timelines.

    C. pictures.

    D. concept maps.

34. When a child understands sounds and how they work, including the idea that spoken words make up sentences and that these sounds communicate a message, she is demonstrating which of the following?

    A. phonemic awareness

    B. phonological awareness

    C. word awareness

    D. oral language competence

35. "For instance" or "for example" are typically found in what types of text?

    A. compare and contrast

    B. problem solution

    C. descriptive

    D. cause and effect

36. Understanding the text structure and features can support

    A. comprehension.

    B. automaticity.

    C. vocabulary development.

    D. phonological awareness.

37. The sketch to stretch activity, which involves readers creating mental images of a concept, is a good instructional strategy to foster

    A. fluency.

    B. imagination.

    C. vocabulary.

    D. comprehension.

38. When readers no longer need to sound out words frequently, but can decode and understand most words, they are in what stage?

    A. logographic-visual

    B. orthographic-morphemic

    C. logographic-morphemic

    D. alphabetic-phonemic

39. The strategy of having a student read the same text three or four times develops

    A. comprehension.

    B. decoding skills.

    C. fluency.

    D. vocabulary.

40. The section of a word that typically comes after the first consonant and after the first vowel is called the

    A. syllable.

    B. suffix.

    C. onset.

    D. rime.

41. When a test measures what it is supposed to measure, it is considered

    A. reliable.

    B. valid.

    C. consistent.

    D. accurate.

42. The hierarchy of ideas or steps in a process may be depicted by a

    A. flow chart.

    B. timeline.

    C. table.

    D. concept map.

43. The ability to communicate an experience that includes past, present, and future events or a cause and effect is called

    A. communicative competency.

    B. storytelling.

    C. narrative discourse.

    D. developmental talk.

44. Words or groups of words that relate to and precede a noun or pronoun and express a relationship to another word or an element in the clause are called

    A. pronouns.

    B. compound words.

    C. participles.

    D. prepositions.

45. A teacher would use what type of book to develop a child's understanding of shapes?

    A. concept

    B. pattern

    C. repetitive

    D. series

46. Children who are writing strings of letters or use letters to label a drawing are typically in what stage?

    A. transitional

    B. pre-literate

    C. emergent

    D. pre-alphabetic

47. Guided reading is typically done

    A. in a whole group.

    B. in a small group.

    C. individually.

    D. as Tier 1 instruction.

48. Which of the following activities would be most appropriate for fostering emergent literacy in a 4-year-old?

    A. singing songs and reciting nursery rhymes

    B. using colored markers to write sight words

    C. writing the alphabet on primary lined paper

    D. using alphabet flash cards to practice letter recognition

49. Syntax deals with

    A. grammar.

    B. meaning.

    C. figurative language.

    D. hyperbole.

50. Assessments that typically provide data to guide instructional decisions are called

    A. formative.

    B. summative.

    C. running records.

    D. benchmarks.

51. The type of writing that focuses on the senses and description is called

    A. persuasive.

    B. narrative.

    C. descriptive.

    D. expository.

52. What are characteristics of fairy tales?

    A. moral or lesson

    B. characters with exaggerated traits, such as extreme strength

    C. typically set in a forest or country setting

    D. characters with clearly defined traits or characteristics

53. What is "and" an example of?

    A. article

    B. conjunction

    C. intersession

    D. preposition

54. The best way to motivate students to read is to

    A. provide incentives.

    B. provide managed choice.

    C. have them watch the movie version first.

    D. send books home.

55. The traits of reading aloud with intonation and inflection are part of

    A. prosody.

    B. automaticity.

    C. comprehension.

    D. accuracy.

56. Which of the following is an instructional strategy designed to develop critical thinking?

    A. sketch to stretch

    B. open-ended essential question

    C. retelling

    D. summarization

57. The "tone" of a piece of writing is called

    A. fluency.

    B. presentation.

    C. voice.

    D. description.

58. Asking a writer to present reasons in a logical order is an example of what type of writing?

    A. expository

    B. narrative

    C. logical

    D. descriptive

59. When children's reading comprehension is 90% or higher, they are at what level of reading?

    A. independent

    B. instructional

    C. frustration

    D. potential

60. What is an individual assessment of oral reading fluency called?

    A. anecdotal record

    B. informal reading inventory

    C. running record

    D. developmental reading assessment

Language Arts and Reading
Practice Test 1: Answer Key

Test Item	Answer	Competency
1.	B	1
2.	B	4
3.	A	3
4.	C	1
5.	B	3
6.	C	1
7.	C	5
8.	C	3
9.	B	1
10.	A	1
11.	D	4
12.	A	4
13.	C	4
14.	A	1
15.	A	4
16.	D	2
17.	B	3
18.	B	2
19.	C	4
20.	B	1
21.	C	2
22.	C	4
23.	C	2
24.	A	3
25.	A	5
26.	A	4
27.	B	2
28.	C	2
29.	A	2
30.	B	5

Test Item	Answer	Competency
31.	A	1
32.	A	3
33.	B	1
34.	B	1
35.	C	3
36.	A	2
37.	D	1
38.	B	3
39.	C	3
40.	D	1
41.	B	5
42.	A	1
43.	C	2
44.	D	4
45.	A	2
46.	C	1
47.	B	1
48.	A	1
49.	A	4
50.	A	5
51.	C	4
52.	D	2
53.	B	4
54.	B	1
55.	A	4
56.	B	4
57.	C	4
58.	A	4
59.	A	3
60.	C	5

Language Arts and Reading
Practice Test 1: Detailed Answers

1. (B)

The answer is concepts of print, as it includes both the directionality and the understanding of book concepts. The alphabetic principle is the understanding that letters represent sounds which form words (D). (Competency 1)

2. (B)

Most vocabulary is learned indirectly, which is why rich experiences, high-quality texts, and opportunities to talk and collaborate are important. (Competency 4)

3. (A)

A concept map would be used to activate students' prior knowledge. A Venn diagram (B) is used to compare things; a story map (C) is used to keep track of events; and a t-chart (D) is usually used for note taking. (Competency 3)

4. (C)

Popcorn reading, a whole group reading activity that involves the teacher calling on students to read aloud to the class, is not an effective instructional strategy. Turn and talk (A), literature circles (B), and buddy reading (D) are better strategies, because they do not single out a reader in front of peers. (Competency 1)

5. (B)

Semantic maps are visual representations of knowledge or experiences on a topic. A KWL chart (A) represents an instructional strategy in which a student or students KWL (already know—want to know—have learned). (Competency 3)

6. (C)

Alphabetic principle is the best answer as it deals with letters and sounds. It is a subset of knowledge under phonological awareness (A), an umbrella term that includes a number of understandings such as oral language. Phonemic awareness (B) is the understanding that words are made up of sounds. Concepts of print (D) is the child's ability to understand concepts of reading and print before they are actually able to decode. (Competency 1)

7. (C)

Stanine scores of 7–9 are above average, 4–6 are average, 1–3 are below average; norms mean the assessment was tested in controlled populations. (Competency 5)

8. (C)

Automaticity is the best answer as it includes the speed or element that is typically measured in words read per minute. Comprehension (A) deals with meaning; accuracy (B) is simply the reader reading without errors; and prosody (D) includes the ability to read with appropriate inflection, tone, and stress. (Competency 3)

9. (B)

Singing and clapping songs are part of the rhyming activities that are good for teaching children rhyming, an emergent literacy skill. (Competency 1)

10. (A)

While most vocabulary is learned indirectly, teaching vocabulary to English language learners is best done explicitly and with intention. (Competency 1)

11. (D)

Reader's theater is the strategy where readers read aloud from a level script to practice reading fluently in a collaborative manner. A literature circle (B) is a collaborative and student-centered reading strategy in which students choose a book together and then each takes on one of four jobs in the Literature Circle. (Competency 4)

12. (A)

Metaphors are literary devices; concept maps (B) are organizational tools; plot (C) is the storyline; a glossary (D) is a text feature. (Competency 4)

13. (C)

Writers in first and second grade begin to increase their writing fluency and write paragraphs with more complex sentences and ideas. (Competency 4)

14. (A)

Project-based learning is an effective way to integrate reading, writing, speaking, listening, and viewing skills. (Competency 1)

15. (A)

Complex sentences contain a subordinate clause. An example is, "She left early to beat the traffic." The phrase "to beat the traffic" is connected to why she left early. A compound sentence (B) is formed when you join two main clauses with a connective (*and, but, so, or,* a comma, or a semi-colon.). A prepositional phrase (C) is composed of a preposition, a noun or pronoun object of the preposition, and an optional modifier of the object. A subordinate clause (D) contains a subject and a verb, but it needs to be attached to a main clause because it cannot make sense on its own. (Competency 4)

16. (D)

Series books, with repeating characters and predictable storylines, are typically good for third graders reading at grade level. Concept books (A) lead readers through a basic concept, which could be in math, reading, or science. Books that have a strong pattern and rhythmic flow (B) help children read along with an adult. (Competency 2)

17. (B)

Logographic-visual is the term used to describe when a child uses illustrations or letters in words to understand the text, without really understanding the letter-symbol relationship. In pseudo-reading (A), children often "pretend" to read, meaning they can recognize signs and stories previously read to them on a page and can therefore point them out and exhibit an understanding of the content. Pragmatics (C) is a group of socially constructed rules that guide how individuals interact with each other, as in taking turns, eye-contact, and greetings. Visualizing (D) refers to children's ability to create pictures in their heads based on text they read or words they hear. (Competency 3)

18. (B)

The index contains the names, subjects, and related information and is typically at the back of a book. A glossary (A) also appears at the end of a book but includes terms and definitions within that book that are either newly introduced, uncommon, or specialized. A bibliography (C) is a list of sources you use when writing a scholarly article or paper or a list of books or articles an author has published on a specific subject. A table of contents (D) is a list of the parts of a book or document, organized in the order in which the parts appear, and listing the page number on which each section starts. (Competency 2)

19. (C)

Direct instruction is the best answer; teaching conventions may include the other components, but are most effectively taught through drawing attention to the conventions and rules. (Competency 4)

20. (B)

Elkonin boxes are used to segment words into individual sounds. (Competency 1)

21. (C)

Myths deal with symbolism and actions of gods; tall tales (A) have gross exaggeration; fables (B) are stories with a moral; fantasies (D) are stories that may be set in other worlds or times and often include magic. (Competency 2)

22. (C)

Interrogative pronouns include "which" and "who," so pronouns (C) is the best answer. Adjectives (A) and adverbs (B) are descriptive, and nouns (D) are more specific. (Competency 4)

23. (C)

Semantic map is the best choice; the others are used to support comprehension in different ways. (Competency 2)

24. (A)

Figures typically show data related to the text. (Competency 3)

25. (A)

The instructional components of K–3 reading are phonemic awareness, oral language, phonics, fluency, comprehension, and vocabulary. (Competency 5)

26. (A)

The stages of the writing process include prewriting or brainstorming, revision, editing, and publishing. (Competency 4)

27. (B)

Fairy tales is the best answer. While the other genres may have stereotypes, they may also have more complex characters. (Competency 2)

28. (C)

Folklore is typically most appropriate for kindergarten as the stories have a beginning, middle, and end, predictable features (which makes the story easier to remember), and can be retold more easily. Folklore is stories, customs, and beliefs that are passed from one generation to the next. Science fiction stories (A) often tell about science and technology of the future. A myth (B) is a story that's told again and again and serves to explain why something is the way it is. Myths exist in every society, as they are basic elements of human culture. A graphic novel (D) is a type of comic book usually with a long storyline similar to those of novels. (Competency 2)

29. (A)

Fables are the stories under the traditional literature genre that include animals as characters and teach lessons. Fantasy (D) typically features the use of magic and might be using myths and legends from almost any culture. With fantasies, their plot involves witches, sorcerers, and mythical and animal creatures talking like humans, as well as other things that never happen in real life. A folktale (B) is an old story that's been told again and again, often for generations. A fairy tale (C) is a story, often intended for children, that features fanciful and wondrous characters such as elves, goblins, wizards, and even, but not necessarily, fairies. (Competency 2)

30. (B)

Benchmark assessments, which are given periodically after specific content is taught, is the best answer, as they are typically formal assessments that measure learning and may predict performance on end-of-year tests. Standardized assessments (A) are any form of test that requires all test-takers to answer the same questions, or a selection of questions from a common bank of questions, in the same way, and that is scored in a "standard" or consistent manner, which makes it possible to compare the relative performance of individual students. Rubrics (C) is a set of criteria for grading assignments. Summative assessments (D) are used to evaluate student learning, skill acquisition, and academic achievement at the conclusion of a defined instructional period. (Competency 5)

31. (A)

Rhyme is the best choice as the two words have ending sounds that are alike. Rhymes would be the same phonogram as in *bite*, *site* or *bright*, *fight*. Onset is the portion of the word before the first vowel, so it would be *br* and *b*. (Competency 1)

32. (A)

Venn diagrams are best for comparing and contrasting. (Competency 3)

33. (B)

Timelines depict events in chronological order. A concept map is a type of graphic organizer used to help students organize and represent knowledge of a subject. Concept maps begin with a main idea (or concept) and then branch out to show how that main idea can be broken down into specific topics. (Competency 1)

34. (B)

Phonological awareness is the umbrella term and so is the best answer choice for this question. Phonemic awareness (A) is the ability to hear, identify, and manipulate individual sounds-phonemes—in spoken words. (Competency 1)

35. (C)

These signal phrases are typically found in descriptive texts. (Competency 3)

36. (A)

Comprehension is the best choice. When readers understand the format and predictable features of a text, they can focus on comprehension. Automaticity (B) is the ability to do things without occupying the mind with the low-level details required. (Competency 2)

37. (D)

The activity is an effective strategy to foster comprehension, as the reader or listener can create visual images to make links to the content being learned. (Competency 1)

38. (B)

The orthographic-morphemic stage is the best choice; logographic-visual (A) is when a reader recognizes the words or logo because of its features; logographic-morphemic (C) is not a stage; alphabetic-phonemic (D) is when the reader develops the concept of letter-sound relationships. (Competency 3)

39. (C)

Repeated readings are typically used to develop fluency. (Competency 3)

40. (D)

Rime is the best answer because a word can be divided into onset (the part of the word before the vowel) and rime (the portion of the word after the vowel). The rime may sometimes be called the *phonogram* or *word family*. (Competency 1)

41. (B)

Validity refers to how well a test measures what it was designed to measure. Reliability (A) refers to the consistency of the results. The other terms are descriptors and not assessment terms. (Competency 5)

42. (A)

Flow chart is the best answer. Timelines (B) show the order; tables (C) organize information; and concept maps (D) are used for a variety of instructional purposes, such as accessing prior knowledge. (Competency 1)

43. (C)

Narrative discourse is the term that is used to describe a trait that, when developed in young children, has a connection with later reading ability. Communicative competency (A) is the correlation between fluency and accuracy. (Competency 2)

44. (D)

Prepositions are words or groups of words that relate to a noun or pronoun and express a relation to another word or element in the clause. (Competency 4)

45. (A)

Concept books typically deal with basic concepts like colors, shapes, numbers, etc. Pattern books feature simple text in a strongly repetitive pattern that allows children to predict what is coming next as they read. (Competency 2)

46. (C)

Emergent is the best answer because emergent writers write letter strings that convey a meaning, while pre-literate children (B) may scribble or write random letter-like forms. Transitional writers (A) are more sophisticated and begin to make the letter-sound connection. Pre-alphabetic (D) is not a writing stage. (Competency 1)

47. (B)

Guided reading works more effectively with a small group. (Competency 1)

48. (A)

Singing songs and reciting nursery rhymes are the most developmentally appropriate activities for working with 4-year-olds. (Competency 1)

49. (A)

Grammar is the best choice; the others deal with semantics. (Competency 4)

50. (A)

Formative assessments can be in a variety of formats, but are used to provide information to guide instructional decisions. (Competency 5)

51. (C)

Descriptive writing is the best answer and is typically expository although the other types may include elements of description. (Competency 4)

52. (D)

Fairy tales have characters with clearly defined traits such as "good" or "evil." There are messages, but not morals (fables). The characters are typically not with extreme traits (tall tales), and while the story may be in a forest or country setting (folk tales), it may also be in a castle, town, or other setting. (Competency 2)

53. (B)

A conjunction joins words and ideas; articles (A) precede nouns, intersession (C) is not a part of speech; and prepositions (D) show relationships. (Competency 4)

54. (B)

Research shows that managed choice and self-selection are motivating factors to encourage students to read. (Competency 1)

55. (A)

Prosody is the best answer as it includes the musical quality of reading aloud; automaticity (B) may include speed and accuracy without the other traits. (Competency 4)

56. (B)

Developing an open-ended essential question allows for development of critical-thinking skills; the others are typically for comprehension. (Competency 4)

57. (C)

Voice is one of the 6 + 1 traits of writing. The others are ideas, conventions, organization, word choice, presentation, and sentence fluency. (Competency 4)

58. (A)

Expository is the best answer; narrative (B) can have a different format; logical (C) and descriptive (D) can fit more than one style. (Competency 4)

59. (A)

When on the independent level, children can read a text by themselves; instructional typically is 75% or higher; and frustration is less than 50% comprehension. (Competency 3)

60. (C)

While assessments of oral reading fluency may be part of an informal reading inventory (B) or a developmental reading assessment (D), running record is the best choice. Anecdotal records (A) are teacher notes based on observation. (Competency 5)

PRACTICE TEST 1

FTCE PreK–3 Mathematics
Subtest 3 (533)

Also available at the REA Study Center (www.rea.com/studycenter)

This practice test is also offered online at the REA Study Center.
We recommend that you take the online version of the test to simulate
test-day conditions and to receive these added benefits:

- **Timed testing conditions**—helps you gauge how much time you
  can spend on each question

- **Automatic scoring**—find out how you did on the test, instantly

- **On-screen detailed explanations of answers**—gives you the
  correct answer and explains why the other answer choices are
  wrong

- **Diagnostic score reports**—pinpoint where you're strongest and
  where you need to focus your study

MATHEMATICS REFERENCE SHEET

Area

 Triangle $A = \dfrac{1}{2}bh$

 Rectangle $A = lw$

 Trapezoid $A = \dfrac{1}{2}h(b_1 + b_2)$

Parallelogram $A = bh$

Circle $A = \pi r^2$

KEY	
b = base	d = diameter
h = height	r = radius
l = length	A = area
w = width	C = circumference
$S.A.$ = surface area	V = volume
	B = area of base
Use 3.14 or $\dfrac{22}{7}$ for π	

Circumference

$C = \pi d = 2\pi r$

Surface Area

1. Surface area of a prism or pyramid equals the sum of the areas of all faces.

Volume

1. Volume of a triangular or rectangular prism equals the <u>Area of the Base</u> (B) times the height (h).

$V = Bh$

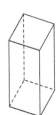 

2. Volume of a pyramid equals $\frac{1}{3}$ times the <u>Area of the Base</u> (B) times the height (h).

$$V = \frac{1}{3} Bh$$

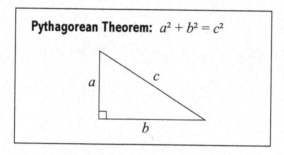

Pythagorean Theorem: $a^2 + b^2 = c^2$

Conversions

1 yard = 3 feet = 36 inches

1 mile = 1,760 yards = 5,280 feet

1 acre = 43,560 square feet

1 hour = 60 minutes

1 minute = 60 seconds

1 cup = 8 fluid ounces

1 pint = 2 cups

1 quart = 2 pints

1 gallon = 4 quarts

1 pound = 16 ounces

1 ton = 2,000 pounds

1 liter = 1000 milliliters = 1000 cubic centimeters

1 meter = 100 centimeters = 1000 millimeters

1 kilometer = 1000 meters

1 gram = 1000 milligrams

1 kilogram = 1000 grams

Metric numbers with four digits are presented without a comma (e.g., 9960 kilometers). For metric numbers greater than four digits, a space is used instead of a comma (e.g., 12 500 liters).

Mathematics Practice Test 1: Answer Sheet

1. Ⓐ Ⓑ Ⓒ Ⓓ
2. Ⓐ Ⓑ Ⓒ Ⓓ
3. Ⓐ Ⓑ Ⓒ Ⓓ
4. Ⓐ Ⓑ Ⓒ Ⓓ
5. Ⓐ Ⓑ Ⓒ Ⓓ
6. Ⓐ Ⓑ Ⓒ Ⓓ
7. Ⓐ Ⓑ Ⓒ Ⓓ
8. Ⓐ Ⓑ Ⓒ Ⓓ
9. Ⓐ Ⓑ Ⓒ Ⓓ
10. Ⓐ Ⓑ Ⓒ Ⓓ
11. Ⓐ Ⓑ Ⓒ Ⓓ
12. Ⓐ Ⓑ Ⓒ Ⓓ
13. Ⓐ Ⓑ Ⓒ Ⓓ
14. Ⓐ Ⓑ Ⓒ Ⓓ
15. Ⓐ Ⓑ Ⓒ Ⓓ
16. Ⓐ Ⓑ Ⓒ Ⓓ
17. Ⓐ Ⓑ Ⓒ Ⓓ

18. Ⓐ Ⓑ Ⓒ Ⓓ
19. Ⓐ Ⓑ Ⓒ Ⓓ
20. Ⓐ Ⓑ Ⓒ Ⓓ
21. Ⓐ Ⓑ Ⓒ Ⓓ
22. Ⓐ Ⓑ Ⓒ Ⓓ
23. Ⓐ Ⓑ Ⓒ Ⓓ
24. Ⓐ Ⓑ Ⓒ Ⓓ
25. Ⓐ Ⓑ Ⓒ Ⓓ
26. Ⓐ Ⓑ Ⓒ Ⓓ
27. Ⓐ Ⓑ Ⓒ Ⓓ
28. Ⓐ Ⓑ Ⓒ Ⓓ
29. Ⓐ Ⓑ Ⓒ Ⓓ
30. Ⓐ Ⓑ Ⓒ Ⓓ
31. Ⓐ Ⓑ Ⓒ Ⓓ
32. Ⓐ Ⓑ Ⓒ Ⓓ
33. Ⓐ Ⓑ Ⓒ Ⓓ
34. Ⓐ Ⓑ Ⓒ Ⓓ

35. Ⓐ Ⓑ Ⓒ Ⓓ
36. Ⓐ Ⓑ Ⓒ Ⓓ
37. Ⓐ Ⓑ Ⓒ Ⓓ
38. Ⓐ Ⓑ Ⓒ Ⓓ
39. Ⓐ Ⓑ Ⓒ Ⓓ
40. Ⓐ Ⓑ Ⓒ Ⓓ
41. Ⓐ Ⓑ Ⓒ Ⓓ
42. Ⓐ Ⓑ Ⓒ Ⓓ
43. Ⓐ Ⓑ Ⓒ Ⓓ
44. Ⓐ Ⓑ Ⓒ Ⓓ
45. Ⓐ Ⓑ Ⓒ Ⓓ
46. Ⓐ Ⓑ Ⓒ Ⓓ
47. Ⓐ Ⓑ Ⓒ Ⓓ
48. Ⓐ Ⓑ Ⓒ Ⓓ
49. Ⓐ Ⓑ Ⓒ Ⓓ
50. Ⓐ Ⓑ Ⓒ Ⓓ

Practice Test 1: Mathematics

TIME: 70 minutes
50 questions*

> **Directions:** Read each question and select the best response.

1. What is the cardinal number for a set?

   A. The first number said when counting objects in the set.

   B. The last number said when counting objects in the set.

   C. The number you skip count by when counting objects in the set.

   D. The number you start with when counting on to find the total objects in the set.

2. What is the best way to introduce the properties of geometric shapes to young children?

   A. Show children examples of various two-dimensional shapes on a Smart Board, then point out the properties of each shape.

   B. Have children complete a worksheet where they match each two-dimensional shape with its properties.

   C. Show children a video that introduces two-dimensional geometric shapes and their properties.

   D. Give small groups of children a set of cut-outs of two-dimensional shapes, then have them sort them into groups based on their similarities.

3. Ms. Sanchez wants the students in her class to investigate symmetry. Which of the following is a good manipulative for her students to use?

   A. Unifix cubes

   B. Cuisenaire rods

   C. base-10 blocks

   D. geoboards

4. Which of the following is an example of a linear model to represent fractions?

   A. pie pieces

   B. two-color counters

   C. pattern blocks

   D. fraction strips

5. Which of the following statements is correct?

   A. All rectangles are rhombuses, but not all rhombuses are rectangles.

   B. All squares are rectangles, but not all rectangles are squares.

   C. All rhombuses are rectangles, but not all rectangles are rhombuses.

   D. All rectangles are squares, but not all squares are rectangles.

---

* This practice test presents slightly more items than you are likely to see on test day. The actual test contains approximately 45 questions. You will only learn exactly how many questions you will get after you take the FTCE tutorial and sign the non-disclosure agreement on test day.

6. A teacher creates groups of students based upon similar mathematical ability. This is an example of what type of grouping?

   A. heterogeneous

   B. homogeneous

   C. eclectic

   D. flexible

7. First graders are measuring the width of a bookshelf using Unifix cubes. They place as many Unifix cubes side-by-side as they need to span the width of the bookshelf and count how many cubes they use. What measurement concepts are they demonstrating?

   A. iterating using standard units

   B. iterating using nonstandard units

   C. tiling using standard units

   D. tiling using nonstandard units

8. A third grade teacher places students into groups to investigate quadrilaterals. Each group member is assigned a different quadrilateral to investigate. Next, students get into a new group with others who were assigned the same quadrilateral. They work together to learn about and become "experts" on their quadrilateral. Students return to their original group to teach group members about the quadrilateral they investigated. Together, they develop shared understanding about types of quadrilaterals. This is an example of which instructional strategy?

   A. jigsaw

   B. connect two

   C. flexible grouping

   D. tiered instruction

9. A child says, *I know an easy way to add 9—just add 10 and then subtract one.* Which mathematical practice is the child demonstrating?

   A. attending to precision

   B. using appropriate tools strategically

   C. looking for and expressing regularity in repeated reasoning

   D. reasoning abstractly and quantitatively

10. A patio has the dimensions shown in the figure below. What is its perimeter?

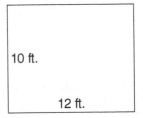

   A. 22 ft.

   B. 120 ft.

   C. 44 ft.

   D. 240 ft.

11. Children grow bean plants in the class garden. One day they use paper strips to measure the height of each plant. They glue the strips onto a class graph to compare the heights of the bean plants. What is this an example of?

   A. measuring with standard units

   B. integrating art with mathematics

   C. integrating science with mathematics

   D. measuring by iterating units

12. What would be the next item in the pattern below?

   A. triangle

   B. circle

   C. square

   D. half circle

13. A four-year-old uses pattern blocks to make the pattern below. What kind of pattern did the child create?

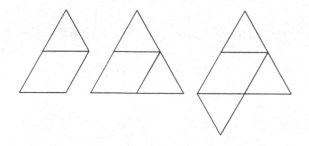

   A. a repeating pattern

   B. a color pattern

   C. a core pattern

   D. a growing pattern

14. Children are learning about graphing. Each child gets a small bag of colored candies. They sort them by color and then arrange them in vertical lines to show how many there are of each color. This is an example of what type of graph?

   A. real graph

   B. pictograph

   C. bar graph

   D. pie graph

15. The table below lists several inputs and outputs for a function machine. What is the rule the machine is using?

INPUT	OUTPUT
7	4
8	5
19	16
29	?

   A. + 3

   B. − 3

   C. + 10

   D. − 10

16. Which type of triangle has no equal sides or equal angles?

   A. equilateral

   B. isosceles

   C. scalene

   D. obtuse

17. What is the core in the following pattern? Clap-Clap-Stomp-Clap-Clap-Stomp-Clap

   A. Clap-Stomp-Clap

   B. Clap-Clap-Stomp

   C. Stomp-Clap-Clap

   D. Clap-Clap-Stomp-Clap

18. Two third graders are solving the following problem:

    There are 130 third graders in our school. There are 26 more girls than boys. How many boys are in third grade? How many girls are in third grade?

    The students draw the picture below to help them solve the problem. How many boys and girls are in third grade?

	Boys

		Girls
    +26

    A. 104 boys, 26 girls

    B. 26 boys, 104 girls

    C. 78 boys, 52 girls

    D. 52 boys, 78 girls

19. Children go outside to collect leaves. You want them to create a class graph. What would be the best type of graph for them to show this data?

    A. histogram

    B. pictograph

    C. line graph

    D. pie graph

20. A child is asked to solve the problem 7 + 3. The child says, "Seven, eight, nine, ten. The answer is ten." The child has just demonstrated

    A. subitizing.

    B. counting on.

    C. cardinality.

    D. counting backwards.

21. A three-year-old says the number words in order from 1 to 10. She has just demonstrated

    A. rote counting.

    B. rational counting.

    C. subitizing.

    D. ordinality.

22. What can be said about angle *A* in the drawing below?

— Angle *A*

    A. It is an acute angle.

    B. It is a right angle.

    C. It is an obtuse angle.

    D. It is a reflex angle.

23. A third grader is trying to remember 6 × 7. He says, "5 × 7 = 35. 35 + 7 = 42, so 6 × 7 = 42." Which property of arithmetic did this child use?

    A. commutative

    B. associative

    C. identity

    D. distributive

24. When Prekindergarten students put cards showing daily activities in temporal order (i.e., *First, I get up. Then, I eat breakfast. Third, I brush my teeth.*), what are the students engaging in?

    A. cardinality

    B. seriation

    C. one-to-one correspondence

    D. subitizing

25. Which property is illustrated in this equation?

    $$a \times 1 = a$$

    A. commutative property of multiplication

    B. identity property of multiplication

    C. associative property of multiplication

    D. distributive property

26. Which property of operations was used in the following example:

$$9 + 3 + 1 = ?$$
$$9 + 1 + 3 = ?$$
$$10 + 3 = 13$$

 A. associative property of addition

 B. commutative property of addition

 C. turn-around property of addition

 D. ten property of addition

27. Which of the following would be the best model to use with third graders who are learning about multiplication?

 A. Unifix cubes

 B. an array

 C. a math balance

 D. tangrams

28. If each circle in the drawing below represents one whole pie, what fraction of leftover pie is represented in the shaded area of the diagram below?

 A. $\dfrac{5}{4}$

 B. $\dfrac{4}{5}$

 C. $\dfrac{5}{8}$

 D. $\dfrac{3}{8}$

29. Which of the following are appropriate mathematical concepts for the PreK–3 curriculum?

 A. multiplying fractions, representing fractions on a number line, and using U.S. customary units to measure

 B. using metric units to measure, composing and decomposing numbers into tens and ones, and extending patterns

 C. representing fractions on a number line, extending patterns, and converting decimals to percentages

 D. decomposing numbers into tens and ones, converting from U.S. customary units to metric units, and representing fractions on a number line

30. Which of the following pairs of fractions are equivalent to each other?

 A. $\dfrac{8}{9}, \dfrac{9}{10}$

 B. $\dfrac{8}{12}, \dfrac{6}{9}$

 C. $\dfrac{7}{11}, \dfrac{9}{13}$

 D. $\dfrac{6}{11}, \dfrac{8}{15}$

31. Which of the following are defining attributes of a parallelogram?

 A. one pair of parallel sides

 B. two pairs of parallel sides and opposite angles equal

 C. two pairs of equal sides and four right angles

 D. four equal sides and opposite angles equal

32. When a child turns the problem 17 − 8 around and asks, "What must I add to 8 to get 17," the child is

    A. using the commutative property of addition.

    B. recognizing the inverse relationship between addition and subtraction.

    C. using the associative property of addition.

    D. recognizing how to decompose numbers in base-ten.

33. Which of the following is an example of an area model for fractions?

    A. Cuisenaire rods

    B. two-color counters

    C. geoboards

    D. ruler

34. Which of the following are correct ways to decompose the number 56 into tens and ones?

        I.   5 tens and 6 ones

        II.   0 tens and 56 ones

        III. 50 tens and 6 ones

        IV. 3 tens and 26 ones

    A. I and II only

    B. I and III only

    C. I, II, and IV

    D. II, III, and IV

35. Second graders are working on subtraction with regrouping. One group is solving the problem 34 − 9. A second group is solving 72 − 56, and a third group is solving 101 − 48. This is an example of

    A. making sense of problems.

    B. procedural fluency.

    C. tiered instruction.

    D. performance-based instruction.

36. What is the most appropriate unit to measure the length of a playground?

    A. meter

    B. inch

    C. kilometer

    D. mile

37. The best strategy to assess children's mathematical thinking is

    A. a checklist the teacher can fill out while observing students.

    B. an interview.

    C. a worksheet.

    D. a class discussion.

38. What is the area of the yard in the figure below?

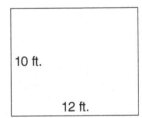

    A. 22 ft.^{2}

    B. 120 ft.^{2}

    C. 44 ft.^{2}

    D. 240 ft.^{2}

39. Put the numbers 2, 6, 3, 7 in the correct blanks to make the equation true.

    _____ + _____ = _____ + _____

    A. 2, 6, 3, 7

    B. 7, 6, 3, 2

    C. 6, 3, 2, 7

    D. 3, 7, 6, 2

40. Which number belongs in the blank to make the equation true?

$$12 - \underline{\hphantom{xx}} = 4 + 5$$

A. 3

B. 9

C. 21

D. 12

41. A milliliter is what fraction of a liter?

A. $\dfrac{1}{10,000}$

B. $\dfrac{1}{1000}$

C. $\dfrac{1}{100}$

D. $\dfrac{1}{10}$

42. The most appropriate unit to measure the capacity of a bathtub is a

A. teaspoon.

B. cup.

C. pint.

D. gallon.

43. What would be the best assessment strategy to determine students' growth in using mathematical practices?

A. a quiz on mathematical practices

B. a bell ringer activity in which students match the practices with their definitions

C. a writing prompt in which students name their favorite practice and tell why it's their favorite

D. a checklist the teacher can fill out while observing students doing mathematics

44. Which of the following is an example of an ABBC pattern?

A.

B.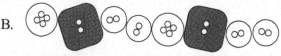

C.

D.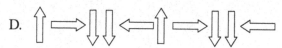

45. What type of triangle is shown in the picture below?

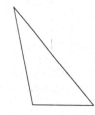

A. obtuse

B. right

C. acute

D. equilateral

46. Which of the following is an example of a unit fraction?

A. $\dfrac{3}{1}$

B. $\dfrac{6}{6}$

C. $\dfrac{3}{4}$

D. $\dfrac{1}{7}$

47. A soda can is an example of a

    A. cylinder.

    B. cone.

    C. pyramid.

    D. prism.

48. Ethan incorrectly solves the following problems. What is his mistake?

$$
\begin{array}{r} 73 \\ -57 \\ \hline 26 \end{array}
\qquad
\begin{array}{r} 92 \\ -64 \\ \hline 38 \end{array}
$$

    A. He regrouped in the ones column, but forgot to change the tens column.

    B. He incorrectly regrouped in the ones column.

    C. He changed the tens column, but forgot to re-group in the ones column.

    D. He incorrectly regrouped in the ones column and forgot to change the tens column.

49. A child rolls a die and without counting each dot, says, "I got a 4." Which of the following does this demonstrate?

    A. rote counting

    B. rational counting

    C. subitizing

    D. ordinality

50. A second grade teacher gives every student in the class a set of cards with one capital letter written on each card. Students are directed to determine if the letter can be divided to show matching halves. This lesson is on

    A. rotation symmetry.

    B. reflection symmetry.

    C. point symmetry.

    D. translation symmetry.

Mathematics Practice Test 1: Answer Key

Test Item	Answer	Competency
1.	B	3
2.	D	1
3.	D	5
4.	D	3
5.	B	5
6.	B	1
7.	D	4
8.	A	1
9.	D	1
10.	C	4
11.	C	1
12.	B	2
13.	D	2
14.	A	4
15.	B	2
16.	C	5
17.	B	2
18.	D	2
19.	B	4
20.	B	3
21.	A	3
22.	A	5
23.	D	3
24.	B	3
25.	B	3

Test Item	Answer	Competency
26.	A	3
27.	B	1
28.	A	3
29.	B	1
30.	B	3
31.	B	5
32.	B	3
33.	C	3
34.	C	3
35.	C	1
36.	A	4
37.	B	1
38.	B	4
39.	C	2
40.	A	2
41.	B	4
42.	D	4
43.	D	1
44.	A	2
45.	A	5
46.	D	3
47.	A	5
48.	A	1
49.	C	3
50.	B	5

Mathematics Practice Test 1: Detailed Answers

1. (B)

Choice (B) is the best answer. *Cardinality* means the last number said when counting a set of objects and tells how many there are in the set. That final number is the cardinal number of the set. (Competency 3)

2. (D)

Choice (D) is the best answer because children's initial mathematical experiences should be with concrete objects. Later they can progress to semi-concrete and abstract thinking. (Competency 1)

3. (D)

Choice (D) is the best answer. Children learn about two types of symmetry in the PreK/Primary years. Reflection symmetry is line or mirror symmetry. Students can place a rubber band down the middle of a geoboard and create a shape on one side of the rubber band. They can then construct what the shape would look like if it was reflected across the line. When investigating rotation symmetry children can create a shape on the geoboard and determine what it would look like if it was rotated by a specific number of degrees. None of the other choices would be good for learning about symmetry. (Competency 5)

4. (D)

Choice (D) is the best answer. A linear fraction model is one in which fractions are length measurements. Fraction strips are a linear model. Pie pieces and pattern blocks are both area models for fractions. Fractions in an area model are portions of an area that can be evenly divided into smaller pieces. Two-color counters are a set model. In a set model, the whole is a group of objects. (Competency 3)

5. (B)

Choice (B) is the best answer. Quadrilaterals are interesting because many of them are special types of other quadrilaterals. A rectangle is a parallelogram with four right angles. Because a rectangle is a parallelogram, it also has two pairs of equal, parallel sides. A square has four equal sides and four right angles. Notice that a shape with four equal sides has two pairs of equal, parallel sides. Because a square has two pairs of equal, parallel sides and four right angles, all squares are also rectangles. However, not all rectangles have four equal sides. Therefore, there are some rectangles that are not squares. (Competency 5)

6. (B)

Choice (B) is the best answer. Homogeneous grouping is grouping students of similar ability together. Heterogeneous grouping is grouping students of differing ability together. (Competency 1)

7. (D)

Choice (D) is the best answer. Standard units refer to U.S. customary or metric measurement units. Young children often measure with nonstandard units like Unifix cubes. When children put out as many copies of a unit as they need to measure an object, they are tiling. In contrast, iterating units requires taking a single example of the unit and repeating it again and again until the object is measured. (Competency 4)

8. (A)

Choice (A) is the best answer. Jigsaw is a strategy in which each student in a group is assigned a specific aspect of a topic. They work with other students in the class who have been assigned the same aspect of the topic, to learn about it and become the expert on it. Students then return to their original group and teach group members about their assigned aspect of the topic. (Competency 1)

9. (D)

Choice (D) is the best answer. When children use properties of operations to solve problems rather than merely relying on a procedure, they are reasoning abstractly and quantitatively. (Competency 1)

10. (C)

Choice (C) is the best answer. The perimeter of any object is the distance required to go all the way around the object. The patio is a rectangle with two sides that are 12 feet long and two sides that are 10 feet long. We can find the perimeter either by adding all of them together: $10 + 12 + 10 + 12 = 44$, or we can add $10 + 12$ and multiply the result by 2. Perimeter is a length so it is measured in feet in this example. (Competency 4)

11. (C)

Choice (C) is the best answer. Measuring is an authentic way to integrate mathematics and science. Measuring with paper strips is an example of using nonstandard units. (Competency 1)

12. (B)

Choice (B) is the best answer. This is a repeating pattern. The core is triangle-circle-circle-square-half circle. The pattern then repeats starting with a triangle. The next shape in the pattern is a circle. (Competency 2)

13. (D)

Choice (D) is the best answer. A growing pattern is also known as a sequence. PreK/Primary students work with arithmetic sequences or growing patterns. These are ones in which the pattern grows by adding or subtracting the same fixed quantity to each term in the sequence. In

this pattern, a triangle is added to each successive term. The next term will have one parallelogram and four triangles. (Competency 2)

14. (A)

Choice (A) is the best answer. A real graph uses actual objects to create the graph. In this example, children use the candies themselves. Real graphs are good ways to introduce graphing to young children because they are the most concrete. The other answer choices are all more abstract. (Competency 4)

15. (B)

Choice (B) is the best answer. A function is a rule that enables the pairing of a single output with any input. The rule indicates what is done to the input to get the output. In this case the rule is "subtract 3." We know that because $7 - 3 = 4$, $8 - 3 = 5$, etc. (Competency 2)

16. (C)

Choice (C) is the best answer. A scalene triangle is one that has no sides or angles that are equal. At least two sides and two angles are equal in an isosceles triangle, and all three sides and angles are equal in an equilateral triangle. An obtuse triangle is one that contains one obtuse angle. An obtuse triangle might be scalene, but not all obtuse triangles are scalene. (Competency 5)

17. (B)

Choice (B) is the best answer. The core in a repeating pattern is the shortest set of elements that repeats. (Competency 2)

18. (D)

Choice (D) is the best answer. The third graders are using a strip diagram to solve the problem. The first rectangle stands for the number of boys. The students know that the number of girls equals the number of boys plus 26 more. That's why they drew a strip for the girls showing a rectangle the same length as the boys with 26 more added. The total number of third graders is 130. First, subtract 130 − 26. That equals 104. That means there are two strips left that are the same length. Divide 104 by 2. That equals 52. There are 52 boys. Now, add 52 + 26 to get the number of girls. There are 78 girls. (Competency 2)

19. (B)

Choice (B) is the best answer. A pie graph (D) shows parts of a whole. Histograms (A) and line graphs (C) are both used for continuous data. The data children collected in this example is discrete data because it can be put into categories. A pictograph is the only answer choice that is used for discrete data. (Competency 4)

20. (B)

Choice (B) is the best answer. When children count on, they start at one of the numbers (usually the larger of the two) and continue counting without having to start at one. Many kindergarten teachers encourage their students to use counting on when learning basic addition facts. (Competency 3)

21. (A)

Choice (A) is the best answer. When children say the number words in order, they are rote counting. They may not be able to match the number word with a specific object when counting. Children can rote count to a higher number than they can rationally count. (Competency 3)

22. (A)

Choice (A) is the best answer. An acute angle is one that is between 0° and 90°. Angle A on the slice of pizza is clearly less than 90°. (Competency 5)

23. (D)

Choice (D) is the best answer. The distributive property of multiplication over addition says $a(b + c) = ab + ac$. This means that the student can either add b and

c and then multiply the result by a **or** the student can multiply b and c by a and then add the results together. In this problem, the student realized that $6 = 5 + 1$. He then distributed the 7 to the 5 and the 1. Written out, it looks like this: $6 \times 7 = (5 + 1)7 = (5 \times 7) + (1 \times 7) = 35 + 7 = 42$. (Competency 3)

24. (B)

Choice (B) is the best answer. Seriation is the ability to organize objects or events based on some attribute. Objects can be ordered by size or length. In this case, events are being ordered based upon when they occur during a typical day. (Competency 3)

25. (B)

Choice (B) is the best answer. The identity property of multiplication says that anytime you multiply a number by one, your answer is the original number. We can think of it as the original number keeping its identity. (Competency 3)

26. (A)

Choice (A) is the best answer. The associative property of addition states that if you are adding two or more numbers, you can add them in any order. Making ten is a strategy that helps students add numbers mentally. Rearranging the 3 and 1 so 9 and 1 can be added to make 10 makes this problem an easy one to calculate without paper and pencil. (Competency 3)

27. (B)

Choice (B) is the best answer because an array is a good strategy to show equal groups. Rows can show the number of groups, and columns can show the number in each group. (Competency 1)

28. (A)

Choice (A) is the best answer. The denominator in a fraction tells us how many parts each whole has been divided into. The numerator tells us how many of those parts we are considering. When naming fractions, it is important to recognize the size of the whole. In this case, one whole pie is completely shaded in. That means that $\frac{4}{4}$ of that pie is shaded. $\frac{1}{4}$ of the second pie is shaded. Therefore, the fraction shown in this picture is $\frac{5}{4}\left(\frac{4}{4}+\frac{1}{4}\right)$. (Competency 3)

29. (B)

Choice (B) is the best answer because PreK/Primary students measure using both U.S. customary and metric units. Composing and decomposing numbers helps them learn place value and develop flexible computational strategies. Extending patterns is an important part of algebraic thinking. (Competency 1)

30. (B)

Choice (B) is the best answer. $\frac{8}{12}$ and $\frac{6}{9}$ are both equivalent to $\frac{2}{3}$. Therefore, they are equivalent to each other. The other choices represent common misconceptions students have about fractions. If students think choice (C) is correct, they may think that adding the same number to the numerator and denominator will yield an equivalent fraction. That is not correct. You must multiply or divide the numerator and denominator by the same number. The pairs in choices (A) and (D) are close to each other in size, but they are not equivalent. (Competency 3)

31. (B)

Choice (B) is the best answer. A parallelogram has two pairs of parallel sides. Because its opposite sides are parallel, its opposite angles are equal. Choice (A) describes a trapezoid. Choices (C) and (D) describe two special types of parallelograms. Choice (C) is a rectangle, and choice (D) is a rhombus. Neither of those is the best answer because they do not describe all parallelograms. Only choice (B) does that. (Competency 5)

32. (B)

Choice (B) is the best answer. Addition and subtraction are inverse operations. This means that any subtraction problem can be thought of as a "think addition" problem. Because addition is based on counting by ones, viewing subtraction as "think addition" can help children learn basic facts. (Competency 3)

33. (C)

Choice (C) is the best answer. Cuisenaire rods (A) and a ruler (D) are both length models. Two-color counters (B) are a set model. Geoboards are an area model for fractions because the fraction represents part of an area that can be evenly divided into smaller pieces. (Competency 3)

34. (C)

Choice (C) is the best answer. We use the base-ten number system. Numbers can be decomposed (broken apart) into tens and ones. 56 is composed of 5 tens and 6 ones. We can also trade all five of the tens for ones, giving us 0 tens and 56 ones. Similarly, we could trade two tens for 20 ones. That would give us 3 tens and 26 ones. A common error is to view 50 as meaning 50 tens instead of 5 tens and 0 ones. (Competency 3)

35. (C)

Choice (C) is the best answer. Tiered instruction is when students work at different levels of the same task. All students are working on the same skill, but are able to work at a level where they can be appropriately challenged. (Competency 1)

36. (A)

Choice (A) is the best answer. While you could measure the length of the playground in inches (B), it would take many inches and would be inefficient. Kilometers (C) and miles (D) both measure distances from place to place. A kilometer is a little more than half a mile, which would make it inappropriate to measure the length of the playground. (Competency 4)

37. (B)

Choice (B) is the best answer because an interview is the best way to ask children to explain their thinking. A checklist (A) is good to record actions, but may not give the teacher much information about the thinking behind the action. During a class discussion (D), some children may not speak. A worksheet (C) doesn't provide an opportunity for follow-up questioning. (Competency 1)

38. (B)

Choice (B) is the best answer. An object's area is the amount of two-dimensional space it takes up. For a rectangle, area is calculated by multiplying the length times the width. Area is measured in square units, which in this case is square feet. (Competency 4)

39. (C)

Choice (C) is the best answer. The equal sign shows equivalence between the two sides of an equation. One way to think about equivalence is as a balance. What needs to go in the blanks on each side of the equal sign so they are balanced? $6 + 3 = 9$ and $2 + 7 = 9$. This is the only option that makes both sides of the equation equivalent. (Competency 2)

40. (A)

Choice (A) is the best answer. When solving a problem like this, students must realize that the equal sign means the expressions on either side of it are equivalent. The equal sign does not mean "the answer is coming." In this problem, $12 - 3 = 9$ and $4 + 5 = 9$. Therefore, both sides of the equation are equivalent. (Competency 2)

41. (B)

Choice (B) is the best answer. The prefix *milli-* means thousandth. Therefore, a milliliter is $\frac{1}{1000}$ of a liter. (Competency 4)

42. (D)

Choice (D) is the best answer. Choices (A), (B), and (C) are all very small units to measure the capacity of a bathtub. While they could be used, they are not the most efficient choice. A gallon is the most appropriate unit to use. (Competency 4)

43. (D)

Choice (D) is the best answer because the Standards for Mathematical Practice (SMPs) describe the varieties of expertise that math teachers should seek to develop in their students. The best way for a teacher to assess the SMPs is to observe students. A checklist can simplify record keeping. (Competency 1)

44. (A)

Choice (A) is the best answer. Variables (letters) can be used to describe patterns. The repeating pattern in choice (A) is heart-star-star-cross. Another way to say that is ABBC. (Competency 2)

45. (A)

Choice (A) is the best answer. An obtuse triangle is a triangle that contains one obtuse angle. An obtuse angle is greater than 90°, but less than 180°. A right triangle (B) contains one 90° angle. Because the angles in a triangle add up to 180°, if one angle equals 90° it is impossible for either of the other angles to be obtuse. An acute triangle is one in which all three angles are acute (C). An equilateral triangle (D) is also an acute triangle, because each angle equals 60°. (Competency 5)

46. (D)

Choice (D) is the best answer. A unit fraction represents a single part of the whole. It is written as $\frac{1}{b}$, where b indicates how many parts the whole has been divided into and 1 indicates that we are considering one of those parts. (Competency 3)

47. (A)

Choice (A) is the best answer. A cylinder is a three-dimensional figure that has two congruent bases that are closed figures. The bases are joined to each other by a curved surface. (Competency 5)

48. (A)

Choice (A) is the best answer because Ethan traded one ten for ten ones but he forgot to show that he had one fewer ten after he traded. (Competency 1)

49. (C)

Choice (C) is the best answer. Subitizing is the ability to look at a common pattern or collection of objects and immediately recognize the quantity they represent without needing to count each one individually. Subitizing helps children with counting on. (Competency 3)

50. (B)

Choice (B) is the best answer. Reflection symmetry is also known as line or mirror symmetry. Objects that have reflection symmetry can pass the "fold test." This means that they can be folded in such a way so that the two sides match up exactly with one another. (Competency 5)

PRACTICE TEST 1

FTCE PreK–3
Science
Subtest 4 (534)

Also available at the REA Study Center (www.rea.com/studycenter)

This practice test is also offered online at the REA Study Center. We recommend that you take the online version of the test to simulate test-day conditions and to receive these added benefits:

- **Timed testing conditions**—helps you gauge how much time you can spend on each question

- **Automatic scoring**—find out how you did on the test, instantly

- **On-screen detailed explanations of answers**—gives you the correct answer and explains why the other answer choices are wrong

- **Diagnostic score reports**—pinpoint where you're strongest and where you need to focus your study

Science Practice Test 1: Answer Sheet

1. Ⓐ Ⓑ Ⓒ Ⓓ
2. Ⓐ Ⓑ Ⓒ Ⓓ
3. Ⓐ Ⓑ Ⓒ Ⓓ
4. Ⓐ Ⓑ Ⓒ Ⓓ
5. Ⓐ Ⓑ Ⓒ Ⓓ
6. Ⓐ Ⓑ Ⓒ Ⓓ
7. Ⓐ Ⓑ Ⓒ Ⓓ
8. Ⓐ Ⓑ Ⓒ Ⓓ
9. Ⓐ Ⓑ Ⓒ Ⓓ
10. Ⓐ Ⓑ Ⓒ Ⓓ
11. Ⓐ Ⓑ Ⓒ Ⓓ
12. Ⓐ Ⓑ Ⓒ Ⓓ
13. Ⓐ Ⓑ Ⓒ Ⓓ
14. Ⓐ Ⓑ Ⓒ Ⓓ
15. Ⓐ Ⓑ Ⓒ Ⓓ
16. Ⓐ Ⓑ Ⓒ Ⓓ
17. Ⓐ Ⓑ Ⓒ Ⓓ

18. Ⓐ Ⓑ Ⓒ Ⓓ
19. Ⓐ Ⓑ Ⓒ Ⓓ
20. Ⓐ Ⓑ Ⓒ Ⓓ
21. Ⓐ Ⓑ Ⓒ Ⓓ
22. Ⓐ Ⓑ Ⓒ Ⓓ
23. Ⓐ Ⓑ Ⓒ Ⓓ
24. Ⓐ Ⓑ Ⓒ Ⓓ
25. Ⓐ Ⓑ Ⓒ Ⓓ
26. Ⓐ Ⓑ Ⓒ Ⓓ
27. Ⓐ Ⓑ Ⓒ Ⓓ
28. Ⓐ Ⓑ Ⓒ Ⓓ
29. Ⓐ Ⓑ Ⓒ Ⓓ
30. Ⓐ Ⓑ Ⓒ Ⓓ
31. Ⓐ Ⓑ Ⓒ Ⓓ
32. Ⓐ Ⓑ Ⓒ Ⓓ
33. Ⓐ Ⓑ Ⓒ Ⓓ
34. Ⓐ Ⓑ Ⓒ Ⓓ

35. Ⓐ Ⓑ Ⓒ Ⓓ
36. Ⓐ Ⓑ Ⓒ Ⓓ
37. Ⓐ Ⓑ Ⓒ Ⓓ
38. Ⓐ Ⓑ Ⓒ Ⓓ
39. Ⓐ Ⓑ Ⓒ Ⓓ
40. Ⓐ Ⓑ Ⓒ Ⓓ
41. Ⓐ Ⓑ Ⓒ Ⓓ
42. Ⓐ Ⓑ Ⓒ Ⓓ
43. Ⓐ Ⓑ Ⓒ Ⓓ
44. Ⓐ Ⓑ Ⓒ Ⓓ
45. Ⓐ Ⓑ Ⓒ Ⓓ
46. Ⓐ Ⓑ Ⓒ Ⓓ
47. Ⓐ Ⓑ Ⓒ Ⓓ
48. Ⓐ Ⓑ Ⓒ Ⓓ
49. Ⓐ Ⓑ Ⓒ Ⓓ
50. Ⓐ Ⓑ Ⓒ Ⓓ

Science: Practice Test 1

TIME: 60 minutes
50 questions*

Directions: Read each question and select the best response.

1. Mr. O'Brien and his second graders create a chart to help with constructing scientific explanations. With the students' help, Mr. O'Brien writes the words *claim*, *evidence*, and *reasoning*, along with brief explanations of each on the chart. This is an example of the use of a(n)

   A. literacy connection chart.

   B. science and engineering practices chart.

   C. process skills chart.

   D. anchor chart.

2. Which of the following is the most important safety procedure needed when investigating what happens when we pour a few drops of vinegar onto baking soda?

   A. Wear safety goggles.

   B. Wash hands before beginning.

   C. Wait until the investigation is finished before tasting the substances.

   D. Designate one child from each group to get the materials so spills are less likely.

3. You find the mass of a cup of chocolate chips using a balance scale. You then microwave the chips until they are fully melted. You find the mass of the melted chocolate. What can you say about how the mass of the chips and the melted chocolate compare?

   A. The mass of the chips is greater than the mass of the melted chocolate.

   B. The mass of the chips is less than the mass of the melted chocolate.

   C. The mass of the chips is the same as the mass of the melted chocolate.

   D. It is impossible to say. It depends upon the type of chocolate chips and what the cup is made of.

4. A first grade teacher wants to assess her students' current understanding about the difference between living and nonliving things prior to instruction. Which of the following would be the best way for her to do that?

   A. Read their science notebooks to see what they have written thus far.

   B. Give them a five-question multiple-choice quiz to see what they know about living and nonliving things.

   C. Give them a real-life problem scenario that requires them to use what they know about living and nonliving things to solve the problem.

   D. Use a set of prepared questions to interview each student individually for a few minutes to find out what they know about living and nonliving things.

---

* The number of items is approximate. You will only learn exactly how many questions you will get after you take the FTCE tutorial and sign the non-disclosure agreement on test day.

5. You hit a baseball with a bat and it flies through the air. What type of force is this?

    A. inertia

    B. contact

    C. at-a-distance

    D. opposing

6. After completing a science unit on weather in Florida, second graders complete the following assessment. Students work in teams of three to design a hurricane-resistant structure. They use what they learned during the unit to inform their design. This is an example of what type of assessment?

    A. performance task

    B. formal assessment

    C. observation

    D. diagnostic assessment

7. Allison's dog had babies. Some of them are white and some are brown. Allison's dog is white. The father of the puppies is brown. What can be said about why the puppies are different colors?

    A. Male puppies get their color from the father and female puppies get their color from the mother.

    B. Traits like color are determined by the environment. The white puppies spent more time in the sun than the brown ones.

    C. Male puppies get their color from the mother and female puppies get their color from the father.

    D. Both parents contribute traits equally to their offspring. If brown is dominant over white, a puppy will only be white if both parents contribute a white allele.

8. Which of the following is the most accurate statement regarding active learning?

    A. Active learning is a synonym for hands-on learning.

    B. Active learning requires students to construct explanations based on sensory experiences.

    C. Active learning occurs on typical lab days in science classrooms.

    D. Active learning requires students to be engaged in activities that utilize gross and fine motor skills.

9. Which of the following is an example of a productive question?

    A. What is your favorite season and why?

    B. What is the definition of a solid?

    C. What patterns do you see in the data you collected?

    D. What steps did you use during your investigation?

10. If you are outside when a tornado strikes, you should

    A. find the nearest tree and wrap your arms around its base.

    B. run to the closest building no matter how far away it is.

    C. stand as tall as you can so you can see which way the tornado is headed.

    D. lie face down on the ground and cover your head and neck with your arms.

11. Students created a class graph from leaves they collected outside. They are now discussing the graph. Ashley says, *There are three more red leaves than yellow leaves.* Which science and engineering practice is Ashley using?

    A. construction explanations and designing solutions

    B. planning and carrying out investigations

    C. engaging in argument from evidence

    D. using mathematics and computational thinking

12. Elijah says, *I saw a puddle in the street by Mr. Ben's house on the way to school. I didn't see any other puddles. I think Mr. Ben must have let water out of his pool.* Elijah's statement is an example of a(n)

    A. observation.

    B. inference.

    C. prediction.

    D. hypothesis.

13. Plants and animals in an ecosystem depend upon one another for survival. Which of the following is NOT an accurate statement about their mutual dependence?

    A. Animals help disperse plant seeds.

    B. Plants are the ultimate source of food for all animals.

    C. Animals produce methane that helps plants grow.

    D. Plants provide shelter and fuel for animals.

14. Which of the following is the best tool to measure wind speed?

    A. trundle wheel

    B. wind vane

    C. anemometer

    D. binoculars

15. Which of the following shows the correct hierarchical organization of animals?

    A. tissues—cells—organs—organ systems

    B. organ systems—tissues—organs—cells

    C. organs—tissues—cells—organ systems

    D. cells—tissues—organs—organ systems

16. Students are discussing whether salt is a solid or a liquid. They do not all agree. What would be the best option to determine which answer is correct?

    A. Students can vote on whether they think salt is a solid or a liquid. The one with the most votes is the winner.

    B. Students can survey their parents/caregivers at home. The next day they can discuss what the adults think.

    C. Students can conduct an investigation to see if salt has the properties of a solid or a liquid.

    D. Students do not have to agree. Scientists have different views. This is a teachable moment for students to learn that different views are welcome.

17. Which of the following is the most accurate statement about the function of the circulatory system in the human body?

    A. The main function is to transport nutrients and wastes to and from the body's cells.

    B. The main function is to pump blood through arteries and veins.

    C. The main function is to carry nutrients from the small intestine.

    D. The main function is to carry messages from the brain to other parts of the body.

18. The space race between the U.S. and the Soviet Union in the last century is an example of a way

    A. economic considerations influence scientific priorities.

    B. political considerations influence scientific priorities.

    C. health considerations influence scientific priorities.

    D. historical considerations influence scientific priorities.

19. The diagram below is an example of a(n)

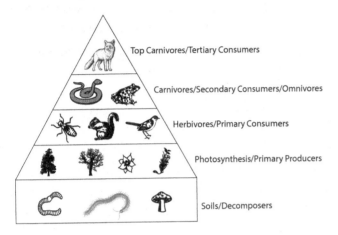

A. food web.

B. food chain.

C. ecosystem.

D. digestion cycle.

20. Which of the following is an example of a renewable resource?

A. coal

B. natural gas

C. wind

D. oil

21. The space program has benefited humans in a variety of ways. One of those is

A. more efficient car engines.

B. better heat resistant materials for firefighters' uniforms.

C. increased government funding to address social issues.

D. decrease in the use of fossil fuels.

22. Is the diagram below a good one to illustrate the water cycle? If not, what is problematic about it?

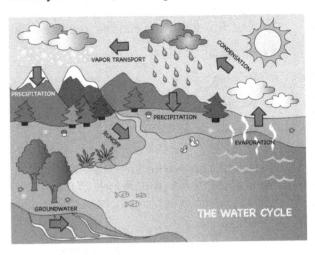

A. It needs to include other types of precipitation besides rain.

B. It makes it appear as if precipitation only occurs over land.

C. It doesn't include the names of each part of the water cycle.

D. There is no problem with the diagram. It accurately depicts the water cycle.

23. The students in your class rub a mineral across an unglazed porcelain tile. They record the color of the powder the mineral leaves behind on the tile. Your students are investigating

A. color.

B. streak.

C. hardness.

D. luster.

24. Students are making a list of the ways living things maintain balance in and control their internal environment. What science concept are they learning about?

A. homeostasis

B. environmental symmetry

C. adaptation

D. hierarchical organization

25. Which of the following is the most accurate statement about precipitation?

    A. Precipitation occurs when ice crystals in clouds become too heavy.

    B. Precipitation occurs when ice crystals in clouds melt.

    C. Precipitation occurs when clouds get pushed together by the wind.

    D. Precipitation occurs when water droplets fall through holes in clouds.

26. Which of the following is an example of physical weathering?

    A. the dissolving of limestone in rain water

    B. the movement of particles of soil when they are hit by raindrops

    C. the peeling away of rocks in sheets or layers

    D. the placement of sediment at the mouth of a river

27. Which of the following is the most accurate statement about why we have seasons on Earth?

    A. The Northern Hemisphere is closer to the Sun during summer than it is in the winter because the Earth tilts on its axis.

    B. The Sun emits more heat during summer than in the winter.

    C. One side of the Earth faces the Sun during the summer and the other side faces away from the Sun.

    D. The Earth's tilt on its axis means that the Sun's rays strike one hemisphere more directly during the summer and the Sun shines for more hours each day.

28. From the new moon to the full moon, the Moon is said to be waxing. This means we are seeing

    A. more of the lighted side each night.

    B. less of the lighted side each night.

    C. the left side of the Moon each night.

    D. a lunar eclipse.

29. A kindergarten teacher sets up a science learning center with a variety of objects and hand lenses. Which science process skill does the center address?

    A. observing

    B. inferring

    C. classifying

    D. measuring

30. Which of the following is an example of a chemical change?

    A. tearing paper

    B. burning a log in the fireplace

    C. dissolving sugar in iced tea

    D. freezing water into ice cubes

31. Cold-blooded animals are ones whose body temperature

    A. is consistently low.

    B. changes in response to temperature changes in the environment.

    C. enables them to live in cold climates.

    D. enables them to live in warm climates.

32. Which of the following is an example of potential energy?

    A. a skier at the top of a hill

    B. a tennis ball traveling through the air

    C. a guitar string that is being plucked

    D. a stream of water from a faucet

33. First graders are sitting on the carpet with their science notebooks after completing an investigation. Their teacher, Ms. Whitaker, asks them to discuss their results with the person sitting next to them. This is an example of which talk strategy?

    A. think-pair-share

    B. jigsaw

    C. turn and talk

    D. numbered heads together

34. Which of the following is an example of a physical change?

    A. pouring vinegar on baking soda

    B. dissolving sugar in tea

    C. a rusting nail

    D. baking a cake

35. The purpose of stems in a vascular plant is to

    A. anchor the plant.

    B. absorb sunlight to make food for the plant.

    C. transport water and nutrients to the leaves.

    D. aid plant reproduction.

36. Which of the following is an example of a mixture?

    A. table salt

    B. water

    C. vinegar

    D. sweetened coffee

37. The students in Ms. Bayer's class are investigating forces. Each of her students has some ideas about forces. Which of the following statements is correct?

    A. A force is a push but not a pull.

    B. A holding force keeps a pencil sitting on a desk.

    C. A force is needed to keep an object moving at a constant speed.

    D. A force is needed to stop a moving object from continuing to move.

38. Which of the following is the best use of a model to help students construct scientific explanations?

    A. make a model of the solar system using Styrofoam balls

    B. use a ball and a lamp to investigate why we have day and night

    C. construct a flower from a cupcake liner, a pipe cleaner, and paper leaves

    D. create a diorama of a specific habitat

39. Plants that have roots and stems to transport nutrients throughout the plant are

    A. nonvascular.

    B. protista.

    C. vascular.

    D. flora.

40. Table salt is an example of a(n)

    A. element.

    B. solution.

    C. mixture.

    D. compound.

41. Which of the following is the most accurate statement regarding the relationship between play and science in a PreK/Primary classroom?

    A. Science should typically be scheduled after children have played outside at recess so they will be more focused and ready to learn.

    B. Science should typically be scheduled before children play outside at recess so they can get the wiggles out after an intense science lesson.

    C. Science uses systematic processes. PreK/Primary classrooms should emphasize those processes and discourage play as it can be dangerous.

    D. Science in PreK/Primary classrooms should include opportunity for unstructured play because that is the way children learn about the world.

42. Which of the following is an example of a vertebrate?

    A. fish

    B. shrimp

    C. spider

    D. centipede

43. Which of the following is the most accurate statement about the nature of science?

    A. Scientific knowledge can be trusted, but it is also open to the possibility that new evidence may arise that causes scientists to change their ideas.

    B. Science is the highest form of knowledge. It can be used to answer any question someone has about the world, both natural and supernatural.

    C. Science is a human endeavor. Scientists base their ideas on evidence, their personal beliefs, and their opinions about the world.

    D. Scientific investigations are one-time events that cannot be repeated. The evidence collected in any scientific investigation can be trusted even if it disagrees with what others found when using similar methods to answer a specific question.

44. Which of the following is the best scientific explanation for why we have night and day?

    A. The Earth orbits completely around the Sun each day.

    B. The Sun orbits completely around the Earth each day.

    C. The Sun stops shining at night and starts again each morning.

    D. The Earth spins entirely around on its axis each day.

45. Pyrite is a mineral that is sometimes called fool's gold because of its color. A sample of pyrite has a mass of 15 g. and a volume of 3 cm³. What is its density?

    A. 5 g/cm³

    B. ⅕ cm³/g

    C. 45 cm³/g

    D. 12 g/cm³

46. Ms. Thompson's kindergarten class has been investigating sound. Jasmine says, *I think sounds are caused by objects wiggling back and forth really fast.* Jasmine's statement is an example of

    A. a claim.

    B. evidence.

    C. reasoning.

    D. argumentation.

47. Which of the following best describes how engineering differs from science?

    A. Engineers design and create solutions to human problems while scientists construct explanations.

    B. Engineers use mathematics and technology when they record and analyze data, but scientists do not.

    C. Engineers and scientists are essentially the same. They both construct explanations and create solutions.

    D. Engineers communicate their results to others while scientists are more focused on their personal research and increasing their own knowledge.

48. In an ecosystem, earthworms are examples of

    A. producers.

    B. consumers.

    C. decomposers.

    D. autotrophs.

49. Which of the following explains why a biome is different from a habitat?

   A. A biome refers to the physical surroundings where a species lives, while a habitat refers to a geographic area with similar weather and vegetation.

   B. A biome refers to a geographic area with similar weather and vegetation, while a habitat refers to the physical surroundings where a species lives.

   C. A biome refers to only the nonliving factors within an ecosystem, while a habitat refers to both the living and nonliving factors.

   D. A biome refers only to the living factors within an ecosystem, while a habitat refers to the nonliving factors.

50. Thanks to sophisticated manufacturing, transportation, and distribution systems, people can buy their favorite fruits and vegetables at any time of the year, even when produce is not in season locally. One by-product of this is

   A. increased pollution from shipping produce long distances.

   B. increased profits for supermarkets.

   C. decreased global mean temperatures.

   D. decreased quality of local ecosystems.

Science Practice Test 1:
Answer Key

Test Item	Answer	Competency
1.	D	1
2.	A	1
3.	C	4
4.	D	1
5.	B	4
6.	A	1
7.	D	5
8.	B	1
9.	C	1
10.	D	3
11.	D	2
12.	B	2
13.	C	5
14.	C	2
15.	D	5
16.	C	2
17.	A	5
18.	B	2
19.	A	5
20.	C	3
21.	B	3
22.	B	3
23.	B	3
24.	A	5
25.	A	3

Test Item	Answer	Competency
26.	C	3
27.	D	3
28.	A	3
29.	A	2
30.	B	4
31.	B	5
32.	A	4
33.	C	1
34.	B	4
35.	C	5
36.	D	4
37.	D	4
38.	B	1
39.	C	5
40.	D	4
41.	D	1
42.	A	5
43.	A	2
44.	D	3
45.	A	4
46.	A	2
47.	A	2
48.	C	5
49.	B	5
50.	A	2

Science Practice Test 1: Detailed Answers

1. **(D)**

   Choice (D) is the best answer. An anchor chart is co-created by the teacher and students during a lesson. It is then displayed in the classroom where children can refer to it. (Competency 1)

2. **(A)**

   Choice (A) is the best answer. Anytime we are doing investigations with acids, like vinegar, children should wear safety goggles to avoid splashing the acid in their eyes. (Competency 1)

3. **(C)**

   Choice (C) is the best answer. When you melt the chocolate chips, they undergo a physical change. The law of conservation of mass states that matter is neither created nor destroyed. You did not add to or take away from the chocolate chips. Because you didn't add or take away matter, the mass of the melted chocolate is the same as the original chips. (Competency 4)

4. **(D)**

   Choice (D) is the best answer. Interviews are a good way to probe students' thinking. Student responses to multiple-choice quizzes don't give a teacher information about student thinking. (Competency 1)

5. **(B)**

   Choice (B) is the best answer. A contact force occurs when objects are touching. The bat striking the ball is a contact force. Some forces operate at a distance without touching. Magnetism is an example. A magnet can pull a paper clip toward it without touching the paper clip. (Competency 4)

6. **(A)**

   Choice (A) is the best answer because students must use science concepts and science and engineering practices to solve a real-world problem. Choice (B) refers to standardized assessments. (Competency 1)

7. **(D)**

   Choice (D) is the best answer. Each parent contributes equally to the genetic make-up of their offspring. Many traits have dominant and recessive alleles. If at least one parent contributes a dominant allele, the offspring will have the dominant version of the trait. The only way the offspring will exhibit the recessive version of the trait is if both parents contribute a recessive allele. (Competency 5)

8. **(B)**

   Choice (B) is the best answer. Active learning engages children in sensory experiences from which they construct new knowledge. (Competency 1)

9. **(C)**

   Choice (C) is the best answer. Productive questions are ones that promote children's reasoning skills and help them construct scientific explanations. Choices (B) and (D) are recall questions. Choice (A) is an opinion. It does not help students construct explanations about seasons. (Competency 1)

10. **(D)**

   Choice (D) is the best answer. Trees and buildings are often picked up by a tornado's strong winds. It is best to lie flat and face-down on low ground if you are outside when a tornado strikes. Cover your head and neck to reduce the likelihood of injury from debris being carried through the air. (Competency 3)

11. (D)

Choice (D) is the best answer. Ashley is using mathematics. She has counted the number of red leaves and yellow leaves and then found the difference between them. (Competency 2)

12. (B)

Choice (B) is the best answer. An inference is a claim or conclusion that is based on evidence. The evidence is that there is a puddle by Mr. Ben's house, but none anywhere else. Therefore, a reasonable inference is that the puddle came from an event like draining a pool which often produces puddles in the street. (Competency 2)

13. (C)

Choice (C) is the best answer. Animals do disperse plant seeds. Plants provide shelter and fuel for animals. They are also the ultimate source of food for all animals because animals either eat plants or eat other animals that eat plants. Methane does not help plants grow. (Competency 5)

14. (C)

Choice (C) is the best answer. A simple anemometer can be constructed with small cups and straws. Wind speed is calculated by the number of revolutions the tool makes in a specific amount of time. (Competency 2)

15. (D)

Choice (D) is the best answer. The basic unit of life is the cell. Groups of similar cells in a multicellular organism are called tissues. Organs are composed of one or more types of tissues. Organs work together in organ systems to perform specific functions that keep the organism alive. (Competency 5)

16. (C)

Choice (C) is the best answer. When scientists have a question, they investigate to find the answer. Scientific knowledge is not determined by popularity. It is based on evidence. (Competency 2)

17. (A)

Choice (A) is the best answer. The circulatory system transports nutrients from the food we eat to the body's cells through the bloodstream. Cellular waste products are picked up and ultimately removed from the body. Blood travels through arteries and veins to carry those nutrients and waste products. (Competency 5)

18. (B)

Choice (B) is the best answer. The U.S. was shocked when the Soviet Union launched a space satellite. Worried that the Soviets would gain a military advantage, the U.S. invested significant amounts of money in space exploration. (Competency 2)

19. (A)

Choice (A) is the best answer. A food web shows all the possible feeding relationships within an ecosystem. (Competency 5)

20. (C)

Choice (C) is the best answer. Renewable resources are ones that are replenishable over decades or shorter timescales. The other choices are all nonrenewable resources. They require millions of years to be replenished. (Competency 3)

21. (B)

Choice (B) is the best answer. Heat-resistant materials for space suits have been adapted for use by firefighters. (Competency 3)

22. (B)

Choice (B) is the best answer. There are many paths a molecule of water can take through the water cycle. Precipitation does not only occur over land. (Competency 3)

23. (B)

Choice (B) is the best answer. Many minerals come in a variety of colors, so it is often not a good property to use to identify a mineral. A mineral's streak is a characteristic property. It is the color of the powder left behind when you rub a mineral on an unglazed porcelain tile. (Competency 3)

24. (A)

Choice (A) is the best answer. Living things maintain balance in their internal environment so all their parts can function effectively to keep the organism alive. (Competency 5)

25. (A)

Choice (A) is the best answer. When ice crystals in clouds become too heavy, they fall toward the ground. The temperature of the atmosphere through which they fall determines if they reach Earth's surface as rain, snow, or sleet. (Competency 3)

26. (C)

Choice (C) is the best answer. When rocks are weathered physically, they are broken into smaller pieces, but their chemical composition does not change. Igneous rock (e.g., granite) peels away in sheets or layers. (Competency 3)

27. (D)

Choice (D) is the best answer. When it is summer, the Sun's rays strike a portion of the Earth at a more direct angle than they do in the winter. This is due to the tilt of Earth's axis. Because the Sun is higher in the sky during the summer, the sunlight that reaches Earth's surface is more concentrated. Days are also longer in the summer than the winter, which means that the Sun's rays strike the hemisphere having summer for more hours each day than they do in the winter. (Competency 3)

28. (A)

Choice (A) is the best answer. In terms of moon phases, waxing means "appearing larger." (Competency 3)

29. (A)

Choice (A) is the best answer. When children observe they use their senses to collect information about the natural world. (Competency 2)

30. (B)

Choice (B) is the best answer. A chemical change is one in which new substances with different properties are produced. When you burn a log, ash, smoke, and energy are produced. Dissolving is a physical change. The sugar is still present even though you may not be able to see it. You can taste it. Phase changes, like freezing or melting, are also physical changes. No new substance is produced. (Competency 4)

31. (B)

Choice (B) is the best answer. The body temperature of cold-blooded animals changes in response to changes in the temperature of their environment. (Competency 5)

32. (A)

Choice (A) is the best answer. Potential energy is possible energy due to an object's position or condition. A skier at the top of the hill has potential energy due to gravity. The other choices are all examples of kinetic energy. (Competency 4)

33. (C)

Choice (C) is the best answer. Turn and talk is a strategy in which students share their thinking with a person sitting next to them. It is sometimes confused with think-pair-share. In think-pair-share, students first silently think of an answer to a question, then share with a partner, and finally share with the larger group. (Competency 1)

34. (B)

Choice (B) is the best answer. Dissolving is a physical change. The sugar and tea have not chemically combined even though you probably can't see the sugar. You can taste it. You can separate the tea and sugar by boiling away the tea. The sugar will remain. (Competency 4)

35. (C)

Choice (C) is the best answer. Stems are found in vascular plants. Their purpose is to transport water and nutrients to plant leaves where photosynthesis occurs. (Competency 5)

36. (D)

Choice (D) is the best answer. The other choices are all examples of compounds—elements that have been chemically combined. The sugar has not combined chemically with the coffee. Sweetened coffee is a solution because the materials are evenly mixed. (Competency 4)

37. (D)

Choice (D) is the best answer. A force must be applied in order to change an object's motion. If there was no opposing force, an object in motion would continue moving at a constant speed. There is no such thing as a holding force. (Competency 4)

38. (B)

Choice (B) is the best answer. Models are used to help students construct explanations of scientific phenomena. The other choices are more like craft projects. Choice (B) will enable students to determine that Earth's rotation causes the day/night cycle. (Competency 1)

39. (C)

Choice (C) is the best answer. Vascular plants are ones that have roots and stems. Nonvascular plants do not have those parts. (Competency 5)

40. (D)

Choice (D) is the best answer. Sodium is a toxic metal and chlorine is a poisonous gas. When they combine chemically, they produce table salt, which is used to season food. The properties of a compound like table salt are very different from the properties of the elements that combine to form it. (Competency 4)

41. (D)

Choice (D) is the best answer. Opportunity for unstructured play should be a feature of all PreK/Primary classrooms. Unstructured play fosters children's creativity and increases their social skills. (Competency 1)

42. (A)

Choice (A) is the best answer. A vertebrate is an animal with an internal skeleton. A fish is the only answer choice that has an internal skeleton. (Competency 5)

43. (A)

Choice (A) is the best answer. Scientific knowledge is durable because scientific explanations are based on lots of evidence, not people's opinions. This means that scientific knowledge can be trusted. However, scientists are open to the possibility that new data may require them to modify their ideas. That's why scientists say their data supports a claim rather than saying data proves a claim. (Competency 2)

44. (D)

Choice (D) is the best answer. The apparent movement of the Sun across the sky each day is caused by Earth's rotation on its axis. The Earth makes one complete rotation in a 24-hour period. As the Earth rotates, different locations face the Sun at different times. (Competency 3)

45. (A)

Choice (A) is the best answer. Density refers to the amount of mass in a given volume of a substance. To calculate density, you divide the mass by the volume ($15 \div 3$). Because density is a ratio, the unit is g/cm^3. (Competency 4)

46. (A)

Choice (A) is the best answer. A claim answers a testable question or problem. In this case, the children were investigating what causes sound. (Competency 2)

47. (A)

Choice (A) is the best answer. Engineers and scientists both use mathematics and technology and communicate their results to others, so choices (B) and (D) cannot be correct. The difference is that scientists try to

construct explanations about how the world works. Engineers focus on designing solutions to human problems. (Competency 2)

48. (C)

Choice (C) is the best answer. Decomposers feed on dead or decaying plants and animals. (Competency 5)

49. (B)

Choice (B) is the best answer. A habitat refers to the physical surroundings where a species lives. A biome is a geographic area that has similar vegetation and weather. The habitats of multiple organisms exist within a single biome. (Competency 5)

50. (A)

Choice (A) is the best answer. Most fresh produce is shipped long distances via semi-trailer trucks. These trucks emit large amounts of carbon dioxide into the atmosphere. (Competency 2)

PRACTICE TEST 1: CORRELATION WITH FTCE COMPETENCIES

Developmental Knowledge

Competency 1: Knowledge of Child Growth, Child Development, and Relationships with Families and the Community
Questions 1, 6, 10, 19, 36, 45, 48, 50

Competency 2: Knowledge of the Profession and Foundations of Early Childhood (PreK–3) Education
Questions 5, 14, 20, 27, 41, 51, 54

Competency 3: Knowledge of Developmentally Appropriate Practices
Questions 9, 16, 32, 39, 44, 46, 49, 53, 55, 56, 57, 59

Competency 4: Knowledge of Developmentally Appropriate Curricula
Questions 24, 37, 43, 47, 52, 58, 60

Competency 5: Knowledge of Developmentally Appropriate Intervention Strategies and Resources Available to Meet the Needs of All Students
Questions 4, 7, 12, 17, 21, 26, 28, 34, 38

Competency 6: Knowledge of Diagnosis, Assessment, and Evaluation
Questions 2, 11, 15, 23, 29, 31, 35, 40, 42

Competency 7: Knowledge of Child Guidance and Classroom Behavioral Management
Questions 3, 8, 13, 18, 22, 25, 30, 33

Language Arts and Reading

Competency 1: Knowledge of Literacy and Literacy Instruction
Questions 1, 4, 6, 9, 10, 14, 20, 31, 33, 34, 37, 40, 42, 46, 47, 48, 54

Competency 2: Knowledge of Fiction and Nonfiction Genres Including Reading Informational Texts (e.g., literary nonfiction, historical, scientific, and technical texts)
Questions 16, 18, 21, 23, 27, 28, 29, 36, 43, 45, 52

Competency 3: Knowledge of Reading Foundational Skills
Questions 3, 5, 8, 17, 24, 32, 35, 38, 39, 59

Competency 4: Knowledge of Language Elements Used for Effective Oral and Written Communication
Questions 2, 11, 12, 13, 15, 19, 22, 26, 43, 44, 49, 51, 53, 55, 56, 57, 58

Competency 5: Knowledge of Assessments to Inform Literary Instruction
Questions 7, 25, 30, 41, 50, 60

Mathematics

Competency 1: Knowledge of Effective Mathematics Instruction
Questions 2, 6, 8, 9, 11, 27, 29, 35, 37, 43, 48

Competency 2: Knowledge of Algebraic Thinking
Questions 12, 13, 15, 17, 18, 39, 40, 44

Competency 3: Knowledge of Number Concepts and Operations in Base Ten
Questions 1, 4, 20, 21, 23, 24, 25, 26, 28, 30, 32, 33, 34, 46, 49

Competency 4: Knowledge of Measurement and Data Collection and Analysis
Questions 7, 10, 14, 19, 36, 38, 41, 42

Competency 5: Knowledge of Geometric and Special Concepts
Questions 3, 5, 16, 22, 31, 45, 47, 50

Science

Competency 1: Knowledge of Effective Science Instruction
Questions 1, 2, 4, 6, 8, 9, 33, 38, 41

Competency 2: Knowledge of the Nature of Science
Questions 11, 12, 14, 16, 18, 29, 43, 46, 47, 50

Competency 3: Knowledge of Earth and Space Sciences
Questions 10, 20, 21, 22, 23, 25, 26, 27, 28, 44

Competency 4: Knowledge of the Physical Sciences
Questions 3, 5, 30, 32, 34, 36, 37, 40, 45

Competency 5: Knowledge of the Life Sciences
Questions 7, 13, 15, 17, 19, 24, 31, 35, 39, 42, 48, 49

PRACTICE TEST 2

FTCE PreK–3 Developmental Knowledge
Subtest 1 (531)

Also available at the REA Study Center (www.rea.com/studycenter)

This practice test is also offered online at the REA Study Center. We recommend that you take the online version of the test to simulate test-day conditions and to receive these added benefits:

- **Timed testing conditions**—helps you gauge how much time you can spend on each question

- **Automatic scoring**—find out how you did on the test, instantly

- **On-screen detailed explanations of answers**—gives you the correct answer and explains why the other answer choices are wrong

- **Diagnostic score reports**—pinpoint where you're strongest and where you need to focus your study

Developmental Knowledge
Practice Test 2: Answer Sheet

1. Ⓐ Ⓑ Ⓒ Ⓓ
2. Ⓐ Ⓑ Ⓒ Ⓓ
3. Ⓐ Ⓑ Ⓒ Ⓓ
4. Ⓐ Ⓑ Ⓒ Ⓓ
5. Ⓐ Ⓑ Ⓒ Ⓓ
6. Ⓐ Ⓑ Ⓒ Ⓓ
7. Ⓐ Ⓑ Ⓒ Ⓓ
8. Ⓐ Ⓑ Ⓒ Ⓓ
9. Ⓐ Ⓑ Ⓒ Ⓓ
10. Ⓐ Ⓑ Ⓒ Ⓓ
11. Ⓐ Ⓑ Ⓒ Ⓓ
12. Ⓐ Ⓑ Ⓒ Ⓓ
13. Ⓐ Ⓑ Ⓒ Ⓓ
14. Ⓐ Ⓑ Ⓒ Ⓓ
15. Ⓐ Ⓑ Ⓒ Ⓓ
16. Ⓐ Ⓑ Ⓒ Ⓓ
17. Ⓐ Ⓑ Ⓒ Ⓓ
18. Ⓐ Ⓑ Ⓒ Ⓓ
19. Ⓐ Ⓑ Ⓒ Ⓓ
20. Ⓐ Ⓑ Ⓒ Ⓓ

21. Ⓐ Ⓑ Ⓒ Ⓓ
22. Ⓐ Ⓑ Ⓒ Ⓓ
23. Ⓐ Ⓑ Ⓒ Ⓓ
24. Ⓐ Ⓑ Ⓒ Ⓓ
25. Ⓐ Ⓑ Ⓒ Ⓓ
26. Ⓐ Ⓑ Ⓒ Ⓓ
27. Ⓐ Ⓑ Ⓒ Ⓓ
28. Ⓐ Ⓑ Ⓒ Ⓓ
29. Ⓐ Ⓑ Ⓒ Ⓓ
30. Ⓐ Ⓑ Ⓒ Ⓓ
31. Ⓐ Ⓑ Ⓒ Ⓓ
32. Ⓐ Ⓑ Ⓒ Ⓓ
33. Ⓐ Ⓑ Ⓒ Ⓓ
34. Ⓐ Ⓑ Ⓒ Ⓓ
35. Ⓐ Ⓑ Ⓒ Ⓓ
36. Ⓐ Ⓑ Ⓒ Ⓓ
37. Ⓐ Ⓑ Ⓒ Ⓓ
38. Ⓐ Ⓑ Ⓒ Ⓓ
39. Ⓐ Ⓑ Ⓒ Ⓓ
40. Ⓐ Ⓑ Ⓒ Ⓓ

41. Ⓐ Ⓑ Ⓒ Ⓓ
42. Ⓐ Ⓑ Ⓒ Ⓓ
43. Ⓐ Ⓑ Ⓒ Ⓓ
44. Ⓐ Ⓑ Ⓒ Ⓓ
45. Ⓐ Ⓑ Ⓒ Ⓓ
46. Ⓐ Ⓑ Ⓒ Ⓓ
47. Ⓐ Ⓑ Ⓒ Ⓓ
48. Ⓐ Ⓑ Ⓒ Ⓓ
49. Ⓐ Ⓑ Ⓒ Ⓓ
50. Ⓐ Ⓑ Ⓒ Ⓓ
51. Ⓐ Ⓑ Ⓒ Ⓓ
52. Ⓐ Ⓑ Ⓒ Ⓓ
53. Ⓐ Ⓑ Ⓒ Ⓓ
54. Ⓐ Ⓑ Ⓒ Ⓓ
55. Ⓐ Ⓑ Ⓒ Ⓓ
56. Ⓐ Ⓑ Ⓒ Ⓓ
57. Ⓐ Ⓑ Ⓒ Ⓓ
58. Ⓐ Ⓑ Ⓒ Ⓓ
59. Ⓐ Ⓑ Ⓒ Ⓓ
60. Ⓐ Ⓑ Ⓒ Ⓓ

Practice Test 2: Developmental Knowledge

TIME: 70 minutes
60 questions*

Directions: Read each question and select the best response.

---

1. Amanda is observing two children working with geometric shapes. She notices that they sort the objects by size, shape, and color. According to Piaget's theory of cognitive development, in what stage might these children be?

   A. sensorimotor

   B. preoperational

   C. concrete operational

   D. formal operational

2. Children aged 4 to 8 typically define friends as those who

   A. engage in common activities or live nearby.

   B. have the traits that are most liked or desired.

   C. share a mutual trust and intimacy.

   D. are about the same age, gender, and ethnicity.

3. Offering space and time for informal conversations among children is recommended when planning for

   A. toddlers.

   B. preschoolers.

   C. infants.

   D. family workshops.

4. One major set of factors that impacts a child's well-being is called

   A. heredity.

   B. genetics.

   C. nature.

   D. temperament.

5. The process of forming a conscience is a goal appropriate for

   A. infants.

   B. toddlers.

   C. preschoolers.

   D. adults.

6. One of the most important recent findings of research on infants is that

   A. loving and learning must be intrinsic and intertwined for an infant to thrive.

   B. they need sleep and nutrition.

   C. the nurture vs. nature debate is still a question.

   D. they may be ready for formal reading instruction.

---

* This practice test presents slightly more items than you are likely to see on test day. The actual test contains approximately 55 questions. You will only learn exactly how many questions you will get after you take the FTCE tutorial and sign the non-disclosure agreement on test day.

7. Mr. Walker is working on developing ways for children to interact socially in relevant ways in his classroom. He is drawing on which theorist's work?

   A. Piaget

   B. Ehri

   C. Montessori

   D. Vygotsky

8. Expressive language

   A. develops at the same time and rate as receptive language.

   B. lags behind receptive language.

   C. develops sooner than receptive language.

   D. is often more advanced than receptive language.

9. The idea that cooperative learning and peer tutoring among children of varying abilities will benefit all—academically and socially—is based on which theorist's work?

   A. Piaget

   B. Maslow

   C. Vygotsky

   D. Gesell

10. Toddlers are known to have increased

    A. aggressiveness.

    B. empathy.

    C. compassion.

    D. resilience.

11. The idea that increasingly complex mental activities of children are derived from social and cultural contexts comes from the work of

    A. Montessori.

    B. Piaget.

    C. Vygotsky.

    D. Bruner.

12. A parent drops off his crying child in the toddler room and needs to leave for work right away. Anaya walks over to the child and picks her up, holding her and singing to her. When the child begins to stop crying, Anaya walks with her over to the book area. She sits down and puts books out on the rug, while holding the child in her lap. Her behavior aligns with which theorist's ideas?

    A. Maslow

    B. Piaget

    C. Vygotsky

    D. Rosenblatt

13. The transition from preoperational thought to understanding concrete operations occurs

    A. during the toddler stage.

    B. during the preschool stage.

    C. during the primary-age stage.

    D. during the intermediate-age stage.

14. Preschoolers typically can express their emotions

    A. and can identify two feelings simultaneously.

    B. but can recognize only one emotion at a time.

    C. and can recognize another's feelings when verbally expressed.

    D. and regulate their feelings and behaviors easily.

15. Research suggests that kindergarten children feel stress in which situations?

    A. circle time

    B. singing time

    C. recess

    D. transitions

16. One effect of extensive adult-directed teaching for typically developing children is they may become

   A. academically behind because of too much rote learning.

   B. unable to take initiative to raise questions and solve problems.

   C. advanced readers who can question and problem-solve.

   D. ahead of their peers and able to help peer teach.

17. Ms. Fuller is observing a group of children engaged in "superhero" play with imaginary guns and swords. They are not actually hurting each other but are just acting out scenes from a recent popular movie. Even so, Ms. Fuller is concerned with the "violent" nature of the children's play. What would be her best course of action?

   A. Stop the play and call their parents.

   B. Observe the play, but actively intervene to help them consider alternative ways of solving problems.

   C. Call a class meeting and tell the children that no one can pretend play with weapons.

   D. Have the school counselor talk with the children who are playing superheroes.

18. Aggression is more likely to occur in

   A. same-age groups.

   B. mixed-age groups.

   C. cooperative groups.

   D. sibling groups.

19. Michael and Juan are playing in the dramatic play center and are developing the rules for taking orders in a restaurant. This feature in symbolic play was identified by which theorist as being essential to play's role in development?

   A. Montessori

   B. Vygotsky

   C. Piaget

   D. Steiner

20. William is working with a 5-year-old child who seems to be committing overregularizations. The child overuses the "-ed" ending for the past tense, i.e., "I runed-to the door." What should William do first?

   A. Begin the process for getting the child exceptional educational services.

   B. Model the proper pronunciation of the word to the child, including repeating the word back in a way that does not demean or embarrass the child.

   C. Correct the child every time he uses the wrong form of a verb.

   D. Call the child's parents and let them know he is concerned.

21. Research has shown that teachers of young children tend to

   A. overestimate children academically, but underestimate them intellectually.

   B. overestimate children intellectually, but underestimate them academically.

   C. underestimate their fine motor skills, but overestimate their gross motor skills.

   D. underestimate children intellectually, but overestimate their gross motor skills.

22. Moral development typically begins during which stage of development?

   A. infant

   B. toddler

   C. preschool

   D. primary

23. The idea that private speech is a characteristic of a child who is egocentric and unable to take the perspectives of others was posited by which theorist?

   A. Piaget

   B. Vygotsky

   C. Bruner

   D. Elkind

24. Recording objective, nonjudgmental facts, concentrating on what was said or not said without subjectivity is part of effective

    A. anecdotal note-taking.

    B. rubric scoring.

    C. summative assessments.

    D. formative notations.

25. You are part of a kindergarten team planning a unit of study on the place of technology in our lives and thinking of activities. One of the teachers says that you should email parents a survey to find out their children's learning styles. She mentions that she learns best auditorily, or by hearing. What is the current research on learning styles?

    A. It is the best way to plan for differentiation.

    B. It is a myth that has been debunked.

    C. It is part of the Universal Design Planning Process.

    D. It is primarily effective for young children.

26. When teachers rely heavily on reward and punishment systems of discipline in the primary classroom, they may

    A. damage children's self-esteem.

    B. develop their children's autonomy.

    C. develop a strong classroom management system.

    D. foster a sense of teamwork.

27. In the primary grades, developmentally appropriate ways of teaching writing to children include

    A. modeling, frequent writing to communicate, with an emphasis on the process.

    B. spelling tests and timed prompts.

    C. spelling and handwriting curriculum.

    D. correcting spelling errors and helping with penmanship.

28. Miss Kara is observing Tommy pretending to cook breakfast for his action figures. After about 2 minutes, he seems to have run out of ideas for the activity. What could Miss Kara do?

    A. Direct him to another center as he is clearly bored.

    B. Transition to another activity such as the listening center.

    C. Sit with him and pretend to have brought a special ingredient for the breakfast.

    D. Begin to work on literacy skills, as he's clearly done with play.

29. Kim wants to assess her 3-year-olds' fine motor skill development. What would be the most developmentally appropriate way?

    A. Have them write their names on a blank piece of paper, noticing their pencil grip.

    B. Observe them as they engage in self-help skills such as buttoning their jackets.

    C. Give them a coloring page and see if they can stay in the lines.

    D. See if they can use their finger and their thumb to grasp.

30. According to the research, a time-out chair in preschool is a developmentally

    A. appropriate practice to keep children safe.

    B. inappropriate practice that should be avoided.

    C. appropriate practice suitable for children older than five.

    D. inappropriate practice for some children.

31. Mr. Paul is having a conference with Tomás's mother. During the conversation, he mentions that Tomás has a difficult time staying on his nap cot during rest time. In fact, he is constantly moving the cot so that there is very little space between him and his friends, or he is getting on another child's cot. His mother explains that Tomás sleeps with her and his siblings in her bed at home regularly. Mr. Paul explains that licensing regulations require Tomás to rest on a nap cot alone. What solution could he offer?

   A. Stop nap time altogether, as it's nearly January.

   B. Put Tomás in a corner away from the other children.

   C. Give Tomás stickers for his behavior chart when he remembers not to get in another child's cot.

   D. Move Tomás to the middle of the room, so that he is in the center of the group.

32. Four-year-old Tommy is pretending to cook breakfast for his action figures. According to research, what is the minimum amount of time he should be able to sustain his play?

   A. 2 minutes

   B. 5 minutes

   C. 10 minutes

   D. 15 minutes

33. A curriculum that is developmentally appropriate likely has

   A. clearly delineated content areas so that children are not confused.

   B. a pacing guide that allows teachers to identify children who are not ready.

   C. integrated content areas in thematic units or topics of study.

   D. differentiated instruction using worksheets and harder books.

34. Jason is creating a class behavior chart for his second graders. He plans to put a sticker by each child's name when he notices positive behaviors. At the end of the week, children who have earned five stickers will get a chance to go to the treasure box. What is this type of management system called?

   A. positive behavioral support system

   B. token economy

   C. conscious discipline system

   D. class economy

35. According to Erikson, when toddlers says "No!" to an adult, they are working on their

   A. autonomy.

   B. vocabulary.

   C. receptive vocabulary.

   D. trust.

36. According to the National Association for the Education of Young Children, assessment should

   A. be informal, as children are young and more formal as they get older.

   B. involve regular and periodic observations of the child in different settings.

   C. include quizzes that are multiple-choice, so the child can choose from the options.

   D. be only done with children who are beginning to read.

37. The first grade Multi-Tiered System of Support Team (MTSS) is reviewing Jason's informal reading inventory and phonics assessments as they work on his Individual Education Plan (IEP). Mr. Alvarez notes that the family has a history of dyslexia. According to research, dyslexia is typically caused by which of the following?

   A. a speech and language disorder

   B. a vision issue in the brain

   C. a phonological processing issue in the brain

   D. a lack of practice with letters and sounds

38. The curriculum model that includes multi-age children from 3 to 6 working individually on tasks and engaging in practical work is credited to

    A. Froebel.

    B. Montessori.

    C. Piaget.

    D. Steiner.

39. A child's ability to rhyme is assessed in a test of

    A. phonological awareness.

    B. phonemic awareness.

    C. alphabetic principle.

    D. onsets and rimes.

40. The first way teachers can begin to promote positive attitudes toward cultural and racial identity is to

    A. teach explicit multicultural curriculum.

    B. bring parents in to explain anti-bias curriculum.

    C. examine their own beliefs and prejudices.

    D. do a survey to find out what attitudes are present.

41. The idea that infants develop a sense of trust or mistrust is based on which theorist's work?

    A. Steiner

    B. Erikson

    C. Piaget

    D. Vygotsky

42. Allowing children to plan names and quantities of materials needed for a group activity fosters

    A. learning concepts of numbers in context.

    B. extra time for the teachers to work with small groups.

    C. learning science concepts of planning.

    D. fine motor skills.

43. Ms. Julie plans to assess her preschoolers' understanding of adding and taking away. What would be the best type of sentence to use?

    A. four and six make ten

    B. four plus six equals ten

    C. four added to six makes ten

    D. four added to six comes to ten

44. Research shows that many families

    A. want to help with their child's learning, but are confused by jargon.

    B. are too busy to help with their child's learning, so they need quick tips.

    C. want the teachers to handle all the teaching, and do not like workshops.

    D. think their children do not need to have formal reading instruction until first grade.

45. A weeklong unit of holidays around the world

    A. may increase stereotypes and misconceptions.

    B. will allow for an introduction of various cultures.

    C. is a good way to honor the students' cultures.

    D. is recommended by the Association for Childhood Education International.

46. Joanna is working in the block group with two babies. One baby keeps picking up the blocks and throwing them at the other baby. Joanna says "Stop" twice, but the baby doesn't stop. What would be her next step?

    A. Put the baby back in her bed as she is clearly tired.

    B. Put away the blocks and put the babies in the board book center.

    C. Try to distract the baby by drawing her attention to a block structure she is building.

    D. Raise her voice so that the baby hears her.

47. Which is best reason for teaching two-year-olds the alphabet song?

   A. It helps them learn the alphabet faster.

   B. It helps them develop listening skills and a sense of rhythm and rhyme.

   C. It helps them learn to read better.

   D. It helps them develop their fine motor skills.

48. For toddlers, what should be the main feature of the curriculum?

   A. social emotional skills

   B. gross motor practice

   C. emergent literacy

   D. basic concepts

49. Tina is lining rocks up "small-large-small-large-small-large." She then groups them into categories by color. What concepts is she likely demonstrating?

   A. science concepts of predictability

   B. math concepts of pattern and order

   C. literacy concepts of sequence

   D. creativity

50. From the scenario in Question No. 49, if Tina is making patterns using the rocks, she is demonstrating

   A. counting and cardinality.

   B. operations and algebraic thinking.

   C. numbers and operations in base ten.

   D. measurement and data.

51. Ms. Kim wants to help her second grade students' parents understand the math unit they are studying. Which activity would promote the best authentic family engagement?

   A. Do a math night where her students demonstrate their learning to their parents through activities that show their understanding at the conceptual level.

   B. Send out an email to the parents with some links on the math concepts being studied.

   C. Ask her team to include the math standards in the newsletter.

   D. Send homework home with the children so they can work with their parents.

52. The idea that children are motivated to find ways to represent their experiences through play, action, and communication is part of what philosophy?

   A. whole-language

   B. reading mastery

   C. child-centered

   D. child-directed

53. Babies typically produce their first word that has meaning around

   A. 6 months.

   B. 9 months.

   C. 12 months.

   D. 16 months.

54. Child-centered theme planning are those ideas that

   A. are related to standards and developmental goals.

   B. emerge from the child's play and life experiences.

   C. are based on the developmental stages of children.

   D. are emotionally relevant.

55. When is the best time for children to learn about spatial concepts, or the properties of objects and relationships among objects?

    A. before preschool

    B. about age 6

    C. around age 8

    D. around age 10

56. The attachment process typically lasts

    A. one year.

    B. two years.

    C. three years.

    D. four years.

57. According to the standards of developmentally appropriate practice, the ratio of adults to infants in a child care setting should be

    A. 1:3.

    B. 1:5.

    C. 1:7.

    D. 1:10.

58. Which theorist developed the concept of "concrete operational stage"?

    A. Vygotsky

    B. Erickson

    C. Piaget

    D. Montessori

59. Donna is developing her lesson plans based on what she believes will be currently relevant, socially meaningful, and intellectually stimulating for her students. This is called

    A. emergent curriculum.

    B. interdisciplinary curriculum.

    C. didactic curriculum.

    D. holistic curriculum.

60. Ms. Jeanie is a kindergarten teacher who has several children whose first language is Spanish. Which decision is most aligned with research and evidence-based practice?

    A. She decides to focus on teaching them English only so that they can help her communicate with their parents.

    B. She understands that they can advance their abilities in both English and Spanish easily if she uses strategies that include realia.

    C. She asks for tablets so that the students can have more time to learn the English alphabet.

    D. She uses an online translator to make her newsletters accessible.

Developmental Knowledge
Practice Test 2: Answer Key

Test Item	Answer	Competency
1.	C	3
2.	A	3
3.	B	5
4.	C	1
5.	C	7
6.	A	1
7.	D	3
8.	B	1
9.	C	5
10.	A	7
11.	C	2
12.	A	3
13.	C	3
14.	B	7
15.	D	5
16.	B	1
17.	B	2
18.	A	7
19.	B	5
20.	B	3
21.	A	4
22.	C	7
23.	A	5
24.	A	6
25.	B	5
26.	A	7
27.	A	3
28.	C	5
29.	B	6
30.	B	7

Test Item	Answer	Competency
31.	D	1
32.	B	5
33.	C	4
34.	B	7
35.	A	2
36.	B	6
37.	C	6
38.	B	4
39.	A	6
40.	C	3
41.	B	2
42.	A	5
43.	A	6
44.	A	1
45.	A	4
46.	C	3
47.	B	2
48.	B	4
49.	B	6
50.	B	6
51.	A	1
52.	A	3
53.	C	1
54.	B	4
55.	A	6
56.	B	2
57.	A	3
58.	C	2
59.	A	4
60.	B	3

Developmental Knowledge
Practice Test 2: Detailed Answers

1. (C)

The best answer is (C). In the Concrete Operational Stage, children develop the concept of seriation, which refers to the ability to sort objects and or other things (e.g., beginning, middle, and end of stories) by various characteristics, such as size, color, type, shape. (Competency 3)

2. (A)

Children who are 4 to 8 years of age typically see friendship in the light of those who engage in activities similar to theirs or who live nearby. As they get older, children begin to see friendship in more nuanced and sophisticated ways. (Competency 3)

3. (B)

When planning for preschoolers, teachers should include time and space for the children to engage in informal conversations. Preschoolers are developing their social-emotional skills and need opportunities to interact often with their peers and others. Play areas should be designed to facilitate talk. (Competency 5)

4. (C)

"Nature" is a broad term that refers to biological, hereditary, or genetic factors and includes choices (A), (B), and (D). (Genetics is not always identical to heredity, since some genetic influences are abnormal, caused by gene mutation.) "Nature" is contrasted with "nurture," which includes factors such as culture, nutrition, parenting styles, and emotional support. (Competency 1)

5. (C)

Preschoolers can begin to distinguish right from wrong and activities can be done to foster their conscience and their sense of what is right. Infants and toddlers have not developed their reasoning skills, so it is important not to label their behavior as deliberately wrong or malicious. (Competency 7)

6. (A)

Honig's (1991) work with families revealed that loving and learning must be intrinsic and intertwined for an infant to thrive. Choice (B) is not based on recent research; choice (C) is still under debate; and choice (D) is untrue. (Competency 1)

7. (D)

Vygotsky's work included a focus on opportunities for children to interact socially with others in order to develop their thinking and language skills. Piaget's stages focus on the individual's construction of concepts. Montessori was also more focused on individual learning. Linnea Ehri's work dealt with stages of word recognition. (Competency 3)

8. (B)

The development of expressive language, or spoken language, lags behind the development of receptive language, or the words that children understand. The implication of this research can be seen in the recommendations that adults and older children talk with young children to build their vocabulary. Additionally, this research supports the practice of talking about picture books or oral reading of chapter books that are above a child's reading ability. (Competency 1)

9. (C)

Vygotsky's theory of the zone of proximal development is based on the idea that children can learn when paired with an individual who is able to scaffold that space between what the child can do on her own and what the child can do with a bit of help. Maslow developed a hierarchy of needs toward personal growth; Piaget developed a theory of cognitive development; and Gesell worked on the idea that a child's developmental age or stage may be different from his chronological age. (Competency 5)

10. (A)

Developmentally, it is common for toddlers to display some aggressive behaviors such as biting or pushing. They are asserting control over their environment and learning about limits. The other answer choices are traits that can be modeled and observed, but may not be as evident as increased aggressiveness. (Competency 7)

11. (C)

Vygotsky asserted that children need social interaction and opportunities to interact with others in order to fully develop their mental processes. Montessori's model included tasks that allowed children to learn through sequenced and well-planned activities, mostly individually rather than socially. Piaget's work focused more on individual cognitive development. Bruner is best known for his work with memory, learning, and perception. (Competency 2)

12. (A)

Maslow's (A) hierarchy of needs theory posits that we have sequential levels of needs that must be met: 1) physiological, 2) security, 3) affiliation, 4) esteem, and 5) self-actualization. Anaya's response demonstrates that she understands a child's need for security and for affiliation, which includes human touch and interaction. (Competency 3)

13. (C)

Piaget observed that children moved from preoperational thought to understanding concrete operations during the primary school years, typically ages 5 to 7. The previous preoperational stage includes toddlers (18 to 24 months) through the preschool years—a time of "magical" non-rational thinking. Intermediate-age students are in middle childhood and should be fully in the concrete operational stage. (Competency 3)

14. (B)

Preschoolers can express their emotions, but are typically only able to recognize one feeling at a time. For instance, it can be difficult for them to express that they are both angry and sad. They are still working on regulating their own emotions as well as identifying emotions that others express. (Competency 7)

15. (D)

Research showed that three of the primary stressors for kindergarten-aged children are transitions, waiting, and worksheets. Understanding this is important as teachers plan for activities, movement, and instruction. (Competency 5)

16. (B)

Children who have adults directing their learning to the extreme or who provide only direct instruction run the risk of developing learned helplessness and being unable to take initiative or to ask questions. Children need opportunities to learn in more unstructured ways, to explore, and to actively engage with their environment. By encountering problems that they need to figure out, children can develop critical thinking and creativity. (Competency 1)

17. (B)

Children often play by imitating the books, movies, and other media to which they are exposed. Since young children are in the stage of seeing things in a didactic way, good vs. evil, the play is not unnatural and should not cause alarm. However, by observing the play and then, if necessary, actively intervening to suggest other story lines, Ms. Fuller can help children consider the consequences of violence and think critically about other possible scenarios. The other choices are either too drastic for the situation or are not age-appropriate. (Competency 2)

18. (A)

Children in same-age groups are more likely to experience aggression than children in groups that are mixed, cooperative, or composed of siblings. The thought is that a mixed group might have children at different developmental stages, so it would have a natural hierarchy that would prevent aggression. Also, having an older child present might provide a model for regulating feelings of anger. Cooperative groups are often the same age, so aggression can sometimes be seen in these. Sibling groups vary a lot depending on the age and gender of the siblings. (Competency 7)

19. (B)

Vygotsky found that symbolic play contains rules or behavioral guidelines that children must follow in order to successfully navigate the play scene. He found that this supported children's ability to restrict their impulsive actions and behave in self-regulated and intentional ways. Piaget differed from this idea in that he felt that play allowed children to explore symbolism and construct personal meaning from the world around them. Montessori noted that pretend play allowed children to act out things they saw in the real world. Steiner asserted that symbolic play allowed children to develop their imaginations. (Competency 5)

20. (B)

This is often a natural and typical developmental action. William should model saying the word correctly back to the student and finding opportunities to draw attention to the proper use without embarrassing the child. ("Oh, so you ran to the door. And who was there?") He might take anecdotal notes to document the progress that the child makes in internalizing the proper use of word endings. (Competency 3)

21. (A)

Teachers of young children tend to overestimate them academically but underestimate them intellectually. For example, they may think a child has a concept of numbers because he can count. Also, researchers have found that children learn from spontaneous play as well as from systematic instruction, so their intellectual ability may be greater than what the formal curriculum contains. Teachers should refrain from judging intellect based only on what a child can do academically. (Competency 4)

22. (C)

Preschoolers begin to develop morality and a conscience as they become more aware of the consequences of their actions and aware of others' feelings. Infants and toddlers are still exploring their environment and developing a self-concept. They are not yet concerned with the feelings of others. Primary-aged children have typically developed at least a beginning sense of morality. (Competency 7)

23. (A)

Piaget asserted that children's private speech was related to their egocentrism and was not connected to learning. Vygotsky postulated that private speech was a way for a child to communicate with herself to self-regulate or to guide thought processes and actions. Bruner is associated with the constructivist theory of active learning, while Elkind dealt with learning theory and personal growth. (Competency 5)

24. (A)

Anecdotal note-taking is a process of recording observed, objective facts and events. Such notes can be used as part of an ongoing informal assessment regarding learning progression or behavior patterns. Rubrics are typically already-developed assessment tools, although notes may be put in the margins. The term "formative notations" is not a valid term, while summative assessments are the final assessment for determining the acquisition of a set of skills or knowledge. (Competency 6)

25. (B)

The learning styles theory has been debunked and may actually not help a child with learning, because it focuses on a perceived preferred modality. Rather than focus on a child's learning style, it is important to engage as many modalities in learning—visual, auditory, kinesthetic, and tactile. This aids in long-term memory retention. One example would be having a child listen to an audiobook while following along by reading a hard copy of the book. (Competency 5)

26. (A)

Reward and punishment systems of discipline and classroom management can negatively impact children's self-esteem. Teachers of young children are encouraged to help children develop a sense of autonomy, so that they have agency and can feel the power to help themselves and begin to self-regulate words and behaviors. (Competency 7)

27. (A)

Teachers should model and provide opportunities for frequent writing to communicate with an emphasis on the process rather than the product. Writing is a developmental process and children move from scribbling to letter strings to more conventional writing as they learn to encode or construct their understanding of the written language. Research on spelling tests has not shown that the words are moved to children's long-term memory unless multisensory strategies are used. Timed prompts are useful for helping children prepare for formal assessments when time is a factor, such as the Florida State Assessments. Handwriting, spelling, and grammar are all important parts of a comprehensive literacy curriculum, but should not replace the writing process. (Competency 3)

28. (C)

Helping or coaching children to develop their ability to play is a way of scaffolding a child's learning as described by Vygotsky. Because he was only playing for two minutes, his apparent boredom or lack of ideas may be alleviated with some guidance. The other answer choices might be options depending on the situation, but none would be ideal. (Competency 5)

29. (B)

It is best to assess fine motor skills by observing children doing everyday tasks. The typical three-year-olds can already hold things and use their pincer grip to grasp. They may not yet have the control to stay within a defined space or to write their names. (Competency 6)

30. (B)

Time-out chairs can cause shame and are developmentally inappropriate practices that should be avoided. There are other strategies to redirect or to help a child learn behaviors appropriate for the situation. The teacher should also examine the situation closely and see what changes or adjustments might be made to avoid negative responses or undesired behaviors. (Competency 7)

31. (D)

Because Tomás sleeps with siblings at home, he may feel uncertain or anxious when he is too far from other children. Mr. Paul can try putting him in the middle of the room so that he can feel the proximity of several other children, which may help Tomás rest better. If that doesn't seem to work, Mr. Paul can see if Tomás wants to try to sleep a little bit away from the others. Mr. Paul should not use stickers as a first option. Developmentally, the children still need at least a quiet or rest period if their mornings are active. If several children do not seem to be resting, Mr. Paul might try shortening the period and offering quiet activities instead. (Competency 1)

32. (B)

According to the research on play, preschoolers should be able to sustain a pretend play episode for a minimum of five minutes. (Competency 5)

33. (C)

Developmentally appropriate curriculum has integrated content areas in thematic units or topics of study. The curriculum is more holistic and interdisciplinary. While there may be a pacing guide or differentiated instruction, the focus is more strengths-based and aligned with the stages of cognitive development. (Competency 4)

34. (B)

A token economy or reward system is grounded in Skinner's behaviorism theory. This type of system may not be effective long-term or for every child, particularly since the children must wait the entire week to see the results of their efforts. The system has been used successfully in situations when children have been identified as having developmental delays or challenges in learning or behavior. With children younger than second grade, one possible obstacle is that they may not understand it; they may not know why they are getting the sticker or how many stickers are needed. Also, they may not be able to stay motivated for an entire week, or the reward many not be appealing. In summary, young children are still developing their executive function, so this type of system may work short-term in some situations, but other strategies should be developed. (Competency 7)

35. (A)

Toddlers are pushing against their world and testing limits to discover what they can do by themselves. By saying "no" (even when they don't actually mean it), toddlers are exerting their sense of being an autonomous self. Adults should be patient and remember that the behavior is natural and necessary for children to develop. Regarding the other choices, "no" is not typically a difficult vocabulary word to learn, and receptive vocabulary means spoken words that a child understands, so those answers are not correct. Trust is linked to the infant stage, according to Erikson. (Competency 2)

36. (B)

Assessment of young children should be as authentic as possible and done in natural ways so that the teacher is assessing the child based on real-world activities. Contrived assessments are not meaningful and often not reliable. (Competency 6)

37. (C)

The best answer is (C). Dyslexia and other reading disabilities are often caused by a phonological processing issue in the brain. It is categorized under Specific Learning Disabilities (SLDs) on IEPs. Individuals can have various levels of severity, but the commonalities include that it affects their reading decoding, fluency, comprehension, writing, and spelling. (Competency 6)

38. (B)

Maria Montessori's curriculum model was built around multi-age grouping, because children from three to six years of age develop rapidly, but often at different rates. Much of the curriculum is designed to be done independently by each child, with the teacher as a coach. Montessori believed that children wanted to imitate what they saw adults in their lives doing, so much of the learning areas are based on practical work. Froebel, who coined the word "kindergarten," believed that children should have an attractive, play-based setting. Piaget did not design curriculum; his work was on the cognitive stages of children's development. Steiner's Waldorf model includes both practical and imaginative play. (Competency 4)

39. (A)

"Phonological awareness" is the umbrella term that includes the ability to rhyme. Phonemic awareness deals with the phonemes or sounds in words. For example, "cat" has three sounds or phonemes. "Shut" also has three, as "sh" is a digraph and makes one sound. The alphabetic principle is the understanding that there is a systematic relationship between letters, sounds, and words. Onsets are the initial phonological units of words, and rimes are the groups of letters that follow. For example, in the word "dog," "d" is the onset and "og" is the rime. Rimes may also be word families. (Competency 6)

40. (C)

Research has revealed that teachers often hold biases that may not be immediately evident. Phrases such as "colorblind" or "I see all children the same" may prevent teachers from seeing children as individuals, with several factors contributing to their individuality. Intentionally working to reframe things in a strengths-based perspective rather than negatively is also helpful. Phrases like "school readiness" can contribute to a deficit mindset. The other possible answers might also be included, but the best first step is to look inward. (Competency 3)

41. (B)

Erikson theorized eight life stages of psychosocial development. These include trust vs. mistrust; autonomy vs. shame and doubt; initiative vs. guilt; industry vs. inferiority; identity vs. role confusion; intimacy vs. isolation; generativity vs. stagnation; and integrity vs. despair. He asserted that if individuals did not successfully navigate each stage, they would encounter difficulty in their development in later stages. Steiner (A) is associated with the Waldorf movement; Piaget's (C) stages involved constructivism and concept-building; and Vygotsky (D) is associated with social learning, scaffolding, and the zone of proximal development. (Competency 2)

42. (A)

Planning involves skills that support the development of concept of number. For example, if the activity involves cutting or gluing, the students would need to determine how many or how much of each item will be needed. (Competency 5)

43. (A)

When working with preschools, the teacher should use words like "make" when exploring math concepts such as combining two amounts to avoid confusion. Mathematical vocabulary such as *plus*, *minus*, and *equal* are typically introduced in the early grades, once the child has gotten a chance to experience the concepts without the abstract vocabulary. (Competency 6)

44. (A)

Many, if not most, parents or caregivers want to help their children with learning, but they may not always have the resources or information. Jargon can add to the confusing world of early learning services and practices, so parents may get frustrated. Additionally, if parents have not had a good experience in the school system either as a child or with their children, they may not feel comfortable helping their child. In some situations, parents may be working long hours or have other stressors that prevent them from working with their child. (Competency 1)

45. (A)

Short studies of holidays and countries, sometimes called "tourist" approaches, don't allow for in-depth learning, but rather focus on the exotic and different. As such, students may be left with stereotypes, simplifications, and misconceptions. (Competency 4)

46. (C)

Throwing blocks or testing the properties of things in their environment is a natural way for a baby to act. By trying to distract the child, Joanna is not discouraging her exploration, but simply trying to redirect it so that everyone stays safe and the child can explore other properties of the blocks. The action of throwing the blocks does not immediately suggest that the baby is tired. By putting the blocks away, Joanna is cutting short the learning that the baby is experiencing and not allowing her to continue an activity that is clearly engaging. Raising her

voice is not a good strategy, as proximity control is a better response. (Competency 3)

47. (B)

Toddlers may memorize the alphabet song, but that does not mean they have learned the alphabet or even the reason for the alphabet. Instead it suggests that they can listen and remember. The song also allows them to work on their rhythm and rhyme, all phonological skills that are necessary precursors to reading. (Competency 2)

48. (B)

Toddlers are just learning to move and act on their environment, so the focus should be on the development of their gross motor skills. Learning activities should be infused with opportunities to move, hop, run, and do cross-lateral movements. While the curriculum may include social emotional content (A), literacy (C), and basic concepts (D), during this time period toddlers are developing their large muscle groups. (Competency 4)

49. (B)

Tina is demonstrating her understanding of the mathematical concept of pattern (small-large-small-large) in her A-B-A-B pattern. She is also demonstrating an understanding of order (attribute) by sorting the rocks by color. The pattern sequence is related to the literacy concept (C), but it is more closely related to the mathematical concept. Creativity (D) is not a concept or skill that could involve some kind of mastery. (Competency 6)

50. (B)

By making patterns with the rocks, the child is demonstrating the concepts of mathematical operations and algebraic thinking. The other answer choices involve concepts associated with counting, numerical manipulations, or graphing. (Competency 6)

51. (A)

Family engagement activities should provide opportunities for the family to be together in a warm, inviting situation. Having a parent night allows children to demonstrate their learning, which develops their confidence and sense of accomplishment. It allows parents to see firsthand what their children are learning in a non-threatening environment. It also allows parents to ask questions and ensure they understand the concepts and methods that are involved. (The email with links to math concepts could be used as a follow-up or for parents who cannot attend the activity.) (Competency 1)

52. (A)

Whole language is an overarching concept that children will be motivated to learn through play, action, and communication with others. The concept was misunderstood by some as meaning that children did not need instruction in reading, but that they would naturally learn to read through exposure and repetition. In recent years, that misunderstanding has been clarified. Regarding the other choices, reading mastery (B) is a systematic, direct reading instruction program, often used with children who have learning difficulties. Child-centered (C) learning means that the adult or teacher designs instruction based on the children's interests or what the teacher knows is developmentally appropriate. Child-directed (D), by contrast, means that the child is directing the activity and the adult is following. These latter two have been confused at times, with child-centered instruction being interpreted as the child making all the choices as to the learning. (Competency 3)

53. (C)

While babies may babble, coo, or imitate, they typically produce their first word that has meaning associated with it around 12 months of age. By 16 months, they have a few more words. It is important to remember that development falls in a range or continuum, and children may develop atypically—that is, either faster or slower than the generally accepted age. (Competency 1)

54. (B)

Child-centered themes emerge from the child's world and are translated into activities and materials that will provoke curiosity and wonder. The teacher will adjust, adding more materials or changing activities, based on the children's responses. The teacher then designs the next theme based on observations and learning. While child-centered themes may align with the standards and developmental goals and are typically emotionally relevant, the essential factor is that the topics of study come from observing the children. (Competency 4)

55. (A)

Through opportunities to interact with their environment, children can begin learning about spatial concepts prior to preschool. Through guided play, children can learn vocabulary words such as "rough," "smooth," "above," and "below." (Competency 6)

56. (B)

According to research, the attachment process typically lasts about two years. Attachment theory states that a strong emotional and physical attachment to at least one primary caregiver is critical to personal development. John Bowlby first coined the term as a result of his studies involving the developmental psychology of children. Attachment patterns that take less or more time are atypical. (Competency 2)

57. (A)

According to the NAEYC's standards of developmentally appropriate practice, the ratio of adults to infants should be one adult for three infants. This allows the adults to monitor and interact with the infants in meaningful ways. As babies get older, the ratio can increase, so that one adult may supervise more children. (Competency 3)

58. (C)

Piaget developed a stage theory of cognitive development, including the concept and stage of concrete operations. This is the third stage in Piaget's theory, and it spans the time of middle childhood—starting around age 7 and continuing until approximately age 11—and is characterized by the development of logical thought. (Competency 2)

59. (A)

Emergent curriculum describes curriculum that emerges from the children's interests, play and life experiences, and developmental levels. The teacher has a lot of autonomy to adjust and include standards in a fluid fashion. An interdisciplinary curriculum includes all content areas in a seamless model. A didactic curriculum is teacher-directed. A holistic curriculum would attempt to help students with academic, social, and emotional skills—which may or may not "emerge" from students' interests and experience. (Competency 4)

60. (B)

Ms. Jeanie understands that the children can grow in both languages if she uses strategies that will foster their learning, such as including realia. She certainly can have them help her communicate with the parents, but that should not be her primary goal. She also might ask for tablets, but there are other programs that would be more beneficial for the students. Finally, she would do well to get a peer-recommended program. (Competency 3)

PRACTICE TEST 2

FTCE PreK–3 Language Arts and Reading
Subtest 2 (532)

Also available at the REA Study Center (www.rea.com/studycenter)

This practice test is also offered online at the REA Study Center. We recommend that you take the online version of the test to simulate test-day conditions and to receive these added benefits:

- **Timed testing conditions**—helps you gauge how much time you can spend on each question

- **Automatic scoring**—find out how you did on the test, instantly

- **On-screen detailed explanations of answers**—gives you the correct answer and explains why the other answer choices are wrong

- **Diagnostic score reports**—pinpoint where you're strongest and where you need to focus your study

Language Arts and Reading
Practice Test 2: Answer Sheet

1. Ⓐ Ⓑ Ⓒ Ⓓ
2. Ⓐ Ⓑ Ⓒ Ⓓ
3. Ⓐ Ⓑ Ⓒ Ⓓ
4. Ⓐ Ⓑ Ⓒ Ⓓ
5. Ⓐ Ⓑ Ⓒ Ⓓ
6. Ⓐ Ⓑ Ⓒ Ⓓ
7. Ⓐ Ⓑ Ⓒ Ⓓ
8. Ⓐ Ⓑ Ⓒ Ⓓ
9. Ⓐ Ⓑ Ⓒ Ⓓ
10. Ⓐ Ⓑ Ⓒ Ⓓ
11. Ⓐ Ⓑ Ⓒ Ⓓ
12. Ⓐ Ⓑ Ⓒ Ⓓ
13. Ⓐ Ⓑ Ⓒ Ⓓ
14. Ⓐ Ⓑ Ⓒ Ⓓ
15. Ⓐ Ⓑ Ⓒ Ⓓ
16. Ⓐ Ⓑ Ⓒ Ⓓ
17. Ⓐ Ⓑ Ⓒ Ⓓ
18. Ⓐ Ⓑ Ⓒ Ⓓ
19. Ⓐ Ⓑ Ⓒ Ⓓ
20. Ⓐ Ⓑ Ⓒ Ⓓ

21. Ⓐ Ⓑ Ⓒ Ⓓ
22. Ⓐ Ⓑ Ⓒ Ⓓ
23. Ⓐ Ⓑ Ⓒ Ⓓ
24. Ⓐ Ⓑ Ⓒ Ⓓ
25. Ⓐ Ⓑ Ⓒ Ⓓ
26. Ⓐ Ⓑ Ⓒ Ⓓ
27. Ⓐ Ⓑ Ⓒ Ⓓ
28. Ⓐ Ⓑ Ⓒ Ⓓ
29. Ⓐ Ⓑ Ⓒ Ⓓ
30. Ⓐ Ⓑ Ⓒ Ⓓ
31. Ⓐ Ⓑ Ⓒ Ⓓ
32. Ⓐ Ⓑ Ⓒ Ⓓ
33. Ⓐ Ⓑ Ⓒ Ⓓ
34. Ⓐ Ⓑ Ⓒ Ⓓ
35. Ⓐ Ⓑ Ⓒ Ⓓ
36. Ⓐ Ⓑ Ⓒ Ⓓ
37. Ⓐ Ⓑ Ⓒ Ⓓ
38. Ⓐ Ⓑ Ⓒ Ⓓ
39. Ⓐ Ⓑ Ⓒ Ⓓ
40. Ⓐ Ⓑ Ⓒ Ⓓ

41. Ⓐ Ⓑ Ⓒ Ⓓ
42. Ⓐ Ⓑ Ⓒ Ⓓ
43. Ⓐ Ⓑ Ⓒ Ⓓ
44. Ⓐ Ⓑ Ⓒ Ⓓ
45. Ⓐ Ⓑ Ⓒ Ⓓ
46. Ⓐ Ⓑ Ⓒ Ⓓ
47. Ⓐ Ⓑ Ⓒ Ⓓ
48. Ⓐ Ⓑ Ⓒ Ⓓ
49. Ⓐ Ⓑ Ⓒ Ⓓ
50. Ⓐ Ⓑ Ⓒ Ⓓ
51. Ⓐ Ⓑ Ⓒ Ⓓ
52. Ⓐ Ⓑ Ⓒ Ⓓ
53. Ⓐ Ⓑ Ⓒ Ⓓ
54. Ⓐ Ⓑ Ⓒ Ⓓ
55. Ⓐ Ⓑ Ⓒ Ⓓ
56. Ⓐ Ⓑ Ⓒ Ⓓ
57. Ⓐ Ⓑ Ⓒ Ⓓ
58. Ⓐ Ⓑ Ⓒ Ⓓ
59. Ⓐ Ⓑ Ⓒ Ⓓ
60. Ⓐ Ⓑ Ⓒ Ⓓ

Practice Test 2: Language Arts and Reading

TIME: 70 minutes
60 questions*

> **Directions:** Read each question and select the best response.

1. Mrs. Jones, a kindergarten teacher, makes a book for the students in her class. Looking at items in her kitchen, she cuts labels from cans of vegetables and soup, as well as the front of boxes of cereal and crackers, and inserts them in page protectors that she's put into a binder. She takes photographs of the signs of common restaurants and stores, prints them, and inserts them in page protectors, too. The final product is a book that she puts into the class library. The book is an example of what?

   A. phonics

   B. environmental print

   C. alphabetic knowledge

   D. leveled text

2. Juan is at the bookstore with his father. He wants to buy a book about shapes and colors. What type of book is this?

   A. fiction

   B. concept

   C. pattern

   D. informational

3. Stacy is reading a book and comes to a word she doesn't know. Which of the following would be most helpful for her to access?

   A. index

   B. glossary

   C. compendium

   D. table of contents

4. Mr. Williams, a second grade teacher, reads aloud two versions of the fairy tale *Cinderella*. What graphic organizer would be best to compare and contrast the versions?

   A. K-W-L chart

   B. timeline

   C. Venn diagram

   D. story map

5. Mr. Rodriquez is working with a small group of students on their reading. The students are reading aloud and he notices that one student is reading slowly and seems to be stumbling over the words. He decides to do a quick, informal assessment and has the child read aloud a passage while using a separate page to mark the child's errors. What assessment is this?

   A. anecdotal note

   B. running record

   C. Informal Reading Inventory

   D. Developmental Reading Assessment

---

* This practice test presents slightly more items than you are likely to see on test day. The actual test contains approximately 55 questions. You will only learn exactly how many questions you will get after you take the FTCE tutorial and sign the non-disclosure agreement on test day.

6. Ms. Donna is planning a center activity to foster her 4-year-olds' learning of spatial concepts and vocabulary. What materials would you advise her to use for a guided play center?

   A. sand and water

   B. books, markers, and paper

   C. wooden blocks

   D. a computer game

7. Five-year-old Gabrielle is in the classroom library looking at books. Mr. David notices that she is moving her finger under the words from left to right, stopping to turn the pages as she pretends to read aloud. She laughs at the illustration and looks back at the cover before returning her attention to the page. What is she demonstrating a knowledge of?

   A. concepts of print

   B. directionality

   C. phonics

   D. humor

8. Miss Juanita is selecting picture books for a mini-lesson to teach the concepts of cause and effect. What genre would provide the best models for writing?

   A. pattern

   B. concept

   C. informational

   D. narrative

9. Students who are reading with 90%–94% accuracy with some instruction and support for comprehension are typically reading at what level?

   A. independent

   B. instructional

   C. frustration

   D. recreational

10. Mr. Martin has a student whose reading is somewhat choppy. To increase his fluency, what strategy would be most effective?

    A. timed readings

    B. practice with high-frequency words

    C. practice with sight words

    D. repeated readings

11. A second grade teacher is planning to review his students' understanding of the sounds that "s" and "h" make when at the beginning of the words "shake," "shook," "shade," and "shower" or at the end of the word "mash." What are these sounds called?

    A. blends

    B. consonants

    C. digraphs

    D. graphemes

12. When students dictate sentences about an event and the teacher records their dictation on chart paper, it is called

    A. interactive writing.

    B. modeled writing.

    C. dictation.

    D. shared writing.

13. Imaginative stories of other worlds that are based in reality are called

    A. fairy tales.

    B. realistic fiction.

    C. folktales.

    D. fantasies.

14. The spelling system is referred to as

    A. orthography.

    B. morphology.

    C. phonology.

    D. phonemology.

15. Which of the following is an alphabetical list of names, subjects, topics, etc., that includes the pages where they can be found?

    A. an index

    B. a glossary

    C. a table of contents

    D. a compendium

16. The musical quality of speech when a passage is read aloud in a smooth and expressive manner with proper phrasing, volume, smoothness, and pacing is called

    A. prosody.

    B. fluency.

    C. comprehension.

    D. singing.

17. The process of putting a piece of writing into a final form through proofing and looking at mechanics is called

    A. drafting.

    B. editing.

    C. revising.

    D. publishing.

18. Thomas has a large number of sight words and high frequency words. While he is reading these quickly and accurately, he cannot answer questions related to the text. He is likely demonstrating

    A. fluency.

    B. vocabulary.

    C. phonics.

    D. automaticity.

19. The stages of the writing process are

    A. publishing, revising, editing, drafting, pre-writing.

    B. scribbling, revising, illustrating, editing, publishing.

    C. brainstorming, drafting, revising, editing, publishing.

    D. descriptive, expository, narrative, persuasive.

20. Jenny writes, "The storm was a wintry soldier marching home." Her word choice is an example of which of the following?

    A. analogy

    B. metaphor

    C. adjective

    D. simile

21. Mr. Milton is teaching a skills block to his second graders. He shows them the word "cat" and then "cats." The word "cat" and the word part "s" are examples of what?

    A. phonemes

    B. morphemes

    C. phonograms

    D. affixes

22. Miss Tonya works on developing her students' prosody by reading aloud a sentence expressively while the students reread it aloud, imitating her expression. This type of strategy is called

    A. echo reading.

    B. choral reading.

    C. shared reading.

    D. modeled reading.

23. William is working with a small group of students who are having trouble with letter formation. What strategy would be a way for him to examine their handwriting skills and to demonstrate how to form the letters legibly?

    A. modeled writing

    B. interactive writing

    C. shared writing

    D. writer's workshop

24. When students begin to understand that there is a connection between letters and sounds, they are demonstrating an understanding of

    A. the alphabetic principle.

    B. phonemes.

    C. concepts of print.

    D. phonology.

25. During a "making words" activity, Mrs. Willard has her students build the word "at." She then has them add letters to make the words "sat," "bat," "rat," and "mat." In this activity, what is the "at" called?

    A. rime

    B. onset

    C. rhyme

    D. syllable

26. When readers read accurately, rapidly, and with expression, they are demonstrating

    A. automaticity.

    B. fluency.

    C. phonics.

    D. sight word knowledge.

27. Mr. Sanders is preparing to work with a small group of children on a phonemic awareness activity. He gives the students counters to represent sounds in words. For the word "chat," how many counters represent the sounds?

    A. four

    B. three

    C. two

    D. one

28. During circle time, Sherwanda, a 5-year-old, tells her classmates about learning to ride her bicycle using training wheels, noting that she is going to try to ride without the training wheels during the upcoming weekend. She is demonstrating

    A. developmental talk.

    B. narrative discourse.

    C. vocabulary development.

    D. phonological awareness.

29. Allison is able to identify all the letters of the alphabet, lowercase and uppercase. According to research, this factor is related to what later ability?

    A. comprehension

    B. fluency

    C. phonemic awareness

    D. decoding

30. Otilia is working in a class of students who are classified as English language learners. Before she begins reading a book aloud, she introduces a story map labeled with "characters," "setting," and "plot." These words are classified as what level?

    A. Tier 1

    B. Tier 2

    C. Tier 3

    D. Tier 4

31. Before reading a book on butterflies aloud to her third graders, Ms. Baker asks them what they know about butterflies to activate their prior knowledge. What graphic organizer would be useful here?

    A. story map

    B. Venn diagram

    C. K-W-L chart

    D. RAFT chart

32. Mr. Milton selects a book to read aloud for several days in a row. He reads it first for the students' enjoyment. During the next few readings, he draws their attention to concepts about print, comprehension, and vocabulary. He is using what instructional practice?

    A. shared reading

    B. interactive reading

    D. modeled reading

    D. repeated reading

33. Kim has 18 first grade students. As she plans for instruction, she determines which books best fit their learning needs. She notices that two of her students seem to be struggling with the books she had selected. She pulls them into a small group and has them work with a simpler text. What is she demonstrating?

    A. modification

    B. differentiation

    C. adaptation

    D. remediation

34. Joey is planning instruction for his reading groups. As he does, he considers the four cueing systems that children rely on as they read. They are

    A. phonological, semantic, syntactic, and pragmatic.

    B. phonemic awareness, phonics, vocabulary, and comprehension.

    C. decoding, analyzing, synthesizing, and inferencing.

    D. proofing, pointing to words, sounding out, and final deciding.

35. Susie is an English language learner and reads aloud a passage about a boy learning to cross the monkey bars. The passage includes the boy saying that the activity was "a piece of cake." What does she need to know to understand the passage?

    A. idioms

    B. simile

    C. analogy

    D. etymology

36. Mr. Reedy is working on a phonics lesson that introduces diphthongs. Which words might be part of this lesson?

    A. chat, shin, think

    B. boy, house, oil

    C. motorcycle, machine, toothpick

    D. right, fight, tie, sigh

37. Ms. Cheek conducts a running record while her second grader is reading aloud. She calculates his accuracy level at 85%. Her student is in what level?

    A. independent

    B. instructional

    C. frustration

    D. recreational

38. During a mini-lesson for a writer's workshop, Ms. Hernandez introduces the phrases "cold as ice," "snug as a bug in a rug," "blind as a bat," and "quick as a fox." What literary concepts are these?

    A. similes

    B. metaphors

    C. idioms

    D. adjectives

39. A component of literacy in which readers identify words quickly and accurately when reading, and spell words efficiently when writing is called

    A. automaticity.

    B. fluency.

    C. decoding.

    D. encoding.

40. Mr. Urbano is planning a lesson to help his students create schema with new information. What is this process called?

    A. accommodation

    B. assimilation

    C. comprehension

    D. prediction

41. When working with students who are English language learners, what strategy is best for introducing new topics?

    A. concept maps

    B. K-W-L charts

    C. mind maps

    D. story maps

42. During circle time, Ms. Lee models when to say "please" and "thank you." She is demonstrating what?

    A. syntax

    B. phonology

    C. semantics

    D. pragmatics

43. Mrs. Bowles is planning for a skills block that includes phonemic awareness instruction. She should include

    A. blending and segmenting words.

    B. spelling simple words.

    C. letter identification.

    D. flashcards.

44. Mr. Chin is planning an activity for students to sequence events in a story. What activity could he use to differentiate for his students?

    A. story boards

    B. worksheets

    C. Elkonin boxes

    D. semantic feature analysis

45. Ms. Lauren notices that Manny is using his knowledge of sound-symbol correspondence to read his classmates' names. She writes a description of the event, noting the date and time. This is an example of

    A. informal observations.

    B. anecdotal notes.

    C. formative assessment.

    D. informal notes.

46. Manny is using his knowledge of sound-symbol correspondence to read his classmates' names and copy them on a clipboard. What skill is he demonstrating?

    A. phonemic awareness

    B. vocabulary

    C. phonics

    D. comprehension

47. Isabella, a second grader, is rereading her rough draft to her writing partner and makes changes based on his comments before she conferences with the teacher. At what stage is she in the writing process?

   A. prewriting

   B. drafting

   C. revising

   D. editing

48. Teachers should include approximately how many hours to teach phonemic awareness strategies to young children?

   A. 10 hours

   B. 20 hours

   C. 40 hours

   D. 60 hours

49. Ms. Westrich is working on helping her students incorporate more elaborate sentence structures in their speech and writing. She writes the sentence, "Although Rowen was afraid, he let go of the rope." This is an example of what kind of sentence?

   A. complex

   B. compound

   C. complex compound

   D. fragment

50. Ashby, a third grader, writes, "They took there dog to the store." Mr. Rickman makes a note of the incorrect use of "there" for "their" and plans a mini-lesson on what type of words?

   A. homographs

   B. homophones

   C. rhyming words

   D. idioms

51. Joanna is assessing two of her kindergarten students' writing. Sebastian can write a complete sentence, with spaces between some words, can spell two high-frequency words correctly, seems to include the beginning and ending sounds in most words, and uses uppercase and lowercase letters. Parker uses random letters that do not correspond to words, draws a picture instead of writing, and uses scribbles to represent cursive writing. What type of informal assessment tool would be most helpful for Joanna to use to evaluate her students?

   A. checklist

   B. brief quiz

   C. portfolio

   D. rubric

52. In the dramatic play center, Keonnia is taking food orders from classmates pretending to be customers. She writes their orders on her paper, using the letter "t" for toast and "j" for juice. She is demonstrating that she understands that writing is a form of communication and that her writing has meaning. What stage of emergent writing is she likely in?

   A. early phonetic

   B. letter strings

   C. phonetic

   D. advanced letter strings

53. Miss Kara is introducing "and" and "but" in a mini-lesson during writer's workshop. These words are examples of

   A. conjunctions.

   B. prepositions.

   C. articles.

   D. phrases.

54. Mr. Pete is working on plans for explicitly teaching his students Tier 2 words. Which list of words are examples of Tier 2 words?

    A. label, write, say

    B. photosynthesis, legislate, matriculation

    C. justify, paragraph, infer

    D. antidisestablishmentarianism, supercalifragilisticexpialidocious, extraordinarily

55. As part of her science report, Margaret is working on a chart to list the amount of water used for her garden each week. This representation would best be done as a

    A. figure.

    B. table.

    C. insert.

    D. illustration.

56. A word which expresses the relationship of a noun or a pronoun to other words of the sentence is called a(n)

    A. preposition.

    B. transition.

    C. article.

    D. conjunction.

57. Mr. Connell is working on a lesson using "pitch," "witch," "stitch," and "glitch." The "tch" is considered a

    A. phoneme.

    B. suffix.

    C. grapheme.

    D. syllable.

58. Reader's theater is a strategy that involves students reading aloud from a script. Teachers may use this strategy to focus on

    A. fluency.

    B. comprehension.

    C. decoding.

    D. background knowledge.

59. Rick is planning a mini-lesson on protagonists. Which genre would be the best example for him to use?

    A. fairy tales

    B. poetry

    C. nonfiction

    D. fantasy

60. Mr. Martin introduces the story *Ruby Bridges* by giving a bit of information on the Civil Rights era in the United States to build the students' background knowledge. This strategy is called

    A. contextual analysis.

    B. semantic feature analysis.

    C. summarizing.

    D. synthesizing.

Language Arts and Reading
Practice Test 2: Answer Key

Test Item	Answer	Competency
1.	B	1
2.	B	2
3.	B	2
4.	C	3
5.	B	5
6.	C	1
7.	A	1
8.	A	2
9.	B	3
10.	D	5
11.	C	1
12.	C	1
13.	D	2
14.	A	1
15.	A	2
16.	A	3
17.	B	4
18.	D	3
19.	C	4
20.	B	2
21.	B	1
22.	A	4
23.	B	1
24.	A	3
25.	A	1
26.	B	3
27.	B	1
28.	B	3
29.	D	4
30.	B	4

Test Item	Answer	Competency
31.	C	2
32.	A	1
33.	B	5
34.	A	3
35.	A	2
36.	B	1
37.	C	5
38.	A	2
39.	A	3
40.	B	3
41.	B	2
42.	D	3
43.	A	1
44.	A	3
45.	B	5
46.	C	3
47.	C	4
48.	B	1
49.	A	4
50.	B	4
51.	D	5
52.	A	4
53.	A	4
54.	B	1
55.	B	2
56.	A	4
57.	C	1
58.	A	3
59.	A	4
60.	A	3

Language Arts and Reading
Practice Test 2: Detailed Answers

1. (B)

Environmental prints are real-world examples of text and can provide a transition from home to school life. Leveled texts (D) are sets of books that cover similar topics over a variety of reading levels to give students information at their comfort level of reading. (Competency 1)

2. (B)

Concept books are books that deal with basic concepts such as shapes, colors, numbers, or counting. Pattern books (C) feature simple text in a strongly repetitive pattern that allows children to predict what is coming next as they read. They may use rhyme, repeated words or phrases, or familiar expressions. (Competency 2)

3. (B)

The glossary is typically found at the back of the book and contains definitions of words found in the text. A compendium (C) is a short but detailed collection of information, usually in a book. (Competency 2)

4. (C)

Venn diagrams are useful for comparing two or more ideas, versions, or events. A Venn diagram is an illustration that uses overlapping or non-overlapping circles to show the relationship between groups of things. (Competency 3)

5. (B)

Running records are informal assessments that can be done quickly to determine whether a reader is at his independent, instructional, or frustration level. Anec-

dotal notes (A) are concise, objective narratives about an incident or person. The Informal Reading Inventory (C) is a method used to assess individual student reading levels. The Developmental Reading Assessment (D) is a standardized reading test used to determine a student's instructional level in reading. (Competency 5)

6. (C)

Wooden blocks are the best choice, as the teacher can use spatial vocabulary such as "under," "over," "next to," "higher," "below" as the children stack the blocks. (Competency 1)

7. (A)

The student is demonstrating an awareness of the concepts of print. This includes the knowledge of what books, print, and written language are, and how they function. Directionality (B) is the realization or knowledge that reading a book is done from left-to-right and top-to-bottom. (Competency 1)

8. (A)

Pattern books are most useful for teaching cause and effect, as they have a "this–now this" format. (Competency 2)

9. (B)

A reader reading between 90% and 94% is considered to be at his instructional level. An independent (A) level is reading with accuracy at 95%–100%. Frustration level (C) is reached when less than 85% of the words are recognized or comprehension falls below 50%. Recreational reading (D) is defined as students choosing what they read, where they read, and when they read. (Competency 3)

10. (D)

Repeated readings is an instructional strategy to build fluency. It takes away the focus on word identification, releases the anxiety associated with having to "get it right," and allows the reader to experience the joy of reading. (Competency 5)

11. (C)

"Sh" is an example of a digraph, which is when two letters combine to make a new sound. A grapheme (D) is a letter of the alphabet, a mark of punctuation, or any other individual symbol in a writing system. (Competency 1)

12. (C)

This is an example of dictation, where the teacher writes down what the students say. Interactive writing (A) is a collaborative teaching/learning strategy in which teacher and students jointly compose a story. Modeled writing (B) is an instructional practice in which the teacher models, in both speaking and writing, how she is creating her own passage. In shared writing (D) the teacher acts as a scribe while the students contribute ideas. (Competency 1)

13. (D)

Fantasy is the genre that is typically set in a complex world with real-life features as well as magical features. A fairy tale (A) is a story that features fanciful and wondrous characters such as elves, goblins, wizards, and even, but not necessarily, fairies. A folktale (C) is a story or legend forming part of an oral tradition. (Competency 2)

14. (A)

Orthography is the study of spelling. Morphology (B) analyzes the structure of words and parts of words, such as stems, root words, prefixes, and suffixes. Phonology (C) is the study of sound patterns and their mean-

ings. Phonemology (D) studies the smallest part of a word. (Competency 1)

15. (A)

The index contains lists of names, words, events, etc., along with the page number on which they can be found. A glossary (B) is a list at the back of a book, explaining or defining difficult or unusual words and expressions used in the text. A compendium (D) is a short but detailed collection of information, usually in a book. (Competency 2)

16. (A)

Prosody is the musical quality of speech or reading aloud that includes all the elements of fluency. Fluency (B) is the ability to read a text easily and with accuracy, speed, expression, and comprehension. (Competency 3)

17. (B)

Editing is the stage after revising but before publishing. (Competency 4)

18. (D)

Automaticity involves quickly decoding words, but the reader may not comprehend the words or content. (Competency 3)

19. (C)

The stages are prewriting (sometimes called brainstorming), drafting, revising, editing, and publishing. Students in the early grades may do a modified version, as revising is a complex process. (Competency 4)

20. (B)

Metaphor is a figure of speech in which a word or phrase is applied to an object or action to which it is not literally applicable. An analogy (A) is a comparison of two things to show their similarities. An adjective (C) is a word that describes a noun or a pronoun. A simile (D) describes something by comparing it to something else accompanied by the words *like* or *as*. (Competency 2)

21. (B)

Morphemes are the smallest unit of meaning. Phonemes (A) are basic sound units of a given language. A phonogram (C) is a letter or combination of letters that represent a sound. An affix (D) is added to the root of a word to change its meaning. It can be a prefix or a suffix. (Competency 1)

22. (A)

Echo reading is when the teacher reads aloud first and students read aloud after him, imitating his phrasing, intonation, and pace. Choral reading (B) is reading aloud in unison with a whole class or group of students. In shared reading (C), learners observe experts reading with fluency and expression while following along or otherwise engaging with the text. In modeled reading (D), the teacher thinks aloud to the children as she processes a reading strategy. (Competency 4)

23. (B)

Interactive writing is an activity during which both the teacher and student are writing. The process involves the sharing of a pen between the teacher and students. It can be done one-on-one or with a small group of students. (Competency 1)

24. (A)

The alphabetic principle is the understanding that letters and sounds represent spoken language. (Competency 3)

25. (A)

A rime is the part of the word containing the vowel and consonant or consonants following the onset.

Rimes (A) are word parts that refer to a spelling pattern, and rimes will rhyme. Rimes begin with a vowel sound and end before the next vowel sound. An onset (B) is the part of a syllable that precedes the vowel of the syllable. A rhyme (C) is a repetition of similar sounding words occurring at the end of lines in poems or songs. (Competency 1)

26. (B)

Fluency is the ability to read accurately, quickly, and with proper inflection, while at the same time comprehending what is read. Automaticity (A) is the ability to do things without occupying the mind with the low-level details required. (Competency 3)

27. (B)

The word "chat" has three sounds, /ch/ /a/ /t/. (Competency 1)

28. (B)

Narrative discourse is the ability to tell about an event that has occurred in the past, is occurring, or will occur in a way that makes sense to the listener. (Competency 3)

29. (D)

Decoding is correlated to alphabet recognition. (Competency 4)

30. (B)

Tier 2 is the academic vocabulary needed for school success. (Competency 4)

31. (C)

The K-W-L chart is useful for assessing the background of students who are ELL. It means what I know, what I want to know, and what I have learned. A RAFT chart (D) can be used to help students understand their roles as writers, their audience, the varied writing formats, and the topic. (Competency 2)

32. (A)

Shared reading involves the teacher reading a book multiple times. The book is often in a big book format, to imitate the lap reading that might be done at home. An interactive read-aloud (B) is a group lesson during which children actively engage in listening and talking about the text throughout the duration of the story. In modeled reading, (D) the teacher thinks aloud and discusses with the students which strategies she is using as she reads to them. (Competency 1)

33. (B)

Differentiation is the decision to modify instruction or materials for learners to meet their needs. Teachers' adaptation (C) refers to the moment-to-moment shifts in teacher behavior in response to an individual or group of students. Usually a modification (A) means a change in what is being taught to or expected from the student. Remedial reading (D) is a short-term intervention of tutoring struggling readers in both an individualized and small group setting. (Competency 5)

34. (A)

The four cueing systems are phonological, semantic, syntactic, and pragmatic. All are needed to read and understand texts. (Competency 3)

35. (A)

This is an example of an idiom, which consists of words that represent another meaning. Idioms can be particularly challenging for ELLs. A simile (B) makes a comparison of two unlike things using the words "like" or "as." An analogy (C) looks at complex subjects and simplifies them through comparison with something easier. Etymology (D) is the study of the origin and history of words. (Competency 2)

36. (B)

Diphthongs are sounds formed by the combination of two vowels in a single syllable, in which the sound begins as one vowel and moves toward another "oil, boy, house." (Competency 1)

37. (C)

Students reading texts at 89% or below are usually in their frustration level. (Competency 5)

38. (A)

A simile is a type of figurative language that includes "as" or "like" to compare two things that are not alike. (Competency 2)

39. (A)

Automaticity is the ability to quickly decode. Decoding (C) involves translating printed words to sounds, or reading, and encoding (D) is just the opposite. It is using individual sounds to build and write words. (Competency 3)

40. (B)

Assimilation is when learners add to their schema. Accommodations (A) change how children learn, not what they learn. Prediction (D) is an activity learners carry out before reading or listening to a text, where they predict what they are going to hear or read. (Competency 3)

41. (B)

The K-W-L chart is good for determining the background knowledge of learners, particularly ELLs. On it is written what I **K**now, what I **W**ant to know, and what I have **L**earned. Concept maps (A) are visual representations students create to connect ideas. Mind maps (C) help students recognize relationships that they couldn't have seen without setting them down on paper. When using a story map (D), students read carefully to learn the details of the passage or book because they specifically are looking for characters, plot, setting, problem and solution. (Competency 2)

42. **(D)**

These are examples of pragmatic language, or language that serves a function. Syntax (A) is the proper order of words in a phrase or sentence. Phonology (B) covers sound patterns and their meanings. Semantics (C) refers to the meaning of what is being read. (Competency 3)

43. **(A)**

Blending and segmenting activities verbally are examples of phonemic awareness activities. (Competency 1)

44. **(A)**

Story boards are excellent for learners at different levels to sequence and comprehend the story. Elkonin boxes (C) help to increase reading skills by challenging students to segment words into their individual sounds and syllables. The semantic feature analysis strategy (D) uses a grid graphic organizer to help students to see connections, make predictions, and master important concepts. (Competency 3)

45. **(B)**

Anecdotal notes are informal records of observations. A teacher objectively compiles this record of observed behavior over time, with no mention of his/her personal opinion. (Competency 5)

46. **(C)**

Phonics involves knowledge of letters and sounds. Phonemic awareness (A) is the specific ability to focus on and manipulate individual sounds (phonemes) in spoken words. (Competency 3)

47. **(C)**

This is the revising stage, when the writer gathers feedback and adjusts or modifies her writing. (Competency 4)

48. **(B)**

Typically 20 hours of instruction is about what a learner needs to master phonemic awareness. (Competency 1)

49. **(A)**

Complex sentences contain a subordinate clause or clause that adds to the information, while the base of the sentence still forms a complete thought. A compound sentence (B) is made up of two or more simple sentences joined with a conjunction such as *but, and, so,* or *however*. A complex compound (C) is a compound sentence that also contains a complex clause. (Competency 4)

50. **(B)**

Homophones are words that sound alike, but are spelled differently. Homographs (A) are words that are spelled the same but have different meanings and may be pronounced differently. An idiom (D) is a group of words expressed, but whose meaning can't be understood from the ordinary meanings of the words (e.g., "break a leg," or "spill the beans"). (Competency 4)

51. **(D)**

Following a rubric would be the best way to assess the writers in the class. A rubric (D) is a matrix or grid of the student's work that is efficient, consistent, objective, and quick. (Competency 5)

52. **(A)**

This writing is the early phonetic stage, as she's using a letter to represent a word and the letter reflects a sound in the word. (Competency 4)

53. (A)

Conjunctions are transition words that join parts of sentences. (Other examples are: *but, and, yet, or, because, although, since, unless, while, where*.) A preposition (B) is a word used to link nouns, pronouns, or phrases to other words within a sentence. The words *a, an*, and *the* are articles (C) that are used to introduce a noun. (Competency 4)

54. (B)

Tier 2 vocabulary are the words that teachers should focus on with systematic, explicit instruction. (Competency 1)

55. (B)

This data would best be represented in a table format, which would organize the information in easy-to-read columns. (Competency 2)

56. (A)

Prepositions are words preceding a noun that express a relation to another word in the clause. For example, in the sentence, "She jumped on the log," *on* is the preposition. (Competency 4)

57. (C)

Graphemes are the smallest written unit that represents a sound and can be one letter or more than one letter. (Competency 4)

58. (A)

Reader's theater is a strategy used to build fluency as it allows students to practice reading aloud using proper pacing, expression, and intonation in an authentic manner. (Competency 3)

59. (A)

Protagonists are the main characters who drive the action, so fairy tales would be the best choice from those given. (Competency 4)

60. (A)

Contextual analysis is putting a book or text in the context of time or place—this provides background knowledge to help students better understand the text. The semantic feature analysis (B) strategy uses a grid to help learners explore how sets of things are related to one another. Synthesizing (D) is when readers change their thinking as they read. (Competency 3)

PRACTICE TEST 2

FTCE PreK–3 Mathematics
Subtest 3 (533)

Also available at the REA Study Center (www.rea.com/studycenter)

This practice test is also offered online at the REA Study Center. We recommend that you take the online version of the test to simulate test-day conditions and to receive these added benefits:

- **Timed testing conditions**—helps you gauge how much time you can spend on each question

- **Automatic scoring**—find out how you did on the test, instantly

- **On-screen detailed explanations of answers**—gives you the correct answer and explains why the other answer choices are wrong

- **Diagnostic score reports**—pinpoint where you're strongest and where you need to focus your study

MATHEMATICS REFERENCE SHEET

Area

 Triangle $A = \frac{1}{2}bh$

 Rectangle $A = lw$

 Trapezoid $A = \frac{1}{2}h(b_1 + b_2)$

 Parallelogram $A = bh$

Circle $A = \pi r^2$

KEY	
b = base	d = diameter
h = height	r = radius
l = length	A = area
w = width	C = circumference
$S.A.$ = surface area	V = volume
	B = area of base

Use 3.14 or $\frac{22}{7}$ for π

Circumference

$C = \pi d = 2\pi r$

Surface Area

1. Surface area of a prism or pyramid equals the sum of the areas of all faces.

Volume

1. Volume of a triangular or rectangular prism equals the <u>Area of the Base</u> (B) times the height (h).

$V = Bh$

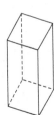 

2. Volume of a pyramid equals $\frac{1}{3}$ times the <u>Area of the Base</u> (*B*) times the height (*h*).

$$V = \frac{1}{3}Bh$$

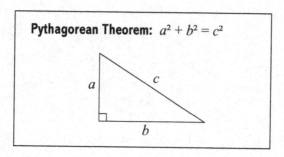

Pythagorean Theorem: $a^2 + b^2 = c^2$

Conversions

1 yard = 3 feet = 36 inches

1 mile = 1,760 yards = 5,280 feet

1 acre = 43,560 square feet

1 hour = 60 minutes

1 minute = 60 seconds

1 cup = 8 fluid ounces

1 pint = 2 cups

1 quart = 2 pints

1 gallon = 4 quarts

1 pound = 16 ounces

1 ton = 2,000 pounds

1 liter = 1000 milliliters = 1000 cubic centimeters

1 meter = 100 centimeters = 1000 millimeters

1 kilometer = 1000 meters

1 gram = 1000 milligrams

1 kilogram = 1000 grams

Metric numbers with four digits are presented without a comma (e.g., 9960 kilometers). For metric numbers greater than four digits, a space is used instead of a comma (e.g., 12 500 liters).

Mathematics Practice Test 2: Answer Sheet

1. Ⓐ Ⓑ Ⓒ Ⓓ

2. Ⓐ Ⓑ Ⓒ Ⓓ

3. Ⓐ Ⓑ Ⓒ Ⓓ

4. Ⓐ Ⓑ Ⓒ Ⓓ

5. Ⓐ Ⓑ Ⓒ Ⓓ

6. Ⓐ Ⓑ Ⓒ Ⓓ

7. Ⓐ Ⓑ Ⓒ Ⓓ

8. Ⓐ Ⓑ Ⓒ Ⓓ

9. Ⓐ Ⓑ Ⓒ Ⓓ

10. Ⓐ Ⓑ Ⓒ Ⓓ

11. Ⓐ Ⓑ Ⓒ Ⓓ

12. Ⓐ Ⓑ Ⓒ Ⓓ

13. Ⓐ Ⓑ Ⓒ Ⓓ

14. Ⓐ Ⓑ Ⓒ Ⓓ

15. Ⓐ Ⓑ Ⓒ Ⓓ

16. Ⓐ Ⓑ Ⓒ Ⓓ

17. Ⓐ Ⓑ Ⓒ Ⓓ

18. Ⓐ Ⓑ Ⓒ Ⓓ

19. Ⓐ Ⓑ Ⓒ Ⓓ

20. Ⓐ Ⓑ Ⓒ Ⓓ

21. Ⓐ Ⓑ Ⓒ Ⓓ

22. Ⓐ Ⓑ Ⓒ Ⓓ

23. Ⓐ Ⓑ Ⓒ Ⓓ

24. Ⓐ Ⓑ Ⓒ Ⓓ

25. Ⓐ Ⓑ Ⓒ Ⓓ

26. Ⓐ Ⓑ Ⓒ Ⓓ

27. Ⓐ Ⓑ Ⓒ Ⓓ

28. Ⓐ Ⓑ Ⓒ Ⓓ

29. Ⓐ Ⓑ Ⓒ Ⓓ

30. Ⓐ Ⓑ Ⓒ Ⓓ

31. Ⓐ Ⓑ Ⓒ Ⓓ

32. Ⓐ Ⓑ Ⓒ Ⓓ

33. Ⓐ Ⓑ Ⓒ Ⓓ

34. Ⓐ Ⓑ Ⓒ Ⓓ

35. Ⓐ Ⓑ Ⓒ Ⓓ

36. Ⓐ Ⓑ Ⓒ Ⓓ

37. Ⓐ Ⓑ Ⓒ Ⓓ

38. Ⓐ Ⓑ Ⓒ Ⓓ

39. Ⓐ Ⓑ Ⓒ Ⓓ

40. Ⓐ Ⓑ Ⓒ Ⓓ

41. Ⓐ Ⓑ Ⓒ Ⓓ

42. Ⓐ Ⓑ Ⓒ Ⓓ

43. Ⓐ Ⓑ Ⓒ Ⓓ

44. Ⓐ Ⓑ Ⓒ Ⓓ

45. Ⓐ Ⓑ Ⓒ Ⓓ

46. Ⓐ Ⓑ Ⓒ Ⓓ

47. Ⓐ Ⓑ Ⓒ Ⓓ

48. Ⓐ Ⓑ Ⓒ Ⓓ

49. Ⓐ Ⓑ Ⓒ Ⓓ

50. Ⓐ Ⓑ Ⓒ Ⓓ

Practice Test 2: Mathematics

TIME: 70 minutes
50 questions*

Directions: Read each question and select the best response.

---

1. Mr. Lincoln's first grade class is partitioning geoboards into halves and fourths. Which type of fraction model are they using?

   A. area

   B. linear

   C. set

   D. length

2. Look at the two images below. What is the relationship between them?

   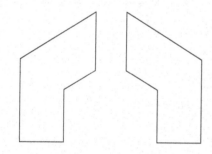

   A. The second one is a flipped version of the first one.

   B. The second one is a congruent version of the first one.

   C. The second one is a rotated version of the first one.

   D. The second one is a scaled version of the first one.

3. Which of the following is correct if we want to round 246 to the nearest hundred?

   A. 200

   B. 240

   C. 300

   D. 400

4. Which of the following is true about the relationship between rote counting and rational counting?

   A. Children can usually rote count to the same number they can rationally count.

   B. Children can usually rote count to a smaller number than they can rationally count.

   C. Children can usually rote count to a greater number than they can rationally count.

   D. There is no relationship between rote counting and rational counting.

5. Which of the following is essentially the same pattern as yellow bear—yellow bear—green bear—red bear?

   A. square—circle—square—triangle

   B. hop—hop—turn around—sit down

   C. clap—clap—stomp—stomp

   D. blue dinosaur—square—yellow bear—triangle

---

* This practice test presents slightly more items than you are likely to see on test day. The actual test contains approximately 45 questions. You will only learn exactly how many questions you will get after you take the FTCE tutorial and sign the non-disclosure agreement on test day.

6. What is the perimeter of the polygon below?

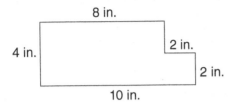

   A. 26 inches

   B. 28 inches

   C. 48 inches

   D. 80 inches

7. A first grade teacher wants to find out what a new student in her class understands about place value. Which of the following would be the best way for her to assess the student's current understanding?

   A. an interview

   B. a portfolio

   C. a test

   D. a checklist

8. What is the area of the shape below?

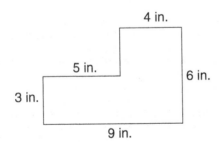

   A. 30 sq. inches

   B. 29 sq. inches

   C. 54 sq. inches

   D. 39 sq. inches

9. Mr. Bartlett wants his second graders to develop the belief that mathematics makes sense. Which of the following should Mr. Bartlett do to help his students embrace that idea?

   A. Encourage them to memorize the correct procedures for solving problems.

   B. Look for key words in problems to determine which operations to use.

   C. Use songs and chants to help students learn mathematical rules.

   D. Encourage students to use drawings or physical models to understand mathematical problems.

10. How long is the worm in the picture below?

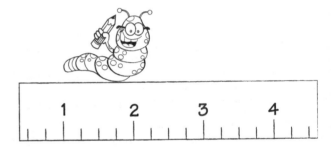

   A. 2 inches

   B. 1 inch

   C. 1¼ inches

   D. 2¼ inches

11. Ms. O'Donnell wants to incorporate technology into her mathematics instruction in ways that will foster student sense-making. Which of the following is she most likely to do?

   A. Allow children to use calculators for basic math facts since everyone has calculators on their phones.

   B. Show online videos to help students learn and remember mathematical procedures.

   C. Have children work with virtual manipulatives as well as physical manipulatives to learn about shapes.

   D. Have children use online programs to practice basic facts.

12. Which of the following is NOT a good tool or manipulative for teaching fractions?

    A. number cubes

    B. pattern blocks

    C. Cuisenaire rods

    D. tangrams

13. Second graders are solving the following problem using base-ten blocks: 36 + 43 + 16 + 27. Ian adds the tens and gets 10 tens. He then adds the ones and gets 22 ones. Ian says the answer is 1022. What is he confused about?

    A. He is not confused. He just made a minor computational error. He should have gotten 11 tens.

    B. He is confused about the need to trade twenty ones for two tens and ten tens for one hundred.

    C. He is confused about the order in which we add. He should have added the ones first.

    D. He is confused about how to correctly read a multi-digit number. He thinks one thousand twenty-two is the same as ten hundred twenty-two.

14. Ms. Santiago has a mathematics center in her classroom where students can use a math balance. Maria places weights of 3 and 2 on one side of the balance and 4 and 1 on the other side. What mathematical concept is the focus of this math center?

    A. math facts

    B. equality

    C. number sense

    D. cardinality

15. What mathematical concept is being shown in the table below?

INPUT	OUTPUT
9	6
4	1
7	4

    A. function

    B. repeating pattern

    C. counting backwards

    D. inequality

16. Juan buys a toy that costs $4.32. He gives the store clerk $5.02. How much change should he receive?

    A. $0.68

    B. $0.70

    C. $0.72

    D. $0.74

17. Which property of multiplication is shown in this equation? $a \times (b \times c) = (a \times b) \times c$.

    A. associative

    B. commutative

    C. identity

    D. distributive

18. Kaitlyn and Shawna are solving the problem 342 – 98. They decide to first calculate 342 – 100 = 242. Kaitlyn says they must add 2 to 242 to get the answer to 342 – 98, but Shawna says they must subtract 2. Maria sees what they are doing and says, *You can't subtract that way!* Which of the following statements best explains which girl is correct and why she is correct?

    A. Kaitlyn is correct because they took away 2 more than they needed to, so they must add it back.

    B. Shawna is correct because 100 is 2 more than 98 so they must take away 2 more.

    C. Maria is correct because you cannot change the problem. You must solve the problem you were given.

    D. Maria is correct because you can only subtract that way when the number you are subtracting is greater than a friendly number like 100, not when it is less than the friendly number.

19. Look at the two images below. What is the relationship between them?

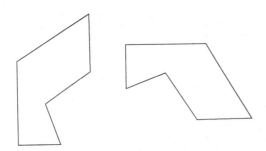

    A. The second one is a flipped version of the first one.

    B. The second one is a congruent version of the first one.

    C. The second one is a rotated version of the first one.

    D. The second one is a scaled version of the first one.

20. Most young children find

    A. counting backwards to be more difficult than counting on.

    B. counting on to be more difficult than counting backwards.

    C. counting backwards to be especially useful for learning addition facts.

    D. counting on to be a good foundation for multiplication.

21. The drawing below is an example of a

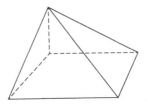

    A. triangular prism.

    B. rectangular prism.

    C. triangular pyramid.

    D. rectangular pyramid.

22. Which of the following is the best model to help young children decompose teen numbers into tens and ones?

    A. Cuisenaire rods

    B. five frame

    C. counting bears

    D. ten frame

23. Students want to create a data display to show the number of children that are in each student's family. Which of the following would be the most appropriate way to display this data?

    A. bar graph

    B. pie graph

    C. line plot

    D. real graph

24. A teacher writes the numeral 17 on the whiteboard. She circles the 1 and asks students to show her that part of the number with counters. Charlie puts out one counter. What can be said about Charlie's response?

    A. It is accurate. He put out the correct number of counters to represent the 1 in 17.

    B. It is incorrect. He does not understand that he needed to put out 10 counters.

    C. It is incorrect. He does not understand that he needed to put out 17 counters.

    D. It is incorrect. He does not understand that he needed to put out 8 counters.

25. Which of the following is a defining attribute of a shape?

    A. color

    B. size

    C. texture

    D. number of angles

26. A kindergarten is solving the following problem, *Alyssa had 3 puzzles. She used her birthday money to buy 8 more puzzles at the store. How many puzzles does she have now?* The kindergartener says, *8, 9, 10, 11. The answer is 11.* What property of addition did this student use?

    A. associative

    B. commutative

    C. distributive

    D. identity

27. Four third graders are discussing the problem 0 ÷ 6. Which of the students has the most accurate idea about this problem?

    A. Allan: 0 ÷ 6 can't be solved. You can't divide 0 by a number.

    B. Marcus: 0 ÷ 6 = 0. You can think of trying to divide 0 cookies among 6 people.

    C. Simone: 0 ÷ 6 can't be solved. You can think of it as what number can I multiply by 6 to get 0.

    D. Jennifer: 0 ÷ 6 = 0. You can think of it as what number can I multiply by 0 to get 6.

28. Third graders are solving the multiplication problem 4 × 5. Isabel draws the diagram below on her paper. What type of drawing is this?

    A. comparison

    B. array

    C. pattern

    D. abstract

29. Four friends are discussing triangles. Which of their statements is the most accurate?

    A. Tamara: A right triangle can't be an isosceles triangle.

    B. Jason: An equilateral triangle is always an acute triangle.

    C. Melissa: An obtuse triangle can be an equilateral triangle.

    D. Zach: A scalene triangle can't be a right triangle.

30. Which expression is equal to 234 + 378?

    A. 156 + 458

    B. 937 − 325

    C. 856 − 245

    D. 208 + 394

31. A third grade teacher writes the following growing pattern on the board: 1, 4, 7, 10, 13. This is an example of what kind of growing pattern?

    A. arithmetic

    B. geometric

    C. algebraic

    D. increasing

32. Which of the following is the correct way to write 602 in expanded form?

    A. 6002

    B. 600 + 20

    C. 600 + 2

    D. 60 + 2

33. Kindergarteners are standing in line to walk to the buses at the end of the day. Marcus says, *I'm first in line, Shante is second, and Amy is third.* Marcus has demonstrated

    A. the use of cardinal numbers.

    B. the use of one-to-one correspondence.

    C. the use of subitizing.

    D. the use of ordinal numbers.

34. Which of the following students is correct about the sum of two odd numbers?

    A. Sean: The sum of two odd numbers is always an odd number.

    B. Melissa: The sum of two odd numbers is an even number if one of the addends is less than 10.

    C. Javier: The sum of two odd numbers is always an even number.

    D. Ebony: The sum of two odd numbers can be even or odd. It just depends on the two numbers you are adding.

35. Which of the following is an example of a U.S. customary unit of measure?

    A. meter

    B. liter

    C. kilogram

    D. pint

36. A third grade teacher places students into groups of three to investigate the properties of triangles. She puts one student who is performing below grade level, one who is at grade level, and one who is performing above grade level in each group. What kind of group did the teacher form?

    A. heterogeneous group

    B. homogeneous group

    C. eclectic group

    D. flexible group

37. Soccer practice starts at 11:30 a.m. on Saturday. If it lasts for 2 hours 55 minutes, what time will it be over?

    A. 2:35 a.m.

    B. 3:05 p.m.

    C. 3:15 a.m.

    D. 2:25 p.m.

38. Which of the following is a true statement about procedural fluency?

    A. It is more important than conceptual understanding in the PreK/Primary grades.

    B. It must be taught prior to teaching for conceptual understanding. Students can't understand until they know the basics.

    C. It means students can use flexible computational strategies in addition to standard algorithms.

    D. It means students learn to decompose and compose numbers and recognize various meanings for the four operations.

39. A kindergarten teacher creates a set of dot plates. She holds up a plate containing two rows with three dots in each row for a few seconds. The teacher then asks, "How many dots did you see?" What topic is being taught using this activity?

    A. rational counting

    B. counting on

    C. subitizing

    D. skip counting

40. When is whole-class instruction in mathematics *most* appropriate?

    A. When students are solving problems with manipulatives.

    B. When the teacher is modeling a mathematical procedure.

    C. When there are students in the classroom with behavior issues.

    D. When the teacher wants to demonstrate the correct way to solve a problem.

41. Students create a class graph to show how many books the entire class has read each month of the school year from August to January. The teacher asks, How many books do you think the class will read during February? This question requires students to

    A. read directly from the graph.

    B. think beyond the information in the graph.

    C. compare information in the graph.

    D. calculate information from the graph.

42. Which of the following is the correct expression to use to solve the following problem?

    5 students are playing on the swings at recess. 3 more come to join them. 4 of the children are called inside by their teacher. How many students are left playing on the swings?

    A. $(5 + 3) + 4$

    B. $(5 + 3) - 4$

    C. $(5 - 3) - 4$

    D. $(3 + 4) - 5$

43. Which of the following is a polygon?

    A. circle

    B. oval

    C. cube

    D. trapezoid

44. The denominator in a fraction tells us

    A. the size of the whole.

    B. how many equal parts we have.

    C. the size of the pieces in the whole.

    D. the number of equal parts in the whole.

45. What is the point called where two faces on a polyhedron meet?

   A. edge

   B. corner

   C. vertex

   D. point

46. A preschool teacher wants to help her students develop one-to-one correspondence. The best way to accomplish this would be?

   A. counting to 20 every day during circle time

   B. singing songs that reinforce the order of the counting sequence

   C. having children match the number of napkins to the number of children at snack time

   D. counting how many crackers are left over at snack time

47. Ms. Nelson's first graders are solving the problem 3 + 4 + 6. *Sam says, "4 + 6 = 10. Then add 3. That's 13."* Which property of addition did Sam use to solve the problem?

   A. commutative

   B. associative

   C. distributive

   D. identity

48. What is the name of the shape below?

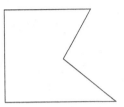

   A. quadrilateral

   B. pentagon

   C. hexagon

   D. heptagon

49. Third graders are practicing multiplying one-digit numbers by multiples of 10. Malcolm solves 3×40 this way: *$3 \times 4 = 12$. $12 \times 10 = 120$.* Which property of multiplication did Malcolm use to solve the problem?

   A. associative

   B. commutative

   C. distributive

   D. identity

50. When students use mathematics problem solving journals, which of the following should be encouraged?

   A. justify their reasoning

   B. use standard algorithms to solve problems

   C. spell words correctly

   D. follow the procedures the teacher has modeled for them

Mathematics Practice Test 2: Answer Key

Test Item	Answer	Competency
1.	A	3
2.	A	5
3.	A	3
4.	C	1
5.	B	2
6.	A	4
7.	A	1
8.	D	4
9.	D	1
10.	C	4
11.	C	1
12.	A	1
13.	B	3
14.	B	2
15.	A	2
16.	B	4
17.	A	2
18.	A	3
19.	C	5
20.	A	3
21.	D	5
22.	D	3
23.	C	4
24.	B	3
25.	D	5

Test Item	Answer	Competency
26.	B	3
27.	B	3
28.	B	1
29.	B	5
30.	B	3
31.	A	2
32.	C	3
33.	D	1
34.	C	2
35.	D	4
36.	A	1
37.	D	4
38.	C	1
39.	C	3
40.	B	1
41.	B	4
42.	B	2
43.	D	5
44.	D	3
45.	A	5
46.	C	3
47.	B	2
48.	B	5
49.	A	3
50.	A	1

Mathematics Practice Test 2: Detailed Answers

1. **(A)**

   Choice (A) is the best answer. Geoboards are an area model for fractions. (Competency 3)

2. **(A)**

   Choice (A) is the best answer. The figure on the right is a mirror image of the figure on the left. The figure on the left was flipped or reflected along an imaginary line to produce the figure on the right. (Competency 5)

3. **(A)**

   Choice (A) is the best answer. 246 is between 200 and 300. If you plot all three numbers on a number line, you will see that 246 is closer to 200 than it is to 300. Procedurally, when rounding to the nearest 100 we only need to consider the value of the tens digit. In this case it is 4. When the digit is 0–4, we round down. When the digit is 5–9, we round up. (Competency 3)

4. **(C)**

   Choice (C) is the best answer. Rote counting involves reciting the number words in sequence. Rational counting involves both one-to-one correspondence and cardinality. (Competency 1)

5. **(B)**

   The bear pattern is an AABC pattern. So is choice (B). Choice (A) is an ABAB pattern; choice (C) is an AABB pattern; and choice (D) is an ABCD pattern. (Competency 2)

6. **(A)**

   Choice (A) is the best answer. The perimeter of a two-dimensional shape can be thought of as the distance required to "walk around" the shape. There are multiple ways to find the perimeter of this shape. One is to add all the sides together. The answer is 26 inches. (Competency 4)

7. **(A)**

   Interviews are a great way to assess students' mathematical thinking because a teacher can probe student responses. (Competency 1)

8. **(D)**

   Choice (D) is the best answer. One way to calculate the area is to divide the shape into two rectangles, one that is 3 in. by 5 in. and another that is 4 in. by 6 in. The area of the first is 15 in.^{2} and the area of the second is 24 in.^{2}. When you add them together, the total area is 39 in.^{2} (Competency 4)

9. **(D)**

   PreK/Primary students should be encouraged to make sense of problems. Drawings and physical manipulatives can help them model the problems they are solving. Teachers should avoid teaching students to look for key words in a problem. Some problems have no key words. (Competency 1)

10. **(C)**

    Choice (C) is the best answer. Each inch is divided into four equal parts. Each of those parts equals ¼ inch. The worm extends from the 1 to the first mark after the 2. It is 1¼ inches long. (Competency 4)

11. (C)

Choice (C) is the best answer. Young children should work with physical manipulatives as much as possible. Virtual manipulatives are online tools students can use to supplement physical models. (Competency 1)

12. (A)

Choice (A) is the best answer. Pattern blocks, Cuisenaire rods, and tangrams can all be used for teaching fractions. Number cubes are not a good choice. (Competency 1)

13. (B)

Choice (B) is the best answer. Ian can trade his 10 tens for a 100. He can trade 20 of his ones for two tens. He now has a 100 and 2 tens and 2 ones. The answer is 122. (Competency 3)

14. (B)

Choice (B) is the best answer. Two expressions are equal if they have the same value. 3 + 2 has the same value as 4 + 1. Balances are a good way for children to develop a strong understanding of the meaning of the equal sign. (Competency 2)

15. (A)

Choice (A) is the best answer. A function is a rule that specifies a single output for each input. In this case the rule is subtract 3. Tables and input-output machines are both used in PreK/Primary classrooms to illustrate functions. (Competency 2)

16. (B)

Choice (B) is the best answer. $5.02 − $4.32 = $0.70. (Competency 4)

17. (A)

Choice (A) is the best answer. The associative property of multiplication says that if I am multiplying three or more numbers, it doesn't matter which two are multiplied first. (Competency 2)

18. (A)

Choice (A) is the best answer. Kaitlyn is correct. The girls were only supposed to subtract 98, but they subtracted 100 (a friendly number). Because they took away two more than they were supposed to, they must add it back. The answer is 244. (Competency 3)

19. (C)

Choice (C) is the best answer. When a shape is rotated in space, it is turned a specific number of degrees. The shape on the left was rotated or turned 90° to produce the shape on the right. (Competency 5)

20. (A)

Choice (A) is the best answer. Counting on relates to the rote counting sequence children learn at a young age. Counting backwards is more difficult because when counting backwards a child must take one away with each number said. (Competency 3)

21. (D)

Choice (D) is the best answer. Prisms and pyramids are named for the shape of their base(s). This drawing has a single base connected to a point in space not in the same plane. That makes it a pyramid. Its base is a rectangle, so it is a rectangular pyramid. (Competency 5)

22. (D)

Choice (D) is the best answer. Children can use a ten frame to show a set of ten and some more. (Competency 3)

23. (C)

Choice (C) is the best answer. A line plot uses a number line to show data. To create the line plot, students can make a number line beginning at 1 and extending to the maximum number of children in the family of some-one in the class. They then place an X above the number for each person with that number of children in the family. (Competency 4)

24. (B)

Choice (B) is the best answer. Charlie's error is common. Children often do not understand that the 1 in the tens place represents a single group of ten or ten ones. (Competency 3)

25. (D)

Choice (D) is the best answer. A defining attribute is a "must-have." Color (A), size (B), and texture (C) are not defining attributes. The number of angles is a defin-ing attribute. So is the number of sides. (Competency 5)

26. (B)

Choice (B) is the best answer. The commutative property is also known as the turnaround property. It says that you can write the addends in an addition prob-lem in any order. This student turned the problem 3 + 8 around to make it 8 + 3. That is because it is easier to count on 3 more from 8 than it is to count on 8 more from 3. (Competency 3)

27. (B)

Choice (B) is the best answer. Students often get mixed up about problems like 0 ÷ 6 and 6 ÷ 0. 0 ÷ 6 can be solved. Marcus is correct. You can think of trying to divide 0 cookies among 6 people. Each person gets 0 cookies. You cannot solve 6 ÷ 0. You cannot divide 6 cookies among 0 people. Jennifer is correct that 0 ÷ 6 = 0. Her reason is not correct, however. There is no number you can multiply by 0 to get 6. (Competency 3)

28. (B)

Choice (B) is the best answer. Arrays are useful for learning about multiplication as equal groups. Rows can

show the number of groups and columns can show how many there are in each group, or they can be reversed. (Competency 1)

29. (B)

Choice (B) is the best answer. An equilateral tri-angle is one in which all sides are equal. All angles are also equal. Since the angles in every triangle add up to 180°, each angle in an equilateral triangle = 60°. There-fore, all equilateral triangles are also acute triangles. (Competency 5)

30. (B)

Choice (B) is the best answer. Both expressions equal 612. (Competency 3)

31. (A)

Choice (A) is the best answer. A growing pattern that increases or decreases by adding or subtracting the same fixed number is arithmetic. In this case, you add 3 to get the next term. A growing pattern that changes by multiplying or dividing by the same fixed number is geometric. (Competency 2)

32. (C)

Choice (C) is the best answer. The 6 in the hun-dreds place = 600. There is a 0 in the tens place. The 2 in the ones place = 2. In expanded form the number is 600 + 2. (Competency 3)

33. (D)

Choice (D) is the best answer. Ordinal numbers tell the position of something in a list. (Competency 1)

34. (C)

Choice (C) is the best answer. Imagine having a number of objects and making as many groups of 2 as you can. If you have one object left over when you do that, the number is odd. If you add two odd numbers, the two left over objects make a group of two, with none left over. This means the answer is an even number. (Competency 2)

35. (D)

Choice (D) is the best answer. A pint is a U.S. customary unit of volume. All the other units in the problem are metric. (Competency 4)

36. (A)

Choice (A) is the best answer. Heterogeneous groups are ones in which students who differ, in this case by academic level, work together. (Competency 1)

37. (D)

Choice (D) is the best answer. Many students realize that 2 hours 55 minutes is 5 minutes less than 3 hours. They count on 3 hours from 11:30 a.m. to get 2:30 p.m. However, they must now subtract 5 minutes. (Competency 4)

38. (C)

Choice (C) is the best answer. Procedural fluency means students can use mathematical rules and procedures to correctly solve problems. They use flexible strategies based on their understanding of mathematics. Conceptual understanding and procedural fluency go hand-in-hand. Both should be emphasized in PreK/Primary classrooms. (Competency 1)

39. (C)

Choice (C) is the best answer. Subitizing is the ability to recognize the total number of objects in a pattern or collection without having to count each object individually. (Competency 3)

40. (B)

Choice (B) is the best answer. Teaching procedures is an appropriate time to use whole class, direct instruction. (Competency 1)

41. (B)

Choice (B) is the best answer. Questions like these require students to make predictions based upon information in the graph. They cannot be directly answered solely from data displayed in the graph. (Competency 4)

42. (B)

Choice (B) is the best answer. This is a two-step problem. Students should first add 5 + 3 and then subtract 4. (Competency 2)

43. (D)

Choice (D) is the best answer. A polygon is a two-dimensional geometric shape composed of line segments. Circles (A) and ovals are two-dimensional shapes, but they are not composed of line segments. A cube (C) is a three-dimensional figure. (Competency 5)

44. (D)

Choice (D) is the best answer. The denominator of a fraction tells us how many equal parts we have divided the whole into. Students sometimes think choice (A) is correct, but it is not. The denominator does not tell us the size of the whole, only how many parts it has been divided into. (Competency 3)

45. (A)

Choice (A) is the best answer. A polyhedron is a three-dimensional figure whose faces are polygons. Faces meet at edges. (Competency 5)

46. (C)

Choice (C) is the best answer. Matching activities are a good way for children to practice one-to-one correspondence. This can occur naturally as children help to prepare snacks. (Competency 3)

47. (B)

Choice (B) is the best answer. The associative property of addition says that when adding three or more numbers, it doesn't matter which two are added first. In this case it makes sense to first add 4 and 6 because they make a friendly number (10). It is then easy to mentally add 3 to get 13. (Competency 2)

48. (B)

Choice (B) is the best answer. A pentagon is a two-dimensional figure with five sides. (Competency 5)

49. (A)

Choice (A) is the best answer. The associative property of multiplication says that when multiplying three or more numbers, it doesn't matter which two are multiplied first. Malcolm broke 40 apart into 4×10. When a student breaks a number apart into its two factors to make a multiplication problem easier to solve, they are using the associative property. (Competency 3)

50. (A)

Choice (A) is the best answer. Several of the Standards for Mathematical Practice highlight the need for students to justify their mathematical thinking. Problem-solving journals are a good place for them to do so. (Competency 1)

PRACTICE TEST 2

FTCE PreK–3 Science
Subtest 4 (534)

Also available at the REA Study Center (www.rea.com/studycenter)

This practice test is also offered online at the REA Study Center.
We recommend that you take the online version of the test to simulate
test-day conditions and to receive these added benefits:

- **Timed testing conditions**—helps you gauge how much time you
  can spend on each question

- **Automatic scoring**—find out how you did on the test, instantly

- **On-screen detailed explanations of answers**—gives you the
  correct answer and explains why the other answer choices are
  wrong

- **Diagnostic score reports**—pinpoint where you're strongest and
  where you need to focus your study

Science Practice Test 2: Answer Sheet

1. Ⓐ Ⓑ Ⓒ Ⓓ

2. Ⓐ Ⓑ Ⓒ Ⓓ

3. Ⓐ Ⓑ Ⓒ Ⓓ

4. Ⓐ Ⓑ Ⓒ Ⓓ

5. Ⓐ Ⓑ Ⓒ Ⓓ

6. Ⓐ Ⓑ Ⓒ Ⓓ

7. Ⓐ Ⓑ Ⓒ Ⓓ

8. Ⓐ Ⓑ Ⓒ Ⓓ

9. Ⓐ Ⓑ Ⓒ Ⓓ

10. Ⓐ Ⓑ Ⓒ Ⓓ

11. Ⓐ Ⓑ Ⓒ Ⓓ

12. Ⓐ Ⓑ Ⓒ Ⓓ

13. Ⓐ Ⓑ Ⓒ Ⓓ

14. Ⓐ Ⓑ Ⓒ Ⓓ

15. Ⓐ Ⓑ Ⓒ Ⓓ

16. Ⓐ Ⓑ Ⓒ Ⓓ

17. Ⓐ Ⓑ Ⓒ Ⓓ

18. Ⓐ Ⓑ Ⓒ Ⓓ

19. Ⓐ Ⓑ Ⓒ Ⓓ

20. Ⓐ Ⓑ Ⓒ Ⓓ

21. Ⓐ Ⓑ Ⓒ Ⓓ

22. Ⓐ Ⓑ Ⓒ Ⓓ

23. Ⓐ Ⓑ Ⓒ Ⓓ

24. Ⓐ Ⓑ Ⓒ Ⓓ

25. Ⓐ Ⓑ Ⓒ Ⓓ

26. Ⓐ Ⓑ Ⓒ Ⓓ

27. Ⓐ Ⓑ Ⓒ Ⓓ

28. Ⓐ Ⓑ Ⓒ Ⓓ

29. Ⓐ Ⓑ Ⓒ Ⓓ

30. Ⓐ Ⓑ Ⓒ Ⓓ

31. Ⓐ Ⓑ Ⓒ Ⓓ

32. Ⓐ Ⓑ Ⓒ Ⓓ

33. Ⓐ Ⓑ Ⓒ Ⓓ

34. Ⓐ Ⓑ Ⓒ Ⓓ

35. Ⓐ Ⓑ Ⓒ Ⓓ

36. Ⓐ Ⓑ Ⓒ Ⓓ

37. Ⓐ Ⓑ Ⓒ Ⓓ

38. Ⓐ Ⓑ Ⓒ Ⓓ

39. Ⓐ Ⓑ Ⓒ Ⓓ

40. Ⓐ Ⓑ Ⓒ Ⓓ

41. Ⓐ Ⓑ Ⓒ Ⓓ

42. Ⓐ Ⓑ Ⓒ Ⓓ

43. Ⓐ Ⓑ Ⓒ Ⓓ

44. Ⓐ Ⓑ Ⓒ Ⓓ

45. Ⓐ Ⓑ Ⓒ Ⓓ

46. Ⓐ Ⓑ Ⓒ Ⓓ

47. Ⓐ Ⓑ Ⓒ Ⓓ

48. Ⓐ Ⓑ Ⓒ Ⓓ

49. Ⓐ Ⓑ Ⓒ Ⓓ

50. Ⓐ Ⓑ Ⓒ Ⓓ

Science: Practice Test 2

TIME: **60 minutes**
          50 questions*

> **Directions:** Read each question and select the best response.

1. Conversational prompts in science are

   A. probing questions that ask students to justify their reasoning.

   B. statements that encourage students to elaborate on their thinking.

   C. prepared prompts that a teacher chooses from when leading a science discussion.

   D. questions students have in their science notebooks to ask others in their group when completing an investigation.

2. A PreK teacher sets up a science center in which students sort rocks into groups based on observable properties. What science process skill is the focus of this center?

   A. measuring

   B. inferring

   C. classifying

   D. hypothesizing

3. A teacher designs an investigation in which students roll a small car with a plastic animal on top of it down a ramp and into a barrier. Students observe that the barrier stops the car, but the plastic animal flies off. What is this lesson most likely about?

   A. Newton's First Law

   B. Newton's Second Law

   C. Newton's Third Law

   D. contact forces

4. A first grade teacher wants to teach students about the differences between living and nonliving things. Which of the following would be the best way for her to begin her instruction?

   A. Take students outside to observe living and nonliving things in the environment.

   B. Read a book that explains the differences between living and nonliving things.

   C. Teach students a song that tells how living and nonliving things differ.

   D. Show students a video about living and nonliving things.

---

* The number of items is approximate. You will only learn exactly how many questions you will get after you take the FTCE tutorial and sign the non-disclosure agreement on test day.

5. A first grade teacher has students write a claim in their science notebooks about how a force changes an object's motion. She reads each student's entry at the end of the day to determine their current understanding about forces and motion. Based upon what she reads, she decides to revise her instructional plan for the next science lesson. This is an example of the use of

A. diagnostic assessment.

B. formative assessment.

C. summative assessment.

D. portfolio assessment.

6. One advantage of space shuttles over earlier spacecraft is that

A. shuttles can be launched from any major airport because they take off like an airplane.

B. shuttles do not pose risks to astronauts unlike earlier spacecraft.

C. shuttles can be used more than once, which makes them more cost-effective.

D. shuttles can fly to the Moon unlike earlier spacecraft.

7. A teacher is searching for biographies about scientists for her classroom library. What should she keep in mind as she searches?

A. Choose books depicting the most famous scientists in history so students learn about their discoveries.

B. Choose books about scientists who represent the full range of diversity within the scientific community.

C. Choose books solely about scientists with the same cultural and linguistic background as students in the school.

D. Choose books that are all at the same reading level so all children can read them.

8. Which of the following is an example of a characteristic property?

A. size

B. shape

C. temperature

D. freezing point

9. Which of the following statements is the most accurate regarding formal and informal learning in PreK/Primary classrooms?

A. Informal learning occurs in PreK classrooms, while formal learning happens in K–3 classrooms.

B. Informal learning happens in PreK/Primary classrooms and formal learning is discouraged.

C. Formal learning happens in PreK/Primary classrooms. Informal learning is what occurs in daycare and after-school programs.

D. Formal and informal learning experiences should both occur in PreK/Primary science classrooms.

10. Which of the following statements is most accurate regarding the relationship between mass and weight?

A. They mean the same thing.

B. Mass is measured by using displacement and weight is measured by using a balance.

C. Mass changes depending upon where you are in the universe, but weight stays the same.

D. Mass stays the same no matter where you are in the universe, but weight changes.

11. Renee says, "I think the metal spoon will be attracted to the magnet." This statement is an example of a(n)

A. observation.

B. inference.

C. prediction.

D. hypothesis.

12. First graders are growing plants. They measure the height of their plant every day and record the measurement in their science notebook. Which of the following would be the best graph to display their data?

    A. picture graph

    B. bar graph

    C. real graph

    D. line graph

13. In an ecosystem, omnivores are organisms that

    A. make their own food to get energy.

    B. eat only plants to get energy.

    C. eat plants and animals to get energy.

    D. eat only animals to get energy.

14. Students roll a toy car down a ramp and then measure how far it rolls on the floor after leaving the ramp. Which would be the best tool for them to use to measure how far the car rolls?

    A. meter stick

    B. ruler

    C. measuring cup

    D. scale

15. Which of the following would be the best reason to have students in a PreK/Primary classroom use a digital camera in science?

    A. to take photos of each other to post on the class webpage

    B. to share information with students who are absent

    C. to view objects in greater detail when hand lenses are not available

    D. to record observations to use as evidence for scientific claims

16. An object's volume refers to

    A. how much matter is in the object.

    B. how much space the object takes up.

    C. the weight of the object.

    D. the average temperature of the object.

17. A child who recognizes the Publix sign is demonstrating what stage of word recognition?

    A. pseudo-reading

    B. logographic-visual

    C. pragmatic

    D. visualization

18. Which of the following statements is most scientifically accurate?

    A. Compounds can be separated by physical means.

    B. Mixtures can be separated by physical means.

    C. Elements can be separated by physical means.

    D. Molecules can be separated by physical means.

19. Which of the following is an important attitude or disposition for scientific thinking?

    A. desire to work alone

    B. faith

    C. openness to new ideas

    D. lack of curiosity

20. Students go outside and collect pine cones. They create a class graph using the pine cones themselves. This is an example of a

    A. real graph.

    B. pictograph.

    C. bar graph.

    D. line plot.

21. Mammals are the only vertebrates who

    A. have live births.

    B. are warm-blooded.

    C. breathe through lungs.

    D. have feet.

22. A thing or an event in an organism's environment that causes it to respond in a specific way is known as a(n)

    A. sensor.

    B. allele.

    C. stimulus.

    D. characteristic.

23. Which of the following is an example of chemical weathering?

    A. tree roots growing in cracks in rocks

    B. freeze/thaw cycles where water seeps into cracks in rocks

    C. peeling away of rock in sheets or layers like granite

    D. dissolving of limestone in acidic rainwater

24. The force of gravity between two objects depends upon

    A. their shape and volume.

    B. their mass and distance.

    C. their volume and mass.

    D. their shape and distance.

25. Organisms in an ecosystem that feed on decaying organisms are known as

    A. producers.

    B. consumers.

    C. decomposers.

    D. omnivores.

26. Students notice that the class garden is far from the outside spigot to get water for the plants. They want to design a system for carrying water to the garden other than using watering cans. Students work in small groups to draw their plan and create a model of their design. What are the students integrating into science?

    A. engineering

    B. technology

    C. art

    D. literacy

27. A teacher designs a lesson in which students create clouds in a bottle. The lesson is most likely about which part of the water cycle?

    A. evaporation

    B. condensation

    C. precipitation

    D. collection

28. You are sitting on the sofa in your living room. What can be said about the forces acting on you?

    A. Gravity pulls you downward toward the center of the Earth and the sofa exerts an upward force on you equal to the force of gravity.

    B. Gravity pulls you downward toward the center of the Earth and the holding force keeps you on the sofa.

    C. Gravity is the only force acting upon you. Sofas can't exert a force.

    D. There are no forces acting upon you because you are not moving.

29. Which of the following is the best way for a teacher to help students confront and change their misconception that day and night occur because the Earth goes around the Sun once each day?

    A. Clearly explain the reason for day and night to students in developmentally appropriate language.

    B. Have students read a passage from their textbook that tells why we have day and night.

    C. Show students a video of the Sun rising, moving across the sky, and setting.

    D. Have students create a model of the Earth and Sun to investigate why we have day and night.

30. Space probes are

    A. unmanned robots that fly by or land on a planet or moon.

    B. manned spacecraft that fly by or land on a planet or moon.

    C. unmanned robots that can explore the Moon but not more distant objects in the solar system.

    D. manned spacecraft that will enable humans to land on distant objects in the solar system.

31. A second grade teacher has several English language learners in his classroom this year. Which of the following would be the best modification to make to his science word wall to support these learners?

    A. Add a picture to each object or concept on the word wall.

    B. Include more words on the word wall than he normally would.

    C. Avoid using the word wall as it is not helpful for English language learners.

    D. Make no changes to his use of the word wall as anything that is good for native English speakers is good for English learners.

32. A city government issues a water restriction during a period of extended drought. This is an example of scientific understanding influencing

    A. economics.

    B. culture.

    C. ethics.

    D. policy.

33. Sound energy is caused by

    A. the breaking of bonds between atoms.

    B. the heating of molecules.

    C. the vibration of an object or substance.

    D. the flow of electrons.

34. A second grade teacher gives pairs of students soil samples and hand lenses to answer the question, What makes up soil? What would be an important safety procedure for this lesson?

    A. wear smocks

    B. only allow one student to examine the soil at a time

    C. remove any dead bugs from the samples before using

    D. wear plastic gloves

35. A tundra biome is one that

    A. can be found in tropical or temperate climates and receives a lot of rain yearly.

    B. contains deep, rich soils that are good for crops and is home to large grazing animals.

    C. can be found in temperature or colder climates and receives moderate rainfall.

    D. has ground that is frozen much of the year and very little precipitation.

36. When we rubbed our hands together, they felt warm. This is an example of a(n)

    A. claim.

    B. evidence.

    C. reason.

    D. explanation.

37. Which of the following is the most important safety consideration regarding the introduction of a live animal into the PreK/Primary science classroom?

    A. The teacher should examine the animal before bringing it into the classroom to be sure it is healthy.

    B. The teacher should model appropriate ways for students to interact with the animal and monitor children's interactions with it to ensure everyone's safety.

    C. The teacher should only bring reptiles since they are less likely to carry diseases than other animals.

    D. The teacher should leave food and water for the animal during school holidays so it can eat and drink when schools are closed for an extended period of time.

38. Which of the following is the most accurate statement about the Sun's heating of land versus water?

    A. Water heats and cools more quickly than land.

    B. Water heats more quickly than land, but cools more slowly.

    C. Water heats more slowly than land, but cools more quickly.

    D. Water heats and cools more slowly than land.

39. The purpose of a plant's flower is to

    A. manufacture food for the plant.

    B. transport nutrients and water throughout the plant.

    C. produce seeds so the plant can reproduce.

    D. cover and protect the plant's seeds.

40. Warm-blooded animals are ones whose body temperature

    A. is consistently high.

    B. remains fairly constant despite temperature changes in the environment.

    C. changes in response to temperature changes in the environment.

    D. enables them to live in warm climates.

41. The main component of soil is

    A. the remains of plants and animals.

    B. air.

    C. weathered rock and mineral fragments called sediment.

    D. water.

42. A teacher is doing a read-aloud using a book about animals who change color to conceal themselves from predators. The science concept the teacher is focusing on is

    A. heredity in the animal world.

    B. how animals respond to their environment.

    C. animal classification.

    D. competition in an ecosystem.

43. Four friends were talking about which objects can be seen in the daytime and nighttime skies. Which student has the most accurate statement?

    A. Antoine: "We only see the Sun in the daytime and the Moon and stars at night."

    B. Michelle: "We only see the Sun in the daytime and the Moon at night, but we can sometimes see the stars in the daytime and the nighttime."

    C. Jared: "We only see the Sun in the daytime and the stars at night, but we can sometimes see the Moon in the daytime and the nighttime."

    D. Ashley: "We can sometimes see the Sun and the Moon in the daytime and the nighttime, but we only see the stars at night."

44. Which of the following is a trait that can be inherited by an organism from its parent?

   A. playing basketball

   B. having curly hair

   C. cooking skill

   D. missing an arm or leg

45. In the human body, the liver

   A. stores liquid waste until it's eliminated from the body.

   B. breaks down starches into simple sugars.

   C. produces bile to help break down food in the small intestine.

   D. produces white blood cells and antibodies to fight infection.

46. Which of the following is an example of kinetic energy?

   A. a skateboarder at the top of a ramp

   B. a stretched rubber band

   C. a bicyclist on a bike path

   D. a car parked in a parking lot

47. One way in which living things differ from nonliving things is that living things

   A. control their internal environment.

   B. are made of atoms and molecules.

   C. contain matter.

   D. have mass and volume.

48. Granite is formed when magma cools below Earth's surface. This means that granite is a(n)

   A. igneous rock.

   B. sedimentary rock.

   C. metamorphic rock.

   D. extrusive rock.

49. Which of the following are examples of a nonvascular plant?

   A. elm trees

   B. mosses

   C. roses

   D. ferns

50. Which of the following is an important characteristic of the nature of science?

   A. Science can answer any question humans have about anything.

   B. Science assumes there are observable patterns in the natural world that can be observed and explained.

   C. Science is a settled discipline. Once we learn something new it does not change.

   D. Science is based on the beliefs and opinions of scientists who use those beliefs to construct scientific explanations.

Science Practice Test 2: Answer Key

Test Item	Answer	Competency
1.	B	1
2.	C	1
3.	A	4
4.	A	1
5.	B	1
6.	C	3
7.	B	1
8.	D	4
9.	D	1
10.	D	4
11.	C	2
12.	D	2
13.	C	5
14.	A	2
15.	D	2
16.	B	4
17.	B	3
18.	B	4
19.	C	2
20.	A	2
21.	A	5
22.	C	5
23.	D	3
24.	B	3
25.	C	5

Test Item	Answer	Competency
26.	A	2
27.	B	3
28.	A	4
29.	D	1
30.	A	3
31.	A	1
32.	D	2
33.	C	4
34.	D	1
35.	D	5
36.	B	2
37.	B	1
38.	D	3
39.	C	5
40.	B	5
41.	C	3
42.	B	5
43.	C	3
44.	B	5
45.	C	5
46.	C	4
47.	A	5
48.	A	3
49.	B	5
50.	B	2

Science Practice Test 2: Detailed Answers

1. **(B)**

Choice (B) is the best answer. Conversational prompts are teacher statements that encourage children to continue the conversation. They can remove the pressure for students who feel they must always have the right answer. (Competency 1)

2. **(C)**

Choice (C) is the best answer. When students sort objects into groups based upon specific properties, they are classifying. (Competency 1)

3. **(A)**

Choice (A) is the best answer. Newton's First Law is also called the Law of Inertia. Objects in motion, like the car and animal, will keep moving in the same direction and at the same speed unless acted on by an outside force. The barrier exerts a force on the car, but not the animal. Therefore, the animal keeps moving at the same speed and in the same direction. (Competency 4)

4. **(A)**

Choice (A) is the best answer. PreK/Primary science instruction should take advantage of children's curiosity and naturalistic exploration. (Competency 1)

5. **(B)**

Choice (B) is the best answer. Formative assessments are used to determine students' progress toward meeting learning goals and to determine how to plan and modify future instruction. (Competency 1)

6. **(C)**

Choice (C) is the best answer. Early spacecraft could only be used for a single mission. Because the space shuttle took off like a rocket and landed like an airplane, it could be used for multiple missions. (Competency 3)

7. **(B)**

Choice (B) is the best answer. No matter what type of community they live in, students need to recognize that scientists are a diverse group of people. (Competency 1)

8. **(D)**

Choice (D) is the best answer. Characteristic properties are ones that are the same for any sample of a substance. Freezing and boiling points are examples of characteristic properties. (Competency 4)

9. **(D)**

Choice (D) is the best answer. Teachers design formal learning experiences in science. Young children also need opportunities to engage in informal, self-directed learning, otherwise known as play. (Competency 1)

10. **(D)**

Choice (D) is the best answer. Mass is the amount of matter in an object that remains the same no matter where you are in the universe. Weight is a measure of the amount of gravity acting on an object. It is determined by the object's mass and the strength of the force of gravity at other locations in the universe. (Competency 4)

11. (C)

Choice (C) is the best answer. A prediction is a statement about what students think will happen. It is based on prior knowledge and reasoning. (Competency 2)

12. (D)

Choice (D) is the best answer. Line graphs can be used to show continuous, numerical data like plant growth over time. The other graph choices are used for categorical data. (Competency 2)

13. (C)

Choice (C) is the best answer. Omnivores are animals that eat both plants and other animals. Herbivores eat only plants, while carnivores only eat other animals. (Competency 5)

14. (A)

Choice (A) is the best answer. A meter stick is the best tool to use. Unlike choices (C) and (D) it measures length. It is better than choice (B) because a ruler would need to be iterated many times to measure the distance the car travels. (Competency 2)

15. (D)

Choice (D) is the best answer. Digital cameras can be used to record data. Students can use the images to construct claims based on evidence. (Competency 2)

16. (B)

Choice (B) is the best answer. Volume refers to the amount of space an object takes up. It should not be confused with mass, which is the amount of matter in an object. (Competency 4)

17. (B)

"Logographic-visual" is the term to describe when a child uses illustrations or letters in words to understand the text, without really understanding the letter-symbol relationship. (Competency 3)

18. (B)

Choice (B) is the best answer. When two substances are mixed together, they each retain their chemical composition and properties and can be separated by physical means. (Competency 4)

19. (C)

Choice (C) is the best answer. Scientists are open to new ideas and are willing to modify their ideas in the face of new evidence that challenges their current thinking. (Competency 2)

20. (A)

Choice (A) is the best answer. A real graph uses actual objects as the data points in the graph. (Competency 2)

21. (A)

Choice (A) is the best answer. Other animals besides mammals breathe through lungs and are warm-blooded. They are the only ones that have live births. (Competency 5)

22. (C)

Choice (C) is the best answer. A stimulus is a thing or event that arouses a specific response in a living thing. (Competency 5)

23. (D)

Choice (D) is the best answer. The other choices are examples of physical weathering. Chemical weathering changes the chemical composition of the rock. (Competency 3)

24. (B)

Choice (B) is the best answer. Objects with greater mass exert a greater gravitational pull on each other. Closer objects exert a greater gravitational pull than objects that are farther away. (Competency 3)

25. (C)

Choice (C) is the best answer. Decomposers are an important component of an ecosystem. They break down organisms into nutrients that can be used by plants. (Competency 5)

26. (A)

Choice (A) is the best answer. When students use science ideas to solve human problems, they are engaging in engineering design. (Competency 2)

27. (B)

Choice (B) is the best answer. Clouds are formed when water vapor rises in the atmosphere, cools, and condenses. (Competency 3)

28. (A)

Choice (A) is the best answer. According to Newton's Third Law, forces come in pairs. When one force acts on an object, there is an opposing force that acts in the opposite direction. (Competency 4)

29. (D)

Choice (D) is the best answer. Students do not change their misconceptions simply by hearing the correct answer. Using models to construct scientific explanations can help students confront their misconceptions. (Competency 1)

30. (A)

Choice (A) is the best answer. Unmanned probes have enabled humans to learn more about distant objects in the solar system. Humans have only traveled as far as the Moon. (Competency 3)

31. (A)

Choice (A) is the best answer. Adding pictures can help English language learners connect the science term with the object or concept. (Competency 1)

32. (D)

Choice (D) is the best answer. Policy decisions at local, state, federal, and international levels can be influenced by scientific understanding. (Competency 2)

33. (C)

Choice (C) is the best answer. Sound energy is produced by vibrations. (Competency 4)

34. (D)

Choice (D) is the best answer. Gloves help keep soil from under children's fingernails or getting into cuts they may have on their hands. (Competency 1)

35. (D)

Choice (D) is the best answer. Tundras are found in very cold climates where the ground is frozen much of the year. They are deserts because they receive little precipitation. (Competency 5)

36. (B)

Choice (B) is the best answer. This statement is an observation made during an investigation. It can be used to support a claim. (Competency 2)

37. (B)

Choice (B) is the best answer. Some students may be unfamiliar with how to safely interact with animals. The teacher can both model this and monitor students' interactions with animals in the classroom. A veterinarian would need to examine the animal to determine whether it is healthy. (Competency 1)

38. (D)

Choice (D) is the best answer. Water has a higher heat capacity than land, which means that it both heats and cools more slowly. (Competency 3)

39. (C)

Choice (C) is the best answer. Flowers produce seeds, which enable the plant to reproduce. (Competency 5)

40. (B)

Choice (B) is the best answer. Warm-blooded animals are ones that maintain a fairly constant body temperature despite temperature changes in the environment. In contrast, the body temperature of cold-blooded animals varies with temperature changes in their environment. (Competency 5)

41. (C)

Choice (C) is the best answer. All the choices are components of soil, but sediment is the major component. (Competency 3)

42. (B)

Choice (B) is the best answer. Animals respond to their environments in a variety of ways. Some animals change color seasonally or quickly to make it more difficult for predators to detect them. (Competency 5)

43. (C)

Choice (C) is the best answer. The Sun is the closest star to Earth. Its light is much brighter than the light coming from distant stars. As the Earth rotates on its axis different locations face the Sun. When the area where we live faces away from the Sun, it is nighttime. The Moon is typically seen during nighttime but can also be seen during the day around the time of the full moon. (Competency 3)

44. (B)

Choice (B) is the best answer. People learn to play sports (A) and cook (C). A parent can help coach them. When someone loses an arm or leg (D), it does not affect their future offspring. Whether someone's hair is naturally curly or straight is an inherited trait. People can temporarily curl or straighten their hair, but it eventually returns to its natural, inherited state. (Competency 5)

45. (C)

Choice (C) is the best answer. The liver is part of the digestive system. Bile is produced in the liver and helps break down food in the small intestine. (Competency 5)

46. (C)

Choice (C) is the best answer. Kinetic energy is energy of motion. All the other choices are examples of potential energy. (Competency 4)

47. (A)

Choice (A) is the best answer. All matter is made of atoms and molecules and has mass and volume. Living things are composed of cells that are complex chemical factories. The cells in an organism's body work together to enable it to control its internal environment. (Competency 5)

48. (A)

Choice (A) is the best answer. Igneous rocks are formed when magma, or liquid rock, cools and hardens. Some igneous rocks form at Earth's surface, but others form below the surface. (Competency 3)

49. (B)

Choice (B) is the best answer. Nonvascular plants are ones that do not transport nutrients via roots and stems. All the other choices are vascular plants. (Competency 5)

50. (B)

Choice (B) is the best answer. Scientists assume pattern and order in the natural world. They seek to explain those patterns. Scientific explanations are based on evidence, not beliefs or opinions. (Competency 2)

PRACTICE TEST 2: CORRELATION WITH FTCE COMPETENCIES

Developmental Knowledge

Competency 1: Knowledge of Child Growth, Child Development, and Relationships with Families and the Community
Questions 4, 6, 8, 16, 31, 44, 51, 53

Competency 2: Knowledge of the Profession and Foundations of Early Childhood (PreK–3) Education
Questions 11, 17, 35, 41, 47, 56, 58

Competency 3: Knowledge of Developmentally Appropriate Practices
Questions 1, 2, 7, 12, 13, 20, 27, 40, 46, 52, 57, 60

Competency 4: Knowledge of Developmentally Appropriate Curricula
Questions 21, 33, 38, 45, 48, 54, 59

Competency 5: Knowledge of Developmentally Appropriate Intervention Strategies and Resources Available to Meet the Needs of All Students
Questions 3, 9, 15, 19, 23, 25, 28, 32, 42

Competency 6: Knowledge of Diagnosis, Assessment, and Evaluation
Questions 24, 29, 36, 37, 39, 43, 49, 50, 55

Competency 7: Knowledge of Child Guidance and Classroom Behavioral Management
Questions 5, 10, 14, 18, 22, 26, 30, 34

Language Arts and Reading

Competency 1: Knowledge of Literacy and Literacy Instruction
Questions 1, 6, 7, 11, 12, 14, 21, 23, 25, 27, 32, 36, 43, 48, 54

Competency 2: Knowledge of Fiction and Nonfiction Genres Including Reading Informational Texts (e.g., literary nonfiction, historical, scientific, and technical texts)
Questions 2, 3, 8, 13, 15, 20, 31, 38, 41, 55, 59

Competency 3: Knowledge of Reading Foundational Skills
Questions 4, 9, 16, 18, 24, 26, 28, 34, 39, 40, 42, 44, 46, 58, 60

Competency 4: Knowledge of Language Elements Used for Effective Oral and Written Communication
Questions 17, 19, 22, 29, 30, 35, 47, 49, 50, 52, 53, 56, 57

Competency 5: Knowledge of Assessments to Inform Literary Instruction
Questions 5, 10, 33, 37, 45, 51

Mathematics

Competency 1: Knowledge of Effective Mathematics Instruction
Questions 4, 7, 9, 11, 12, 28, 33, 36, 38, 40, 50

Competency 2: Knowledge of Algebraic Thinking
Questions 5, 14, 15, 17, 31, 34, 42, 47

Competency 3: Knowledge of Number Concepts and Operations in Base Ten
Questions 1, 3, 13, 18, 20, 22, 24, 26, 27, 30, 32, 39, 44, 46, 49

Competency 4: Knowledge of Measurement and Data Collection and Analysis
Questions 6, 8, 10, 16, 23, 35, 37, 41

Competency 5: Knowledge of Geometric and Special Concepts
Questions 2, 19, 21, 25, 29, 43, 45, 48

Science

Competency 1: Knowledge of Effective Science Instruction
Questions 1, 2, 4, 5, 7, 9, 29, 31, 34, 37

Competency 2: Knowledge of the Nature of Science
Questions 11, 12, 14, 15, 19, 20, 26, 32, 36, 50

Competency 3: Knowledge of Earth and Space Sciences
Questions 6, 17, 23, 24, 27, 30, 38, 41, 43, 48

Competency 4: Knowledge of the Physical Sciences
Questions 3, 8, 10, 16, 18, 28, 33, 46

Competency 5: Knowledge of the Life Sciences
Questions 13, 21, 22, 25, 35, 39, 40, 42, 44, 45, 47, 49

NOTES